Stalinism

Blackwell Essential Readings in History

This series comprises concise collections of key articles on important historical topics. Designed as a complement to standard survey histories, the volumes are intended to help introduce students to the range of scholarly debate in a subject area. Each collection includes a general introduction and brief contextual headnotes to each article, offering a coherent, critical framework for study.

Published

The German Reformation: The Essential Readings
C. Scott Dixon

The English Civil War: The Essential Readings
Peter Gaunt

The Italian Renaissance: The Essential Readings
Paula Findlen

The Scientific Revolution: The Essential Readings
Marcus Hellyer

Stalinism: The Essential Readings
David L. Hoffmann

The Cold War: The Essential Readings
Klaus Larres and Ann Lane

The Third Reich: The Essential Readings
Christian Leitz

The Counter-Reformation: The Essential Readings
David M. Luebke

The Crusades: The Essential Readings
Thomas F. Madden

The Russian Revolution: The Essential Readings
Martin Miller

The French Revolution: The Essential Readings
Ronald Schechter

Cromwell and the Interregnum: The Essential Readings
David L. Smith

Stalinism

The Essential Readings

Edited by David L. Hoffmann

Blackwell
Publishing

Editorial material and organization © 2003 David L. Hoffmann

350 Main Street, Malden, MA 02148-5018, USA
108 Cowley Road, Oxford OX4 1JF, UK
550 Swanston Street, Carlton South, Melbourne, Victoria 3053, Australia
Kurfürstendamm 57, 10707 Berlin, Germany

First published 2003 by Blackwell Publishers Ltd, a Blackwell Publishing
company

Library of Congress Cataloging-in-Publication Data

Stalinism : the essential readings / edited by David L. Hoffmann.
     p.   cm. – (Blackwell essential readings in history)
Includes bibliographical references and index.
   ISBN 0–631–22890–X — ISBN 0–631–22891–8 (pbk.)
   1. Soviet Union—Politics and government – 1936–1953. 2. Soviet
Union—Social conditions.   I. Hoffmann, David L. (David Lloyd), 1961–
II. Series.
   DK 267 .S6946 2003
   947.084—dc21

                                                2002009489

A catalogue record for this title is available from the British Library.

Set in 10½ on 12 pt Photina
by SNP Best-set Typesetter Ltd., Hong Kong

For further information on
Blackwell Publishing, visit our website:
http://www.blackwellpublishing.com

To my daughter Sarah

Contents

Acknowledgments   ix

Glossary   xi

Introduction: Interpretations of Stalinism   1
David L. Hoffmann

Part I   The Origins of Stalinism   9

1   **Stalin's Role**   11
    Stalin and his Stalinism: Power and Authority in the Soviet
    Union, 1930–1953   13
    Ronald Grigor Suny

2   **Social Origins**   37
    Grappling with Stalinism   39
    Moshe Lewin

3   **Socialist Ideology**   63
    The Soviet Tragedy: A History of Socialism in Russia   65
    Martin Malia

4   **The Foreign Threat**   81
    The Objectives of the Great Terror, 1937–1938   83
    Oleg Khlevnyuk

5   **The Welfare State**   105
    Magnetic Mountain: Stalinism as a Civilization   107
    Stephen Kotkin

6   **State Violence**   127
State Violence as Technique: The Logic of Violence in Soviet
Totalitarianism   129
Peter Holquist

Part II   The Consequences of Stalinism   157

7   **Resistance and Conformity**   159
Everyday Stalinism: Ordinary Life in Extraordinary Times   161
Sheila Fitzpatrick

8   **Stalinist Subjectivity**   179
Working, Struggling, Becoming: Stalin-Era Autobiographical
Texts   181
Jochen Hellbeck

9   **Women and Gender**   211
Women in Soviet Society: Equality, Development, and
Social Change   213
Gail Warshofsky Lapidus

10   **Ethnicity and Nationality**   237
Nature and Nurture in a Socialist Utopia: Delineating the
Soviet Socio-Ethnic Body in the Age of Socialism   239
Amir Weiner

11   **The Postwar Years**   275
Russia after the War: Hopes, Illusions, and Disappointments   277
Elena Zubkova

Index   302

Acknowledgments

The editor and publishers wish to thank the following for permission to use copyright material:

Ronald Grigor Suny, "Stalin and his Stalinism: power and authority in the Soviet Union, 1930–53," from *Stalinism and Nazism: Dictatorships in Comparison*, edited by I. Kershaw and M. Lewin pp. 26–52. Copyright © 1997 Cambridge University Press. Reprinted with permission of the publisher and author.

Moshe Lewin, *The Making of the Soviet System: Essays in the Social History of Interwar Russia*, pp. 286–338. Copyright © 1985 The Harvester Press Ltd.

Martin Malia, *The Soviet Tragedy: A History of Socialism in Russia, 1917–1991*, pp. 178–81, 217–26. Copyright © 1994 Martin Malia. Reprinted with permission of The Free Press, a Division of Simon & Schuster, Inc.

Oleg Khlevnyuk, "The Objectives of the Great Terror, 1937–1938," from *Soviet History, 1917–53*, edited by Julian Cooper, Maureen Perrie, and E. A. Rees. Published by St. Martin's Press. Copyright © 1995 Macmillan Press Ltd. Reprinted with permission of Macmillan Ltd.

Stephen Kotkin, *Magnetic Mountain: Stalinism as a Civilization*, pp. 6–9, 16–23, and 381–93. Copyright © 1997 The Regents of the University of California. Reprinted with permission of The Regents of the University of California and the University of California Press.

Peter Holquist, "State Violence as Technique: The Logic of Violence in Soviet Totalitarianism," from *Landscaping the Human Garden*, edited by Amir Weiner. Copyright © 2003 by the Board of Trustees of the Leland Stanford Jr. University. Reprinted with the permission of Stanford University Press, www.sup.org.

Sheila Fitzpatrick, *Everyday Stalinism: Ordinary Life in Extraordinary Times: Soviet Russia in the 1930s*, pp. 218–27. Copyright © 1999 Oxford University Press, Inc. Reprinted by permission of Oxford University Press, Inc.

Jochen Hellbeck, "Working, Struggling, Becoming: Stalin-Era Autobiographical Texts," *The Russian Review*, vol. 60(3), July 2001, pp. 340–59. Copyright © 2001 *The Russian Review*. Reprinted by permission of the author and publisher.

Gail Lapidus, *Women in Soviet Society: Equality, Development, and Social Change*, pp. 95–119. Copyright © 1978 The Regents of the University of California. Reprinted with permission of The Regents of the University of California and the University of California Press.

Amir Weiner, "Nature, Nurture and Memory in a Socialist Utopia: Delineating the Soviet Socio-Ethnic Body in the Age of Socialism," *American Historical Review*, October 1999, pp. 1114–55. Copyright © 1999 American Historical Association. Reprinted by permission of the author and publisher.

Elena Zubkova, *Russia After the War: Hopes, Illusions, and Disappointments, 1945–1957*, pp. 20–39. Translated by Hugh Ragsdale. Copyright © 1998 M. E. Sharpe.

Every effort has been made to trace copyright holders and to obtain their permission for the use of copyright material. The authors and publishers will gladly receive any information enabling them to rectify any error or omission in subsequent editions.

Glossary

apparatchiki – see *apparaty*.

apparaty – Soviet bureaucrats or functionaries.

Bolsheviks – Communists.

Bukharin, Nikolai – Communist Party leader and rival of Stalin; executed during Great Purges.

byt – everyday life.

Central Committee – governing body of the Communist Party; elected by Party congresses.

Cheka – Soviet secret police; subsequently renamed OGPU and NKVD.

CPSU – Communist Party of the Soviet Union.

Decembrists – Russian officers who revolted against the tsarist autocracy in 1825.

de-Cossackization – elimination of Cossacks (frontier people).

dekulakization – elimination of kulaks (wealthy peasants) through dispossession and deportation.

Enlightenment – eighteenth-century philosophical movement that stressed the application of reason to human affairs.

Ezhov, Nikolai – head of Soviet secret police (NKVD) during the Great Terror.

First Five-Year Plan – plan of rapid industrialization, 1928–32.

Great Break – Stalin's radical policy change in the late 1920s; initiated collectivization, rapid industrialization, and attack on non-Communist authorities.

Great Patriotic War – term for Second World War in the Soviet Union.

Great Purges – arrests and executions of Communist Party members; part of the Great Terror, 1936–8.

Great Terror – widespread arrests and executions, 1936–8; included the Great Purges of Communist Party members.

Great War – First World War.

Gulag – system of forced labor camps.

Homo Sovieticus – Soviet Man.

Ivan groznyi – see Ivan the Terrible.

Ivan the Terrible – sixteenth-century Russian tsar.

Kamenev, Lev – a Communist Party leader; executed during the Great Purges.

kolkhoz – collective farm.

kolkhozniki – collective farm peasants.

Komsomol – Communist youth organization.

Khrushchev, Nikita – succeeded Stalin as leader of the Communist Party and Soviet Union.

Kirov, Sergei – popular leader of Leningrad Party organization; seen by some as potential rival to Stalin; murdered in 1934.

krai – region; territorial administrative unit.

kraikom – regional Communist Party committee.

kulaks – wealthy peasants; deemed exploiters and class enemies by the Soviet government.

Lenin, Vladimir – founder and leader of Bolshevik/Communist Party until his death in 1924.

MTS – machine tractor stations.

nachal'stvo – authorities; command.

Narkomnats – Commissariat of Nationalities.

Narkomyust – Commissariat of Justice.

NKVD – Soviet secret police; previously called OGPU.

New Economic Policy (NEP) – policy enacted by Lenin in 1921; allowed for limited private enterprise and free trade.

Nepmen – private entrepreneurs of NEP period.

obkom – provincial Communist Party committee.

oblast – province; territorial administrative unit.

OGPU – Soviet secret police; subsequently called NKVD.

OUN – Organization of Ukrainian Nationalists.

Peter the Great – eighteenth-century Russian tsar.

philosophes – French philosophers of the eighteenth-century Enlightenment.

Politburo – Communist Party's highest decision-making body; elected by Central Committee.

proletariat – industrial working class.

raikom – district Communist Party committee.

raion – district; territorial administrative unit.

Shklovsky, Viktor – literary theorist and leader of the Russian Formalist movement in the early 1920s.

smychka – alliance; term use by Communists to refer to their idea of an alliance between workers and peasants in the 1920s.

sovkhozy – state collective farms.

spravka – list; inventory.

Stakhanovites – hero workers; named for record-breaking coal miner, Aleksei Stakhanov.

stakhanovtsy – see Stakhanovites.

troiki – tribunals during the Great Terror.

Trotsky, Lev – a Communist Party leader and rival of Stalin; expelled from the Party in 1927 and subsequently deported from the country.

Tsar – title of pre-revolutionary hereditary monarchs.

UPA – Ukrainian Insurgent Army.

velikii perelom – see Great Break.

Vlasov army – anti-Soviet Russian army during the Second World War.

vozhd' – leader.

zemstvos – organs of local self-government in the late pre-revolutionary period.

Zinoviev, Grigorii – a Communist Party leader; executed during the Great Purges.

Introduction: Interpretations of Stalinism

David L. Hoffmann

For scholars of Soviet history, no problem looms larger than that of Stalinism. How was it that the October Revolution of 1917, which seemed to promise human liberation and equality, resulted not in a communist utopia but instead in a Stalinist dictatorship? Why did this attempt to create a perfect society lead to gulag prison camps, bloody purges, and unprecedented levels of state repression? For decades historians have grappled with these questions, and have put forward a range of competing explanations. Some have blamed Stalin personally, others have focused on socialist ideology or the international threat, still others have explored Stalinism's social and cultural origins. Stalinism, then, represents not only the most central problem in Soviet history, but one rich in historiographical controversy and interpretation as well.

This book presents various explanations of Stalinism written both by eminent historians and by younger scholars who have conducted research in newly opened Russian archives. The articles and excerpts offer a range of interpretations as to what caused Stalinism and what were its social consequences. Taken together these interpretations provide an important lesson in historical causality. Underlying each explanation of Stalinism are assumptions regarding the forces that cause events to happen. Interpretations that stress Stalin's personal role assume that history is shaped by individuals. Explanations that emphasize socialist ideology see ideas and ideological systems as driving history. Social historians of Stalinism focus on characteristics of Soviet society, while cultural historians highlight Soviet cultural constructs or modern political culture more generally.

Stalinism can be defined as a set of tenets, policies, and practices instituted by the Soviet government during the years in which Stalin was in power, 1928–53. It was characterized by extreme coercion employed for the purpose of economic and social transformation. Among the particular features of Stalinism were the abolition of private property and free trade; the collectivization of agriculture; a planned, state-run economy and rapid industrialization; the wholesale liquidation of so-called exploiting classes, involving massive deportations and incarcerations; large-scale political terror against alleged enemies, including those within the Communist Party itself; a cult of personality deifying Stalin; and Stalin's virtually unlimited dictatorship over the country.

The range of phenomena included under the name Stalinism alerts us to the fact that not all aspects of Stalinism can be explained by a single cause. Indeed, historians generally eschew monocausal explanations, and instead see a variety of forces as shaping history. Even a single Stalinist policy, such as collectivization, may be best explained by an array of factors – Soviet leaders' ideological aversion to private agriculture, national security imperatives to industrialize quickly, a short-term economic crisis that prompted government grain requisitioning, and a penchant among modern policymakers for economic planning and state control. But because the study of history represents an attempt to understand the world and what makes things happen, historians are obliged to weigh these causal factors and argue which of them predominated or how they worked in combination to produce a certain outcome.

During the Cold War, debates as to what caused Stalinism were highly politicized. At issue were the legitimacy of the Soviet government and the culpability of socialist ideology.[1] The totalitarian model, the dominant paradigm of the Cold War era, posited an all-powerful government ruling over an atomized, defenseless society. This model explained how a government that lacked popular support and legitimacy could nonetheless remain in power. Many totalitarian theorists emphasized the role of socialist ideology, thereby implicitly or explicitly condemning it for Stalinist brutality and terror. Such interpretations saw Stalinism as the logical result of the October Revolution, when, according to this view, the Bolsheviks (later renamed Communists) seized power in an

---

[1] Socialist ideology encompasses a range of political thought, of which Marxism became the leading strain. The political party of Russian Marxists led by Vladimir Lenin (and subsequently by Stalin) was called the Bolsheviks, renamed Communists after the October Revolution. Communist leaders never claimed to have achieved communism; according to Marxism a communist utopia would emerge only as the last stage of history. But Stalin did claim to have established socialism in the Soviet Union by the mid-1930s.

illegitimate coup d'état and proceeded to impose their ideological vision upon the population.[2]

In the 1970s and 1980s, revisionist scholars challenged the totalitarian model, and presented Soviet society as more than a passive object controlled by an all-powerful state. One revisionist trend emphasized the role of workers and soldiers in the October Revolution and their support for the Bolsheviks. This research portrayed the Bolshevik rise to power as a popular revolution rather than a coup d'état, and thus attributed to the Soviet government a substantial degree of legitimacy.[3] Another strain of revisionist scholarship stressed that Stalinism was not the logical outcome of the Revolution, and that more moderate alternatives existed within the Communist Party. These scholars drew a distinction between Bolshevism and Stalinism, and implicitly exonerated socialist ideology from the crimes of Stalinism.[4]

Of course revisionism required that Stalinism be explained in some other way. If the October Revolution was not an illegitimate seizure of power that created a ruthless dictatorship, and if socialist ideology did not necessarily lead to Stalinist excesses, then revisionists still had to explain the origins of the Stalinist dictatorship and terror. While revisionist scholars generally held Stalin accountable for betraying the ideals of the Revolution, many also looked for deeper causes of Stalinism. Some focused on Stalin's control of Communist Party personnel, or on support within the Soviet bureaucracy for him and his policies.[5]

[2] Merle Fainsod, *How Russia is Ruled* (Cambridge, Mass., 1953); Carl J. Friedrich and Zbigniew K. Brzezinski, *Totalitarian Dictatorship and Autocracy* (Cambridge, Mass., 1956); A. Avtorkhanov, *Stalin and the Soviet Communist Party: A Study in the Technology of Power* (London, 1959); Alexander Solzhenitsyn, *The Gulag Archipelago 1918–1956*, trans. Thomas. P. Whitney and Harry Willetts, vols. 1–3 (New York, 1973–8); Adam Ulam, *The Bolsheviks: The Intellectual and Political History of the Triumph of Communism in Russia* (New York, 1973).

[3] Marc Ferro, *October 1917: A Social History of the Russian Revolution* (London, 1980); Ronald G. Suny, "Towards a Social History of the October Revolution," *American Historical Review*, vol. 88, no. 1 (1983); S. A. Smith, *Red Petrograd: Revolution in the Factories, 1917–1918* (New York, 1983); Alexander Rabinowitch, *The Bolsheviks Come to Power: The Revolution of 1917 in Petrograd* (New York, 1978); Allan K. Wildman, *The End of the Russian Imperial Army: The Road to Soviet Power and Peace* (Princeton, 1987); Diane Koenker and William G. Rosenberg, *Strikes and Revolution in Russia, 1917* (Princeton, 1989).

[4] Stephen F. Cohen, "Bolshevism and Stalinism," and Robert C. Tucker, "Stalinism as Revolution from Above," in Tucker, ed., *Stalinism: Essays in Historical Interpretation* (New York, 1977); Roy Medvedev, *Let History Judge: The Origins and Consequences of Stalinism* (New York, 1971); Moshe Lewin, *Lenin's Last Struggle* (London, 1969); Giuseppe Boffa, *The Stalin Phenomenon* (Ithaca, 1992). In this volume, see the selection by Suny.

[5] T. H. Rigby, "Stalinism and the Mono-Organizational Society," and Moshe Lewin, "The Social Background of Stalinism," in Tucker, ed.; Graeme Gill, *The Origins of the Stalinist Political System* (New York, 1990). Even prior to revisionist scholarship, Stalin's

Others sought the social origins of Stalinism, portraying Soviet society, with its backward peasant population, as a fertile breeding ground for the patriarchal authoritarianism of Stalinism.[6] Even more radical revisionists suggested that certain segments within Soviet society supported or even advocated Stalinist policies such as rapid industrialization, collectivization, and purging.[7]

While revisionism provided a far more sophisticated picture of Stalinism than did the totalitarian model, not all aspects of revisionist scholarship were accepted by the scholarly community. Sheila Fitzpatrick, the leading scholar in the field and one who first raised the possibility that Stalinist policies emanated from Soviet society, herself rejected the idea that collectivization and industrialization should be described as a "revolution from below" and instead argued these policies were clearly the initiative of the Stalinist leadership.[8] On the alleged link between peasant patriarchalism and Stalinism, further research revealed that the Soviet Union's largely peasant society, far from supporting Stalin's rule, opposed Stalinist policies and engaged in active or passive resistance.[9] Some scholars such as Martin Malia rejected revisionist social history altogether and insisted that Stalinism was indeed the logical result of an attempt to put socialist ideology into practice.[10] A more general turn in the historical profession away from social history toward cultural history has also contributed to post-revisionist scholarship which no longer seeks the origins of Stalinism in Soviet society.[11]

accumulation of power within the bureaucracy had been well documented; see E. H. Carr, *Socialism in One Country 1924–1926*, vol. 1 (London, 1958); Robert V. Daniels, *The Conscience of the Revolution: Communist Opposition in Soviet Russia* (Cambridge, Mass., 1960). Trotsky was the first to blame Stalinism on the "triumph of the bureaucracy;" see Leon Trotsky, *The Revolution Betrayed: What is the Soviet Union and Where is it Going?* (New York, 1937).

[6] See Lewin's article in this volume.

[7] William J. Chase, *Workers, Society, and the Soviet State: Labor and Life in Moscow, 1918–1929* (Urbana, Ill., 1987); Lynne Viola, *The Best Sons of the Fatherland: Workers in the Vanguard of Collectivization* (New York, 1987); Robert Thurston, "The Stakhanovite Movement: Background to the Great Terror in the Factories, 1935–1938," and Roberta T. Manning, "The Great Purges in a Rural District: Belyi Raion Revisited," in J. Arch Getty and Manning, eds., *Stalinist Terror: New Perspectives* (New York, 1993).

[8] Sheila Fitzpatrick, "New Perspectives on Stalinism," *The Russian Review*, vol. 45, no. 4 (1987).

[9] Lynne Viola, "*Bab'i Bunty* and Peasant Women's Protest during Collectivization," *The Russian Review*, vol. 45, no. 1 (1986); Sheila Fitzpatrick, *Stalin's Peasants: Resistance and Survival in the Russian Village after Collectivization* (New York, 1994); David L. Hoffmann, *Peasant Metropolis: Social Identities in Moscow, 1929–1941* (Ithaca, 1994).

[10] See Malia in this volume.

[11] Recent cultural history that provides new perspectives on Stalinism includes Katerina Clark, *Petersburg: Crucible of Cultural Revolution* (Cambridge, Mass., 1995); Boris Groys, *The Total Art of Stalinism: Avant-Garde, Aesthetic Dictatorship, and Beyond* (Princeton,

One important trend within post-revisionism attempts to place Stalinism in an international comparative context. During the Cold War scholars tended to assume a fundamental disjuncture between the Soviet Union and Western democracies, and they therefore highlighted the distinctive features of Soviet history.[12] But now that these Cold War dichotomies are less salient, it is possible to see striking parallels, as well as important differences, between Stalinist social practices and those of other modern states. Recent work on Stalinism has demonstrated that it, like other twentieth-century governmental systems, deployed technologies of social cataloguing and intervention that were new to the modern era. These technologies grew out of Enlightenment thought and European disciplinary culture, which promoted social intervention in the name of rational social reform. State intervention in society vastly increased during the First World War, when the advent of mass warfare prompted political leaders across Europe to expand both welfare programs and excisionary coercion to ensure a loyal and militarily fit population. The Soviet state, formed at this moment of wartime mobilization, institutionalized many of these interventionist practices and used them to pursue its own ideological agenda. New scholarship thus maintains that Stalinism, with its radical interventionism to reshape society, cannot be understood apart from the rise of modern state welfare and state violence.[13]

Equally exciting new work is being done on the consequences of Stalinism – how Stalinist policies affected the population and how people responded to these policies. Here the opening of former Soviet

1992); Michael David-Fox, "What is Cultural Revolution?" *The Russian Review*, vol. 58, no. 2 (1999); Karen Petrone, *Life Has Become More Joyous, Comrades: Celebrations in the Time of Stalin* (Bloomington, 2000); James von Geldern and Richard Stites, eds., *Mass Culture in Soviet Russia: Tales, Poems, Songs, Movies, Plays, and Folklore, 1917–1953* (Bloomington, 1995); Catriona Kelly and David Shepherd, *Russian Cultural Studies: An Introduction* (Oxford, 1998); Stefan Plaggenborg, *Revolutionskultur: Menschenbilder und Kulturelle Praxis in Sowjetrussland Zwischen Oktoberrevolution und Stalinimus* (Koln, 1996). For further discussion of the shift to cultural history, see Sheila Fitzpatrick, ed., *Stalinism: New Directions* (London, 2000), pp. 7–11.

[12] The totalitarian model did posit a fundamental similarity between Nazi Germany and Stalinist Russia, but it counter-posed these systems to Western liberal democracies. Modernization theory represents the one attempt during the Cold War to see similar processes of industrialization and urbanization as shaping both Western democracies and the Soviet Union (as well as other non-Western countries); see, for example, Cyril E. Black, ed., *The Transformation of Russian Society: Aspects of Social Change since 1861* (Cambridge, Mass., 1960). This theory, however, was criticized for its ethnocentrism and determinism; it implied that all countries would ultimately become like modern Western societies.

[13] I discuss these ideas further in "European Modernity and Soviet Socialism," in David L. Hoffmann and Yanni Kotsonis, eds., *Russian Modernity: Politics, Knowledge, Practices* (New York, 2000). In this volume, see Kotkin, Holquist, and Weiner.

archives has proven especially important for research. Using previously classified documents, scholars have discovered widespread opposition to Stalinism, including worker strikes, peasant protests, and popular expressions of contempt for Stalin and the ruling elite, not to mention more passive forms of resistance to the Stalinist system.[14] Additional new sources such as diaries have provided valuable insights into how people experienced and understood Stalinism, and how some individuals came to internalize Stalinist ideas and values.[15]

Other important work, both past and present, explores the impact of Stalinism on particular groups within Soviet society. The Stalinist gender order, as constructed during the 1930s, meant the large-scale recruitment of women into the industrial workforce, but Soviet propaganda simultaneously emphasized women's reproductive obligations. Gail Warshofsky Lapidus's classic book on this topic, excerpted in this volume, still offers the most succinct discussion of women's double burden under Stalinism, but it has been joined by important new research as well.[16] Studies of Stalinist nationality policy represent some of the most vibrant new scholarship in the field. These studies explore the treatment of national minorities, and reveal the ways the Soviet government inadvertently fostered the very national conscious it hoped to supercede.[17] Amir Weiner's article in this volume is pathbreaking not only in situating Soviet conceptions of ethnicity within the larger utopian project, but in its analysis of the Second World War's impact on the Soviet purification drive. The excerpt from Elena Zubkova's book also exemplifies pioneering research on the postwar Stalin years, a period scholars are only beginning to investigate.

Stalinism is such a large topic that a great deal of important scholarship could not be included in this volume. Among the most significant of this work is Robert Davies's multi-volume history of Stalinist indus-

---

[14] Jeffrey J. Rossman, "The Teikovo Cotton Workers' Strike of April 1932: Class, Gender and Identity Politics in Stalin's Russia," *The Russian Review*, vol. 56, no. 1 (1997); Lynne Viola, *Peasant Rebels Under Stalin: Collectivization and the Culture of Peasant Resistance* (New York, 1996); Sarah Davies, *Popular Opinion in Stalin's Russia: Terror, Propaganda, and Dissent, 1934–1941* (New York, 1997); Golfo Alexopoulos, "Portrait of a Con Artist as a Soviet Man," *Slavic Review*, vol. 57, no. 4 (1998). In this volume, see Fitzpatrick.

[15] Nataliia Kozlova, "Krest'ianskii syn," *Sotsiologicheskie issledovaniia* 1994, no. 6; Veronique Garros et al., eds., *Intimacy and Terror: Soviet Diaries of the 1930s* (New York, 1995). In this volume, see Hellbeck.

[16] See, for example, Wendy Goldman, *Women, the State and Revolution: Soviet Family Policy and Social Life, 1917–1936* (New York, 1993); Melanie Ilic, *Women Workers in the Soviet Interwar Economy: From 'Protection' to 'Equality'* (New York, 1999).

[17] See, for example, Yuri Slezkine, "The USSR as a Communal Apartment, or How a Socialist State Promoted Ethnic Particularism," *Slavic Review*, vol. 53, no. 2 (1994); Ronald Grigor Suny, *The Revenge of the Past: Nationalism Revolution, and the Collapse of the Soviet Union* (Stanford, 1993); Terry Martin, *The Affirmative Action Empire: Nations and Nationalism in the Soviet Union, 1923–1939* (Ithaca, 2001).

trialization. Covering all aspects of Soviet economic history during the industrialization drive, Davies's work, along with contributions by other British economic historians, constitutes one of the most valuable bodies of scholarship on Stalinism.[18] This research is nicely complemented by several important studies of Soviet workers during Soviet industrialization, and by recent work on Soviet trade and consumption during the Stalin era.[19] Regrettably scholarship on Stalinist diplomatic and military history also could not be included in this volume.[20] Instead the focus will be on the political and social history of Stalinism.

Stalinism was one of the most central phenomena of Russian history and of the twentieth-century world; it was also one of the deadliest, involving the incarceration and execution of millions of people. It is therefore appropriate that Stalinism has been the subject of intense scrutiny and lively scholarly debate. Historians have the role of trying to understand the past – what happened, why things occurred, and what they mean. In the case of the Stalinist past, historians struggle to understand it, not only, as is so often intoned, to avoid repeating it, but also to come to terms with it, and perhaps even to help work through the collective trauma it inflicted. Stalinism represents one of the darkest and most complex pages of human history, and it therefore deserves our most careful attention and thought. This volume seeks to facilitate that task by presenting a range of interpretations as to the origins and consequences of Stalinism.

[18] R. W. Davies, *The Industrialization of Soviet Russia* (Cambridge, Mass., 1980 and London, 1989–1996). See also Alec Nove, *An Economic History of the USSR* (New York, 1969); E. A. Rees, *Stalinism and Soviet Rail Transport, 1928–1941* (London, 1995); Stephen Wheatcroft et al., "Soviet Industrialization Reconsidered: Some Preliminary Conclusions about Economic Development 1926–1941," *Economic History Review*, 1986, no. 2.

[19] On labor history, see Lewis H. Siegelbaum, *Stakhanovism and the Politics of Productivity* (New York, 1988); Hiroaki Kuromiya, *Stalin's Industrial Revolution: Politics and Workers, 1928–1932* (New York, 1988), and *Freedom and Terror in the Donbas: A Ukrainian-Russian Border Region, 1870s–1990s* (New York, 1998); Francesco Benvenuti, *Fuoco sui Sabotatori! Stachanovismo e Organizzazione Industriale in URSS, 1934–1938* (Rome, 1988); Donald A. Filtzer, *Soviet Workers and Stalinist Industrialization: The Formation of Modern Soviet Production Relations, 1928–1941* (London, 1986). On Stalinist trade, see E. A. Osokina, *Our Daily Bread: Socialist Distribution and the Art of Survival in Stalin's Russia, 1927–1941* (Armonk, NY, 2001); Julie Hessler, "Cultured Trade: The Stalinist Turn Towards Consumerism," in Fitzpatrick, ed.; Amy E. Randall, "Revolutionary Bolshevik Work: Stakhanovism in Retail Trade," *The Russian Review*, vol. 59, no. 3 (2000).

[20] See, for example, Jonathan Haslam, *The Soviet Union and the Struggle for Collective Security in Europe, 1933–1939* (London, 1984); Gabriel Gorodetsky; *Grand Delusion: Stalin and the German Invasion of Russia* (New Haven, 1999); William Taubman, *Stalin's American Policy: From Entente to Détente to Cold War* (New York, 1982); John Erickson, *The Road to Stalingrad* (London, 1975), and *The Road to Berlin: Continuing the History of Stalin's War with Germany* (Boulder, Co., 1983).

Part I The Origins of Stalinism

Stalin's Role

Stalin and his Stalinism: Power and Authority in the Soviet Union, 1930–1953

Ronald Grigor Suny

Excerpted from Ronald Grigor Suny, "Stalin and his Stalinism: Power and Authority in the Soviet Union, 1930–53," in Ian Kershaw and Moshe Lewin, eds., *Stalinism and Nazism: Dictatorships in Comparison* (New York: Cambridge University Press, 1997).

Editor's Introduction

In explaining Stalinism, many historians focus on Joseph Stalin himself – his mindset, his methods, and his personality. Characterizations of Stalin highlight both his Machiavellian thinking and his malicious nature. Stalin is thus portrayed as an evil genius – someone whose cunning and ability to wield power were matched only by his vindictiveness toward potential rivals. In this view, the brutality and terror of the Stalinist system derived principally from Stalin himself. As an omnipotent but paranoid leader, Stalin arrested and executed millions of innocent people, including many of his fellow Communist Party members. Through this exercise of mass terror, he ensured that no one opposed his policies or challenged his personal dictatorship.

Such explanations generally emphasize Stalin's ruthless maneuvering to account not only for his bloody reign but for his rise to power in the first place. Apart from his guile, Stalin seemed an unlikely successor to Lenin. He lacked the theoretical brilliance and oratorical skills of Trotsky and other leading Communists. Many Party members saw him primarily as a functionary – someone skilled in organizational matters though unsuited for leadership. But Stalin proved to be an extremely effective political infighter. By aligning first with one group and then another, he succeeded in discrediting and eliminating rivals, until he emerged in the late 1920s as the supreme leader of the country.[1] Stalin was aided in his rise to power by his appointment as the Communist Party's General Secretary – the person in charge of personnel matters. Initially seen as an administrative post, Stalin used this position to promote his own loyalists within the Party and thus to build his base of support.[2]

Other historians have questioned whether Stalin's rise can be attributed solely to his manipulation and ruthlessness. They point out that Stalin, with his blunt and dogmatic style, actually appealed to many rank-and-file Communists, and that his shifting positions were responses to changing political and economic circumstances instead of purely tactical moves to outflank his opponents.[3] Scholars have also noted that both Stalin's political shifts and his intolerance of dissent were common to other Communist leaders, and hence reflected emergency circumstances and Party culture as much as Stalin's personal predisposition. As Chris Ward writes, "Stalin's personality cannot be divorced from the world in which he functioned."[4] Of course, it was Stalin who took the Party's intolerance of dissent to such extremes that he executed thousands of fellow Communists during the Great Purges of the late 1930s. The question of Stalin's personal role, then, is one still very much debated by historians.

In the selection that follows, Ronald Grigor Suny, a specialist on Stalin and Soviet nationalities, synthesizes old and new evidence regarding Stalin's method of rule and his personal imprint on the system that bears his name. Suny maintains that, contrary to the totalitarian model, the Stalinist system did not completely control or atomize Soviet society. While Stalin concentrated enormous power at the top, that power was diffused downward through lower-level Soviet officials. Factory directors and collective farm managers had to accommodate workers and peasants to some degree, and this accommodation left room for the average Soviet citizen to maneuver within the system.

While he rejects the totalitarian model, Suny still emphasizes the extremely negative characteristics of Stalinism and attributes these to Stalin personally. He argues that Stalin drastically departed from Lenin's policies and practices; his article thus exemplifies the revisionist argument

[1] Adam B. Ulam, *Stalin: The Man and His Era* (Boston, 1989); Anton Antonov-Ovseyenko, *The Time of Stalin: Portrait of a Tyranny*, trans. George Saunders (New York, 1980); Dmitrii Volkogonov, *Stalin: Triumph and Tragedy*, trans. Harold Shukman (New York, 1991).

[2] Leonard Schapiro, *The Communist Party of the Soviet Union* (New York, 1960); T. H. Rigby, *Communist Party Membership in the U.S.S.R., 1917–1967* (Princeton, 1968). As Suny writes in the selection below, Stalin was the ultimate "man of the machine."

[3] Robert C. Tucker, *Stalin in Power: The Revolution from Above 1928–1941* (New York, 1990); Michal Reiman, *The Birth of Stalinism: The USSR on the Eve of the "Second Revolution,"* trans. George Saunders (London, 1987). For more on economic debates within the Party, see Alexander Erlich, *The Soviet Industrialization Debate 1924–1928* (Cambridge, Mass., 1960).

[4] Chris Ward, *Stalin's Russia* (New York, 1993), p. 32.

that there was a fundamental discontinuity between Bolshevism and Stalinism. Suny highlights a range of areas – collectivization of the peasantry, suppression of national minorities, cultural conservatism, and a turn away from internationalism – where Stalin deviated from the original orientation of Lenin and the Bolsheviks. Indeed, as Suny points out, Stalin eventually executed most of the original Bolsheviks during the Great Purges, which made his break with Bolshevism even more complete.

In his discussion of the Great Purges, Suny stresses Stalin's personal mistrust and vindictiveness toward others. He cites Stalin's letters demanding the execution of alleged conspirators as well as Party leaders' accounts noting Stalin's suspiciousness and insecurity. Quoting another scholar, he calls Stalin's "gloomy personality" and "paranoid tendencies" crucial causes of Stalinist terror. He also concludes that, despite debates among historians about the political dynamics behind the Great Purges, that Stalin's will and ambition were the principle catalyst. Through the purges, Stalin established unlimited despotism over the Party as well as the country. As Suny describes, a number of high-ranking Party members opposed Stalin's policies prior to the purges, but afterwards any opposition to Stalin became unthinkable.

In addition to making the argument that Stalin personally shaped the Stalinist system, Suny's article provides a good overview of the Stalin period. He describes the "Stalin revolution" – Stalin's elimination of private trade and creation of a state-run economy. This economic program, which included the coercive collectivization of agriculture, facilitated rapid industrialization but caused great deprivation and suffering among the population. Suny also discusses another important element of Stalinism, the Stalin cult – a propaganda effort that presented Stalin as a wise and charismatic leader. This cult bolstered Stalin's legitimacy and helped establish him as Lenin's heir even as he deviated from Leninism in practice. After analyzing Stalin's cultural conservatism and use of terror during the purges, Suny turns finally to the Second World War and postwar years, which saw Stalin's power grow even greater. The exigencies of war promoted further concentration of authority in Stalin's hands, and the victory over Nazi Germany raised Stalin's stature to new heights. But as Suny notes, overcentralization and Stalin's own mental deterioration exacerbated the mistrust and rigidity that plagued the Stalinist system.

Stalin and his Stalinism: Power and Authority in the Soviet Union, 1930–1953

Ronald Grigor Suny

The deceptively simple question to be answered in this essay is: how did Stalin rule? How did he maintain his authority while establishing a personal autocracy? His extraordinary and brutal political achievement was to act in the name of the Communist party and its central committee against that party and central committee, while remaining the unchallenged head of party and state and, evidently, a vastly popular leader. At the end of the process his absolute grip on power allowed him to declare black white and completely reverse the foreign policy of the Soviet Union and the line of the Comintern by embracing Nazi Germany in a non-aggression pact. The colossal and costly destruction he brought upon the country on the eve and in the early days of the Second World War gave rise to no organised opposition, and the centralised apparatus of control that he had created was not only able to weather the Nazi invasion but to organise a victory that would preserve the essence of the system he forged for another half-century.

The simplest, though inadequate, answer to the question, would be that Stalin's power was maintained through the exercise of terror and monopolistic control of the means of communication throughout society. Though certainly an important part of the answer, an exclusive focus on terror and propaganda does not explain how Stalin won his authority within the party in the 1920s and maintained it among his own supporters even before the advent of the Great Terror. Once initiated, terror operated through collaboration, and Stalin's associates almost never attempted to free themselves from the source of their fears. Terror was supported by many within and outside the party who believed that extraordinary means against vicious and hidden enemies were required. Tens of millions regarded Stalin as the indispensable leader of the 'socialist' camp, perhaps someone to be feared as was Ivan *groznyi*, a leader who filled the hearts of enemies with awe.[1] . . .

The author wishes to express his gratitude to Lewis Siegelbaum and Moshe Lewin for their careful and critical readings of earlier drafts.

[1] Michael Cherniavsky, 'Ivan the Terrible as Renaissance Prince', *Slavic Review*, 27, 2 (June 1968), pp. 195–211.

Building Hegemony in the 1930s

Though the relative peace, stability, and economic improvement of the NEP years, in contrast to the preceding seven years of war, revolution, and civil war, had given the Leninist state a degree of acceptance and authority in the eyes of many, that acceptance was fragile and based on the compromises and limits of what the Communists almost invariably saw as a transitional period, a temporary retreat from socialism. The launching of the Stalin revolution, first in the countryside and then in industry, destroyed the basis of the regime's fragile relationship with the great majority of the population (the *smychka*) and created a new crisis of legitimacy and authority.

By ending NEP and almost all private production and trade, Stalin created the first modern non-market, state-run economy, one that simultaneously eliminated rival sources of power and resistance to the will of the central authorities. 'Industrialists' no longer held property in the means of production. Workers could no longer effectively organise in order to raise the price of labour. Farmers could no longer withhold grain to affect market prices. Yet all of these groups devised ways within the command economy to exercise limited degrees of power, autonomy, and resistance. Workers, to take one example, were able to undermine harsh factory regimes by taking their skills, so desired by managers, to another workplace. Bosses, caught between demands from above for higher productivity, had to satisfy, however inadequately, some of the needs and demands of their workers and even permit a degree of worker autonomy on the shop floor.[2] Much of the time and effort of Soviet officials was concerned with raising output and productivity, and successive state strategies required accommodations and concessions as often as additional pressure and repression.[3] Thus, while power was actively being concentrated at the top by Stalin, it was being diffused downward and outward throughout the economic and political systems by thousands of *vintiki* (little screws) who had their own requirements for survival and 'making out'. The state grew; in Moshe Lewin's sense, it 'swallowed' society; but at the same time it was unable to realise the vision presented by totalitarian theory of complete atomisation of society. The limits of state power were met when people refused to work

[2] Hiroaki Kuromiya, *Stalin's Industrial Revolution: Politics and Workers, 1928–1932* (Cambridge: Cambridge University Press 1988).
[3] Much of the work of Lewis Siegelbaum has explored the various strategies by which the regime attempted to raise productivity. See, for example, his 'Soviet Norm Determination in Theory and Practice, 1917–1941', *Soviet Studies*, 36 (1984), pp. 48–67; and *Stakhanovism and the Politics of Productivity in the USSR, 1935–1941* (Cambridge: Cambridge University Press 1988).

efficiently, migrated from place to place by the millions, or informally worked out ways to resist pressure from above.

Stalin came to power in the absence of a broad consensus on the legitimacy and necessity of his personal rule. Using the instruments of state power to mobilise people in a grand programme of social transformation, the regime confidently conceived of itself as possessing a popular and historically sanctioned mandate and worked assiduously to increase support for itself through education and propaganda, leadership cults, election campaigns, broad national discussions (e.g., on the constitution), public celebrations (like the Pushkin centennial of 1937), show trials, and political rituals.[4] Most importantly, the party/state made real concessions to the populace and satisfied the ambitions and aspirations of many (certainly not all) for social mobility and an improved living standard. Peasants who became workers and workers who became managers and party bosses were moving up, while many of their envied social 'betters' of the past were experiencing an enforced downward mobility.[5]

In the Stalinist formulation the 'revolution from above' of the 1930s, though initiated by the state, was supported from below by millions of peasants and workers struggling to create a new society based on collective farms and socialist industry. The state-initiated industrialisation of the 1930s mobilised millions of men and women into the most mammoth building project in modern times, and a romance of dams and powerstations, new cities on the steppe and in Siberia, created enthusiasts among the new workers and managers. The enormous difficulties that the breakthrough into 'socialism' entailed – resistance from farmers, famine, economic bottlenecks and breakdowns – were seen as the work of enemies and saboteurs, rather than inherent in the party's policies or a by-product of popular recalcitrance and massive coercion. Though the disjuncture between these forced images of imagined harmony and purpose and the hardships and dislocations of actual worksites created unease among many who attempted to govern a vast country, the sheer scale of the transformation and its construction as a human epic engendered the broad social support that the regime had sought for two decades.[6]

---

[4] Christel Lane, *The Rites of Rulers: Ritual in Industrial Society – the Soviet Case* (Cambridge: Cambridge University Press 1981).

[5] Social mobility has been a frequent theme in the work of Sheila Fitzpatrick. See, for example, *Education and Social Mobility in the Soviet Union, 1921–1934* (Cambridge: Cambridge University Press 1979); and 'Stalin and the Making of a New Elite, 1928–1939', *Slavic Review*, 38, 3 (September 1979), pp. 377–402.

[6] As the Harvard Project interviews in the early 1950s demonstrated, and as Donna Bahry has emphasised in a recent study, 'one of the cardinal values defining the Soviet

The naked exercise of unrestrained power was key to Stalin's victory, but his regime simultaneously worked to create authority and acceptance, borrowing from and supplementing the repertoire of justifications from Lenin's day. While appropriating the mantle of Lenin and much of the rhetoric of Bolshevism, however, Stalin revised, suppressed, and even reversed much of the legacy of Lenin. Internationalism turned into nationalism; the *smychka* between the workers and the peasants was buried in the ferocity of collectivisation; radical transformation of the family and the place of women ended with reassertion of the most conservative 'family values'. And in the process almost all of Lenin's closest associates fell victim to the self-proclaimed keeper of the Leninist flame.

Within ten years of his dispute with Lenin, Stalin transformed nationality policy from a series of concessions to non-Russians into a powerful weapon of imperial state-building. He reversed Lenin's focus on 'Great Russian chauvinism' as the principal danger in nationality relations and emphasised instead the dangers from the nationalism of non-Russians. In 1923, he turned on M. Kh. Sultan-Galiev, a former associate in Narkomnats and a spokesman for the aspirations of Muslim Communists, accused him of *national-uklonizm* (national deviationism), had him 'tried' before a party conference, arrested, and expelled from the party.[7] Five years later, the state police 'discovered' a new plot, the 'Sultan-Galiev counter-revolutionary organisation', and in the next decade the OGPU and its successor, the NKVD, 'unmasked' dozens of conspiratorial groups promoting nationalism from Ukraine to Central Asia.[8] In a letter to Levon Mirzoian, first secretary of the Kazakh *kraikom*, in 1933, Stalin called for intensifying the struggle against local

---

system's claim to legitimacy was industrial transformation . . . [R]apid industrialization appeared to have near-universal backing' (Donna Bahry, 'Society Transformed? Rethinking the Social Roots of Perestroika', *Slavic Review*, 52, 3 (Fall 1993), p. 524).

[7] *Tainy natsional'noi politiki TsK RKP: 'Chetvertoe soveshchanie TsK RKP s otvetstvennymi rabotnikami natsional'nykh respublik i oblastei v g. Moskve 9–12 iiunia 1923 g.': Stenograficheskii otchet* (Moscow: Insan 1992); N. Tagirov, 'Sultan-Galiev: Pravda i domysly', *Kommunist Tatarii*, no. 9 (September 1989), pp. 68–76; 'Shchitaem svoim revoliutsionnym dolgom', *Kommunist Tatarii*, no. 6 (June 1990), pp. 51–5; Alexandre A. Bennigsen and S. Enders Wimbush, *Muslim National Communism in the Soviet Union: A Revolutionary Strategy for the Colonial World* (Chicago: University of Chicago Press 1979); Stephen Blank, 'Stalin's First Victim: The Trial of Sultangaliev', *Russian History/Histoire Russe*, 17, 2 (Summer 1990), pp. 155–78; Douglas Taylor Northrop, 'Reconsidering Sultan-Galiev', in *Selected Topics in Soviet Ethnopolitics*, eds. Gail Lapidus and Corbin Lydey (Berkeley: University of California 1992), pp. 1–44.

[8] 'V komissii Politbiuro TsK KPSS po dopolnitel'nomu izucheniiu materialov, sviazannykh s repressiiami, imevshimi mesto v period 30–40-kh i nachala 50-kh godov', *Izvestiia TsK KPSS*, no. 9 (1990), pp. 71–6; 'O tak nazyvaemom "national-uklonizme"', *Izvestiia TsK KPSS*, no. 9 (1990), pp. 76–84.

Kazakh nationalism 'in order to create the conditions for the sowing of Leninist internationalism'.[9] Five years later, after having carried out purges against Kazakh intellectuals and 'deviationist' party members, Mirzoian himself was arrested and executed.[10]

Stalinism was both a revolutionising system, unwilling to accept backward Russia as it was (and here it differs from many traditionally authoritarian dictatorships), and a conservative, restorative one, anxious to reestablish hierarchies, affirm certain traditional values like patriotism and patriarchy, and create political legitimacy based on more than victorious revolution.[11] The revolution and the restoration were both evident in the 1930s, with the former powerfully present in the First Five-Year Plan period and the latter dominating in the middle 1930s. The unresolved tensions between those aspects of Stalinism that extended the revolutionary egalitarian, participatory impulses of 1917 and those that resurrected stratification and authoritarianism remained in irresolvable tension with one another.

The ultimate 'man of the machine', Stalin was one of the least likely candidates for charismatic hero. Short in stature, reticent in meetings and on public occasions, neither a talented orator like Trotsky or Zinoviev, nor an attractive and engaging personality, like Lenin or Bukharin, Stalin did not himself project an image of a leader – until it was created for him (and by him) through the cult. First the promotion of a cult of Lenin, which Stalin actively encouraged, then his identification as a loyal Leninist, and eventually his merger with and substitution for the image of Lenin were important props for Stalin's authority both within the party and in society.[12] All this was accomplished in a political culture based on the pre-revolutionary Bolshevik traditions in

---

[9] Ibid., p. 79.

[10] Boris Levytsky (comp.), *The Stalinist Terror in the Thirties: Documentation from the Soviet Press* (Stanford: Hoover Institution Press 1974), pp. 176–9; Martha Brill Olcott, *The Kazakhs* (Stanford: Hoover Institution Press 1987), pp. 218–19.

[11] Nowhere was this more evident than in the state's shifting strategies toward women and the family. See Wendy Z. Goldman, 'Women, Abortion and the State, 1917–36', in *Russia's Women: Accommodation, Resistance, Transformation*, eds. Barbara Evans Clements, Barbara Alpern Engel, and Christine D. Worobec (Berkeley–Los Angeles: University of California Press 1991); and her *Women, the State and Revolution: Soviet Family Policy and Social Life, 1917–1936* (Cambridge: Cambridge University Press 1993).

[12] Robert C. Tucker, 'The Rise of Stalin's Personality Cult', *American Historical Review*, 84, 2 (April 1979), pp. 347–66. A key role in the effort to link Stalin with the legacy of Lenin was played by Stalin's assistant, Tovstukha, who worked in the Lenin Institute from 1924 to 1926, helped edit the first two volumes of Lenin's collected works, edited the first nine editions of Stalin's collection of articles *Problemy leninizma*, and wrote the first official Soviet biography of Stalin (1927) (Rosenfeldt, *Knowledge and Power*, pp. 170–4; *Pravda*, 10 August 1935, pp. 1, 3; 'I. B. Rusanova, I. P. Tovstukha. K 80-letiiu so dnia rozhdeniia', *Voprosy istorii KPSS*, no. 4 (1969), pp. 128–30).

which emphasis on personality, the exaggerated importance of the leader, and the attendant sacral notions of infallibility were all alien.

The ideological props of the Stalin dictatorship were both a radically revised Marxism and a pro-Russian nationalism and etatism. Class warfare was seen as inevitable and intensifying rather than diminishing as the country approached socialism. As long as the country was surrounded by hostile capitalist states, it was claimed, state power had to be built up. When the Soviet Union was declared to be socialist by Stalin in 1936, the positive achievement of reaching a stage of history higher than the rest of the world was tempered by the constant reminders that the enemies of socialism existed both within and outside the country, that they are deceptive and concealed, and must be 'unmasked'. Repeated references to dangers and insecurity and to the need for 'vigilance' justified the enormous reliance on the 'steel gauntlets of Ezhov'.

Inventing Opposition

The enthusiasm for industrialisation was tempered by much less support for Stalin's agrarian revolution. The open resistance to collectivisation among the peasants was reflected in less dramatic form by quiet forms of opposition within the party. The oligarchy that carried out the Stalin revolution was a very narrow political elite but not one that had effectively closed the party to debate and consideration of alternatives. Between the fall of Bukharin in 1928–9 and the death of Kirov in December 1934, Stalin-faction rule produced and reproduced oppositions and potential oppositions. The real disagreements with the General Line of rapid industrialisation and full collectivisation and dekulakisation were fuelled by the evident failures and costs of implementing these policies. In his own statements Stalin refused to accept any blame for the economic chaos or the famine. Because 'the last remnants of moribund classes', some of whom had 'even managed to worm their way into the party', were actively sabotaging the building of socialism, more repression was needed.

> The abolition of classes is not achieved by the extinction of the class struggle, but its intensification . . . We must bear in mind that the growth of the power of the Soviet state will intensify the resistance of the last remnants of the dying classes.[13]

[13] Originally this was an idea put forth by Trotsky. I. V. Stalin, 'Itogi pervoi piatiletki: Doklad 7 ianvaria 1933 g.', *Sochineniia*, 12, pp. 211–12.

In a letter replying to the Cossack writer Mikhail Sholokhov's protests against the systematic brutality of the grain collection, Stalin took a hard line:

> One must take into account . . . the other side. And that other side amounts to the fact that the respected corn-growers of your region (and not only your region) have gone on a sit-down strike (sabotage!) and shown no concern about leaving the workers, the Red Army, without grain. The fact that the sabotage was peaceful and outwardly bloodless in no way alters the realities – that the respected grain-growers have in essence carried out a 'peaceful' war with Soviet power. A war by starvation (*voina na izmor*), dear Comrade Sholokhov.[14]

The growing gap between the public statements and images put forth by the state, on the one hand, and the real destruction in the countryside, on the other, prompted prominent party members to resist the cover-up of the failures. Already in late 1930 some in the leadership of the RSFSR and the Transcaucasian federation expressed misgivings, which in turn were interpreted by the Stalin centre as a widespread and united oppositional tendency (the Syrtsov–Lominadze Right–Left Bloc).[15] Swift retribution (demotion in these cases) did not deter a number of other critical foci from emerging, notably the Riutin Platform and Appeal (1932) and the Smirnov, Tolmachev, and Eismont opposition (1932). Within the Central Committee and the Politburo more moderate elements opposed the rapid tempos in industry and proposed a more conciliatory attitude toward society, particularly the peasantry.

[14] Quoted by Khrushchev, 8 March 1963; *Pravda*, 10 March 1963; Jonathan Haslam, 'Political Opposition to Stalin and the Origins of the Terror in Russia, 1932–1936', *The Historical Journal*, 29, 2 (1986), p. 403.

[15] R. W. Davies, "The Syrtsov–Lominadze Affair', *Soviet Studies*, 33, 1 (January 1981), pp. 29–50. Indicative of the mood in the party is a conversation with Lominadze reported by a friend: 'When I saw him, with another of his friends, in 1931, he was boldly critical of Stalin's leadership. Now that opposition from both Left and Right had been suppressed, he thought the next logical step was a radical reform of the Party and its personnel.

"What about the General Secretary?" asked his friend.

"If there is a spring cleaning, every piece of furniture has to be removed, including the biggest one."

"But who could replace him?"

"That's up to the Congress." It was time for younger men to take a share of the responsibility – men who had some practical experience but had been less involved in the struggle between the factions.

Needless to say, this was extremely risky talk. It even occurred to me that Lominadze saw himself as a suitable successor to Stalin' (Joseph Berger, *Shipwreck of a Generation: The Memoirs of Joseph Berger* (London: Harvill Press 1971); American edition: *Nothing But the Truth* (New York: John Day 1971), p. 166).

The short-lived attempt to organise opposition to Stalin by Martem'ian Ivanovich Riutin never went further than a few meetings of like-minded party members, the formation of an organisation – the Union of Marxist–Leninists, the discussion of Riutin's report, 'Stalin and the Crisis of the Proletarian Dictatorship', and an appeal to party members to join their efforts. Riutin condemned Stalin's emerging dictatorship as the negation of the collective leadership of the Central Committee and the principal cause of the growing disillusionment of the people with socialism. He believed that the only way to save Bolshevism was to remove Stalin and his clique by force. If Riutin was right that 'the faith of the masses in socialism has been broken, its readiness to defend selflessly the proletarian revolution from all enemies weakens each year', then the regime had either to move immediately toward conciliation and the rebuilding of confidence or turn to even more radical and repressive measures.[16]

Riutin's circle is an unusual instance of coherence and organisation among those who opposed Stalin."[17] Much more evident was a broad, inchoate discontent with Stalin's rule that permeated political and intellectual circles. Several loyal Stalinists, like Kaminskii, Kosior, Vareikis, and Bauman, harboured serious doubts about Stalin's agricultural policies. Others, like Mykola Skrypnyk, a co-founder of the Ukrainian Communist Party who had sided with Stalin in the 1920s and early 1930s, were critical of the growing ethnocentrism in the party and state and the evident pro-Russianness of Stalin's nationality poli-

---

[16] On Riutin, see: 'Stalin i krizis proletarskoi diktatury' [Platform of the Union of Marxist–Leninists (the Riutin Group)], *Izvestiia TsK KPSS*, no. 8 (1990), pp. 200–7; no. 9, pp. 165–83; no. 10, pp. 191–206; no. 11, pp. 161–86; no. 12, pp. 180–99, with commentary, pp. 200–2; M. Riutin, 'Ko vsem chlenam VKP (b)', reprinted in *Osmyslit kult Stalina*, ed. Kh. Kobo (Moscow: Progress 1989), pp. 618–23; 'O dele tak nazyvaemogo "Soiuza Marksistov–Leninistev"', *Izvestiia TsK KPSS*, no. 6 (1989), pp. 103–15. See also, the biography of Riutin by B. A. Starkov in *Izvestiia TsK KPSS*, no. 3 (1990), pp. 150–63, followed by Riutin's letters, pp. 163–78.

[17] The members of the Riutin group were arrested a few weeks after their first meeting. Riutin had been expelled from the party in 1930, and his seventeen associates were expelled by the Central Control Commission on 9 October 1932, for 'having attempted to set up a bourgeois, kulak organization to re-establish capitalism and, in particular, the kulak system in the USSR by means of underground activity under the fraudulent banner of "Marxism–Leninism"'. A number of accounts hold that Stalin demanded the death penalty for Riutin but was thwarted by Kirov and other moderates (Boris I. Nicolaevsky, *Power and the Soviet Elite: 'The Letter of an Old Bolshevik' and Other Essays* (New York: Frederick A. Praeger 1965), pp. 3–65; Arkadii Vaksberg, 'Kak zhivoi s zhivymi', *Literaturnaia gazeta*, 29 June 1988; Lev Razgon, 'Nakonets!' *Moskovskie novosti*, 26 June 1988; Dmitrii Volkogonov, *Triumf i tragediia: Politicheskii portret I. V. Stalina*, I, part 2 (Moscow: Novosti 1989), pp. 85–6). Riutin was sentenced to ten years' solitary confinement. On 10 January 1937, he was secretly tried and shot.

cies.[18] Perhaps most ominously, tensions arose between the Red Army commander, Mikhail Tukhachevskii, who called in 1930 for expansion of the armed forces, particularly aviation and tank armies, and Stalin and Voroshilov, who opposed what they called 'Red militarism'.[19] During the famine in Ukraine high military officers, like Iakir, angered Stalin by reporting their upset at peasant resistance, which, they felt, could spread to the troops, and by demanding that more grain be kept in the region.[20]

Even among Stalin's closest supporters there were fractures, though their precise nature remains mysterious. The open disagreement at the Seventeenth Party Congress (January–February 1934) between Orjonikidze and Molotov over industrial targets was a rare public sign of a deeper split between moderates and radicals.[21] The popular Kirov, the only real rival left to Stalin by 1932, was in all his public and political appearances completely loyal to the General Secretary, though he often emphasised the need for 'revolutionary legality', which was understood to be a lessening of repressive measures.[22] Stalin still represented for the majority of party members the militant turn toward socialism – collectivisation, rapid industrialisation, the destruction of organised political opposition. However, his personal proclivity toward the use of force seemed to some to have gone beyond the broad bounds of Bolshevik practice.

The private letters from the vacationing Stalin to his closest comrade Molotov (from 1930 and 1933) reveal in a striking way the less public characteristics of the dictator and his methods of rule. He wrote short, terse memoranda to Molotov on the important matters that were before the Politburo, and apparently did the same with Kaganovich, Orjonikidze, and others. 'From the boss (*khoziain*) we are receiving regular and frequent directives', Kaganovich wrote to Orjonikidze in 1932.[23] While he preferred to work through his own narrow circle of friends – Molotov, who was his principal executor, Voroshilov, Mikoyan,

---

[18] Skrypnyk committed suicide in 1933, as Ukrainian national communists were systematically being purged.

[19] R. W. Davies, *The Industrialisation of Soviet Russia, 3: The Soviet Economy in Turmoil, 1929–1930* (Cambridge, Mass: Harvard University Press 1989), pp. 446–7. In May 1932 Stalin apologised to Tukhachevskii and endorsed some of his proposed reforms.

[20] Eventually some grain was sent to Ukraine in January 1933 along with the new party boss, Postyshev.

[21] Kendall E. Bailes, *Technology and Society under Lenin and Stalin: Origins of the Soviet Technical Intelligentsia, 1917–1941* (Princeton: Princeton University Press 1978), pp. 275–80; J. Arch Getty, *Origins of the Great Purges* (Cambridge: Cambridge University Press 1985), pp. 13–17.

[22] S. Kirov, *Stati i rechi, 1934* (Moscow 1934).

[23] 'Pis'ma Stalina Molotovu', p. 94.

Orjonikidze, Kaganovich – Stalin was quick to turn on any of them if he felt challenged. In 1933 he severely criticised Orjonikidze for objecting to remarks by Vyshinskii that attacked those working in the industrial and agricultural ministries: 'The behaviour of Sergo (and Iakovlev) in the story of the "completeness of production" is impossible to call anything else but anti-party, because it has as its objective goal the defence of reactionary elements of the party *against* the CC VKP(b).'[24] Because Kaganovich had sided with Orjonikidze, he too fell under Stalin's wrath. Nothing came of this dispute at the time, nor of the more serious accusations made against Mikhail Kalinin.

The OGPU was carrying out investigations in 1930 into a series of anti-Soviet 'parties' made up of former Mensheviks, industrial specialists, and Ukrainian activists.[25] Stalin received regular reports from Iagoda and insisted that Molotov circulate them among the members of the Central Committee and the Central Control Commission, as well as among 'the more active of our *khoziaistvenniki* (economic managers)'. He told Molotov that he was convinced that these conspiratorial elements were linked with the Rightists within the party.

> It is absolutely essential to shoot Kondrat'ev, Groman and a pair of the other bastards (*merzavtsy*) . . . It is absolutely essential to shoot the whole group of wreckers in meat production and to publish this information in the press.[26]

He personally demanded the arrests of the former Menshevik Sukhanov, his Communist wife (who, he says, must have known what was going on in their home), Bazarov, Ramzin, and others. The concocted stories of anti-Soviet conspiracies were fed throughout the top bureaucracy and created an atmosphere of suspicion that justified the use of precisely the kinds of harsh measures that Stalin advocated.

Fear and the need for vigilance, which were created both by the police findings and by the real and imagined weaknesses and insecurities of the Soviet Union, bound the Communists together around the leader who projected an image of Bolshevik toughness. At the same time the Stalinist settlement involved the creation of a highly hierarchical system of rewards and privileges, of access to information and influence, that effectively disenfranchised the great mass of the population and privileged a small number of party and state officials, intellectuals, and managers. The end of rationing in 1934–5 forced everyone below the privileged upper levels of society to forage in government stores and peasant markets for what they could afford. Social inequalities grew in

[24] Ibid., p. 94.
[25] Ibid., p. 103.
[26] Ibid., p. 103.

an economy of permanent shortages where money talked less effectively than one's position and personal connections. A 'ruling class without tenure', in Lewin's phrase,[27] grew increasingly dependent on being in favour with those even higher up. They were under a constant threat of demotion, expulsion from the party, arrest and even death. Their success required absolute and unquestioning obedience, enforcement of the decisions from the top with determination, even ruthlessness, on those below, and a willingness to acquiesce and participate in what can only be considered criminal activity (denunciations of the innocent, approval of lawlessness, collaboration with a regime based on deception).[28] Their dilemma was that it was dangerous for them to be anything but responsive to the top, and yet their position and requirements to increase production and satisfy the demands of the top and the centre pulled them toward making arrangements with the bottom and the periphery.

Conservative Revolutionary

Neither a consistent moderate nor radical, Stalin himself shifted from centre-right (during his alliance with Bukharin in the mid-1920s) to left (during the period of the so-called 'cultural revolution' at the end of the 1920s and the early 1930s) and then back to a more moderate position around 1931–2. Responding to a growing mood among party leaders concerned with industry, Stalin announced in June 1931 a major change in the party's wage policy (the end of *uravnilovka*, levelling the wages, and the introduction of greater differentials between skilled and unskilled workers in order to end labour migration) and a much more tolerant and supportive policy toward the technical intelligentsia.[29] Whether or not this policy shift was imposed on Stalin or corresponded to a genuine reevaluation of his position, during the next half-decade he steadily began to reverse the more radical policies of the end of the 1920s and the early 1930s and pull back from egalitarianism and collectivism toward a promotion of hierarchy, cultural traditionalism, and social conservatism that has come to be known as the 'Great Retreat'.

---

[27] Moshe Lewin, 'The Social Background of Stalinism', in *Stalinism: Essays in Historical Interpretation*, ed. Robert C. Tucker, (New York: W. W. Norton 1977), p. 130.

[28] Roi Medvedev, *Oni okruzhali Stalina* (Moscow 1990); English translation: *All Stalin's Men* (Garden City, NY: Doubleday 1984).

[29] I. V. Stalin, 'Novaia obstanovka – novye zadachi khoziaistvennogo stroitel'stva', *Sochineniia*, 13 (Moscow: Gosudarstvennoe izdatel'stvo politicheskoi literatury 1951), pp. 51–80. Bailes shows how this conciliatory move was initiated by Orjonikidze and others involved in industrial production (*Technology and Society*, pp. 144–55).

On a variety of fronts the Stalinists retreated from their forward positions of just a few years earlier. Though the collective farms remained firmly under the tutelage of the state and continued to operate essentially as grain-collection apparatuses,[30] a series of decisions allowed the collective-farm peasants to possess some livestock, to sell their surpluses on the market, and to own their houses and work household plots. While workers were increasingly restricted in their movements through the 1930s, an essentially 'bourgeois' system of remuneration was created: 'from each according to his ability, to each according to his work'. Workers were encouraged to compete with one another in order not only to maximise output, but to win material rewards, and various collective forms of organising work and payment were eliminated.[31] Progressive piece-work was introduced in the spring of 1934, and while real wages fell for most workers a significant number of *udarniki* (shock workers) and *stakhanovtsy* participated in the more 'joyous' life that Stalin had promised.[32] Worker power declined and that of managers and technicians increased.[33] 'The Party wanted the bosses to be efficient, powerful, harsh, impetuous, and capable of exerting pressure crudely and ruthlessly and getting results "whatever the cost" . . . The formation of the despotic manager was actually a process in which not leaders but *rulers* were made.'[34] In the words of Mikhail Kaganovich, 'The ground must shake when the factory director enters the plant.'

The severe economic crisis of the winter of 1932–3, as well as the coming to power of Hitler in Germany, helped accelerate the swing toward state policies that favoured the educated and ambitious and eased the pressure on others. By the middle of the year arrests and deportations declined; production targets for the Second Five-Year Plan were reduced; and consumer goods were given higher priority. As one historian sums it up:

[30] Moshe Lewin, '"Taking Grain": Soviet Policies of Agricultural Procurements Before the War', *The Making of the Soviet System: Essays in the Social History of Interwar Russia* (New York: Pantheon 1985), pp. 142–77. 'Peasants in Stalin's times were indeed legally bound to their place of work, submitted to a special legal regimen, and – through the kolkhoz – to a form of collective responsibility with regard to state duties. They were transformed, not unlike as in pre-emancipation times, into an estate placed at the very bottom of the social ladder' (p. 176).

[31] Lewis H. Siegelbaum, 'Production Collectives and Communes and the "Imperatives" of Soviet Industrialization, 1929–1931', *Slavic Review*, 45, 1 (Spring 1986), pp. 65–84.

[32] Lewis H. Siegelbaum, *Stakhanovism and the Politics of Productivity in the USSR, 1935–1941* (Cambridge: Cambridge University Press 1988), particularly chapter 6, 'Stakhanovites in the Cultural Mythology of the 1930s'.

[33] Hiroaki Kuromiya, *Stalin's Industrial Revolution*, pp. 50–77.

[34] Moshe Lewin, 'Society, State, and Ideology during the First Five-Year Plan', in *Cultural Revolution in Russia, 1928–1931*, ed. Sheila Fitzpatrick (Bloomington: Indiana University Press 1978), p. 74.

In the mid-1930s Soviet society struck a balance that would carry it through the turmoil of the purges, the Great War and reconstruction. The coercive policies of the Cultural Revolution [1928–31] were replaced or supplemented by the use of inducements. Benefits were quickly apparent: education opened professional opportunities; a stable countryside improved dietary standards; increased production and income encouraged consumerism. A lightened mood swept the nation. Women wore make-up; young people revived ballroom dancing. Life, as Stalin said, and Lebedev-Kumach's popular song repeated, had become better and happier.[35]

A new Soviet middle class developed with its own form of 'bourgeois values'. More attention was paid to private life. From Stakhanovite workers, with their newly acquired bicycles and wristwatches, to factory managers and their wives, who were on the receiving end of Stalin's 'Big Deal', a certain level of security and material improvement, 'a sense of pride and participation', wedded them to the order created by Stalin.[36]

James van Geldern emphasises how Soviet citizens were turned into spectators in the 1930s, rather than active participants. Formal, meaningless voting, viewing the leaders atop Lenin's mausoleum, were 'rituals of participation', public observations of political spectacles.[37] New heroes, from aviators to polar explorers, and extended public dramas – like the rescue of downed female fliers and ice-bound sailors – riveted public attention and reinforced the values of the modernising party/state. An empire was created disguised as a voluntary federation of free peoples, with a reconstructed Moscow at its centre, and festivals of reaffirmation, like the Moscow Olympiad of Folk Music, periodically reminding people of the unbreakable unity of a diverse, continent-size country. Ideas of progress – the conquest of recalcitrant nature, the overcoming of peasant 'darkness' and the isolation of remote villages, the building of the Moscow Metro – enhanced the heroic nature of Soviet leaders and the efforts of the Soviet people. Sacrifice and vigilance went along with pride in *nashi dostizheniia* (our achievements). The image of the motherland (*rodina*) was revived, gradually displacing that of the international community of proletarians, until in 1943 Stalin cavalierly dissolved Lenin's Third International. In 1939, he had pro-

---

[35] James van Geldern, 'The Centre and the Periphery: Cultural and Social Geography in the Mass Culture of the 1930s', in *New Directions in Soviet History*, ed. Stephen White, (Cambridge: Cambridge University Press 1992), p. 62.

[36] Siegelbaum, *Stakhanovism and the Politics of Productivity*, pp. 210–46. The idea of the 'Big Deal', Stalin's exchange of material goods and security for loyalty, is the theme of Vera Dunham, *In Stalin's Time: Middleclass Values in Soviet Fiction* (Cambridge: Cambridge University Press 1976).

[37] Van Geldern, "The Centre and the Periphery', p. 71.

posed, as a joke to Ribbentrop: 'Let's drink to the new anti-Cominternist
– Stalin!'[38]

In his public rhetoric of these years Stalin maintained his severity and
toughness, qualities that had long been part of Bolshevik culture, but
showed that under pressure he could be more flexible and accommo-
dating. He seemed not only a competent commander to many but indeed
an indispensable leader in a time of political stress and economic crisis.
A high party official, Barmin, wrote about this period (1932): 'Loyalty
to Stalin was based principally on the conviction that there was no one
to take his place, that any change of leadership would be extremely dangerous, and that the country must continue in its present course, since
to stop now or attempt a retreat would mean the loss of everything.'[39]
Rumours that Stalin, had suggested that he resign (probably after the
suicide of his second wife, Nadezhda Allilueva, in November 1932) were
embellished by reports of his associates rallying around him.[40]

The years of upheaval and uncertainty of the early 1930s were
clearly coming to an end by the opening of the Seventeenth Party Congress in late January 1934. Though the full story has yet to be told, there
appears to have been a movement at the Congress to replace Stalin with
Kirov, but Kirov's differences with Stalin were not great enough for the
Leningrad leader to repudiate the General Secretary as many others
wished. Though many still feared the trend toward personal autocracy
by Stalin, the oligarchic bureaucratic system seemed more secure than
ever; oppositions had been rendered impotent; and a new emphasis on
'revolutionary legality' seemed to promise a more orderly, procedural,
less disruptive mode of governance. But, as Lewin notes:

> Stalin was not ready to accept the role of just a cog, however powerful, in
> his own machine. A top bureaucrat is a chief executive, in the framework
> of a constraining committee . . . But Stalin had had the power, and the

---

[38] *Sto sorok besed s Molotovym: Iz dnevnika F. Chueva* (Moscow: Terra 1991), p. 19; *Molotov
Remembers: Inside Kremlin Politics: Conversations with Felix Chuev*, ed. Albert Resis
(Chicago: Ivan R. Dee 1993), p. 12.

[39] A. Barmin, *One Who Survived* (New York, 1945). When the Menshevik Fedor Dan
asked Bukharin in 1936 why he and other communists had so blindly trusted Stalin,
Bukharin answered, 'You don't understand this; it is completely different. It is not he who
is trusted but a man whom the party trusts; it happened that he became a kind of symbol
of the party, [and] the lower ranks, the workers, the people believe in him; maybe this is
our fault but that is how it happened, that is why we all climb into his mouth . . . knowing
for sure that he will eat us. And he knows this and only chooses the right moment' ('On
pozhret nas', from the archive of L. O. Dan in the Institute of Social History, Amsterdam,
published in *Osmyslit' kult Stalina*, ed. Kobo, p. 610).

[40] On Stalin's relationship with his second wife, see ' "Nadezhde Sergeevne Alliluevoi,
lichno ot Stalina" (Perepiska 1928–1931 godov)', *Istochnik: Dokumenty russkoi istorii*,
no. 0 (1993), pp. 9–22.

taste for it – for ever more of it – since he had led the early stage of the shattering breakthrough and gotten full control over the state in the process. At this point, the traits of his gloomy personality, with clear paranoid tendencies become crucial. Once at the top and in full control, he was not a man to accept changes in the pattern of his personal power . . . He therefore took the road of shaking up, of destabilising the machinery and its upper layers, in order to block the process fatally working against his personal predilection for autocracy.[41]

Terror and Autocracy

The half-dozen years before the murder of Kirov (December 1934) might be seen as the prehistory of Stalinism, the period of formation of the political structures and social conditions that created the possibility for a regime of extreme centralisation of power, overwhelming dominance of a weakened society, and particular ferocity. The unlimited despotism of Stalinism was the product of the Great Purges, which simultaneously eliminated all possible resistance and created a new and more loyal elite with which the tyrant could rule.

There is no consensus among scholars as to the motivations behind the Purges. Interpretations range from the idea that purging was a permanent and necessary component of totalitarianism in lieu of elections (Zbigniew Brzezinski) to seeing the Great Terror as an extreme form of political infighting (J. Arch Getty).[42] Dissatisfaction with Stalin's rule and with the harsh material conditions was palpable in the mid-1930s, and the regime was faced with the difficulties of controlling the family circles and local feudatories (particularly in the union republics). One of the effects of the Purges was the replacement of an older political and economic elite with a younger, potentially more loyal one.[43] The largest number were promoted workers and party rank-and-file, young technicians, who would make up the Soviet elite through the post-Stalin period until the early 1980s.[44] 'Stalin – and, for that matter, the majority of Soviet citizens', writes Sheila Fitzpatrick,

[41] Lewin, 'The Social Background of Stalinism', pp. 130–1.

[42] Getty, *Origins of the Great Purges*, p. 206. For a range of views on the purges, particularly of the so-called 'revisionists', see J. Arch Getty and Roberta T. Manning (eds.) *Stalinist Terror: New Perspectives* (Cambridge: Cambridge University Press 1993).

[43] A. L. Unger, 'Stalin's Renewal of the Leading Stratum: A Note on the Great Purge', *Soviet Studies*, 20,3 (January 1969), pp. 321–30; Bailes, *Technology and Society*, pp. 268–71, 412–13; Sheila Fitzpatrick, 'Stalin and the Making of a New Elite, 1928–1939', *Slavic Review*, 38, 3 (September 1979), pp. 377–402.

[44] Bailes criticises Fitzpatrick for not distinguishing between those who rose into the intelligentsia through formal education, many of whom were workers (the *vydvizhentsy*), and the *praktiki*, who were elevated through their work experience ('Stalin and the Making of a New Elite: A Comment', *Slavic Review*, 39, 2 (June 1980), pp. 286–9).

saw the cadres of the mid-1930s less in their old role as revolutionaries than in the current role as bosses. There is even some evidence that Stalin saw them as Soviet boyars (feudal lords) and himself as a latter-day Ivan the Terrible, who had to destroy the boyars to build a modern nation state and a new service nobility.[45]

Yet neither arguments from social context nor functionalist deductions from effects to causes have successfully eliminated the principal catalyst to the Terror, the will and ambition of Stalin. The Great Purges have been seen traditionally as an effort 'to achieve an unrestricted personal dictatorship with a totality of power that [Stalin] did not yet possess in 1934.'[46] Stalin guided and prodded the arrests, show trials, and executions forward, aided by the closest members of his entourage: Molotov, Kaganovich, Zhdanov, Malenkov, Mikoyan, and Ezhov.[47] Here personality and politics merged, and the degree of excess repression was dictated by the peculiar demands of Stalin himself, who could not tolerate limits on his will set by the very ruling elite that he had brought to power.[48]

Whatever his authentic political aspirations, Stalin was marked by his deep suspiciousness and insecurity. As Bukharin told the old Mensheviks Fedor and Lydia Dan, Stalin

is even unhappy because he cannot convince everyone, and even himself, that he is greater than everyone, and this is his unhappiness, perhaps the most human feature in him, perhaps the only human feature in him, but already not human. Here is something diabolical: because of his great 'unhappiness' he cannot but avenge himself on people, on all

---

[45] Sheila Fitzpatrick, *The Russian Revolution* (Oxford: Oxford University Press 1982), p. 159. Comparisons to the Russian past – autocracy, the service nobility, the collective-farm peasantry as serfs – are used metaphorically by Moshe Lewin and are central to the analysis of Robert C. Tucker in *Stalin in Power: The Revolution from Above, 1928–1941* (New York: W. W. Norton 1973).

[46] Robert C. Tucker, 'Introduction', in *The Great Purge Trial* eds. Tucker and Stephen F. Cohen (New York 1965), p. xxix. This is essentially the argument of the second volume of his Stalin biography, as well as the view of Robert Conquest in *The Great Terror: Stalin's Purge of the Thirties* (New York: Macmillan 1968); *The Great Terror: A Reassessment* (New York: Oxford University Press 1990).

[47] Boris A. Starkov, 'Narkom Ezhov', in *Stalinist Terror*, eds. Getty and Manning, pp. 21–39.

[48] Stalin's personal involvement in the details of the Terror has been indisputably demonstrated by archival documents released in the late 1980s and early 1990s. One such note to Ezhov will suffice to give the type of intervention that the *vozhd'* engaged in. In May 1937, he wrote: 'One might think that prison for Beloborodov is a podium for reading speeches, statements which refer to the activities of all sorts of people but not to himself. Isn't it time to squeeze this gentleman and make him tell about his dirty deeds? Where is he, in prison or in a hotel?' (*Dialog* (Leningrad), no. 4 (1990), p. 21; cited in Starkov, 'Narkom Ezhov', p. 29).

people, but especially on those who are somehow higher, better than he . . .[49]

The Purges destroyed primarily those in power. 'It is one of the mysteries of Stalinism', Lewin summarises,

> that it turned much of the fury of its bloody purges against this very real mainstay of the regime. There were among the *apparaty*, probably, still too many former members of other parties or of the original Leninist party, too many participants and victors of the civil war who remembered who had done what during those days of glory. Too many thus could feel the right to be considered founders of the regime and base on it part of the claims to a say in decisions and to security in their positions. Probably, also letting the new and sprawling administration settle and get encrusted in their chairs and habits could also encourage them to try and curtail the power of the very top and the personalised ruling style of the chief of the state – and this was probably a real prospect the paranoid leader did not relish.[50]

Stalin's initiation and personal direction of the Purges was the catalyst to thousands of smaller settlings of scores.[51] In the context of deep and recurring social tensions the state gave the green light to resentments against the privileged, the intelligentsia, other ethnicities, outsiders. The requirement to find enemies, to blame and punish, worked together with self-protection and self-promotion (and plain sadism) to expand the Purges into a political holocaust. At the end the Soviet Union resembled a ruined landscape, seriously weakened economically, intellectually, and militarily, but at the same time dominated by a towering state apparatus made up of new loyal *apparatchiki*, disciplined by the police, and presided over by a single will.

Victory and Decline, Finale and Conclusion

By the outbreak of the Second World War the central government, the military, the republics and local governments, the economic infrastructure had all been brutally disciplined. Obedience and conformity had eliminated most initiative and originality. Ruling through his like-minded lieutenants, Stalin relied on specialists whenever he needed

[49] 'On pozhret nas', p. 610.

[50] Moshe Lewin, 'Grappling with Stalinism', *The Making of the Soviet System*, pp. 308–9.

[51] Sheila Fitzpatrick, 'How the Mice Buried the Cat: Scenes from the Great Purges of 1937 in the Russian Provinces', *Russian Review*, 52, 3 (July 1993), pp. 299–320.

expertise or greater competence. After decimating the high command of the armed forces, his control over his military was greater than Hitler over his, at least at the beginning of the war. He intervened and interfered in both minute and major decisions, and was often abrupt and threatening, yet he was more willing to rely on his generals than was Hitler, who became progressively more involved with operational command and more contemptuous of the military leaders. 'Hitler's generals', writes Severyn Bialer, 'exercised less influence on the decisions of their High Command at the moment they were most able to act effectively; Stalin's generals exercised more'.[52] Stalin stood at the centre of all strategic, logistical, and political decisions. He was chairman of the State Defence Committee, which included the highest party officials (Molotov, Beria, Malenkov, Voroshilov, Kaganovich, and later Voznesenskii and Mikoyan); the chairman of Stavka, the supreme military headquarters; General Secretary of the party and chairman of the Politburo; chairman of the Council of Ministers and People's Commissar of Defence. Real business often took place in late-night meetings at Stalin's apartment or dacha, and the exigencies of total war reinforced and accelerated the centralisation of power.[53]

Official propaganda convincingly identified the victory over Nazism with the superiority of the Soviet system, its organic link with *rodina* (the motherland), and the personal genius of Stalin. The triumph over fascism provided the Communists with another source of legitimation and authority. New Russia and the Soviet Union were melded into a single image. Patriotism and accommodation with established religious and national traditions, along with the toning down of revolutionary radicalism, contributed to a powerful ideological amalgam that outlasted Stalin himself. In the post-war decades the war became the central moment of Soviet history, eclipsing the revolution and the *velikii perelom* of the early 1930s.[54] And though there would be sporadic uses of repression and terror against individuals or groups (the 'Leningrad Affair' of 1947, the 'Doctors' Plot' of 1953), as well as a series of ethnic deportations of repatriated Armenians, Kurds, Meskhetian Turks, and

---

[52] Severyn Bialer, *Stalin and His Generals* (New York: Pegasus 1969), p. 43. 'As supreme head of army command, Hitler was centrally involved in the formulation of day-to-day tactics in a way which occupied no other head of state during the Second World War. For the German army, this was catastrophic. The command structure which he had devised placed him in charge of both the general management of military campaigns and its detailed tactics' (Ian Kershaw, *Hitler* (London and New York: Longman 1991), p. 175).

[53] Milovan Djilas, *Conversations with Stalin* (New York: Harcourt, Brace & World 1962), passim.

[54] Nina Tumarkin, "The Great Patriotic War as Myth and Memory', *Atlantic Monthly*, 267, 6 (June 1991), pp. 26, 28, 37, 40, 42, 44.

others, no massive terror on the scale of 1937 was employed after the war.

Whatever benefits accrued to the Soviet system from the unity of decision-making at the top must be weighed against the costs of over-centralisation and the resultant paralysis lower down in the apparatus. In the years of the Cold War, as Stalin deteriorated physically and men-tally, the entire country – its foreign policy, internal politics, cultural life, and economic slowdown – reflected the moods of its leader and was affected by his growing isolation, arbitrariness, and inactivity. No one could feel secure. The ruling elite was concerned with plots, intrigues, and rivalries between Stalin's closest associates, the rise and fall of clients and patrons. 'All of us around Stalin', writes Khrushchev, 'were temporary people. As long as he trusted us to a certain degree, we were allowed to go on living and working. But the moment he stopped trusting you, Stalin would start to scrutinize you until the cup of his distrust overflowed.'[55] In his last years Stalin turned against Molotov and Mikoyan, grew suspicious of Beria, Voroshilov, Kaganovich, and Malenkov. Khrushchev overheard him say, 'I'm finished. I trust no one, not even myself.'[56]

The Stalinist system was restored and consolidated after the devasta-tion of the war years. As a single political cultural synthesis became hegemonic and the more disruptive violence of the pre-war period receded, pervasive fear, which disciplined people into obedient silence, coexisted with genuine acceptance of the system. The figure of Stalin stood symbolically for ideal behaviour in an ideal society. Enemies were still omnipresent; a single simplified reading of historical reality was at hand in the *Kratkii kurs* (the short history of the Communist party) and the official biography of Stalin; and the USSR was still the future in the present.

Further Reading: Stalin

Isaac Deutscher, *Stalin: A Political Biography*, 2nd edn. (New York, 1966).
Lars T. Lih, Oleg V. Naumov, and Oleg V. Khlevniuk, eds., *Stalin's Letters to Molotov* (New Haven, 1995).
Norman M. Naimark, "Cold War Studies and New Archival Materials on Stalin," *The Russian Review*, vol. 61, no. 1 (2002).
Alfred J. Rieber, "Stalin, Man of the Borderlands," *American Historical Review*, vol. 106, no. 5 (2001).

[55] *Khrushchev Remembers*, trans. and ed. Strobe Talbott (Boston: Little, Brown and Co. 1970), p. 307.
[56] Ibid.

Robert C. Tucker, *Stalin in Power: The Revolution from Above, 1928–1941* (New York, 1990).

Adam B. Ulam, *Stalin: The Man and His Era* (Boston, 1989).

Dmitrii Volkogonov, *Stalin: Triumph and Tragedy*, trans. Harold Shukman (New York, 1991).

Social Origins

2

Grappling with Stalinism

Moshe Lewin

Excerpted from Moshe Lewin, "Grappling with Stalinism," in
Lewin, *The Making of the Soviet System: Essays in the Social History
of Interwar Russia* (New York: Pantheon Books, 1985).

Editor's Introduction

Traditionally, historians in all fields focused on elite politics – the lives of
rulers, the decisions of statesmen, the ideas of philosophers. In the case
of Soviet history, scholars wrote biographies of Stalin and histories of the
Communist Party. But beginning in the 1960s, many historians turned to
social history – the lives and behaviors of the common people. Social
historians believed that common peasants and workers also deserved to
be studied, and that their mentalities, attitudes, and actions helped to
shape history. By the 1970s and 1980s, scholars of the Soviet Union also
began to examine social history, and to look beyond the ideas and actions
of Communist Party leaders to explain the October Revolution and
Stalinism.

   As discussed in the introduction, social history in the Soviet field was
attached to revisionism – the scholarly trend that overturned the totalitarian model. Revisionist scholars presented Soviet society as more than
a collection of passive, atomized individuals whose thoughts and behavior were completely controlled by the state. Revisionists who studied the
October Revolution highlighted the role of workers and the ways in which
their support for the Bolsheviks (Communists) played a crucial role in
the establishment of the Soviet government. This scholarship altered the
totalitarian view that the Bolsheviks seized power in an illegitimate coup
d'état with no popular backing. It also called into question the assumption that Stalinism followed automatically from Bolshevism, and required
a new explanation for the origins of Stalinism.

   Moshe Lewin is a leading revisionist scholar and pioneer in the
social history of Stalinism. While he does not ignore the importance of
high politics, and in fact has written on political struggles within the

Communist Party leadership, his work seeks to place Stalinism in its broader social context. Lewin thus goes beyond narrow studies of the Communist Party to examine the character of Soviet society, and social influences on the Soviet state. For Lewin, it was the interplay between the state and society that shaped fundamental aspects of Stalinism. The Soviet state had the power to initiate social change, as it did with collectivization, but the social turmoil that resulted and the nature of society itself profoundly affected the Stalinist system.

In the selection below, Lewin emphasizes the overwhelmingly peasant character of Soviet society and its contribution to Stalinism. He points out that peasants made up the vast majority of the population, and that millions of peasants migrated to cities during Stalinist collectivization and industrialization in the early 1930s. This mass migration meant that even many urban residents, including industrial workers, students, and Soviet officials, were in fact former peasants who had just recently left their villages. Peasant in-migrants, according to Lewin, were ill-equipped to deal with modern urban life, and relied upon their traditional peasant ways of thinking even in the city. He describes the Russian peasant (or *muzhik*) as at best semi-literate and having a mentality based on religion tinged with magic and sorcery. Because the Soviet government had to accommodate this widespread peasant mentality, it resorted to quasi-religious forms such as the Stalin cult – propaganda that deified Stalin.

Another detrimental social force identified by Lewin was a new class of bureaucrats (or *apparaty*). These bureaucrats sought to enhance their own power and privileges, and in the process contributed to the rigidity and hierarchy of the Stalinist system. Of course many bureaucrats and even high-ranking Communist Party officials were subsequently shot during the Great Purges, so their elite status did not last. Lewin describes the Great Purges as a type of demonology, whereby Party officials were unmasked as "enemies of the people." At show trials, purge victims were depicted as sinners who had strayed from the Party line and become involved in treasonous activities against the Soviet government. While Lewin notes that this secular inquisition was orchestrated by Stalin, he argues that it appealed to a population made up of peasants and former peasants who remained superstitious and ready to blame the country's hardships on evil forces and demons.

Lewin thus concludes that the primitivized condition of Soviet society contributed to Stalinism. The Soviet population was made up primarily of uneducated peasants, and the country's underdeveloped economic and social structures were further weakened by the Civil War and the brutalities of collectivization. Rapid industrialization and urbanization only exacerbated the situation in the short run, as uprooted peasants flooded the cities, bringing with them rural superstitions and uncultured behavior. This population was not ready to support democracy or social-ism. Instead it bred authoritarianism, as the state took control of all economic and social functions, and Stalin himself assumed complete autocratic power.

Grappling with Stalinism

Moshe Lewin

An Enigma

Rather than deal with the phenomenon of Stalinism in any exhaustive way, the aim here is to introduce into the study and discussion of the system and period in Soviet history some elements, not necessarily original, that have not been fully "employed" yet in our search for an adequate explanation of what still continues to be, to a large extent, enigmatic. Facts and ideas derived from the study of the social history of Russia prompts one to get more "historical" in thinking about Russia, to incorporate factors from the past which, it may turn out, were still unextinguished and mightily at work in the earlier stages of the regime and not yet fully accounted for as driving forces that shaped events and structures about to follow.

In fact, a statement like that may even sound a bit trite. But it is a fact that most of the thinking about Russia turned to some general concepts and to political and ideological factors that looked more attractive and, somehow, pushed historical insights aside. Some of those attitudes and theses acquired even the dubious status of obsessions and outright fallacies. One widespread approach insisted on Leninism – and on the Leninist conception of party organization – as the root of Stalinism and Stalin. The former seemed to have implied the latter, carrying the next stage in its womb almost by definition. Thus Leninism, a political ideology, is presented as the main "culprit" – the primary cause of a specific unfolding of Russian postrevolutionary history, a demiurge that exhibits its potential, explains itself, and makes history – without much of an input from social and historical factors. It was lost on many observers that powerful factors were at work, before and after the revolution, that shaped events, leadership, and ideology itself, and they could have affected Leninism and Stalinism in different ways, including the ways the two phenomena related to each other. The aura of a successful revolution – or, if one was opposed to it, its opprobrium – contributed to the not uncommon phenomenon of singling out an outstanding event for its intense heat and spectacular quality and seeing in it an absolute divide in historical development, which supposedly cut the links with the past radically. Wasn't this the essence of what was aimed at – and held from now on to be solely responsible for all the future chapters? In the eyes of some of the participants, it actually was responsible only for the nicer things that followed, the less palatable being put at the doorsteps of either "deviations" or "vestiges of the past," which were bound to disappear without a trace anyway. Eric Hobsbawm pointed to the fallacies that overconcentration on revolutions or similar shattering events can beget. And one could add more fallacies that stem from abusing the portmanteau device of "vestiges of the past," of which some Soviet writers are still very fond. Religion, greed for predominantly material possessions, criminal behavior – these are some examples of the supposed "vestiges" for which the regime did not wish to carry the blame. Western scholars rarely "bought" this later type of explanation, but they did often accept the impact of revolution as a quasi-absolute breaking point and perpetuated it in their specializations and departmental divisions, thus causing a considerable loss in interpretative power.

Another widespread approach, mostly interested in leaders, resulted in a set of one-sided conclusions which are to be expected whenever personal ambition and power struggles at the top of the social and political ladder are made into the very substance of historical inquiry. Unavoidably, fascination with the mighty and highly visible makes deeply seated matrices of social relations and profound cultural and long-term economic trends less interesting or, at best, relegates them to the background.

Overreliance on certain types of class analysis by Bolsheviks and their heirs, as well as by some scholars abroad, also became a source of considerable political and conceptual difficulties, especially for the actors and leaders of the events in Russia. An all too eager "application" of a class analysis taken from an armory developed in and for a rather advanced capitalist society, when tried in a society still in the early stages of some expected course of history, in transition or in flux, where a mixture of forms coexisted or meshed, could easily misfire. Tsarist Russia was exhibiting precisely such traits, and the new Soviet rulers still used the same analytical tools and desperately tried to discern in their postrevolutionary society either full-blown classes or at least their clearly discernable prefiguration which could lead to the preferred future or drive the system dangerously back into restoration. This was done in order to gain an insight into the historical process and use it as basis for policy making, but it remains a fact that the postrevolutionary Soviet leadership often looked the other way, in the wrong direction, made a long list of blunders, and, at a later stage, especially during the great purges, ended up compromising the analytical tools altogether by monumentally abusing them.

Again, the analysis suffered either because society after the civil war was too undifferentiated, too homogenous, or too archaic or else, as in the early 1930s, too unsettled by a state of flux and upheavals to yield credible results to a scrutiny misguided by inappropriate concepts.

E. H. Carr also thought that Marxian class analysis was inoperative in the Soviet conditions, although for a different reason: It was not this or another ruling class that dominated Soviet society but rather the state that played the dominant role and made or unmade the social structure, without itself yielding to such domination or to a class analysis. Carr's reasoning reflected a reality which became, appropriately, a center of analysis in the study of Eastern European regimes, tsarist and Soviet included. The growing role of the state in the advanced capitalist and democratic systems added justification to this kind of focus for the developing countries.

There is no intention to declare the approaches mentioned here to be irrelevant or not worthy of pursuing. It is rather this or another form of exaggeration or overemphasis that is contested, and what is underlined is the need to refine the tools, or to introduce new, indispensable data and additional factors. In the case of the state, too, it is the overconcentration on it that is deplored, which leads to unilateral interpretations making it into more autonomous a factor than it actually was or is, into a mold that is not shaped by anything but itself, and into a primary cause that develops and changes by its own devices. That a state can be mighty and dominate the social system, especially at some specific breakthrough periods, is beyond doubt. Situations when the state does unleash itself and acts as a powerful and destructive break on social development were observed often enough, as well as being a prime mover and agent of development. But absolutizing such an interpretation would overpoliticize the analysis, obscure what a longer-term view could well disprove or, at least, seriously modify. A temporary, seeming unshackling of constraints is not really a license for full freedom of action. One can claim that state-induced – or accelerated – social and economic changes would end up in imposing adaptations on state institutions and on the whole state system itself; constraints on them not only do exist but actually form a system of which the state is a part and which limit, frustrate, or otherwise circumscribe its operations. Economic, social, and cultural phenomena have to be introduced into the analysis, even if the object of study is a powerful and arbitrary destructive despot. The validity of such historical interpretation does not stop when human rights are curtailed and when oppressive bureaucracies take over the forefront of the stage.

Our treatment cannot offer any full-fledged analysis that would aim at correcting all the aforementioned shortcomings. But the need to do so is worth underlining. Historical studies can help to restore the balance and come up with more satisfactory interpretations by exercising some of the arcana of their métier, telling the story of events but also sorting out trends, dealing with ideologies but without detaching them from institutions and social structures, studying personalities without forgetting the networks of their helpers as well as the broader masses even if some leaders are scornful of them, and dealing with states as important parts of social systems that change in them and with them. . . .

The Muzhik – a Headache Again

By the end of the 1920s the day of reckoning seemed to be nearing. Debates on strategy of development, unavoidably enmeshed in a contest for power, and ideological battles with the very soul of the regime at stake, turned around three main planks: (1) how to industrialize, (2) without making the peasantry explode and (3) without letting state and party get out of hand. The last point turned around the character of the system and its by now obvious potential to become an oppressive superstate. Left and right, openly or implicitly, had this worry on their mind. The future Stalinist faction and its chief did not show much sign of sharing such worries. They would discover the price of this omission some seven or eight years later. For the time being it was precisely the organized forces of the state, and all the levers at its command, that would be launched into operating and managing the new "big drive."

In all those future plans and strategies, the *muzhik* was again to become, as so often in the past, the pivotal factor. What to do with him? Was he really the main carrier of an eventual capitalist restoration? Would he support the regime that was trying to overcome a crisis which the same *muzhik* had supposedly created? Would he support the new accumulation process for which he was to pay a higher price?

In the events that followed, known as the collectivization drive – the term "collectivization" certainly being a misnomer – a clash of the main forces on the Russian historical arena could not be averted. The state launched an onslaught on the peasantry – a feat of "social engineering" which by far overshadowed Stolypin's "engineering from above" in scale, daring, and violence. The results were momentous for both the peasantry and the regime.

Had this clash been the only or simply the main front the process could have been handled with less damaging results. But the collectivization of the peasants was only a part of a larger, rather unplanned "offensive." Simultaneously with battling the *muzhik*'s mentality and forcing on him new forms of life and labor, the regime launched an accelerated industrialization, developed new cities and expanded the old ones, educated new important layers of professionals indispensable for the whole process – technicians, scientists, skilled workers, administrators – and constantly expanded the state machinery, its bureaucracies and agencies. The Leviathan was now coming of age, exceeding the worst expectations of earlier critics. There had been similar phenomena in Russian history before, but here all records were probably beaten as far as the scope of state action and the pervasiveness of terror were concerned, as well as the durability of the results. In the process of disciplining the masses of new workers, of the unwilling peasants in the kolkhozy, in the process of indoctrinating, training, terrorizing, and coercing, the growing *apparaty* were themselves submitted to such strains that much of the medicine they were applying to others were applied to them too – including a bloodletting soon to be administered in such doses that it pointed to pathology in the whole system. This so-called second October produced such a cascade of crises and disequilibria that, clearly, the capacity of the regime to act rationally and to cope seemed to have reached its limits. The avalanche of tasks, growing in complexity, was poured on the shoulders of *apparaty*, whose numbers grew but whose abilities could not keep pace with such requirements; in fact, its quality had to fall because of the influx of raw recruits. All these factors contributed to the polity veering precipitously into a frame and system of violence capped by a capricious autocrat.

In the official language of those days the peasantry appeared as the honorable ally of the working class, and now even a more honorable "kolkhoz peasantry," but it also was considered to have been the main cause of all the obstacles the regime found on its way. In this capacity they were presented as "petit bourgeois," and no one could remonstrate that this was one and the same mass of peasants, supposedly carriers of a new socialist essence as well as of the quite opposite spirit that also kept infecting the working class, officialdom, and even the party.

Out of the peasant mass a special stratum of "super-*muzhiki*" was singled out, better known as "kulaks" – yet another of those abuses of class analysis of which a long list could be supplied. (See Chapter 5 [of the original publication].) The small apex of better-off peasants, who in Soviet conditions were producers still basically relying on the labor of members of their families, with an average of about ten hectares, two to three cows, two to three horses, one, rarely two or more hired laborers – for an average family of eight to ten people. To construct from them a "capitalist class," or even a "semicapitalist" one, demanded stretching concepts well into the realm of the chimerical (although there was no need to doubt their distaste for the kolkhoz). Yet, as officially decreed, it was with the elimination of these kulaks "as a class," supposedly the last rampart of capitalism, that the country ushered in the era of socialism. So it was not in October when the real thing was eliminated but in Stalin's "big drive," when a placebo was removed, that socialism came true. Was it really socialism that was attained by an ideological manipulation of this kind?

The problem can best be visualized by reminding ourselves that, according to official data, about 400 million rubles' worth of property was confiscated from this "rural capitalism." The figure was later revised upward, but the modesty of these sums tell the story. One big industrial plant cost more, but the damage to the economy caused by the expropriation and elimination of over a million of the best farmers was staggering. A trait that was characteristic of much of what was done is worth pointing to: speed and a rush into large-scale units for which the countryside was not ripe. Nationalization of productive capacity operated prematurely can cause heavy social and political damage; but there is still a difference between nationalizing a big, bureaucratically organized, industrial corporation, where no more than a change of the board of directors might be needed, and nationalizing huts, cows, and plows. In this latter case, as we know, the act of the state did actually destroy a class of producers, leaving the inheritor with nothing but dust.

This remark applies not only to the expropriation of the kulak but to the whole collectivization process. The fallacy of collectivization Soviet style consisted in imposing on small-scale farmers large-scale forms and methods before the appropriate technical means and cadres had become available and without appropriate transitional stages. Most peasants lived and worked in family-run small farms as well as being incorporated, in a particularly Russian way, in a communal landholding system. Over generations they also had acquired a mentality, culture, and ethics stemming from this mode of life and work and a system of religious beliefs, mainly a specific rural Christianity, heavily tinged with magical practices and sorcery. The leap from sorcery to higher mathematics, to put it in terms often used in the 1920s, demanded much more than just the application of state power. Many thought that communal forms, although age-old and geared to the needs of a primitive and overpopulated countryside, could have been used as a steppingstone to something more modern at some later stage. Yet, befitting the impetuosity of the day, this way was discarded. Speeding up by force becoming, for a time, the cure-all, the price tag attached to this approach was constantly the same: a new and considerable regression in the sphere of agriculture, paralleled by other walks of life, especially the spheres of culture, ideology, and politics.

We remember that the resistant mentality of the peasant was not only a problem in running kolkhozy. Thanks to the vast industrial effort

– we do not forget this major fact – they came to towns in the millions. The majority of the new industrial working class, many of the officials, the student body, and a considerable proportion of the new professional classes would be recruited from peasants. They were the material from which the classes of the growing industrial society were constituted. Would they shed their traditional cultural-religious outlook after only a short period of schooling? And in the environment of the fast growing cities of those 1920s, as well as the building sites and overcrowded labor camps of the 1930s? A massive feat of social mobility would, in the short run, produce rather an equally massive disorientation, quite inimical to a quick and serious shedding of old habits. And the phenomena of accelerated restructuring we are studying, as well as their effects, are all "short-run" – and so is our central theme itself. The impact of breathtaking social change will be contradictory, and it is only with hindsight that the long-term aspects can be separated from the shorter waves of change. Some superficial new veneer that is easy to acquire should not be mistaken for change in deeper cultural and psychological layers that take much longer to mature.

As some 17 million peasants settled in cities between 1928 and 1935 alone – not to mention many more millions that came and left the towns during those years and later – the population of the urban sector was thereby doubled in this incredibly short time. Obviously, these people were getting or beginning to get "deruralized," but at the same time, as I have described elsewhere (see Chapter 10 [of the original publication]), they did "ruralize" the towns, especially the factories. Miscalculations in planning, themselves related to the whipping speedup, were responsible for the excessive scope and suddenness of this process. It was therefore not a simple migration to cities, usually seen as acts of progress and social advance. It was to become all very positive, again, "in the long run." For the time being, the cities and other places were flooded by streams of people – many of them desperate because of their dislike of kolkhozy, or because of dekulakization – that outstripped the power of absorption of those cities and strained to the utmost their institutions and material means. The new arrivals had thus to face a rough and unhospitable environment, a deteriorating economic situation, inadequate lodging – not to mention the complexities of the Soviet industrial and urban system for which the rural mind was badly equipped.

It all amounted to a massive uprooting, cultural and psychological shock, causing widespread disorientation, a crisis of values, and the concomitant phenomena of delinquency, hooliganism, cynicism, mass anomie, and the attraction of not too palatable countercultures.

Such phenomena are crucial for the understanding of the 1930s. Although we deal here, to some extent, with a textbook case of rapid industrialization and urbanization anywhere, the scale and concentration in time, as well as the political circumstances, were very different and unique. The strain and tension imposed on people and on the political system nationally were immense. At this juncture it was what happened to people that was crucial for the understanding of the polity. People, mostly, as said, of rural origin, had to adapt and somehow rebuild their ethical and cultural values, to regain control of their lives and their sanity. For this purpose all that was available from the past and present environments would be used in different doses, the problem being that not much from the old luggage was of use, whereas the new environment too had its capabilities to offer good values greatly impaired. The burden of response and solutions was landing in the lap of the state – itself, to say the least, in high fever, strained to the utmost, relying too much on crude coercion and primitive propaganda, and displaying quite a basket of pathological syndromes. In the midst of this schooling and building, training and pushing, the acculturation process was partly blocked, and a temporary phenomenon for which the term "deculturation" could be suitable set in. This term could account for both the phenomena of massive uprooting experienced by peasants losing old values and cultural molds and not acquiring new ones quickly enough as well as for the results of political and cultural terror and crude propaganda: drabness; uniformity; sloganeering; crude language and mores, both below and higher up; foul countercultures; drinking and criminal behavior.

It is worth repeating that the state operating in this kind of cultural "void" (of its own making, to a large extent) experienced effects of those trends all through its own agencies and *apparaty*. It was therefore going to mobilize all it could to master the tides and to go on ruling. This would demand quite a lot of doing – and would amount to and account for the last chapter in the making of the Stalinist state.

One Ideology – or More?

One of the strategies of social control was the creation or the expansion of a strong scaffolding of bosses, all through the system, called *nachal'stvo* by the people as well as by the interested parties themselves. The term came from the political dictionary and practice of tsarist Russia and was going to both prop up as well as actually typify the system. But to counter the effects of "deculturation" in towns and of similar phenomena and the loss of incentives in the countryside, a more subtle policy was needed. The regime had to offer and inculcate values, to extirpate some and instill some other beliefs, and to legitimize its policies and its very character in the eyes of the populace, at a time when it was both socially lifting up and downgrading millions of people. Success would not be easy in this sphere, and it would demand pressures and compromises on the cultural and ideological fronts and further transformations of the character of the polity.

A comparison with the history of the Christian church and of other great religions in the earlier stages of their development can offer a useful illustration to what was involved in Soviet Russia's efforts to combat the effects of "the petit bourgeois tides" and the demoralizing results of mass anomie and value crisis. "Neither the prophet nor the priest," wrote Reinhard Bendix in his book on Max Weber, "can afford to reject all compromise with the traditional beliefs of the masses."[1] The same goes for regimes, however radical, engaged in the process of changing social relations. In its old fight against forms of paganism and, more broadly, against the whole preliterate popular culture, the church finished by adapting many of its ways to folkways and adopting many elements from the popular religion in order to win out on substance by conceding some points tactically. Whether these points were just trifles or much more is beyond our pursuits here, but the church did use its miracles to compete with their magic, its exorcism to outdo their healers, its versions of devils, witches, and sorcerers to eliminate their spirits and deities. The list of those adaptations and adoptions is much longer, but our concern is with some comparable phenomena in the 1930s in the Soviet Union. Obviously, here was the twentieth century, not the tenth, and things did not occur in centuries but were concentrated in a few years. In addition, the acting forces were not heathen peasants versus a Christian church and kingdom but Christian peasants versus an atheistic government which was not going to introduce a religion – just use methods and structures similar to the religious and church experience for its own purposes. Still, the analogy is quite striking.

Another parallel with church history, which we will go into only very briefly, concerns the phenomena of transformation of sects into churches and the emergence of sects inside established churches, a process that was recurrent in all religions. It can throw a searching light on the transformation of the revolutionary Bolshevik party from a network of clandestine committees into a mighty bureaucracy, with a powerful hierarchy on one pole and a rightless "laity" on the other, with privileges at the top and obligatory catechesis handed from above for the use of the lower rungs, and finally with a laicized version of . . . sin, apostates, and inquisition.

---

[1] Reinhard Bendix, *Max Weber: An Intellectual Portrait* (1960; reprint ed., Berkeley: University of California Press, 1978), p. 92.

The first visible effort undertaken to compete with popular religion (or the existing religions in general) for the minds of the rural and urban dwellers, on lines that justify our analogy, began initially as a semiconscious strategy with actions like the erecting of Lenin's mausoleum and the encouragement of pilgrimages to Lenin's embalmed body. All these despite the protests and sense of outrage against such practices expressed by Lenin's widow and other old Bolsheviks. Despite also the official disdain for the Orthodox church's practice of venerating relics of saints (*moshchi*).

In the 1920s an interesting and lively debate initiated by the writer Veresaev in *Krasnaya nov'*[2] raised the problem of replacing religious ceremonies, above all those related to the life-cycle rituals that played such an important role especially in the countryside, by something secular and modern, specially conceived for this purpose. In the lively debate warnings were sounded against coercive or artificial methods, against the cultural and psychological damage that can be caused when depriving people of the old but deeply felt and needed symbolisms without replacing them by something acceptable to the recipients.

One discussant even cautioned against replacing one authoritarian and dogmatic set of rituals with another equally authoritarian and dogmatic. The whole operation, in order to make good sense to him, should have consisted only in replacing something authoritarian and conservative by a ceremony that expressed and carried human emancipation onto a higher level – not by another ritual of indoctrination.[3]

The warnings expressed in this interesting debate were not heeded. What was emerging in public life, especially in the 1930s, were ceremonies and a style that looked strikingly as if it had been borrowed from the old: processions with "icons" of living and dead leaders, ritualized public ceremonials, pompous displays of a kind of secular liturgy, the growing use of a vocabulary soaked with religious and semireligious overtones. The frontiers of the country became now "sanctified" (*svyashchennye*); government requirements, such as grain procurements, became "commandments" (*zapovedi*) – modest but ever expanding steps into a strategy aimed at replacing the old national and religious belief system and ritual by a quasi-cult of a secular state. This was to be observed in full blossom already during the later 1930s, which also saw the pinnacle of what can now be seen as the centerpiece of Stalinism and its main achievement: the hectic building of a superstate, heavily spiced by its so-called excesses.

2 V. Veresaev, "Ob obryadakh," *Krasnaia nov'*, no. 11 (1926).
3 Letter to Veresaev, in *ibid.*

Not much effort is needed to relate the "Stalin cult" to this broader strategy of "sanctifying" the state. The Stalin cult became a linchpin in this revamped secular orthodoxy. Sermons, vows, adulation, and panegyrics cotributed a peculiar "Byzantine" flavor to the neo-autocracy. But besides being a very serious dent in the official Marxist–Leninist ideology, which had no place for such developments, the strategy did not seem sufficient or convincing enough in the battle for people's minds and for the legitimization of the regime. Marxism–Leninism could not convincingly explain the new cult, and both were unable or felt unable to make palatable and acceptable the superstate, the rigid bureaucratic hierarchy, the bureaucratic takeover of all vestiges of popular sovereignty, the appearance of privileged strata in society and at the upper echelons of the bureaucratic ladder. Many saw treason in such trends, which were discernible already since the early postrevolutionary days, and in fact, by standards of the official creed and its erstwhile commitments, such tendencies were shocking. To mend the ideological fences a strategy of ideological diversion was conceived and applied. First came the taming of the critical potential of the official creed itself through its transformation into a strictly controlled catechesis, only as allowed and amended by the "supreme authority."

An additional prop was then sought in those chapters of the imperial past which best suited the new situation and the self-image of the new leader: the great tsars, builders and despots, Ivan the Terrible and Peter the Great, seemed to fit the bill. The imperial past was thus tapped for whatever it could offer in the operation of integrating the peasants, building an industry, and erecting a powerful state, with a despot at its helm, not unlike those days of yore which offered a glitter of regalia, an imperial pomp and an Oprichnina,* with its rake applied against critics and foes.

The imperial past was screened not only for the uses of quasi-religious devices to sustain a modern autocracy (*samoderzhavie*), but also for what it could offer in terms of sustaining nationality (*narodnost'*), too,† as well as to mount a brand of great power nationalism complete with the chant of glory to "Great Russia" (*Velikaya Rus'*), as the Soviet anthem still says.

There was an obvious craving at the top – which probably ascribed the same to the masses – for this kind of supportive symbols and ide-

---

* The Oprichnina was, among other things, the personal and secret police established by Ivan the Terrible to deal with his enemies, and to administer lands confiscated from the boyars for the benefit of the state.

† "Autocracy, Nationality, Orthodoxy" was the official state motto expressing the ideology of tsardom under Nicholas I. One could use the principle of "partyness" to replace "Orthodoxy," but there is no need to overdraw the parallel. The similarity is there anyway.

ologies. It was not just a coolly conceived strategy but a deep psychological need felt by the ruler himself, who might have felt a genuine affinity with those great predecessors – and who certainly believed he was much better.

We can see already that more than one ideology was "drafted" to serve the great restructuring of those years, ideologies that actually were incompatible and therefore necessitated additional constructs.

An attentive observer could soon discern the emergence of yet another ideological production that borrowed elements from the Marxist–Leninist and imperial–national (or nationalist) rhetoric, coupled with some original ingredients – to express the interests and outlook of the growing bureaucracy. This was to be expected, especially at the top of the hierarchy, even if it was not immediately made public or even not allowed clear and full expression by the shattering purges that hit those *apparaty* and hindered them from settling to rule and enjoy their privileges unmolested.

Despite the shakiness in its ranks caused by the general flux of the times and the purges, official ideology could not offer a sufficient expression for what the bureaucracy was doing and was standing for or for its interests as perceived by it. "Statehood" (*gosudarstvennost'*) would become the central theme which would show what the real goal was and how to assure the internal cohesion of the carrier of this statehood. An important element, though, could be borrowed from the theoretical founding fathers, namely, nationalization of the main means of production as a socialist principle *par excellence*. It was not that important that this was not, really, the central tenet of socialism. But it suited the interest of the bureaucracy to use this formula because it did, in fact, express the source of the state's power and the position of its servants as guardians of the national patrimony. This was a good basis for defending their special role and thus special privileges, justifying the growing self-image and self-importance of the new mandarins of the state: the party apparatchik; the *otvetrabotnik*; and the *krupnyi gosudarstvennyi deyatel'*.* This ideology began its career from the defense of the party apparatus against the onslaught of the opposition in the 1920s, continued through the repudiation of egalitarianism in the early 1930s, blossomed in the imposition and glorification of "one-man management" (*edinonachalie*), and finally found the right casuistry in the thesis that the state would whither away sometime in the future, but not before its powers had expanded to the utmost during the ongoing historical

---

* An *apparatchik* is a paid official of the party, though this is not what they would call themselves officially; probably rather *partrabotnik*. An *otvetrabotnik* is an employee of some rank and responsibility. *Krupnyi gosudarstvennyi deyatel'* – "prominent state leader" – is a term reserved for top government and party officials of ministerial rank and higher.

stage. The bureaucracy's sovereignty in the system was thinly camou-flaged by extolling the importance of leadership and management, which looked like a simple variation on the theme of the party's leading role. The socialist credential of such principles could be questioned, of course, as well as the principle of state ownership of the means of production. Such ownership, mainly of land, had a precedent in earlier stages of historical development; it could become – and actually was – the basis of all kind of regimes, including the early Moscow princedom and tsardom.

There are some internal, less known, and still unresearched parts of the bureaucratic ideology which operated already in the 1930s and are going stronger today. They concern the justification of open and covert material and other privileges, justification for their life and career practices, deference to authority and superiors, ideas concerning their position in the state compared with that of other classes, and other elements that are not treated in official handbooks and histories but constitute a potent ideological reality.

It is one of the mysteries of Stalinism that it turned much of the fury of its bloody purges against this very real mainstay of the regime. There were among the *apparaty*, probably, still too many former members of other parties or of the original Leninist party, too many participants and victors of the civil war who remembered who had done what during those days of glory. Too many thus could feel the right to be considered founders of the regime and base on it part of the claims to a say in decisions and to security in their positions. Probably, also, letting the new and sprawling administration settle and get encrusted in their chairs and habits could also encourage them to try and curtail the power of the very top and the personalized ruling style of the chief of state – and this was probably a real prospect the para-noid leader did not relish. I have already briefly proposed the idea that a modern bureaucracy needs and enjoys "tenure," which was denied to it in the most cruel ways by the autocrat. In fact, autocracy could not really block for too long a sociological trend which finally prevailed in Russia beginning with Khrushchev (see Chapter 11 [of the original publication]).

For the time being, in the midst of a difficult contest with the peasantry, the strenuous efforts to discipline labor during the height of the purge of the party and the government apparatus, yet another, a fourth ideology was put to use. This was felt to be necessary to justify the existence not only of the superstate but of the specific means employed in erecting it: terrorism and mass repression. This was a dip into the darker and irrational traditions and urges of individuals and whole polities, used to glue together an unpalatable reality, an impossible mixture of ideologies and a gruesome and counterrevolutionary onslaught on people and principles. The device, this time, was worthy of a great shaman. The show trials epitomized the visible part of this construct. It made the mythology of the "enemies of the people" look real, when real people, mostly Lenin's comrades and leaders of the revolution, actually confessed to the most improbable crimes. The procedure thus seemed to rehabilitate the mythology, when in fact it only proved what it tried to conceal. As there was no basis in reality to all the accusations, only confession could serve as proof when any analytical or juridical content was missing. Bukharin, during his own trial in 1938, called this procedure "the medieval principle." And rightly so, as this "principle" was the basis for the witch trials and the inquisitorial persecutions of schismatics.

The parallel with such trials was perfect. The victims were depicted as sinners who had sold their souls to the devil and committed the basest of treasons. Torture was also used before those trials, but especially massively, with or without any trials, after Stalin personally authorized in 1937 the use of "physical pressure" against all those traitors.

In this context it is worth remembering that not just some action – however innocent – but even a shadow of doubt about the party line and the leader's wisdom was already the beginning of treason – because doubt was bound to end up serving foreign intelligence services and was thus worthy of being cut down prophylactically, even if it was still buried somewhere in the subconscious. Condoning somebody's doubt without reporting it to the authorities was equally reprehensible – and punishable.

All this is fully documented and well known. What is less realized is that the whole activity, including ferreting out the very function of doubt, using scapegoats to whitewash the regime, producing mythical enemies, belonged to a fourth, independent, and fully operative ideology which was offering now to the mass of people, disoriented by the shocks that were showered on them in those years, both poles of a Manichaean equation: the forces of progress with the idolized leader at the helm; and the array of evil forces, spirits or demons, to explain away all that went wrong or caused suffering, thereby to mobilize the nation around the regime's work of construction and destruction.

We know that many responded by offering a stream of denunciations, although we may never know how many did the denouncing or the arresting or how many were arrested or perished. But the effort here on the part of the regime – or was it mainly caused by the pathological mind of the top leader? – was geared to tapping the psychological and cultural predispositions of a disoriented population in the midst of a crisis of values and a cultural no man's land by making them accept a "demonology" offered by the regime. It also shows how the system that engaged in a contest with a superstitious folk still believing in the evil force (*nechistaya sila*) could catch the bug itself and sink in the deepest superstitions and aberrations which could neither be blamed on any scapegoats nor left at the doorsteps of the popular mentality.

A Social Structure Breeding Authoritarianism

In this chapter we have tried to introduce into the inquiry into the Stalinist phenomenon trends that operated in the longer span of Russian history, the mechanism that undid the previous system but also, and this is our contention, continued to affect the new regime. We have also considered the results of the revolution and the civil war, which not only eliminated the previous ruling classes but also brought into the historical arena a new social layer to run the state and a new type of a ruling institution, the party. Also as a result of those two events the whole socioeconomic system, and in many ways the political system as well, reverted to an earlier, precapitalist stage of social development. Therefore this supposedly postcapitalistic system, although recognizing that its predecessor was not that advanced, was in fact departing from a level of development that had inherited only a fraction of the acquisitions of twentieth-century Russia. This state of affairs influenced the respective positions of "state" and "society," the new state being welded onto and facing, mainly, a socially homogeneous, communautary peasantry, and the relations between the two might be considered as defining and constraining much of what was possible and what was actually going to happen in the next stages.

At the next crisis – and the gist of the argument is that the whole context was imbalanced and crisis-prone – a new acceleration created a third complex of factors and trends that closed certain avenues of development and strongly favored others and, in conjunction with many of the props of the previous stages, finally resulted in the combination of development and terror, a bureaucratic state and an autocratic rule that became known as Stalinism. Stalinism, therefore, with its wholesale statization, destruction of cadres, coercive collectivization, concentration camps, and massive slave labor, emerged in a relatively "primitivized" society that had been pushed up by accelerated industrialization, causing the characteristic twin results of the period: an acculturation that was marred by considerable deculturation; an industrial leap forward that was seriously hampered by a stagnating agriculture, a massive upward mobility with a no less massive loss of status for many others, growing literacy, but a general state of immensely downgraded liberties. In fact, it was going to be, for a generation, a cruelly oppressive police state.

Each floor of the historical structure had contributed to this result. Tsarist Russia had a growing and dynamic capitalist sector that was too weak as yet to chew up the peasantry and to transform the system into a full-fledged capitalist market society. As Lenin saw it, a very advanced modern industrial and financial sector was strongly clogged by a web of constraints coming from the state, or from the economic backwardness of the countryside, where the availability of an enormous surplus of cheap peasant labor prevented most of the gentry from modernizing their estates – and contributed to their loss of substance and of importance in the economy of the country.

The revolution destroyed both sides of the equation: the capitalist sector, and those relations that constituted the "semifeudal" building blocks. But what was it that replaced them? For the time being, it was to be the results of "two retreating curves," whereby the new regime inherited from the past, among other things, a peasantry which was liberated from its shackles but had retreated into a mold more "rural" than before and an urban society deprived of many of its experienced and sophisticated layers.

The situation was thus more propitious than before for an enhanced role of the state and more – not less – authoritarian than before the revolution. The whole social matrix was then breeding just this: authoritarianism. It is the context of a "homogenized," illiterate, and semiliterate society and a "simplified" social structure, facing a web of bureaucracies themselves rather heterogeneous socially, with many holdovers from the previous system, with many new arrivals from the lower classes. The whole government machinery, although itself reflecting in many ways the social and economic decline, still was capable of what the bulk of society was not: using the tools of the twentieth century for ruling and conceiving of their situation and aims in modern, often scholarly terms. All this, as already stated, was conducive to authoritarian relations between the sides, almost by spontaneous and natural reflex. Studies of the emerging administrations after October, in all spheres of governmental action, including the party, shows it convincingly: the tone of command (helped by experiences from the civil war) and bureaucratic supremacy came to the officials, whatever their social origins, naturally and easily. If anything, this trend was going to grow, reaching its apogee in "high Stalinism." Paradoxically, although the socialist ideology influenced some to oppose such trends, others could see in this same ideology a justification for firm, even tough and domineering attitudes, befitting those who know what is best for the popular classes, who were not privy to concepts on the intricacies of historical development.

How the initiated analyzed the situation – although we do not forget that initially they differed quite seriously among themselves – is relevant to the study of the regime. The leader felt, as we have noted, that the state was given a broader scope and monopolistic position when facing the enfeebled social basis. But this situation also created in the leadership of the state, not despite but because of their forward-looking and modernizing ideology, a sense of vulnerability and, finally, a paranoid fear of its own masses. Whether this was objectively justified is an interesting topic for debate. But it certainly was exaggerated – or tended to become so – by the habit of using the tools of class analysis conceived in and for a developed capitalist society. In the social structure after the civil war, with its leveled-down peasantry and its cities, from which higher classes disappeared, the practice of looking desperately for a full-fledged class configuration which did not exist enhanced the sense of vulnerability, hindered the appearance of more appropriate analytical tools, and contributed in many ways to the strengthening of factors of stress and disequilibrium in the system. Misuse of tools of analysis, we claim, was one of the causes of the loss of self-control and of accrued irrationality that came to plague the country during a long period, finally driving the system into a state of acute morbidity.

It is difficult to imagine how such social realities, such hard givens of the initial stage, would not deeply influence the further stages. The structural pattern does not predetermine all policies, nor does it deny certain choices. But it certainly limits those choices and, at least, eliminates certain more desirable alternatives. One does not see a possibility of any democratic solutions in those days – even if Lenin wanted one.[4] More pertinently, socialist solutions were not available either. Officially, a transition period was necessary for it, but finally it was the almost wholesale nationalization that was decreed to be the attribute of socialism. What this meant, in reality, was a statization, which is something different, although in itself not so unexpected in Russia. But the ideological veil helped here to accelerate a broad nationalization that was, by any standard, premature in most of the sectors, not

[4] See Stephen F. Cohen and Robert C. Tucker, eds., *The Great Purge Trial* (New York: Grosset & Dunlap, 1965), pp. 653–67. This remark does not aim to explain events and results in the polity by claiming that consequences flow predictably and unavoidably from the described social setting in a rigidly predetermined manner. The broad outlines of the emerging type of polity are, of course, deeply influenced by this setting, which presents obvious limiting factors. But inside such a general framework choices and alternatives exist, and much depends on the quality of decisions and on the abilities of the battling factions.

only during the civil war but also later, including in the 1930s. And "premature nationalization" – an idea which cannot be developed here – is one of the underlying factors of a specific type of bureaucratization that went with the enhancement of state power and rigid controls of the population.

Under these conditions, one wonders whether the failure of the Bolsheviks consisted in having relinquished their Octobrist ideals – we are aware how many of them fought against and paid dearly for trying to slow down the trend away from original hopes – or whether they perished because they did not know how to handle an authoritarian state and prevent it from veering into something worse, thereby closing avenues for a social democracy in Russia for an era of unknown length.

The full effects of this kind of failure become clear after a furious acceleration of economic growth was launched in a society little prepared for it all – and precisely because it was so little prepared. The effort to operate a leap in a situation we showed to have been "unbalanced" was the source of deep waves of change and crises, which we have tried to describe. The ensuing additional destabilizations, some of which were underlined in our treatment, helped tilt the scale to an ever growing reliance on "administrative methods," which were, of course, more than just coercion. They created an additional temptation to abuse the levers of coercion and prefer them to other tools, a temptation the regime had no incentives anymore to refuse. If we accept this picture of growing strains, contradictions, and imbalances in the whole system, which were foreshadowed already in the pre-1928 period but expanded in the next one under the impact of the "big drive," then further statization, bureaucratization, more coercion, and the making of a quite archaic personal despot, can be seen as a response to conditions quite favorable for these trends. What happens in agriculture should make the emergence and deepening of the state's totalitarian grip and other of its traits clearer, as this branch – and its carrier, the peasantry – is a key mechanism in this process. In another important sphere of life, the cities, the sudden and unplanned influx to towns described as the ruralization of the cities, and its consequences for social cohesion, culture, standard of living, social and individual psychology, values, collective and personal neuroses, and, finally, criminality can be seen as facets of a "deculturation" that characterized many of the cities. During a number of years the countryside was subjected partly to similar, partly to some specific transformations. The aim of the shattering collectivization policy was twofold: to organize the peasants in more productive larger units and forms and thus to help break the country's dependence on the *muzhik*. *Raskrest'yanit'* – "depeasantizing" – was the name of the game. The breaking in of the peasant was the least successful of the policies of the Soviet state, although polite formulas are misplaced here. What followed was a creation of a system that was more oriented to and more successful in squeezing than in producing. The peasantry denied the kolkhoz fields its zeal, and concentrated it on the tiny family plots. In this way the *muzhik* perpetuated himself as a social class of an archaic character, except that the economic basis for this was only 3.8 percent of the total sowing – and on this 3.8 percent, the peasant's family and the whole nation depended for their food to a ridiculously high degree well into the 1950s. Forceful extraction of unpaid labor, and a residual method of payment (payment only at the end of the year, in unpredictable quantity, and only after the state, creditors, and the kolkhoz took their share) deeply affected the character of the peasants and made them remember the NEP with nostalgia. From their point of view, collectivization brought them a loss of status and a drop in their standard of living. A whole system of social, economic, and legal restrictions annulled all they had achieved in three previous revolutions, and they kept asking themselves, as their interest in land and in agriculture became atrophied, what their position was in this state, what their social identity was. They were not salaried workers (whom the system officially considered its mainstay); they were not cooperators (everything was controlled and prescribed from above, and elections of kolkhoz officials were just a formality); and they were not the independent producers, the patrons (*khozyaeva*), as they had been during the NEP. Some kind of hybrid, some kind of ridiculous mini-*muzhik* suffering from such a deep sense of depersonalization and loss of identity – such was one of the results of this forceful socioengineering. At the same time a situation somewhat parallel to what occurred in the days of Peter the Great emerged and lasted well into Khrushchev's days. Peter tried and had to build his industrial plants on the basis of serf labor. Stalin carried on his industrialization, especially his industrialization of agriculture, on the basis of extracting unpaid surpluses, leaving only "residual remuneration" to *kolkhozniki* – which in no way could be a voluntarily accepted deal. Thus labor-oppressive practices emerged in the countryside and to a lesser extent (and in different forms) in industry as well. A labor-oppressive regimen or numerous elements thereof in the system at large also enabled and was supplemented by a wide sector of slave labor in the camps.

This complex of phenomena belongs to the repulsive and regressive elements in the Soviet industrial and social development. Stalinism was the epitome of such traits, and without them it would not have existed. When its main architect passed away and many traits of his system were dismantled, Russia found itself advancing and powerful, but the grip of the initial social backslide of 1917–21, strongly conducive and favorable to the authoritarian, ubiquitous state system of the 1930s, has not yet been broken to this day – far from it – and the result has been periodic slowdowns, decline, and conservative blockages in the country's development and social relations.

Further Reading: The Social History of the Stalin Era

Kendall E. Bailes, *Technology and Society under Lenin and Stalin: Origins of the Soviet Technical Intelligentsia, 1917–1941* (Princeton, 1978).

R. W. Davies, *The Industrialization of Soviet Russia 2: The Soviet Collective Farm 1929–1930* (London, 1981).

Donald Filtzer, *Soviet Workers and Stalinist Industrialization: The Formation of Modern Soviet Production Relations, 1928–1941* (London, 1986).

Sheila Fitzpatrick, *Education and Social Mobility in the Soviet Union, 1921–1934* (New York, 1979).

Sheila Fitzpatrick, "Ascribing Class: The Construction of Social Identity in Soviet Russia," *The Journal of Modern History*, vol. 65, no. 4 (1993).

David L. Hoffmann, *Peasant Metropolis: Social Identities in Moscow, 1929–1941* (Ithaca, 1994).

Hiroaki Kuromiya, *Stalin's Industrial Revolution: Politics and Workers, 1928–1932* (New York, 1988).

Moshe Lewin, *Russian Peasants and Soviet Power: A Study of Collectivization*, trans. Irene Nove (Evanston, 1968).

William G. Rosenberg and Lewis H. Siegelbaums, eds., *Social Dimensions of Soviet Industrialization* (Bloomington, 1993).

Lewis H. Siegelbaum, *Stakhanovism and the Politics of Productivity in the USSR, 1935–1941* (New York, 1988).

Socialist Ideology

3

The Soviet Tragedy: A History of Socialism in Russia

Martin Malia

Excerpted from Martin Malia, *The Soviet Tragedy: A History of Socialism in Russia, 1917–1991* (New York: The Free Press, 1994).

Editor's Introduction

Another important interpretation of Stalinism sees socialist ideology as its primary cause. The Cold War itself was in large part an ideological confrontation between American capitalism and Soviet socialism, so it is not surprising that historians would emphasize the role of ideology in Soviet history, including in the origins of Stalinism. This emphasis on ideology did not go unchallenged, as illustrated by the preceding articles by Suny and Lewin, but it nonetheless influenced historical explanations of Stalinism throughout much of the Cold War era. With the end of the Cold War and the collapse of the Soviet Union, one might have expected a de-emphasis on ideology and a turn away from predominantly ideological explanations of Soviet history. In the short run, however, the opposite occurred. The collapse of the Soviet Union sparked a wave of Cold War triumphalism in which conservative commentators proclaimed victory over socialism. Some historians also adopted this triumphalist tone, as they reiterated the centrality of socialist ideology to the Soviet system and to its failure.[1]

The Soviet Union's collapse also tended to undercut social historians and revisionists in the Soviet history field. Social historians' approach, with its focus on social classes and movements from below, had been heavily informed by Marxism and its belief in the determinacy of socio-economic

[1] Zbigniew Brzezinski, "The Grand Failure," and Richard Pipes, "The Fall of the Soviet Union," in Lee Edwards, ed., *The Collapse of Communism* (Stanford, 2000); Robert Conquest, "Academe and the Soviet Myth," in John H. Moore, ed., *Legacies of the Collapse of Marxism* (Fairfax, VA, 1994).

factors. The Soviet collapse spelled the virtual demise of Marxism as a scholarly as well as a political philosophy, and it thereby hastened the turn away from social history. Moreover, the rapidity of the Soviet system's collapse weakened revisionists' claims that social groups had supported the October Revolution and the Soviet government. Once Mikhail Gorbachev lifted censorship and coercion, the Soviet people were quick to forsake socialism, and this seemed to confirm that it never had any popular backing, and that indeed the Soviet system had been imposed by ideologues who illegitimately seized power in 1917.

The fact that by 1991 the "Great Socialist Experiment" had failed, that the Soviet planned economy had stagnated completely, that people rejected socialism altogether, also seemed to indicate that socialist ideology was unworkable. As such, the conservative view that it was an artificial ideology, imposed forcibly on an unwilling population, gained more credence. Many Russians themselves were eager to adopt this position, as they dismissed the entire Soviet era as a giant ideological mistake, as a 74-year wrong turn on Russia's historical path. Such a view neglected the fact that the Soviet system had operated for three-quarters of a century, had industrialized the country (albeit at a tremendous human cost), had educated a largely illiterate population and created a modern urban society, and had transformed the country into a military superpower, capable of defeating Nazi Germany and rivaling the United States for world domination. But in the immediate aftermath of the Soviet collapse, the tendency to judge the past through the lens of the present was overwhelming, and this perspective lent support to historical explanations that emphasized ideology.

In his book, *The Soviet Tragedy*, Martin Malia provides the most forceful statement on the importance of ideology to Stalinism and the Soviet system as a whole. Malia begins with a brilliant discussion of the ideas of socialism as they developed in Europe and in Russia itself. He conveys both the intellectual and moral appeal of socialism, and explains the rise of Marxism, which became the leading strain of socialist thought. In the excerpt that follows, Malia argues for the centrality of socialist ideology to the Stalinist system. He raises the question of Stalin's personal influence on the system, and asks whether the criminality of Stalinism was due to Stalin's criminal character. But he responds that, while Stalin was indeed a terrible man, Stalinism was not simply the work of one person and instead comprised an entire system of hyper-bureaucratic and terroristic control.

Malia also considers whether Stalinism should be explained as a legacy of the tsarist autocracy. Some scholars indeed argue that Stalinist authoritarianism derived from Russian autocratic traditions and from Stalin's conscious emulation of Ivan the Terrible and Peter the Great.[2] But Malia refutes this explanation as well, pointing out that the admittedly despotic measures of these tsars were intended to increase state power and their own control, and fell far short of the complete social and human transformation to which Stalin aspired. Stalin sought not only to modernize Russia but to create a new world of socialism; his aspiration to transform humankind came not from the tsars but from socialist ideology.

Malia notes that this belief in Marxian socialism belonged not only to Stalin, but to the Communist Party as a whole. All Party members endeavored to remake society according to their ideological vision. This vision foresaw bloody class warfare with the agents of capitalism, so it was not Stalin alone who introduced the massive use of coercion into the system. In fact it was the Party that served as the military–political vehicle that waged class war. And it was according to the socialist program of abolishing private property and the market that Stalin and the Party conducted their "Great Offensive" – the collectivization and industrialization drives launched at the end of the 1920s. Hence according to Malia, Stalinism was not a deviation from socialism, as revisionists claim, but rather the logical result of the Soviet attempt to put socialist ideology into practice.

Malia concludes by asking whether Stalinism was indeed socialism. He notes that the Soviet system under Stalin clearly achieved non-capitalism; it suppressed the fundamental elements of capitalism – private property, profit, and the market. In this sense Stalinism realized the instrumental program of socialism. At the same time, Stalinism did not impart the supposed moral benefits of socialism – material abundance, human freedom, equality, and an end of exploitation. On the contrary, Stalinism impoverished, imprisoned, and exploited people; by the standards of socialist morality it was worse than capitalism. Malia accounts for this contradictory outcome by arguing that the means and ends of socialism were themselves in contradiction. By following the socialist program, Stalin and the Communist Party arrived not at socialist liberation and equality but at a totalitarian dictatorship that repressed civil society and individual autonomy in the name of socialism.

---

[2] Robert C. Tucker, *Stalin in Power: The Revolution from Above, 1928–1941* (New York, 1990); George Backer, *The Deadly Parallel: Stalin and Ivan the Terrible* (New York, 1950).

The Soviet Tragedy: A History of Socialism in Russia

Martin Malia

The Stalin Question

Stalin's rule during this decisive decade has been called the Second Russian Revolution, and the designation is quite apt. It has also been called "primitive socialist accumulation by the methods of Tamerlane,"[1] and this is even more apt. Yet neither label really conveys the specificity of the event: The transformation of Russia during the thirties was unprecedented in scope, to the same degree as the means employed to achieve it were unique in their mixture of the insane and the criminal with – it must be admitted – the grandiose and the epic.

This poses another major problem of historical interpretation.[2] The previous chapter [in the original publication] argued that the choice of a coercive road to socialism was no accident but the logical course for a Bolshevik Party in a crisis of survival. Yet it does not automatically follow that the extraordinarily brutal manner in which Stalin implemented that choice was equally governed by the Party's ethos. The pace at which collectivization and industrialization were forced was not the outcome of an automatic process but the result of conscious decisions. And after 1929 Stalin's power was so great that he personally made, or at least supervised, the most crucial of those decisions.

So the question of the logic of the system versus Stalin's personal role does not end with the Great Break but continues throughout the thirties, from the collectivization to the Purges. How much of the criminality of the collectivization was due to Stalin's own criminal character? How much of the madness of the Purge was due to his own possible insanity? Surely – this line of inquiry goes – neither Lenin nor Trotsky (both hard Bolsheviks who could quite conceivably have adopted a coercive policy in 1929) would have deliberately starved the peasants or murdered revolutionary comrades. The personal paranoia and the individual sadism of Stalin the man must constitute the decisive element that made his reign seem, in Bukharin's metaphor, like the return of Genghis Khan.[3]

---

[1] Nikolai Valentinov in *Sotsialisticheskii vestnik* (New York, April, 1961).

[2] Robert C. Tucker, *Stalinism: Essays in Historical Interpretation* (New York: Norton, 1977), pp. 77–108.

[3] Adam Ulam, *Stalin: The Man and His Era* (New York, 1973), p. 307.

To this argumentation is often added the theme that Stalin's Second Revolution (unlike the first Revolution of 1917) was a revolution from above, and revolution from above is the time-honored Russian method of catching up with the advanced West.[4] Thus Stalinism represented a reversion to the more extreme phases of Russian autocracy, as under Ivan the Terrible or Peter the Great. And at a superficial glance this explanation seems eminently plausible. Indeed, Stalin himself liked to compare his rough nation-building with that of these two tsars, Peter for the Plan and Ivan for the Terror. Yet it would be prudent to reserve judgement on this matter until Stalin's own record has been examined, and to seek the sources of Stalinism, in the first instance, not in remote centuries but in the actual circumstances that produced the revolution from above. Here, in this line of inquiry, Stalin's personality is far more germane than are the ghosts of autocrats past.

Even so, caution is in order on this score, too, for Stalin's lugubrious figure, like Hitler's equally macabre one, can easily overshadow his period and the system he represented. Thus "Stalinism" in common parlance too often means a style of rule – an extreme personal tyranny, an exceptional despotism, or a superdictatorship – created and sustained by the man, Stalin. But these Greek and Roman terms do not do justice, any more than does the invocation of Genghis Khan, to the historical particularity of the Stalin phenomenon.

So Stalinism must also be viewed as a *system* of hyperbureaucratic and terroristic control. Yet even when this is done, the system's genesis is still too often explained not by structural factors but by the tyrant's overweening ambition. The consequence of this is that once the evil author of the "ism" has disappeared, the system itself may be considered to have ended. Thus in both Western and Soviet usage, as we have seen, Stalinism was at times held to be a completely different phenomenon from Bolshevism and Leninism.[5] In Soviet parlance this assessment was expressed as "the cult of personality," which meant that an otherwise sound socialism was "distorted" by the undue and accidental power of one leader. So the logics of backwardness, of the monolithic Party, of primitive socialist accumulation, and of the ideocratic partocracy were all obscured by a logic of abstract tyranny, the "cult."

This approach might be called the "bad man" theory of history. Its appeal is to simplify a painful past by personalizing it and concentrating

---

[4] Alexander Gerschenkron, *Economic Backwardness in Historical Perspective* (Cambridge, Mass., 1962). See also Igor Kliamkin, "Kakaia doroga vedet k khramu," *Novyi mir* (November, 1987), pp. 67–92.
[5] See introduction [in the original publication].

it in a single focus of evil.* But, as just noted, the defect of this universal penchant is that it obscures the deeper system behind the man, or at least subordinates it to his continuing presence. Thus, what came before him and what came after can be viewed as a different system, and the belief arises that once the focus of evil has disappeared this system can recover a healthy normality. Hence, the "bad man" approach to Stalinism is related to the aberration thesis. Indeed, Stalin's evil personality is at the heart of the "aberration" thesis because there is no alternative way to explain how an otherwise healthy organism went awry. Stalin climbed to dictatorship because he was, as Bukharin liked to see it, "an unprincipled intriguer who subordinates everything to the preservation of his own power."[6]

Now, Stalin was a bad man, indeed a very bad man, and he grew steadily worse with age. But much more than this is needed to explain the momentous policies of his twenty-five-year reign. He had to have a context of institutions and ideas within which to work and through which to vent whatever dark drives haunted his psyche. Moreover, we must assume that there were quite a number of other individuals in Russia and in the Party who had equally harsh childhoods and cruel fathers, who were equally neurotic and thirsty for power, but who did not become politically significant figures. Psychology does not translate into politics unless there is first a political problem to be met. In explaining any political leader's policies we must accept, just as he does when he acts, the primacy of political motivation. Political leaders who use their power simply to act out their psychoses do not keep power very long, as the cases of Peter III, or Paul I, and on back to Emperor Commodus, serve to illustrate. But Stalin lasted a quarter of a century, and by any mundane standards of judgement he must be considered a world-historical success: After all, he built socialism, defeated fascism, and created a Soviet empire. Psychological reductionism in history works no better than socioeconomic reductionism. One of the purposes of this chapter, therefore, is to derive Stalin's policies from the Soviet system rather than to work the relationship the other way around. . . .

---

* The personalization of history is not confined to negative phenomena. There is also a "good man" view of history, of which a striking example was the Western cult of Gorbachev, which for six years sustained the illusion that Communism was reforming itself when in fact it was collapsing. Indeed, personalization of public life is well-nigh universal – from Romulus to George Washington – because it seems to make reality easily comprehensible to everybody.

[6] Stephen F. Cohen, *Bukharin and The Bolshevik Revolution: A Political Biography, 1888–1938* (New York, 1973), p. 322.

These considerations now make it possible to address the questions of interpretation posed at the beginning of this chapter. First there is the matter of autocratic continuity and periodic revolution from above in Russian history. The phenomenon, of course, is undeniable; but the real problem is how we explain it, and how we relate one episode of revolution to another. And on this score analogy is too often confused with cause, as if some metaphysical essence were operating from Ivan to Peter to Stalin.[7] Nor does Stalin's own penchant for this type of thinking prove much. His self-comparisons with Peter and Ivan served to illustrate and justify what he had already decided to do for other reasons; they were hardly his inspiration when he set out to do it. At that point his ideological references were Marxism and socialism and, especially, Lenin the Leader.

Thus it is very easy to establish empirically the sources of Stalin's policies in the Bolshevik tradition; but it is extremely difficult, if not impossible, to find empirical transmission belts leading to those policies from Ivan or Peter. The most that one can say in support of a traditional Russian input into Stalinism is that roughly analogous situations of backwardness produced roughly analogous responses. But this is a far cry from saying that the earlier responses caused the later one, or that the later response in some mysterious manner reincarnated the earlier ones. The nature of Russia's industrial backwardness in the 1930s is as different from that of her military backwardness in the eighteenth or the sixteenth century as are the politics of ideocratic partocracy from those of divine-right absolutism.

Moreover, the intensification of autocracy has hardly been the only theme in Russian history. In particular, from Peter's time to 1917 Russia was moving steadily in the opposite direction, towards a more pluralistic and "European" order. The process of the "unbinding" (*raskreposhchenie*) of the Russian universal service order proceeded from the gentry's emancipation from compulsory state service in 1762 to the peasant's emancipation from serfdom in 1861, and from local self-government through the *zemstvos* and a largely independent judiciary in 1864 to the legislative Duma of 1905 – in short, to the creation of a civil society.

Furthermore, if we move from loose analogies to a closer look at actual comparisons, it should be clear that revolution from above on Stalin's titanic scale has no precedent in Russia, or anywhere else for that matter. Both Ivan the Terrible and Peter the Great worked with a

---

[7] Alexander Yanov, *The Origins of Autocracy: Ivan the Terrible in Russian History* (Berkeley and Los Angeles: University of California Press, 1981).

universal service state.[8] A country with no natural frontiers, with a poor agricultural base, and with only a minuscule urban population was constrained to general mobilization of both its material and human resources in order to survive as an independent entity, and later in order to expand. This meant that the peasants were enserfed to the gentry in order to permit the latter to serve in the armies of the autocratic tsar, while the gentry's possession of its lands and serfs was conditional on that same service. Russia's was the harshest system of universal service anywhere in Europe, though it was not without partial parallels farther West, particularly in Prussia.

Peter the Great tightened the requirements of state service for all social classes, from the gentry to the serfs, in order to give Russia for the first time a standing army on the Western model. But he did not substantially alter the basic structure of the system; rather, he gave the form of a European ancien régime to the already existing Muscovite service state. He could do this because the difference between the militarized systems of Russian autocracy and of Western absolutism was not all that great at the time. But he in no way replaced the old Russian order with a new one of his own devising. The revolutionary aspect of his rule lay in cultural Westernization rather than in social and political reorganization.

Ivan the Terrible's policies, to be sure, were more socially destructive than Peter's. The old hereditary boyar aristocracy was effectively broken as a cohesive group and replaced by the service gentry; Ivan's "political police," the oprichnina, acquired a separate territorial realm-within-a-realm where autocratic caprice was the supreme law; and the whole Muscovite system was put under such strain that soon after Ivan's death it collapsed in the great smuta of 1605–13. Although we can surmise that Ivan's policies were due to the pressure of the unsuccessful Livonian war with Poland and Sweden, we do not really know his motives; but it is not very likely that they add up to a "modernizing" response to the European challenge, as was clearly the case with Peter's. The ultimate result of Ivan's policies, moreover, was not revolutionary, for the Muscovite order restored by the Romanovs after the smuta was fundamentally the same as that which had existed before Ivan.

Stalin's revolution from above, in contrast, cannot be situated in any continuum with the social order that preceded it, whether under the NEP or the Old Regime. But just as important is the radical ideological envelope of Stalinism: in reality it is ideology that explains both the total scope and the inordinate cost of Stalin's revolution. Peter and Ivan, on the other hand, in their justifications of autocracy, used only the most

---

[8] See chapter 2 [of the original publication].

conventional arguments of the European tradition: either the Christian duty of submission to divinely ordained power or the imperatives of natural law. Thus, even though Stalin, like Peter (though not like Ivan), was responding to the pressures of economic backwardness and military lag, his overall ambition to bring history to its culmination with the new world of socialism is quite incommensurate with his predecessor's limited, purely national projects.

Similarly, a secondary role must be assigned to Stalin's personality in explaining his system. Before 1929 the worst that could be said about his character was what Lenin had said – that Stalin was "too rude" for state responsibilities – though Lenin deemed such rudeness quite acceptable among Bolsheviks. To be sure, the overall record of Stalin's career shows him to be cruel to the point of sadism, and suspicious to the point of paranoia. Still, this was not apparent at the start of his Great Offensive. It is thus best to assume that his character was not a constant, but that it evolved under the pressure of the unprecedented risks of the Offensive.

In 1932, in the midst of that Offensive, Stalin's wife committed suicide after a violent argument that apparently concerned his policies toward the peasants. Even though he was hardly a sensitive man, this must have produced some effect on him, and for the worse. And the carnage of the collectivization no doubt hardened him even more. Later, he told Winston Churchill that the ordeal had been as frightful as the war.[9] We may also assume that for one so deep in crime as was Stalin by the time of the terror famine, any further crime could only come more easily. As with a drug, ever larger doses of crime could only produce a lesser effect, and murder could degenerate into mere habit. Thus, although Stalin's criminality did not simply derive from his character, his criminal character may have increasingly derived from his crimes.

But more important than history or psychology is the institutional setting in which Stalin operated, a setting that bred both cruelty and paranoia. The Party, as its agitprop ceaselessly proclaimed, was in a class war to the death. It was surrounded by enemies without and within: international capital, petty bourgeois kulaks, bourgeois wreckers, and deviationists within the Party. Stalin no doubt personally aggravated this mood of universal struggle and suspicion, but he by no means created it; it derived, rather, from the Party's whole heritage. This was a Party with which his "rude" character meshed only too readily.

To discover the impetus behind the Great Break, therefore, we must return to what had been the driving force of Communism since it first

[9] Ulam, *Stalin*, p. 290.

discovered its vocation in the militant and military frenzy of 1918. What fueled Bolshevism's Second Offensive was what had fueled the first: the vocation of the Party itself as the military–political vehicle for bringing humanity into socialism. The Party had no other reason for existing. By 1929, after twelve years of vainly waiting for socialism to appear, the time had come to force the hand of history and to build the future by an act of will. The alternative was not Bukharin's "growing into socialism"; the alternative was the withering away of the Party's ideological momentum in an interminable effort to wait out the muzhik. And with the dissipation of ideology, the Party's will to monopolize power would have eroded as well.

So the second episode of War Communism was launched, but it unfolded with a much greater sweep and intensity than the first. And the tone of the operation was quite different: Whereas 1918 had seen a hot hysteria, unpremeditated and unrehearsed, 1930 saw a colder hysteria, prepared and channeled to a high degree. This was because the tasks to be accomplished in 1930 were more complicated than those in 1918, and the Party-army was now more numerous, disciplined, and stronger. Let us recall the sequence of causation leading to this Second Offensive.

The Revolution and War Communism made Russia much more backward than she had been before 1917. Thus, when the market was reborn after 1921, the peasants became the arbiters of the country's economic destiny. By 1926 the regime had no choice but to increase investment in industry, if only to renovate an obsolete and decaying plant; but the Party at the same time wished to build socialism to give itself a worker and urban "base." Yet the Party's ideological distrust of both the market and kulak "capitalism" led it to set prices too low to keep the peasants producing. Thus in 1927 foodstuffs became scarce in the cities just as industrial expansion was taking off. The solution of raising state prices and relying on the market for the rest was rejected, since this would have made the Party and its industrial program hostage to uncontrollable, "anarchic," and "capitalist" forces. Therefore, it was decided to take the peasants' grain by coercion through immediate and full collectivization. Once this choice had been made, it also became necessary to accelerate industrial expansion to the maximum. And these two decisions together meant suppressing the market as well as all social classes that lived off it, from the kulaks to the nepmen.

But this amounted to a total "solution" to all problems at once through the total subordination of the whole of society to the Party-state. Thus one step inexorably led to another, all the way to the creation of a new, totalitarian order. There is no overall logic of Russian history leading to this result; but there *is* such a logic of Bolshevism – realizable should circumstances permit the Party to act out fully its Marxist fantasy. In 1918–21 the circumstances of economic breakdown cut the process of Bolshevik self-realization short. In 1929–1933 the circumstances of a stronger Party and an economy in reasonable health (at least at the start) permitted the Party to take the Marxist logic to its resolution.

This does not mean, however, that the Party consciously desired or even anticipated what it found when it reached that culmination. Instead, as in 1918, it improvised its way into discovering what its true program was. Soviet socialism was built not out of any genuine plan but as if driven by Hegel's "cunning of reason" – that is, the outcome of the Offensive was determined by the logic of the system itself, a logic leading the Party in ways not fully apparent to its leaders. Thus Stalin and his men moved by a process of trial and error, and from one crisis to another, to arrive at the unproductive kolkhoz system and the military–industrial complex they had created by 1935. And when they got there, of course, they had no choice but to proclaim that these were the "socialist" results they had aimed at all along.

In fact, for a time they were not sure they would reach this "socialism" at all. Stalin knew at the start that his Offensive was a high-risk gamble that put the survival of the system at stake. To be sure, Lenin had gambled everything in October and again at Brest-Litovsk, but at that time there was much less to lose than in 1929 when a Soviet state existed. And, indeed, by 1931–2 it looked as though Stalin would lose his gamble, for the early blunders in both agriculture and industry had thrown the country into such chaos that it seemed, once again, as if the whole system might collapse. It was only in 1933, after the fall harvest had been brought in and such industrial projects as Magnitogorsk had at last begun producing, that Stalin won his gamble. It was only in January 1934, at the Seventeenth Party Congress, that the Party could draw its first confident breath since January 1930 and proclaim the "victory" of its Offensive.

Thus another crisis of survival was surmounted. And it was surmounted because, at the height of the danger, the Party in a visceral reflex had closed ranks behind the Leader. Preobrazhenskii and most of his colleagues on the Left rallied to Stalin because he was implementing, however crudely, their platform, and because they could not bear to be left out of the building of socialism. One of them, Iurii Piatakov, not only became Sergo Ordzhonikidze's deputy but was indeed the real brains behind the industrialization drive. Bukharin and most of the Right, despite their declared commitment to the peasant and the market, did the same because they too could not bear being left out of the Great Offensive, no matter how botched its execution and how uncouth its leader. It is noteworthy that not one prominent Bolshevik resigned from the Party or publicly protested its crimes. Only Trotsky, who by now had been expelled from the country, openly campaigned against Stalin's "mistakes" – but as distortions of his, Trotsky's, correct policies.

Yet what really brought the Party through the crisis were not these holdovers but the likes of Nikita Khrushchev and their simpler faith. In 1928, during the Shakhty affair, Khrushchev was active against "wreckers" in his home region of the Donbas; shortly thereafter he moved to Kiev to become head of the Organization Department of the Ukrainian Party. In 1929 an Industrial Academy (in effect, a school for adult education) opened in Moscow to train Party cadres of working-class background to assume responsibilities in the now revolutionary economy, and Khrushchev became one of its first students. There he participated in expelling a group of fellow students as "Right deviation-ists." In 1931, on the recommendation of the former General Secretary of the Ukrainian Party, Kaganovich, he became a Party district secre-tary in Moscow and helped clean out the supporters of his Rightist pre-decessor, Riutin (of whom more shortly).

In 1934, at the age of 39, Khrushchev was rewarded by election to the Central Committee at the Congress of Victors. Soon thereafter he succeeded Kaganovich (who had been promoted to higher things) as Moscow Party chief and thus took over supervision of the construction of the Moscow Metro. It is upwardly mobile worker-peasants turned Party-workers like Khrushchev that Stalin called the "salt of the earth." Like the Leader himself, they could quite sincerely see themselves as the proletariat in power; and they could feel just as sincerely that they had an inherent right to exercise their class dictatorship for the building of socialism and the betterment of all mankind.

*   *   *

But was the result of their efforts really "socialism?" It was clearly not "capitalism;" but is that enough to qualify it as true "socialism?" Social-ist opinion outside Russian was divided over this question at the time, and it has bedeviled all discussion of socialism ever since. With Stalin's achievement the discourse of world socialism entered a wholly new phase.

From the 1830s to the First Five-Year Plan, socialism was a state that lay in the future; with Stalin's victory for the first time it could be alleged that socialism actually existed in the present. It had passed from the status of a prospective utopia to that of a palpable reality, and from the status of a movement to a society. Or at least the Soviet regime claimed that this had occurred. From that time onward, therefore, any socialist had to define his position in terms not just of the Soviet "experiment" but of the Soviet "achievement." But what are the criteria for deciding Soviet socialism's ontological status?

The Soviet Union had indubitably arrived at noncapitalism. It had suppressed private property, profit, and the market, and this is clearly the instrumental program of integral socialism. But most of the positive moral benefits that were supposed to result from this program had not appeared; on the contrary, a large number of unanticipated negative consequences could be observed. There was no growth of material abundance, but rather an increase of penury. There was no advance of human freedom, but instead a regression into servitude. There was no triumph of equality, but rather a new stratification of the population as a function of the Party's purposes. There was no end of the exploitation of man by man; indeed, to this was added the exploitation of everybody by the Party-state.

In short, the Party had built socialism, and it turned out not to be socialism. Or, to be more precise, the Party had realized the instrumental program of socialism, but socialism's moral program still remained in the future. Indeed, the new present was arguably worse, in terms of socialist morality, than the old capitalist past.

There are several ways of coping with this unexpectedly contradictory outcome. One is to deny that any contradiction existed at all, and to claim that the moral consequences of socialism did in reality follow from the practical program. This is the course that was adopted by the Soviet regime, and it is difficult to see how it could have done otherwise without admitting that it had failed and that the system was a fraud.

Another solution is to say that the central objective of the Soviet Revolution was realization of the instrumental program of non-capitalism – namely, the end of private property – and that since this had been achieved, the Soviet order was a real, if incomplete, socialism. This is the course taken by Trotsky, Bukharin, and a multitude of later commentators, both in Russia and abroad, from Roy Medvedev and Gorbachev to any number of Western authorities. This solution, of course, embraces the already mentioned aberration thesis; the bad-man theory of history; and/or the heavy heritage of Russian autocracy, bureaucracy, and backwardness. And until 1991 it entailed the belief that in the fullness of time the moral program of socialism would be added to the instrumental one. It is this hopeful and consoling *via media* that has been far and away the most popular solution to the Soviet conundrum, both in the East and in the West.

But there is a third solution, which is to say that the instrumental program of socialism leads quite logically to the perversion of its moral program. In other words, the failure of integral socialism stems not from its having been tried out first in the wrong place, Russia, but from the socialist idea per se. And the reason for this failure is that socialism as full noncapitalism is intrinsically impossible. For the suppression of private property, profit, and the market is tantamount to the suppression of civil society and all individual autonomy. And although this can be approximated for a time, it requires an inordinate application of force that cannot be sustained indefinitely.

As a practical matter, therefore, socialism leads not to an assault on the specific abuses of "capitalism" but to an assault on reality *tout court*. It becomes, in effect, an effort to suppress the real world, and this is something that cannot succeed in the long run. But for a protracted period this effort *can* succeed in creating a surreal world, one defined by the paradox that inefficiency, poverty, and brutality can be officially presented as the *summum bonum* of society, and one where society is unable to challenge this fraud.

It is this resolution of the Soviet conundrum that East European dissidents adopted when they were first able to speak up after Stalin's death. And it is on this solution that the majority of the people of Eastern Europe acted in 1989–91 when they concluded that the system could not be reformed but had to be abolished, and that the basic social realities of private property, profit, and the market had to be restored if ever the East was to make an exit from the failed surreality of "really-existing" socialism.

But it would take a half-century for all of this to become clear. In the meantime the regime's greatest successes were still before it. In 1934–5 Stalin gave his country a new breathing spell, a mini-NEP – but only in the psychological sphere. With a second and more sober Five-Year Plan under way, rationing could now come to an end. The Leader therefore proclaimed in a new slogan that "life has become better, life has become more joyous." But this was only a respite before he moved to complete his work through the Great Purges.

Further Reading: Marxist Ideology and Stalinism

Giuseppe Boffa, "The Role of Ideology," in Robert V. Daniels, ed., *The Stalin Revolution*, 3rd edn. (Lexington, Mass., 1990).

Leszek Kolakowski, "Marxist Roots of Stalinism," in Robert C. Tucker, ed., *Stalinism: Essays in Historical Interpretation* (New York, 1977).

Wolfgang Leonhardt, *Three Faces of Marxism* (New York, 1974).

Alfred G. Meyer, *Communism*, 4th edn. (New York, 1984).

Robert C. Tucker, ed., *The Marx–Engels Reader* (New York, 1972).

Robert C. Tucker, *The Soviet Political Mind: Studies in Stalinism and Post-Stalin Change* (New York, 1963).

The Foreign Threat

4

The Objectives of the Great Terror, 1937–1938

Oleg Khlevnyuk

Originally appeared as Oleg Khlevnyuk, "The Objectives of the Great Terror, 1937–1938," in Julian Cooper, Maureen Perrie, and E. A. Rees, *Soviet History, 1917–1953: Essays in Honour of R. W. Davies* (London: Macmillan Press, 1995).

Editor's Introduction

The aspect of Stalinism that has attracted more attention than any other is the Great Terror – one of the most deadly and bizarre episodes in all human history. In the late 1930s, millions of innocent people, including many high ranking Communist Party members, were imprisoned or shot by the Soviet secret police. The Great Terror is the term given to this massive use of state violence which included both the Great Purges of Party members and wide-ranging arrests and executions of average Soviet citizens. Many historians have sought to explain why the terror took place. While no one denies Stalin's involvement in the terror, scholars attribute varying degrees of responsibility to him. Some scholars believe that Stalin masterminded all aspects of the terror and was personally responsible for the murder of millions of people. Other scholars, while not exonerating Stalin, stress systemic or political factors that caused or at least fueled the terror.

The totalitarian model presented terror as an integral part of the Soviet system. One totalitarian theorist even postulated that purging was a permanent and necessary component of Soviet totalitarianism – a hypothesis proven wrong when bloody purges ceased after Stalin's death.[1] Radical revisionists have also looked beyond Stalin to explain why the Great Terror

---

[1] Zbigniew Brzezinski, *The Permanent Purge: Politics in Soviet Totalitarianism* (Cambridge, Mass., 1956). Some historians of the totalitarian school nonetheless stress Stalin's role; see Robert Conquest, *The Great Terror: A Reassessment* (New York, 1990).

occurred. J. Arch Getty, for example, argues that the Great Purges were not a planned, coherent policy controlled by Stalin, but rather an extreme form of political infighting within the Party. What began as an attempt by Stalin and other leaders to consolidate control over local Party organizations spun out of control after rank-and-file Communists were encouraged to denounce their local bosses and Party members began to settle scores with one another. Getty and another revisionist, Gabor Rittersporn, also stress the extreme social tensions within the country and widespread fear of conspiracies and foreign spies to explain how the purges turned deadly.[2]

Oleg Khlevnyuk's pioneering research in the former Communist Party archives has shed a great deal of light on Stalin's use of terror. In the following selection, Khlevnyuk cites previously classified documents of the Politburo (the Communist Party's supreme council) to argue that the Great Terror was clearly orchestrated from the top. The Politburo in fact sent quotas for arrests and executions to the NKVD (the Soviet secret police), which carried out the terror. These quotas were directed at specific groups within the population – expelled Party members, former opposition party members, certain national minorities, former kulaks, criminals, and other "anti-Soviet elements." Both the Great Purges within the Party and the Great Terror overall, then, were centrally controlled efforts to eliminate purported enemies of the ruling Politburo. Khlevnyuk acknowledges that local authorities in some cases over-fulfilled their quotas, but he maintains that it would be wrong to attribute the terror to local initiative, given that the Politburo ceaselessly demanded increased "struggle with the enemy."

In addition to demonstrating that the terror was controlled from the center, Khlevnyuk presents evidence that it was directed by Stalin himself. Stalin was the author of many of the Politburo directives on the terror, and he personally approved lists of individuals and groups to be arrested and executed. Khlevnyuk also assesses Stalin's objectives in carrying out the Great Terror. While not dismissing the possibility that Stalin's paranoia or vindictiveness contributed to the terror, Khlevnyuk makes the case that Stalin launched the terror to eliminate any potential opposition in the event of war. By examining the particular groups targeted by the terror, he concludes that Stalin and his inner circle sought to remove all strata of the population that were hostile or potentially hostile to them. Stalin

---

[2] J. Arch Getty, *Origins of the Great Purges: The Soviet Communist Party Reconsidered, 1933–1938* (New York, 1985); Gabor T. Rittersporn, *Stalinist Simplifications and Soviet Complications: Social Tensions and Political Conflicts in the U.S.S.R., 1933–1953* (Chur, NY, 1991); and "The Omnipresent Conspiracy: On Soviet Imagery of Politics and Social Relations in the 1930s," in Nick Lampert and Rittersporn, eds., *Stalinism: Its Nature and Aftermath: Essays in Honour of Moshe Lewin* (Armonk, NY, 1991).

considered these targeted groups a potential "fifth column" of internal opposition in the event of war with a foreign country. Viacheslav Molotov, one of Stalin's closest supporters within the Politburo, made this very argument late in his life when he recalled the Great Terror; he maintained that it was absolutely necessary to eliminate anyone who could not be counted on to support the Soviet government, especially given the growing threat of fascism and likelihood of war.

Ever since the October Revolution in 1917, the foreign threat had loomed large in the minds of Communist leaders. During the Civil War which followed the Revolution, several foreign countries, including the United States, Britain, France and Japan, had sent troops to intervene on the side of anti-Communist forces. This foreign intervention confirmed the Communists' fears that the capitalist countries were eager to over-throw and eliminate the fledgling Soviet state. Throughout the 1920s and 1930s, the threat posed by "capitalist encirclement" weighed on Com-munist leaders, including Stalin himself who continually warned of both internal and external enemies. This threat became much more concrete with the rising international tensions of the late 1930s. Hitler, who came to power in Germany in 1933, made no secret of the fact that he planned military aggression to expand eastward. His military build-up and bel-ligerent moves in the second half of the 1930s made this threat more imminent. At the same time, Japan was engaged in its own military aggres-sion in Manchuria and increasingly threatened Soviet territory as well.

At the time of the Great Terror, then, the foreign threat and likelihood of war were very tangible to Communist leaders. They could not help but think of the possible consequences for themselves in the event of war. Khlevnyuk cites the classic Stalin biography by Isaac Deutscher, who imagines a conversation between Stalin and the ghost of Nicholas II, the Russian tsar overthrown by the 1917 Revolution.[3] The Revolution had been precipitated by the horrendous military losses suffered by the tsarist army during the First World War. Military defeats had discredited the tsar and emboldened his opponents, among them the Bolsheviks (Commu-nists) who ultimately came to power and who executed the tsar and his family during the Civil War. In the event of another great war, Stalin too had to worry about internal challenges to his leadership. Eliminating potential opponents within the Party and the population as a whole served as a preemptive strike against any such opposition.

Khlevnyuk is not seeking to justify the use of terror through his expla-nation of Stalin's motives. By killing millions of people, including many high-ranking Party officials and army officers, Stalin greatly weakened the country on the eve of the Second World War, and hence undermined the

---

[3] Isaac Deutscher, *Stalin: A Political Biography*, 2nd edn. (New York, 1966).

ability of his regime to withstand the Nazi invasion. Nonetheless, the foreign threat in the late 1930s was genuine, and it provided an impetus for dealing with internal enemies, real or imagined. That Stalin chose the Great Terror as his method for dealing with enemies remains a matter for historical and moral judgment. But Khlevnyuk makes a strong case that Stalin's motives for using terror went beyond any personal vendettas or paranoia.

It is possible to see the foreign threat as a cause for all of Stalinism, not just the Great Terror. Given Russia's crushing defeat in the First World War, and the extreme international tensions of the interwar period, some scholars have argued that Stalinism was necessary to prepare the country militarily. At the time of the First World War, Russia was far less indus-trialized than western European countries, Germany in particular, and its weaknesses in industry and transportation contributed greatly to its mil-itary defeats. Following the Revolution, all Communist leaders and many non-Communist engineers and technical specialists agreed that the Soviet Union needed to industrialize quickly. The precise pace of industrializa-tion and the means by which to achieve it remained topics of debate, but when Stalin launched his highly coercive collectivization and industrializa-tion campaigns at the end of the 1920s, he received the support of most Party members. One historian, Theodore von Laue, has in fact argued that Stalinism was a logical if horrific response to the intense foreign threat of the interwar period and the need to industrialize at any cost.[4]

As with the Great Terror, the causes of Stalin's forced collectivization and industrialization drives remain important topics for historians to discuss. To point out the foreign threat does not necessarily negate the importance of Communist ideology or Stalin's personal predilections. Still, it is important to consider the foreign threat as one factor that, either by itself or in conjunction with other factors, caused Stalinism. Khlevnyuk's pioneering research on the Great Terror provides important evidence for making this historical judgment.

---

[4] Theodore von Laue, *Why Lenin? Why Stalin? Why Gorbachev?: The Rise and Fall of the Soviet System* (New York, 1993); von Laue, "Stalin in Focus," *Slavic Review*, vol. 42, no. 3 (1983).

The Objectives of the Great Terror, 1937–1938

Oleg Khlevnyuk

The mass repression in the Soviet Union in 1937–8, variously referred to as the Great Terror or the 'Ezhovshchina', has produced a volume of monographs, articles and memoirs, which have examined the phenomena from a diversity of viewpoints.[1] However, many of the circumstances surrounding this tragedy remain obscure. In particular there is little information concerning the mechanism whereby the repression was organised and carried out. Most of the NKVD's documents for this period remain in the KGB's archives and are not available for researchers. In the still closed Presidential archives there is a large volume of material concerning the activities of the Politburo and Stalin in 1937–8. In republican, provincial and local archives there is a wealth of material on how central directives were implemented in the localities.

The detailed study of these problems will require much time and effort by historians. That work has only just started. The lack of information and insufficient research mean that many questions cannot yet be fully answered. Some of the most intriguing questions concern the relationship between centralism and 'local initiative' in the events of 1937–8. More work is needed to determine the system whereby the victims of repression were selected, the objectives of the purgers, as well as the question of the actual number of the victims who were repressed.

In the present article, which draws on new documents including those from the Politburo's special files (*osobye papki*), an attempt is made to present in general outline the mechanism of repression in 1937–8, and on this basis to determine what were the objectives of the organisers of the terror.

Almost all historians are agreed in fixing the commencement of the new stage of Stalinist repression at the end of the summer–beginning

This chapter was originally translated by E. A. Rees.

[1] See for example R. A. Medvedev, *Let History Judge: The Origins and Consequences of Stalinism* (New York, 1971); R. Conquest, *The Great Terror: A Reassessment* (New York, 1990); J. A. Getty, *The Origins of the Great Purges: The Soviet Communist Party Reconsidered, 1933–1938* (New York, 1985); G. T. Rittersporn, *Stalinist Simplifications and Soviet Complications: Social Tensions and Political Conflicts in the USSR, 1933–1953* (Philadelphia, 1991); J. A. Getty and R. T. Manning (eds), *Stalinist Terror: New Perspectives* (Cambridge, 1993).

of the autumn of 1936. In June Stalin instructed the NKVD to organise a new political trial of Trotskyists and Zinovievists.[2] On 29 June the
Central Committee of the CPSU dispatched to the localities a secret letter
concerning 'the terrorist activities of the Trotskyist–Zinovievist counterrevolutionary bloc',[3] on the basis of which many former oppositionists were repressed. In August in Moscow there took place the trial of the
so-called 'anti-Soviet joint Trotskyist–Zinovievist centre'. All 16 of the
accused, including L. B. Kamenev and G. E. Zinoviev, were shot. In
the country there followed a wave of new arrests.

On 26 September on Stalin's insistence the Politburo removed G. G.
Yagoda from the post of People's Commissar of Internal Affairs (NKVD
USSR) and appointed in his place N. I. Ezhov, who for several years, at
Stalin's behest, had exercised a supervisory role over the NKVD. On 29
September Stalin signed the Politburo decree, 'Concerning the counter-
revolutionary Trotskyist–Zinovievist elements'.[4] The decree in effect
demanded the total destruction of former oppositionists.

In the following few months mass arrests were carried out in the economic, state and party institutions. In January 1937 there took place
the second great Moscow trial of the so-called 'Parallel Anti-Soviet
Trotskyist Centre'.

The first results of the purge were reviewed by the Central Committee plenum of February–March 1937. On the eve of the plenum the
Sector of Leading Party Organs of the Central Committee, headed by
G. M. Malenkov, compiled inventories (*spravki*) of nomenklatura officials
of various departments. The *spravki* comprised several lists. In the first
were listed the names of leading officials, who had already been dismissed from their posts, expelled from the party and arrested. In the
remaining lists were given the names of other officials who had not yet
been arrested but who had committed various 'sins': who had participated in the different oppositions, who 'had deviated', who had in the
past been members of other parties etc.[5] The majority of those named
in these lists were soon to be repressed.

The *spravka* which Malenkov prepared for Stalin and dated 15
February 1937 noted the great number of former party members in the
USSR. (Many of the facts and theses from the *spravka* were noted by
Stalin in his speeches to the February–March plenum.) Malenkov wrote:

> It should be noted in particular that at the present time in the country
> there number over 1,500,000 former members and candidate members

[2] *Izvestiya TsK KPSS*, 1989, no. 8, p. 84.
[3] Ibid., pp. 100–15.
[4] Ibid., no. 9, p. 39.
[5] RTsKhIDNI, 17/71/43, 44, 45, 46 etc.

of the party, who have been expelled and mechanically dismissed at various times from 1922 onwards. In many enterprises there are concentrated a significant number of former communists, with the result that sometimes they exceed the numerical composition of the party organisations which work in these enterprises'.

For example at the Kolomenskyi locomotive building works, the *spravka* noted, compared to 1,408 communists there were 2,000 former party members; at the Krasnoe Sormovo works there were 2,200 members and 550 former members, at the Moscow Ball Bearing Works 1,084 members and 452 former members, etc.[6]

Many of the participants at the February–March plenum spoke of the presence in the country of a great number of 'anti-Soviet elements', and 'offenders'. The secretary of the West Siberia kraikom R. I. Eikhe reported that in 11 years from 1926 to 1937 in the krai 93,000 individuals were expelled from the party whilst in the krai party organisation at the beginning of 1937 there were 44,000 communists. 'Amongst those expelled', Eikhe declared, 'there are no small number of direct enemies of the party. They were in the party, they acquired certain political habits and will attempt to utilise this against us.' In the krai, Eikhe continued, there lived also a great number of exiles, former kulaks. Amongst these there remained 'a not insignificant group of inveterate enemies, who will attempt by all means to continue the struggle'.[7] The secretary of the party organisation of Turkmeniya, Popok, also spoke of the evident danger which was posed by former kulaks who had returned from imprisonment and exile: The great number of kulaks who passed through Solovki and other camps and now as 'honourable' toilers return home, demand allotment of their land, making all kinds of demands, going to the kolkhoz and demanding admission to the kolkhoz.'[8] At the plenum others emphasised the fact of the existence of millions of believers in the country with many priests who retained no small influence.[9] The necessity of continuing the struggle with enemies was indicated by the main reports to the plenum from Stalin, Molotov and Ezhov.

In the months following the February–March plenum the policy of unmasking and arresting former oppositionists continued. On 23 May 1937 the Politburo sanctioned the expulsion from Moscow, Leningrad and Kiev to the 'non-industrial regions of the Union' of all those expelled from the party for membership of the various oppositions together with

[6] RTsKhIDNI, 17/2/773, 115.
[7] *Voprosy istorii*, 1993, no. 6, pp. 5–6.
[8] Ibid., p. 25.
[9] Ibid., no. 5, pp. 4–5, 14–15; no. 6, pp. 8, 21–2.

those accused of 'anti-Soviet manifestations (the dissemination of hostile views in lectures and in the press)'. Those expelled also included the families of those sentenced to be shot for political crimes, and those sentenced to imprisonment for five years and upwards. On 8 June the Politburo sanctioned the expulsion from the Azov–Black Sea krai to Kazakhstan of the families of 'arrested Trotskyists and rightists'.[10] In March–June 1937 there continued the arrest of party and state leaders at various levels. Mass arrests now began in earnest in the leadership of the Red Army.

Up until the middle of 1937, therefore, the main blow of repression was directed against members of the party, mainly those who had in their time participated in the oppositions or who had shown some kind of dissent with Stalinist policies. Repression began also in the organs of power: inside the NKVD many of Yagoda's people were arrested, in the army cases were fabricated against a number of senior military officers. The new stage in the purge was heralded by the decision of the Politburo of 28 June 1937, 'Concerning the uncovering in West Siberia of a counter-revolutionary insurrectionary organisation amongst exiled kulaks'. The resolution ordered the shooting of all 'activists of the insurrectionary organisation'. To speed up the investigation of their cases a troika was established comprising the head of the NKVD of Western Siberia (Mironov), the procurator of the krai (Barkov) and the party secretary of the krai (Eikhe).[11]

Within a few days the practice of establishing troiki was extended to the whole country. On 2 July 1937 a Politburo resolution 'Concerning anti-Soviet elements' sanctioned the carrying out of operations which became a pivot of the mass repression of 1937–8. By a resolution of the Politburo the following telegram was sent to the secretaries of the oblast committees, krai committees and the Central Committees of national communist parties:

> It is noted that the majority of former kulaks and criminals, who were exiled, at one time from various oblasts to the northern and Siberian regions and then with the completion of the sentences of exile have returned to their oblasti – are the main instigators of all kinds of anti-Soviet and diversionary crimes.

The Central Committee ordered the secretaries of oblasti and krai organisations and all oblast, krai and republican representatives of the NKVD to take account of all kulaks and criminals who returned to their areas of domicile so that the most hostile of them should be immediately

[10] *Protokoly zasedanii Politbyuro, osobaya papka.*
[11] Ibid.

arrested and shot. These cases were to be handled administratively through the troiki, whilst the remainder, the less active but still hostile elements, were to be resettled and sent to the regions designated by the NKVD.

The Central Committee required the local authorities within five days to present to the Central Committee the composition of the troiki, and the number to be shot as well as the number to be exiled.[12]

In the following weeks lists of the troiki and information concerning the number of 'anti-Soviet elements' were received from the localities, and on this basis orders were prepared within the NKVD for the implementation of the operation. On 30 July Ezhov's deputy in the NKVD, M. P. Frinovskii, who had been assigned responsibility for implementing this action, sent to the Politburo for its approval the NKVD's operational order N00447, 'Concerning the operation for repressing former kulaks, criminals and other anti-Soviet elements'. The order fixed the beginning of the operation, depending on region, from 5–15 August; it was to be completed in four months' time.

Above all the order laid down 'the contingents to be subject to repression'. In reality it included all who in whatever degree had struggled against Soviet power or had been victims of former repressions: kulaks, those released from or who had fled from exile, former members of disbanded parties (SRs, Georgian Mensheviks, Mussavats, Dashnaks etc.), former White Guards, surviving tsarist officials, those arrested, charged with terror and spying-diversionary activities, political prisoners, those held in labour camps etc. On one of the later places in this list were included criminals.

All those to be repressed, in accordance with this order, were divided into two categories: first those subject to immediate arrest and shooting; second those subject to imprisonment in labour camps or prison for periods from 8 to 10 years. All oblasti, krais and republics in the order were assigned quotas (*limity*) for those to be repressed for each of the two categories (on the basis of information concerning the number of 'anti-Soviet elements', which the local authorities had sent to Moscow). A total of 259,450 individuals were to be arrested, of these 72,950 were to be shot (including 10,000 in the camps). These figures were deliberately incomplete since the quotas omitted a number of regions of the country. The order gave local leaders the right to request from Moscow additional quotas for repression. Moreover, to those imprisoned in camps or in exile might be added the families of the repressed.

Troiki were established in the republics, krais and oblasti to decide the fate of those arrested. As a rule they included the narkom or adminis-

[12] *Trud*, 4 June, 1992, p. 1.

trative head of the NKVD, the secretary of the corresponding party organisation and the procurator of the republic, krai or oblast. The troiki were accorded extraordinary powers, to pass sentences (including shootings) and issue orders for their implementation without any check. On 31 July this order of the NKVD was approved by the Politburo.[13]

From the end of August the Central Committee received from local leaders requests to increase the quotas for repression. From 27 August to 15 December the Politburo sanctioned increasing the quotas for various regions for the first category by almost 22,500 and for the second category by 16,800 individuals.[14]

Besides the general operation to liquidate 'anti-Soviet elements' there were organised several special actions. On 20 July 1937 the Politburo ordered the NKVD to arrest all Germans, who were working in defence factories and to deport some of them abroad. On 9 August the Politburo confirmed the order of the NKVD USSR 'Concerning the liquidation of the Polish diversionist group and organisation POV' (Polish Organisation of Military Personnel). On 19 September the Politburo approved the NKVD order 'Concerning measures in connection with the terrorist diversionary and spying activities of Japanese agents of the so-called Harbintsy' (former workers of the Chinese Eastern Railway, who had been resettled in the USSR following the sale of the Chinese Eastern Railway to Japan in 1935).[15]

In the second half of 1937 there was carried out also the mass expulsion from frontier regions of 'unreliable elements'. The largest expulsion was the deportation from the Far Eastern krai of the entire Korean population to Kazakhstan and Uzbekistan which was implemented on the basis of the Central Committee – Sovnarkom resolution of 21 August 1937 with the stated aim of 'suppressing penetration by Japanese espionage in the Far Eastern krai'.[16]

An important component part of the mechanism of mass repression was the conducting of numerous trials both in the capital and in the localities. As distinct from the secret courts and the absolutely secret sessions of the troiki open trials fulfilled an important propaganda role. Therefore sanction for the conducting of the main trials was given directly by the Politburo. It also as a rule determined in advance the sentence, most commonly shooting. The Politburo was especially active in

---

[13] Ibid.

[14] *Protokoly zasedanii Politbyuro, osobaya papka.* See also *Moskovskie novosti,* 21 June 1992, pp. 18–19.

[15] *Protokoly zasedanii Politbyuro, osobaya papka.* On the fate of the Harbintsy see: A. Suturin, *Delo kraevogo masshtaba* (Khabarovsk, 1991) pp. 195–213.

[16] See *Belaya kniga o deportatsii koreiskogo naseleniya Rossii v 30–40-kh godakh* (M., 1992) tom. 1.

the second half of 1937 in sanctioning the organisation of these trials. From 8 August to 17 December 1937 the Politburo approved the conducting of about 40 trials in various regions of the country.[17]

At the beginning of 1938 signals were issued from Moscow, which it seemed, indicated a cessation of the purge. On 9 January the Politburo ruled as incorrect the dismissal from work of relatives of individuals, arrested for counterrevolutionary crimes, only on the grounds of their being relatives, and charged the USSR's Procurator, A.Ya. Vyshinskii to give corresponding instructions to the organs of the procuracy.[18] On 19 January the press published the resolution of the Central Committee, 'Concerning the mistakes of party organisations in the expulsion of communists from the party, of the formal-bureaucratic attitude to appeals of those expelled from the CPSU and of measures for correcting these deficiencies', which demanded greater attention to the fate of party members. Certain token measures in connection with these resolutions was undertaken by the leadership of the USSR's Procuracy and by Narkomyust.[19]

The true meaning of these political manoeuvres still remains obscure. Certain indications concerning the preparation of the campaign allow us to assert that the operation against the 'anti-Soviet elements', as noted above, was to be completed in four months, i.e. by November–December 1937 (depending on region). It is possible, that having this circumstance in mind Stalin was prepared at the beginning of 1938 to terminate the purge and that he wished to give a clear signal to this effect to the January plenum of the Central Committee. In support of such a proposition might be cited the fact that the announcement of the 'relaxation' at the beginning of 1939 at the XVIII party congress was also carried through on the basis of the slogan for a more attentive attitude to the fate of communists. The report on this question at the January plenum and at the XVIII party congress were both made by G. M. Malenkov.

[17] It is difficult to give precise figures for the number of trials sanctioned by the Politburo since in a number of cases the resolution does not give a precise figure. For example on 14 November 1937 the Politburo instructed the Archangel obkom to conduct two or three cases of 'wreckers in the timber industry'. From the decisions of the Politburo it is also not always clear whether they had in mind an open trial. For example on 15 November the Politburo charged the Novosibirsk obkom that 'those apprehended concerning the explosion at Prokop'evsk should be brought before the court and shot, the shooting to be publicised in the Novosibirsk press' (*Protokoly zasedanii Politbyuro, osobaya papka*).

[18] RTsKhIDNI, 17/3/994, 56. This resolution was formulated as a resolution of Sovnarkom USSR of 10 January 1938 (GARF, 5446/57/53, 27).

[19] P. H. Solomon Jnr., 'Soviet Criminal Justice and the Great Terror', *Slavic Review*, vol. 46, no. 3, 1987, pp. 405–6.

Whatever the truth of this argument the resolution of the January plenum of 1938 remained no more than a political declaration. The purge could not be completed in four months. On 31 January 1938 the Politburo adopted the proposal of the NKVD USSR 'Concerning the confirmation of additional numbers of those subject to repression of former kulaks, criminals and active anti-Soviet elements'. By 15 March (in the Far East by 1st April) it was prescribed, within the operation for eliminating 'anti-Soviet elements', to repress an additional 57,200 individuals, of whom 48,000 were to be shot. Correspondingly the powers of the troiki, who were to carry out this work, were extended.[20] Also on 31 January the Politburo authorised the NKVD to extend until 15 April the operation for destroying the so-called 'counterrevolutionary nationalist contingent-Poles, Letts, Germans, Estonians, Finns, Greeks, Iranians, Harbintsy, Chinese and Romanians'. Furthermore, the Politburo charged the NKVD that it should complete by 15 April analogous operations and destroy (*pogromit'*) the cadres of Bulgarians and Macedonians, both those of foreign origin and those who were citizens of the USSR.[21]

After confirming these new quotas for repression the history of the previous year was repeated: local leaders began to request increasing the quotas and extending the duration of the operation. From 1 February to 29 August 1939 the Politburo approved additions to the January quotas for those to be repressed by about 90,000 people.[22] And this meant also in fact approving the breaching of the April deadline on the duration of the operation.

In 1938 the campaign of political trials was continued. For the year as a whole the Politburo sanctioned the conducting of about 30 trials, of which seven were in January 1938.

Only in the autumn of 1938 was the terror reined in. The examination of cases by the troiki was forbidden by the directive of Sovnarkom-Central Committee of 15 November 1938.[23] The joint Sovnarkom-Central Committee resolution of 17 November 1938 forbade the carrying out of 'mass operations for arrest and exile'.[24] On 24 November Ezhov was released from his post as narkom of the NKVD. The great terror was brought to an end.

This brief enumeration, which does not cover all the actions, that comprised what is known as the great terror, allows us to make some observations.

[20] *Moskovskie novosti*, 21 June 1992, p. 19.
[21] *Ibid.*
[22] *Protokoly zasedanii Politbyuro, osobaya papka*. It is not possible to determine precisely what proportion of these were subject to be shot, since in many cases the Politburo confirmed general figures for the first and second category.
[23] For the text of this directive see *Moskovskie novosti*, 21 June 1992, p. 19.
[24] *Istoricheskii arkhiv*, 1992, no. 1, pp. 125–8.

The mass repression of 1937–8 was unquestionably an action directed from the centre; which was planned and administered from Moscow. The Politburo gave orders for the carrying out of the various operations, it approved the operational orders of the NKVD, it sanctioned the organisation of the most important trials. The question of the activities and reorganisations of the NKVD, and the appointment of the responsible officials of this commissariat, occupied in 1937–8, to judge from the protocols, the leading place in the Politburo's work.

The activity of the troiki, as already noted, was regulated by means of quotas on the numbers to be incarcerated in camps and those to be shot. Sentences imposed on a significant proportion of those tried by the Military Collegium of the USSR's Supreme Court, the military tribunals and other 'judicial bodies' were in fact determined in advance by the Politburo's Commission for Legal Matters and confirmed by the Politburo. In this period the Commission for Legal Matters presented its protocols for the approval of the Politburo once a month on average. The texts of these protocols remain unavailable. But evidently they include the 383 lists 'of many thousands of party, soviet, Komsomol, military and economic workers' which, as N. S. Khrushchev revealed at the XX party congress, Ezhov sent to Stalin to be approved.[25] (Ezhov was included in the composition of the Politburo Commission on Legal Matters on 23 January 1937[26] and evidently during the repression played a leading part in it). An example of one of these lists was given in the speech by the deputy chairman of the Committee of Party Control Z. T. Serdyuk at the XXII party congress in October 1961:

Comrade Stalin,
    I send for your approval four lists of individuals which are to be sent to the Court of the Military Collegium.
1. List 1 (general)
2. List 2 (former military officials)
3. List 3 (former workers of the NKVD)
4. List 4 (wives of enemies of the people)
I request that you sanction that they all be sentenced to the first category.
                                    Ezhov.[27]

In spite of the fact that the majority of directives concerning the terror were formulated as decisions of the Politburo their true author,

---

[25] *Reabilitatsiya. Politicheskie protsessy 30–50 kh. godov,* (M., 1991) p. 39.
[26] *Protokoly zasedanii Politbyuro, osobaya papka.*
[27] *XXII s"ezd Kommunisticheskoi partii Sovetskogo Soyuza; Stenograficheskii otchet,* t. III (M., 1962) p. 152.

judging from the existing documents, was Stalin. The Politburo itself in the years of the terror evidently met irregularly. On 14 April 1937 there was adopted the resolution 'with the aim of preparing for the Politburo and in case of especial urgency – also for the resolution of questions of a secret character . . . to create attached to the Politburo of the CC CPSU a permanent commission comprising of comrades Stalin, Molotov, Voroshilov, Kaganovich, L., and Ezhov'.[28] The inclusion in this group of Ezhov (who, incidentally, became only a candidate member of the Politburo several months later) testifies to the fact that this simplified procedure was designed primarily to examine questions relating to the NKVD's activity. This was so in practice. Several resolutions, judging by all the evidence, Stalin adopted in fact on his own. The directives of the Central Committee to the localities about the arrests and organisation of trials bore Stalin's signature.[29] In a number of cases Stalin dispatched telegrams with instructions from himself in person. For example on 27 August 1937 in reply to a request from the secretary of the Western obkom of the party, Korotchenko, concerning a trial of 'wreckers active in agriculture in Andreevskii raion' Stalin telegraphed: 'I advise you to sentence the wreckers of Andreevskii raion to be shot, and the shootings to be publicised in the local press.' A similar telegram from Stalin personally the same day was sent to Krasnoyarsk obkom.[30] With a great measure of confidence it is possible to assert that when the documents from the Presidential archive are available, much more evidence will be revealed concerning Stalin's leading role in the organisation of the terror.

The centralised initiation and direction of the terror as a whole does not mean that there were no elements of a spontaneous character. Indeed they existed in all such actions – during the course of collectivisation, and forcible grain requisitioning in 1932–3, in the so-called struggle against 'terrorism' following the murder of Kirov etc. In official language these phenomena were referred to as 'excesses' (*peregib*) or as breaches of socialist legality. To the 'excesses' of the mass repression of 1937–8 it is possible to adduce the high number of deaths during interrogation or the exceeding by local organs of the quotas for arrests and shootings established by Moscow etc. For example, according to incomplete information, the troika of the NKVD of Turkmeniya from August 1937 to September 1938 tried 13,259 individuals although they had a limit of only 6,277.[31] This fact of exceeding the quota by more than double, and also the murder of prisoners under investigation, which was

---

[28] RTsKhIDNI, 17/3/986, 16.
[29] *Tsentr khraneniya sovremennoi dokumentatsii*, 89/48/2, 3, 7, 9, 11, 12, 15, 16, 17, 20.
[30] *Izvestiya*, 10 June 1992, p. 7.
[31] *Protokoly zasedanii Sekretariata Tsk VKP (b) osobaya papka.*

concealed by the local organs and not given in accounts, must be taken into consideration in assessing the total number of those repressed.

However, as a whole such spontaneity or initiative by local authorities was planned, deriving from the nature of the orders which were issued by the centre, from the constant demands of Moscow to 'strengthen the struggle with the enemy', from the assignment to the NKVD of the primary task of ruthlessly implementing and breaking all minor attempts to oppose the terror. Up to a certain point the leadership of the country in fact encouraged breaches of their own directives, untying the NKVD's hand, although it was fully cognisant of the fact that the terror went beyond the limits established by the 'control figures'.

As the mass terror of 1937–8 was an action which was directed from the centre, it is logical to ask what aims did it serve for the organisers of the repression and in particular for Stalin. This problem has been repeatedly examined in the literature. Historians have directed attention to such facts as the elimination of a significant proportion of those communists with pre-revolutionary party service, the growing threat of a new war, the replacement of the ruling elite, the unstable state of Stalin's own psychology etc. What we know today regarding the mechanisms of the 'Great Terror' allows us to assert that the main aim of the mass repression of 1937–8 was the removal of all strata of the population, which in the opinion of the country's leaders were hostile or potentially hostile.

The purge at the end of the 1930s was carried out in accordance with the policy of repression implemented in earlier years. The actions that followed one another – expulsions from the party and the arrest of oppositionists, collectivisation and 'dekulakisation', the struggle with 'sabotage of grain requisitioning' and 'theft of socialist property', arrests and exile after the murder of Kirov, mass expulsions from the party and arrests in the course of the exchange of party documents etc. – affected many millions of people. By the middle of the 1930s in the country, as already noted, there were 1.5 million former party members, millions of prisoners in the labour camps and in the so called labour settlements. There were also millions of people who were free but who at various times had been brought to legal account etc. A great problem for the government was the return from exile of 'kulaks' who by the middle of the 1930s were being released and under the new Constitution had their rights restored. Thus the number of those with a grudge (*obizhennyi*) and thus under suspicion (together with their families) included a significant proportion of the country's population. In the conditions of a threat of a new war many of them were considered as a potential 'fifth column'. Amongst those who fell under the constant suspicion of the

Kremlin leadership were the immigrants, representatives of national minorities, many of whom had certain contacts with their co-nationals who lived abroad.

With certain of the formerly repressed individuals the government attempted reconciliation. The resolution of TsIK and Sovnarkom USSR of 16 January 1936 for example foresaw lighter punishments or early release of some of those sentenced by the notorious law of 7 August 1932 concerning the safeguarding of socialist property.[32] The narkom of Justice Krylenko and chairman of the Supreme Court of the RSFSR Bulat, informed M. I. Kalinin, chairman of TsIK USSR, that in implementing this resolution by July 1936 (the resolution foresaw the work would be completed in six months) more than 115,000 cases were to be reexamined. Almost 49,000 of those imprisoned had their sentences cut and about 38,000 were released. This aroused amongst several hundred of prisoners the expectation of being granted a full amnesty.[33]

A still larger action of a similar kind occurred when the mass repression was in full swing. On 23 October 1937 the Politburo charged the USSR's Procuracy and Narkomyust to carry out for the whole union and autonomous republics, krais and oblasti a check on criminal cases, which involved those who had held positions in the village soviets, kolkhozy, MTS, as well as village and kolkhoz activists. They were to check all cases beginning from 1934. At the same time the Politburo undertook to drop cases and free from punishment those kolkhozniki accused of minor offenses (property, administrative infringements etc.).[34] This action continued for more than two years.[35] The examination of criminal cases involved 1.5 million people. By 10 March 1940 were delivered *spravki* concerning the quashing of convictions on almost 450,000 people and releasing from prison almost 30,000. The cases against 128,000 people were closed, whilst 25,000 had their punishments reduced.[36]

On 22 October 1938 Sovnarkom USSR adopted a resolution which authorised the granting of passports to the children of those in special labour settlements and in exile on attaining 16 years of age 'on the general basis and not to place in their way obstacles to go to education

---

[32] Approved by the Politburo on 15 January 1936 (RTsKhIDNI, 17/3/974, 174).

[33] RTsKhIDNI, 78/7/207, 1–2.

[34] *Protokoly zasedanii Politbyuro, osobaya papka.*

[35] On 27 July 1939 Sovnarkom USSR adopted a resolution 'Concerning the reexamination of cases of individuals from the kolkhozy and village aktiv, judged in 1934–1937', which recognised the unsatisfactory course of presenting evidence for gaining convictions and demanded the completion of this work in its entirety for the whole country by 1 November 1939 (GARF, 17/57/60, 1).

[36] GARF, 5446/30/277, 24–8.

or to work', although it preserved restrictions on departure to so called 'regime localities'. Before the war about 100,000 people were released from exile by this resolution.[37]

However, the Stalinist leadership always considered terror as its main method of struggle with a potential 'fifth column'. The cruel repression of 1937–8 was above all determined by biographical particulars. The basis for shooting or dispatch to the camps might be an unsuitable pre-revolutionary past, participation in the civil war on the side of the Bolsheviks' enemies, membership of other political parties or oppositionist groups within the CPSU, previous convictions, membership of 'suspect' nationalities (Germans, Poles, Koreans etc.), finally family connections and association with representatives of the enumerated categories. Corresponding accounting of all these contingents of the population through the years was done by the NKVD and the party organs. Following orders from Moscow to the localities the lists were compiled and on this basis arrests were carried out.

Already in the order of the NKVD N00447 'Concerning the operation for the repression of former kulaks, criminals and active anti-Soviet elements' the organs of the NKVD were instructed to investigate 'all criminal contacts of those arrested'. As revealed by numerous memoirs and documents the fulfilment of this task was one of the main objectives of the NKVD's staff. Adopting torture, they fabricated numerous cases of 'counterrevolutionary organisations', in which were numbered the friends, co-workers and relatives of those arrested. On this basis new arrests were carried out. The repression was thus extended to those strata of the population which formally were not subject to the purge. Some of those judged in the purge by biographical data were rehabilitated at the end of 1938–9.

It was by these crude means that the repression was carried out amongst members of the party and leading workers both in the centre and in the localities. At first those arrested were those who in their time had participated in oppositions or had some 'political deviation' (the lists of such workers, compiled on the basis of the study of archival material, was in the hands of the NKVD). Then on the basis of their testimony, obtained in many cases by torture and duress, new arrests were carried out. For 1936 alone 134,000 people were expelled from the party, in 1937 more than 117,000 and in 1938 more than 90,000.[38] Some of them were reinstated. However, many were arrested after their expulsion. As a result of the purge of the party the composition of the ruling

---

[37] V. N. Zemskov, 'Kulatskaya ssylka v 30-e gody', *Sotsiologicheskie issledovaniya*, 1991, no. 10, p. 19–20.

[38] RTsKhIDNI, 17/117/873, 23.

elite changed substantially. At the beginning of 1939 the Sector of Leading Party Organs accounted 32,899 leading workers, which were included in the nomenklatura of the Central Committee (narkoms of the USSR and RSFSR, their deputies, heads of chief administrations and obedinenie of the commissariats and their deputies, administrators of trusts and their deputies, directors and chief engineers of many industrial enterprises, directors of MTS and sovkhozy, heads of the political departments (*politotdely*) of the sovkhozy, directors of higher educational institutions and scientific-research institutes, chairmen of oblast and krai ispolkoms, heads and deputy heads of departments of ispolkoms, heads of railway lines and construction projects etc.). Of these 43 per cent were promoted to work in 1937–8. Still more significant was the replacement of the leading party workers. Of 333 secretaries of obkoms, kraikoms and Central Committees of national communist parties who were working at the beginning of 1939 194 were promoted in 1937–8; of 10,902 secretaries of raikoms, gorkoms and okrugkoms of the party 6,909 were appointed to their posts in 1937–8.[39] The changes in the apparat took place through the advancement of young officials and workers.

Not all by any means of the leaders who were repressed suffered for 'political unreliability' (past political sins or close contact with former oppositionists). As with other strata of the population there were amongst the leading workers who suffered many who had an unblemished biography. Researchers have repeatedly noted that with the help of the terror the Stalinist leadership resolved a real existing problem of replacing the older cadres with younger and more educated people.[40] For Stalin such a cadres revolution also had political significance. On the one hand, the promotees, younger cadres advanced as a consequence of the repression, were more amenable to the *vozhd'* than the old guard. On the other hand it was possible to place all responsibility for former lawlessness, economic errors, the difficulties of life of ordinary Soviet people on the repressed leaders.

Those leaders who were repressed did indeed bear their share of responsibility for what had taken place in the country. The dictatorship created the conditions which allowed incredible abuses of power to occur, and many officials took full advantage of this. Having previously encouraged the tyranny of local leaders, the Moscow *vozhd'* in the years of terror turned against these leaders and actively demonstrated his resolution to 'defend' the people from bureaucrats and enemies. For example on 14 May 1937 the Politburo examined the question of the

---

[39] RTsKhIDNI, 477/1/41, 62–83; 477/1/51, 153–4.
[40] S. Fitzpatrick, 'Stalin and the Making of a New Elite' in S. Fitzpatrick, *The Cultural Front: Power and Culture in Revolutionary Russia* (Ithaca, 1992) pp. 149–82.

cases of assaults on kolkhozniki in various raions of Kursk oblast and adopted a proposal submitted by Vyshinskii

> on the adoption by the courts in cases of assaults on kolkhozniki and their public humiliation, of deprivation of freedom as a means of punishment, reviewing sentences that imposed insufficiently harsh punishments in these cases. To publish in the local press sentences for the most important cases, connected with assaults on kolkhozniki and their public humiliation.[41]

On 10 June 1937 the Politburo examined the cases of a number of officials of Shiryaevskii raion in Odessa oblast who were accused of humiliating kolkhozniki. The Procurator of the USSR was charged to send investigators to Shiryaevskii raion to examine the most important cases and to complete the investigation in ten days time. The matter was heard by the Ukrainian Supreme Court in open session in the locality. The sentences were published in the press, both local and central.[42] A specially secret point of this resolution envisaged the sentencing of all the guilty in the case to loss of liberty from 3 to 10 years imprisonment.[43] This policy appears to have been applied widely. In numerous open trials which were carried out in all regions of the country, those judged – mainly local leaders – were most often accused of abuse of power and coercion. The victims of their oppression – ordinary citizens – often gave evidence in the courts. The reports of such 'show-trials' were carried in the press.[44]

This policy it seems bore fruit. In the memoirs of a peasant woman from Novosibirsk oblast, M.D. Mal'tseva, who herself was subject to 'dekulakisation' and exile, she recounts the period of mass repression of the 1930s:

> People suffered so much in that time, but one never heard people criticising Stalin; only the local leaders were blamed; only they were criticised. Because of them we all suffered, and how many people died because of them is unknown. I don't know, perhaps I am wrong, but I say that in 1938 many were taken, perhaps because they heeded our tears, since there were good reasons to take them, that's what I think.[45]

Similar opinions, it seems, were widespread.

[41] RTsKhIDNI, 17/3/987, 229.
[42] RTsKhIDNI, 17/3/987, 492.
[43] Protokoly zasedanii Politbyuro, osobaya papka.
[44] S. Fitzpatrick, 'How the Mice Buried the Cat: Scenes from the Great Purges of 1937 in the Russian Provinces', The Russian Review, vol. 52, July 1993, pp. 299–320.
[45] Vozvrashchenie pamyati. Istoriko-publitsisticheskii al'manakh (Novosibirsk, 1991) pp. 209–10.

With the aim of discovering the reasons for the instigation of the mass repression of 1937–8 it is necessary to take into account the following circumstance. Terror and force were one of the basic methods for creating the Stalinist system. In this or that measure with their help were resolved practically all social-economic and political problems – the securing of social stability, raising industrial production, ensuring Stalin's personal power etc. These and other factors at each stage underwrote the existence of state terror and mass repression. However each of the terror campaigns in turn raised the level of coercion higher, since so to speak the 'usual level' had its concrete reason. For example the mass exile of peasants at the beginning of the 1930s served the purpose of collectivising the countryside. The terror at the end of 1932–3 was a means of escaping from the sharp social-economic and political crisis which developed between the first and second Five-Year Plans. The mass repression of 1937–8 also had its direct causes, as noted above.

In the mind of the Stalinist leadership this was precisely a purge of society, an attempt by one blow to rid themselves of all those who in this or that measure had been subject to coercion in the preceding years or had fallen under suspicion on some other count. This operation was conceived as a means of eliminating a potential 'fifth column' in a period when the threat of war was increasing, and also as a means of disposing of loyal cadres who for various reasons were no longer needed by Stalin.

This view of the purges as a means of eliminating a potential 'fifth column' is not new. The argument was forcefully advanced by the American ambassador in Moscow in the 1930s, Joseph E. Davies.[46] Trotsky, whose writings Stalin avidly read, repeatedly warned of the danger of a prolonged war (whether in the case of victory or defeat), in the absence of a revolutionary upsurge in the west, leading to a capitalist restoration, 'a bourgeois Bonapartist counter-revolution' in the USSR.[47] Isaac Deutscher in his classic biography of Stalin gives an imag-

---

[46] Joseph E. Davies, *Mission to Moscow* (London, 1942).

[47] L. D. Trotsky, *The Revolution Betrayed* (London, 1967) p. 229. Trotsky quoted the following passage from *The Fourth International and War*, published in 1935: 'Under the influence of the critical need of the state for articles of prime necessity, the individualistic tendencies of the peasant economy will receive a considerable reinforcement, and the centrifugal forces within the collective farms will increase with every month . . . In the heated atmosphere of war, we may expect . . . the attracting of foreign allied capital, a breach in the monopoly of foreign trade, a weakening of state control of the trusts, a sharpening of competition between the trusts, conflicts between the trusts and the workers, etc. . . . . In other words, in the case of a long war, if the world proletariat is passive, the inner social contradictions of the Soviet Union not only might, but must lead to a bourgeois Bonapartist counterrevolution.'

inary conversation between Stalin and the ghost of Nicholas II where the relationship between war and regime stability is discussed.[48]

It might be noted further that this was indeed the whole thrust of Stalin's two reports to the Central Committee plenum in February–March 1937, as well as the reports of Molotov, Ezhov, Kaganovich and others. The revelations from the archives now strongly reinforce that view. It is supported by evidence from the directives of the highest leadership of the country concerning the implementation of the purge in 1937–8, by the way these actions were understood by contemporaries, and by the explanations given later by Stalin's own colleagues.[49]

Writing his final, agonized letter to Stalin in December 1937, appealing for his life to be spared, emphasising his loyalty and respect for Stalin personally, Bukharin noted the 'great and courageous idea of a general purge', associated with war preparations and paradoxically the transition to democracy, heralded by the Stalin Constitution. The purge, he noted, directed at the guilty, those under suspicion and those who might waver, should ensure a 'full guarantee' for the leadership in the event of an emergency.[50]

The most explicit statements in support of this view were uttered by Molotov in the 1970s, when he declared:

> 1937 was necessary. If you take into account that after the revolution we chopped right and left, achieved victory, but the survivals of enemies of various tendencies remained and in the face of the growing threat of fascist aggression they might unite. We were driven in 1937 by the consideration that in the time of war we would not have a fifth column . . .

> And there suffered not only the clear Rightists, not to speak of the Trotskyists, but there suffered also many who vacillated, those who did not firmly follow the line and in whom there was no confidence that at a critical moment they would not desert and become, so to speak, part of the 'fifth column'.

> Stalin, in my opinion, pursued an absolutely correct line: so what if one or two extra heads were chopped off (*puskai lishnyaya golova sletit*), there would be no vacillation in the time of war and after the war.[51]

[48] I. Deutscher, *Stalin: A Political Biography* (Harmondsworth, 1968), pp. 373–4.

[49] M. Sholokhov for example wrote in 16 February 1938 to Stalin: 'Cases of apprehension as part of the purge of the rear need also to be rechecked. Those apprehended include not only active Whiteguardists, emigres, executioners in a word those whom it is necessary to apprehend, but under this rubrik have been taken away also true Soviet people' (*Istochnik*, 1993, no. 4, p. 18).

[50] *Istochnik*, 1993, no. 0, p. 23.

[51] *Sto sorok besed s Molotovym. Iz dnevnikov F. Chueva* (M., 1991), pp. 390, 391, 416. See also the memoirs of G. Dimitrov in *Sovershenno sekretno*, no. 12, 1990, pp. 18–20.

The complex relationship between war and revolution, which had almost seen the tsarist regime toppled in 1905 and which finally brought its demise in 1917, was a relationship of which Stalin was acutely aware. The lesson of history had to be learnt lest history repeat itself.

Further Reading: The Great Terror

Robert Conquest, *The Great Terror: A Reassessment* (New York, 1990).

J. Arch Getty, "'Excesses are not Permitted': Mass Terror and Stalinist Governance in the Late 1930s," *The Russian Review*, vol. 61, no. 1 (2002).

J. Arch Getty, *Origins of the Great Purges: The Soviet Communist Party Reconsidered, 1933–1938* (New York, 1985).

J. Arch Getty and Oleg V. Naumov, eds., *The Road to Terror: Stalin and the Self-Destruction of the Bolsheviks, 1932–1939* (New Haven, 1999).

James R. Harris, *The Great Urals: Regionalism and the Evolution of the Soviet System* (Ithaca, 1999).

Oleg V. Khlevniuk, *In Stalin's Shadow: The Career of 'Sergo' Ordzhonikidze* (Armonk, NY, 1995).

Hiroaki Kuromiya, *Freedom and Terror in the Donbas: A Ukrainian–Russian Borderland, 1870s–1990s* (New York, 1998).

Gabor T. Rittersporn, *Stalinist Simplifications and Soviet Complications: Social Tensions and Political Conflicts in the U.S.S.R., 1933–1953* (Chur, NY, 1991).

Peter H. Solomon, Jr., *Soviet Criminal Justice Under Stalin* (New York, 1996).

Robert Thurston, *Life and Terror in Stalin's Russia, 1934–1941* (New Haven, 1995).

The Welfare State

5

Magnetic Mountain: Stalinism as a Civilization

Stephen Kotkin

Excerpted from Stephen Kotkin, *Magnetic Mountain: Stalinism as a Civilization* (Berkeley: University of California Press, 1995).

Editor's Introduction

The end of the Cold War and collapse of the Soviet Union has generated not only new archival research on Stalinism but new conceptual frameworks as well. Some scholars have begun to reintegrate Soviet history into the more general course of European history and to view Stalinist state practices as having roots in the aims and technologies of the modern state. This approach, while continuing to stress the fundamental ideological and operational differences of the Stalinist system, sees Stalinism not as the anomalous product of factors unique to the Soviet Union but rather as a particular incarnation of more general intellectual and political developments in modern Europe.

Among the most significant of these developments were new forms of social science and medical knowledge which prompted European reformers to reconceptualize the population as a social entity to be rationally studied and managed. Social statistics, for example, provided government officials and non-government professionals with a statistical representation of their societies and a confidence that they could reshape or even transform those societies for the betterment of the country as a whole. The belief that populations and newly identified social problems could be understood and acted upon scientifically gave rise to a new ethos of social intervention. This ethos was widely shared among social thinkers and state officials of various political orientations, and it underlay a range of state welfare programs introduced throughout Europe in the late nineteenth and early twentieth centuries.[1]

A comparative examination of the Stalinist system reveals that it shared both this interventionist ethos and many of the state welfare programs developed in western European countries. Welfare programs provided valuable benefits to the retired, disabled, and unemployed. But the welfare state also entailed highly normative assumptions about the way people should live, and intervention in people's lives to impose purportedly scientific norms upon them. State welfare practices thus included public health inspections, sanitary regulations, quarantines, home visits from medical personnel, instruction on infant care and childraising, state removal of children from parents deemed negligent, and other normative interventions to establish a rational and productive order in people's lives. When attached to an ideological agenda of social and human transformation, as in the Soviet case, state intervention to reorder human society could take extreme forms and have dire consequences.

In the selection that follows, Stephen Kotkin first put forward the argument that Stalinism was an extreme, socialist form of the European welfare state. Taking as his starting points the Enlightenment and French Revolution, Kotkin places Stalinism squarely in the context of Europe's intellectual and political heritage. He explains that the very idea of reshaping society originated with eighteenth-century Enlightenment thinkers, who believed they could apply science to create a rational social order.[2] The French Revolution in turn gave this idea force by demonstrating that revolutionary politics could bring about social transformation. Revolutionaries in Russia drew inspiration from the French Revolution, and after they themselves came to power in 1917, they pursued their own version of a rational and just social order – one which sought to eliminate capitalist exploitation and social classes.

Kotkin points out that the class divisions that Stalin and his fellow Communist leaders sought to overcome were also a central part of European history – a legacy of nineteenth-century industrialization which had destroyed the alleged organic unity of traditional agrarian societies and replaced it with class-stratified cities. An array of European thinkers pondered how to recover social unity, Karl Marx being just one of many

[1] For further discussion, see David L. Hoffmann, "European Modernity and Soviet Socialism," in Hoffmann and Yanni Kotsonis, eds., *Russian Modernity: Politics, Knowledge, Practices* (New York, 2000).

[2] Conservative thinkers have also pointed to the Enlightenment as the ultimate source of Stalinism; see Richard Pipes, *Communism: A History* (New York, 2001). In contrast to this conservative or Burkean framework, which warns against any attempt to change social traditions, Kotkin is operating from a leftist or Foucauldian orientation. This approach critiques the Enlightenment not for its attack on traditional norms but for its imposition of new behavioral standards, which, far from being objective, were in fact highly normative and contrary to their purported goal of human liberation.

who grappled with this problem.[3] Marx envisioned violent revolution as the means to overthrow the capitalist system, and ultimately to achieve a classless, socialist society. In the mid-1930s, Stalin declared that the bases of socialism had been achieved and that collectivization and the state-run economy had succeeded in eliminating the exploiting classes and class conflict.

The Stalinist system also established extensive state welfare benefits, again putting into practice ideas and programs that originated in western Europe. These benefits included state-sponsored disability and retirement pensions, free medical care, state-funded housing, and guaranteed employment for all citizens. Kotkin therefore concludes that Stalinism was not an anomaly resulting from Stalin's evilness, Russia's social backwardness, or Marxist ideology. Instead the Soviet Union under Stalin embodied, more than any other country, the elements of "progressive modernity" – a coordinated, purposeful economy and a government of national unity dedicated to the well-being of the population and country as a whole.[4] In the book from which this excerpt is drawn, Kotkin focuses mostly upon the socialist elements of the Stalinist order which distinguished the Soviet Union from other countries and made Stalinism a distinct "civilization." But his work nonetheless put forward a new comparative framework from which to approach Soviet history, and he and other scholars have pursued that framework subsequently.[5]

[3] Katerina Clark places Marxist thought in its broader intellectual context of "Romantic Anticapitalism" – a term she uses to describe the ideas of a variety of thinkers who criticized capitalist society for its alienation, individualism, and commodification of culture. Romantic anticapitalism informed the thinking of many western European and prerevolutionary Russian intellectuals, Marxist and non-Marxist alike, and hence contributed to the intellectual and cultural ecosystem from which Stalinism emerged. Clark's book represents something of a landmark work in that it places Soviet cultural history in this broader comparative framework; Katerina Clark, *Petersburg: Crucible of Cultural Revolution* (Cambridge, Mass., 1995).

[4] The paradigm of neo-traditionalism has been counter-posed to an understanding of Stalinism as exemplifying elements of modernity. But these two historiographical approaches are not necessarily mutually exclusive. Neo-traditionalism involved the use of traditions for modern mobilizational purposes; it was only after industrialization and urbanization largely destroyed traditional folk culture, that political leaders invented traditions to galvanize popular support in the age of mass politics and mass warfare. For more on neo-traditionalism, see Terry Martin, "Modernization or Neo-traditionalism? Ascribed Nationality and Soviet Primordialism," in Hoffmann and Kotsonis, eds.

[5] Stephen Kotkin, "Modern Times: The Soviet Union and the Interwar Conjuncture," *Kritika*, vol. 2, no. 1 (2001); Peter Holquist, "'Information is the Alpha and Omega of our Work': Bolshevik Surveillance in its Pan-European Context," *The Journal of Modern History*, vol. 69 (1997); Amir Weiner, "Nature, Nurture, and Memory in a Socialist Utopia: Delineating the Soviet Socio-Ethnic Body in the Age of Socialism," *The American Historical Review*, vol. 104, no. 4 (1999) – excerpted in this volume; David L. Hoffmann, "Mothers in the Motherland: Stalinist Pronatalism in its Pan-European Context," *Journal of Social History*, vol. 34 (2000).

Kotkin's excerpt below also highlights the importance of subjectivity as a topic for investigation. In examining the Soviet city of Magnitogorsk (which means Magnetic Mountain in Russian), he stresses the ways that, under Stalinism, average citizens developed a sense of themselves as subjects. Soviet citizens had no choice but to engage with the political, economic, and social structures of everyday life under Stalinism. Whether they eagerly participated in, circumvented, or resisted the Stalinist system, people's identity and behavior were defined in relation to it. Soviet power in this sense was productive as well as repressive; it created possibilities and new modes of self-identification, even if many people identified themselves in opposition to it.[6] As Kotkin writes, the historian of Stalinism needs to explain how the aspirations of Stalin and his fellow leaders interacted with those of ordinary people in the Soviet version of the welfare state.

---

[6] For an example of scholarship on Stalinist subjectivity, see Hellbeck in this volume.

Magnetic Mountain: Stalinism as a Civilization

Stephen Kotkin

Science, Utopia, and Revolutionary Politics

It is impossible to comprehend Stalinism without reference to the eighteenth-century European Enlightenment, an outpouring of impassioned public discussion that took as its point of departure the seventeenth-century innovation of modern "science." Applying the new models of nature to the political world, many thinkers during the Enlightenment embarked on a quest for an explicitly "rational social order," a well-regulated organization of human beings independent of the "arbitrary" authority of a sovereign. Arguably it was the French *philosophe* Condorcet – the first to give wide currency to the expression "science of society" – who conferred the prestige of Newtonian science on the search for a rational social order. For Condorcet, among others, science offered "the means to transform the social world" at the same time as it "suggested the model of the rational social organization to be implemented." Above all, science promised not simply the possibility of immediate improvement but "a vision of constant progress."[1]

What gave this worldview tremendous force was, of course, the French revolution, which appeared to offer a mechanism for realizing the vision of a rational social order. To be sure, the revolution brought forth a variety of applications, including the ideas and practices of liberalism, a "radical" strand of republicanism rooted in notions of equality, and Bonapartist dictatorship. But each of these different traditions emerged from the common source of what came to be called "revolutionary politics." This innovation signaled a simple yet profound discovery: that politics could be used to direct and possibly even remake society.[2]

[1] Keith Baker, *Condorcet: From Natural Philosophy to Social Mathematics* (Chicago: University of Chicago Press, 1975), pp. 385–6. Baker notes the important role that Condorcet reserved for the "scientific elite," who were charged with guiding social progress – a mission reminiscent of the one assumed in Russia by the Bolshevik party. According to Condorcet, the elite, made up of people of "superior intellect," was somehow to be bound by the principle of democratic consent, but no mechanism was specified. The centrality of the Enlightenment and Condorcet for understanding the Russian revolution was impressed upon me by Martin Malia.

[2] Lynn Hunt, *Politics, Culture, and Class in the French Revolution* (Berkeley: University of California Press, 1984), p. 3.

Many of the Russian revolutionaries were guided by a highly developed awareness of the bewitching French experience and conceived of their own actions as an elaboration of that great chain of events, in the direction of what they imagined to be a more genuine version of radical democracy. Rather than a democratic order in the name of the nation, which allegedly concealed the class rule of the bourgeoisie, the Russian revolutionaries envisioned what was supposed to be a more inclusive order founded on the putative universality of the proletariat. Paradoxically, the goal of greater inclusiveness was to be reached by means of fierce class warfare and exclusion. Nonetheless, in the reinvention of revolutionary politics on the basis of class, the Russian revolutionaries were still following the central vision of the Enlightenment. The Russian revolution, too, was about using politics as a means for creating a rational, and therefore just, social order.

Not only did the revolution in the Russian empire partake of the most highly valued traditions in European history, but even the revolution's ostensibly exotic class character was quintessentially European, an effect of the nineteenth-century fossil-fuel industrialization that had swept England and the continent and rendered problematic the universalism of the Enlightenment's vision. Indeed, far from beginning with the Russian revolution, the task of reconstituting "the nation" by alleviating, or somehow overcoming, deep class divisions had been a central preoccupation throughout Europe for nearly a century – especially in the great "kingdom of the ideal," German-speaking Central Europe, where the inspiration for a specifically proletarian revolution originated.

It was, of course, Karl Marx who combined the Enlightenment's application of scientific rationality to society with the French revolution's discovery of the magic of politics and proclaimed the definitive science of society aimed at bringing about the ultimate political revolution that would eliminate the class divisions wrought by industrialization. Profoundly influenced by the great elaborator of the French revolution, Georg W. F. Hegel, who had articulated a dynamic vision of the progressive movement of history, Marx named his design for a future, classless society "socialism" – a term already in wide use that signified either the amelioration *or*, more often, the complete transcendence of what were the truly appalling living conditions of Europe's working majority.[3]

Emphasizing transcendence, Marx and his followers believed his conception of socialism to be new. In a famous essay entitled "Socialism: Utopian and Scientific" (1880), Friedrich Engels argued that if with Hegel the world began to be viewed as a developmental process, with the

---

[3] George Lichtheim, *The Origins of Socialism* (New York: Praeger, 1969).

onset of industrialization and the rise of the working class in the 1830s socialism had ceased to be "an accidental discovery of this or that ingenious brain" and had become instead "the necessary outcome" of a larger historical struggle governed by scientific laws. Accordingly, the task for critical analysis was no longer to imagine a society as perfect as possible but to lay bare the present pattern of socioeconomic relations in which the next "stage" of historical development was already nascent. Marx, according to Engels, had done just that for the "capitalist mode of production," and thus with Marx "socialism had become scientific."[4]

Engels's distinction between utopian and scientific socialism, which was embraced by the Soviet state, has been dismissed by philosophers who argue that Marxian socialism was in fact no less utopian than the unattainable visions of Fourier or Owen. Far from having been "science," the argument goes, Marxism was nothing more than a bogus religion claiming falsely to be science.[5] But the historian should not so quickly dismiss Marxism's claim to be scientific. This claim inspired millions of people, both inside and outside the Soviet Union, and informed the thinking of much of what went on under Stalin (and after), from the establishment of economic planning and school curricula to the capacity for opposition to the regime.

If the scientificity of Marxian socialism needs to be taken seriously, however, so does its utopian aspect. Like the Enlightenment mentality out of which it grew, Marxian socialism was an attractive schema for realizing the kingdom of heaven on earth. Of course, as a supreme rationalist of the nineteenth-century type, Marx himself never wrote a utopia. But he asserted that a utopian society would – indeed must – come about for the sake of humankind, and his voluminous, often esoteric writings inspired the most extensive effort ever to realize just such an outcome in the eastern fringes of Europe. That the scientific utopianism of Marx found an appreciative audience in the Russian empire was due to the specificities of Russian history, especially to certain intensely felt aspirations that predated the 1917 revolution and found expression in the revolutionary process. . . .

Stalinism in fact revived the revolutionary utopianism that had been so encouraged during the Civil War but that had suffered a blow in 1921 when the "Peasant Brest-Litovsk" policy of replacing grain requisition-

---

[4] The pamphlet, an extract from the polemic commonly known as *Anti-Dühring* (1878), can be found in Robert C. Tucker, ed., *The Marx–Engels Readers*, 2d ed. (New York: Norton, 1978), pp. 683–717.

[5] Leszek Kolakowski, *Main Currents of Marxism*, vol. 3 (New York: Oxford University Press, 1981), pp. 523–30.

ing by a tax-in-kind was extended beyond Tambov province.[6] The extension of the tax-in-kind was followed by other measures that together coalesced into what was dubbed the New Economic Policy (NEP), which partially legalized the anathema of private trade and the market, reversed much of the holy-grail policy of nationalization of urban property and industry, yet failed to generate convincing signs of the anticipated new world associated with socialism.[7] During the NEP, the dictatorship of the proletariat was beset by high unemployment, rising prostitution, millions of orphaned children (many of whom roamed the country engaging in criminal activities and forming gangs), and an explosion of private trade. The authorities were largely at a loss as to what to do about these ills and the disappointment they fostered.[8]

Back at the Tenth Party Congress in March 1921, when the hesitant steps that led to the NEP were taken over strenuous objections, Lenin had asked apologetically, "How could one start a socialist revolution in a country like ours without dreamers?"[9] As the 1920s wore on, many

[6] In August–September 1920, after the Civil War was essentially won and the threat of a restoration of landowner rights ended, there had been a massive uprising by a peasant army against the Bolsheviks. This peasant or "Green Army" which mobilized around 20,000 troops and was similar in organization to the Red Army, was defeated by a Red Army force more than double its size. At the same time, central authorities also made concessions in Tambov, introducing a NEP *avant la lettre*. Oliver Radkey, *The Unknown Civil War in Soviet Russia: A Study of the Green Movement in the Tambov Region, 1920–1921* (Stanford: Hoover Institution, 1976). The analogy to the capitulatory treaty signed with the Germans in March 1918 – a desperate gamble that paid off when the Germans surrendered to the Allies in November – was made by Bukharin, and repeated by Riazanov during the debate on the tax-in-kind decree at the Tenth Party Congress. *Desiatyi s"ezd Rossiiskoi kommunisticheskoi partii: Stenograficheskii otchet* (Moscow, 1926), p. 255. In many regions, including Siberia, Central Asia, and Ukraine, the introduction of the tax-in-kind was purposely delayed for as long as a year.
[7] The NEP was not introduced by a single decree. Laws and decrees were issued like an avalanche throughout 1922 and 1923. These were notable for the many restrictions they carried against trade in certain goods, and the many limitations they maintained on private manufacturing and the hiring of labor. In 1923, moreover, the regime began backing away from some of the provisions of the NEP, and though the NEP did receive something of a second wind in 1924–5, it was again partially rolled back in 1926. This ambivalence and grudging tolerance characterized the entire existence of the NEP. It should also be kept in mind that during this time, the regime remained a dictatorship; there may have been a "cultural" NEP, but there was no "political" NEP. See E. H. Carr, *The Bolshevik Revolution, 1917–1923*, vol. 2 (New York: Macmillan, 1952), pp. 269–359.
[8] Alan Ball, *Russia's Last Capitalists: The Nepmen, 1921–1929* (Berkeley: University of California Press, 1987); Roger Pethybridge, *One Step Backwards, Two Steps Forward: Soviet Society and Politics under the New Economic Policy* (Oxford: Clarendon Press, 1990).
[9] On the question of what was deemed within and outside the realm of possibility in the Russian context, see the perceptive comments by Silvana Malle, *The Economic Organization of War Communism, 1918–1921* (Cambridge: Cambridge University Press, 1985), pp. 495–6.

people had begun to wonder just what had happened to the great dream of a new Russia and to the powerful class rhetoric of haves versus have-nots, oppressors versus oppressed, for not only had industrial production barely managed to climb back to 1914 levels, but the most striking results of the revolution seemed to be the formation of a new urban bourgeoisie, the Nepmen, and an incipient alliance (*smychka!*) between what few party officials there were in the countryside and a new rural bourgeoisie, the kulaks.[10]

To be sure, the NEP had a constituency, which stretched beyond the so-called Nepmen and kulaks to embrace elements of the expanding state bureaucracy (largely the Commissariats of Finance and Agriculture) and certain sections of the Communist party.[11] The country had recovered. But even to many of those who supported the NEP, the socialist revolution seemed to have lost much of its momentum. Proposals for putting the revolution back on track, either largely within or even outside the NEP framework, were hotly debated throughout the decade,[12] but it was unclear what, if anything, might come of them – until 1929, when the country was suddenly launched on what was called the Great Break (*velikii perelom*).

The precipitating factor behind this colossal improvisation may have been the grain crises of the late 1920s. But the Great Break's significance extended well beyond the regime's self-inflicted showdown with the peasantry, a confrontation that, it needs to be recalled, took place against the background of deep-seated anxieties about capitalist encirclement and the Red Army's inability to fight a war against the advanced European countries. In the context of this perceived vulnerability, the Great Break promised not only to secure the regime's political control over the countryside but also to bring about in the shortest possible time what Russia had not been able to achieve in several centuries: to become an undisputed great power and, what was more, an example for the rest of the world to admire and emulate, by building socialism.[13]

That the initial launching of this remarkable turn of events could have been determined essentially by one man turned out to be another

---

[10] The contradictions of the NEP, especially when juxtaposed against the apparent certainties of the Civil War (at least in retrospect), are treated, along with the crucial importance of the institutional nexus of the Red Army, in Mark von Hagen, *Soldiers in the Proletarian Dictatorship: The Red Army and the Soviet Socialist State, 1917–1930* (Ithaca: Cornell University Press, 1990).

[11] The mood during the NEP both inside and outside party circles has been well-described by Nikolai Valentinov [Volskii], *Novaia ekonomicheskaia politika i krizis partii posle smerti Lenina* (Stanford: Hoover Institution Press, 1971).

[12] Alexander Erlich, *The Soviet Industrialization Debate, 1924–1928* (Cambridge, Mass.: Harvard University Press, 1960).

[13] Further discussion of the Great Break appears in the introduction to part 1.

of the unforeseen yet central developments of the revolution during the 1920s. Lenin, the socialist revolution's undisputed moral and political leader and the symbol of the new Russia, fell ill and died (exerting virtually no influence on policy matters during the last two years of his life). After a nasty struggle, Stalin emerged as Lenin's successor, filling a role already created by his predecessor but then remaking it into a personal despotism.[14] This Stalin achieved not only by his oft-remarked dominance of the bureaucracy, but also by his careful attention to questions of ideology and their relation to political power.[15] Not Bukharin, the party's "theorist," nor Trotsky (by far the most original mind among the Bolsheviks) but Stalin first systematized the "foundations of Leninism" – and through constant maneuvering made sure he was recognized as Leninism's main arbiter.[16]

Whatever concessions or apologies Stalin continued to make at meetings of the politburo or Central Committee, as soon as the meetings adjourned he retreated to his office atop the apparat and acted virtually

---

[14] Since the 1960s, there has been much talk in the historiography of the "alternatives" to Stalin, with attention focusing on Trotsky and Bukharin. Despite being a Jew, Trotsky did probably have the potential to become paramount leader following Lenin's death, but for a variety of reasons he lost out. Bukharin never had such a chance. Discussion of a "Bukharin alternative" is not simply a matter of whether he had an alternative "plan" of action, but whether Stalin might have chosen to follow it, for once Trotsky was defeated, there was no alternative to Stalin's rule, barring accidental death or assassination. For an analysis of the succession problem that represents a step forward, see Lars Lih, "Political Testament of Lenin and Bukharin and the Meaning of NEP," *Slavic Review* 50, no. 2 (1991): 240–52.

[15] For a handy review of the explanations of Stalin's rise to supremacy, see Chris Ward, *Stalin's Russia* (London: Edward Arnold, 1993), pp. 7–38. Documents being released from formerly secret archives are liable to shed considerable new light on this critical problem.

[16] I. V. Stalin, "Ob osnovakh Leninisma," lectures at Sverdlov University published in *Pravda*, 26 and 30 April 1924; and 9, 11, 14, 15, 18 May 1924; reprinted in *Sochineniia*, vol. 6 (Moscow, 1947), pp. 69–188. In addition to systematizing Leninism (in strikingly defensive terms), Stalin apparently invented, and certainly popularized, the denigrating term "Trotskyism" (see *Sochineniia*, pp. 342–57), which sealed Trotsky's fate. It should be kept in mind that Leninism as an ideology was not formed automatically. Stalin's vigorous handling of the formulation of Leninism has been remarked on by Robert Tucker, *Stalin as Revolutionary, 1879–1929* (New York: Norton, 1973), pp. 316–18, 324. Significantly, although Lev Kamenev by virtue of his position as boss of the Moscow party organization was nominally in charge of the Marx–Engels–Lenin Institute, he gave it little attention. The institute and its critically important documents were assiduously controlled by aides to Stalin from inside the apparat. See Larry Holmes and William Burgess, "Scholarly Voice or Political Echo? Soviet Party History in the 1920s," *Russian History/Histoire Russe* 9 (1982): 378–98; Niels Erik Rosenfeldt, "'The Consistory of the Communist Church': The Origins and Development of Stalin's Secret Chancellery," ibid., pp. 308–24.

as he saw fit. Yet he always made sure that everything he did was explained and justified within what he effectively characterized as the Leninist legacy. When Stalin mobilized the powerful class-war rhetoric of the revolution's "heroic age" – kept alive after 1921 in patterns of dress, images, songs, festivals, names, storytelling, a new pantheon of heroes – and launched a vicious campaign against the kulaks, he had no conceptual difficulty in presenting this, or the concurrent decisions to push forward with the forcible collectivization of agriculture and accelerate the pace of industrialization, as a continuation of the work begun by Lenin and October.[17] He went further, however, and, in re-revolutioning the revolution, skillfully invoked scattered remarks by Lenin on the importance of national strength and *explicitly* tied the building of socialism to imperial Russian history.[18]

As masterful a political infighter as Stalin proved to be, he could scarcely have succeeded in garnering the required support for such an immense mobilization without the vision of building socialism he was able to articulate, and the genuine passions that such a bold plan for a bountiful world, remade along class lines, evoked among many people. As the decade of the 1930s began, the great eastern country's time in the sun seemed to have truly arrived. The terrible ordeals of the "imperialist war," Civil War, epidemics and famine had not, after all, been in vain. The Stalin revolution seemed like the second, and potentially more lasting, dawn of a just, pure, merry, and beautiful Russia, where he who was nothing would become everything.

[17] More serious were the considerations that (1) just such a course had been advocated by the so-called left opposition, which Stalin had vanquished as part of his bid for absolute power; and (2) that certain circles in the party, upon whom he had relied to destroy the opposition, were against the leftist course. Stalin rhetorically dismissed the resemblance of the Big Drive to the program of the left opposition, at the same time shifting attention onto those whom he castigated as the "right opposition."

[18] Stalin's revolution has been called a "revolution from above," a characterization that was officially incorporated by the Soviet regime in the short course party history published in late 1937 as a description of collectivization. In fact, such a notion had been advanced by an émigré Orthodox Christian socialist, Georgii Fedotov, *Problemy budushchei Rossii* tom 1 (1931; St. Petersburg, 1991), p. 229. (I am grateful to Professor Wada Haruki for bringing this source to my attention.) Echoing such commentators, Robert Tucker has treated the oft-noted resemblance to past tsars invoked by Stalin not as the result of efforts to generate legitimacy for state policies by means of crafted historical analogies but as a factual model that inspired Stalin's actions and as an accurate characterization of the social, political, economic, and cultural order formed under him. Such a view tends to downplay considerations of property, class, and socialism. Tucker, *Stalin in Power: The Revolution from Above, 1928–1941* (New York: Norton, 1990). For a discussion of the concept "revolution from above" in Russian history, see E. H. Carr, *Socialism in One Country*, vol. 1 (New York: Macmillan, 1958), pp. 9–10.

The City and the Welfare State

Nowhere was the euphoric sense of the revolution's renewed possibilities in the 1930s more in evidence than at Magnetic Mountain. Numerous other instant cities were also created, such as Komsomolsk-na-Amure, Novokuznetsk (Stalinsk), and Karaganda, while virtually all established urban centers underwent such dramatic expansion and transformation that they became in effect new cities.[19] (Indeed, according to the January 1939 census, in the twelve years since the December 1926 census the registered urban population of the Soviet Union jumped from 26.3 to 55.9 million.)[20] But Magnitogorsk remained the quintessential emblem of the grand transformation whereby the Enlightenment goal of using science to perfect society, having been bonded to the French revolution's discovery of political mobilization and filtered through industrialization and the attendant rise of the working class, had become a reality one could participate in first-hand. This prospect transfixed large numbers of foreign observers, as well as many of the inhabitants of the USSR.

That Magnitogorsk, as the encapsulation of the building of socialism, appeared to embody the Enlightenment dream, once improved, would have been reason enough for the world attention it received. At the same

[19] A partial list of new Soviet cities built between the wars can be found in "Goroda postroenny pri sovetskoi vlasti," *Bloknot agitatora*, no. 1 (1948): 23–33. In some ways even Moscow had come to resemble Magnitogorsk. B. I. Nikolskii, artistic director of the Magnitogorsk theater, speaking at a party meeting of the city's Kirov *raikom* in 1936 remarked that "I am an old Muscovite. I lived forty years in Moscow. When the Maly theater suggested I go to Magnitogorsk, I must confess, my face did not express joy or great desire." But Nikolskii went on to assert that the difference between Moscow and Magnitogorsk was "not that great." He observed that "living in Magnitogorsk, you don't feel as you do living on Moscow's Kuznetskii Most, but as if you were living a bit farther out, in the outskirts, say, on the Boulevard of Enthusiasts, where gigantic construction is going on." *Magnitogorskii rabochii*, 21 December 1936.

[20] Data from the suppressed 1937 census have finally become available, confirming the long suspected need to modify downward the total population in 1939. But such a correction would have little effect on the magnitude of the expansion of the urban population. Even considering that some of the urban growth was the result of reclassification, the USSR certainly underwent the largest urban expansion in a single decade that the world had known up to that time. See Chauncy Harris, *Cities of the Soviet Union: Studies in Their Functions, Size, Density, and Growth* (Chicago: Association of American Geographers, 1972), pp. 1, 61, 89–90; Adolf G. Rashin, "Rost gorodskogo naseleniia v SSSR (1926–1959 gg.)," *Istoricheskie zapiski*, no. 66 (1960): 269–77; E. Andreev et al., "Opyt otsenki chislennosti naseleniia SSSR 1926–1941 gg. (kratkie rezultaty issledovaniia)," *Vestnik statistiki*, 1990, no. 7, pp. 34–58; and V. A. Isupov, "Igra bez pravil: Perepisi naseleniia SSSR v 30-e gody," *Sovetskaia istoriia: Problemy i uroki* (Novosibirsk, 1992), pp. 149–67. An often unremarked point is that the population of Gulag sites was apparently classified as urban.

time, Magnitogorsk also appeared to exemplify the unique benefits supposedly derived from the advance of urbanism. Before the revolution in Russia, cities were feared as anomalies of development and dangerous threats to the sociopolitical order, but after 1917 they came to be viewed as the epitomes of progress and therefore the prime bulwarks for the existing order. More than that, cities were welcomed as the training grounds for producing the armies of model citizens whose collective activities would increase the Soviet state's great-power potential. Even though on the eve of the war in 1941, still only one-third of the population lived in cities, the revolution in Russia was a decidedly urban-centered one.

Revolutionary Russia's embrace of the city could claim an extended genealogy in the experience of Europe, where cities had long been celebrated as the principal agents of civilization.[21] Before the Enlightenment gave birth to the notion of a science of society, a tradition of trying to imagine the ideal city arose whereby cities served as the settings for, and the objects of, analyses of how best to organize human affairs, a goal that presupposed continual regulation by centralized authority.[22] It was this legacy that helped make possible, and in turn came to be elaborated by, the Enlightenment (which took place more or less simultaneously throughout the great urban centers of Europe).[23] This legacy also made feasible the programs for the state regulation of society in the name of the commonweal, beginning in the nineteenth century with efforts to

[21] For an example and continuation of this tendency, see Jacques le Goff, "The Town as an Agent of Civilization," in Carlo Cipolla, ed., *The Fontana Economic History of Europe and the Middle Ages* (New York, 1972), pp. 77–106. A handy survey of the development of the social scientific study of the city in the United States, beginning with the writings of sociologists at the University of Chicago in the first decades of the twentieth century, is provided by Ulf Hannerz, *Exploring the City: Inquiries toward an Urban Anthropology* (New York: Columbia University Press, 1980). Hannerz omits any comment on the fact that the analysts of the city live in it, or that his own advocacy of an urban anthropology is an artifact of city life.

[22] As the great urbanist Lewis Mumford pointed out, until the late nineteenth century, discussion of the city was largely limited to Utopian literature. "City," in *International Encyclopedia of the Social Sciences*, vol. 2 (New York: Macmillan and the Free Press, 1968), p. 448. Echoing Mumford, the literary critic Northrop Frye also pointed out that Utopia "is primarily a vision of an orderly city and a city-dominated society." Frye, "Varieties of Literary Utopias," *Daedalus* 94 (1965): 323–47; quote from 328.

[23] Lewis Mumford, *The City in History: Its Origins, Its Transformations, and Its Prospects* (New York: Harcourt Brace Jovanovich, 1961). Gwendolyn Wright and Paul Rabinow have asserted that the advent of the writings on cities was connected with the fifteenth- and sixteenth-century rise of administrative states (out of the great postfeudal territorial monarchies), and with the corresponding new problem then posed of administering not just territories but also inhabitants. Wright and Rabinow, "Spatialization of Power," *Skyline*, 1982.

confront the special problems of urban life and urban populations and continuing into the twentieth.

In the grand narratives of European history, the nineteenth century most often appears as the period when the twin challenges of the French and Industrial revolutions transformed the various old regimes into modern polities with parliaments, political parties, and universal male suffrage – in short, into what today we recognize as "democracy." Such a narrative of the birth of "the bourgeois world," which triumphed in the Great War when all remaining old regimes collapsed, has been given substantial support by the fact that European states, their elites, and opposition groups were themselves preoccupied with the problem of how to respond politically to the new conditions brought about by the French and Industrial revolutions.[24]

There is, however, another story, one that begins before 1789 and continues well after 1914: the formation of the welfare state. This other, parallel development is largely one of social regulation – procedures, rules, categories, and social practices, almost all of which arose outside the state but came to be taken over by it – as well as self-imposed normalization and micro-level resistance. A far less visible historical drama, not of political parties and parliamentary clashes but of identities and the clever tactics used in the invention of daily life, the formation of the welfare state was linked to the efforts at pacification in Europe's colonies, a process that took place simultaneously and exerted a reciprocal influence on the articulation of social-control and welfare-related programs "at home."[25]

---

[24] To be sure, in recent years a streak of revisionism appeared that has questioned whether feudalization of the bourgeoisie, rather than *embourgeoisement* of the old regimes, should be the basic story line. In this vigorously argued challenge to the standard view, however, the interpretive categories do not change; only the emphasis does. Arno J. Mayer, *The Persistence of the Old Regime* (New York: Pantheon, 1981). Rather than focus on the bourgeoisie as a class, one scholar has advocated concentrating on private property, the market, the public sphere, law, and voluntary associations – in short, on what he calls "the silent bourgeois revolution," which might better be termed the civic revolution. David Blackbourn, "The Discreet Charm of the Bourgeoisie: Reappraising German History in the Nineteenth Century," in David Blackbourn and Geoff Eley, *The Peculiarities of German History: Bourgeois Society and Politics in Nineteenth-Century Germany* (New York: Oxford, 1984), pp. 174–205.

[25] Further discussion of this and related issues can be found in the innovative analysis of urban planning and administration in French-controlled Morocco by Paul Rabinow. In contrast to the approach taken in this monograph, Rabinow focuses on the class of administrators (thus offering a kind of intellectual history), rather than on the social relations and contestations that the administrators' actions helped produce in the urban milieus in which they conducted experiments. Rabinow, *French Modern: Norms and Forms of the Social Environment* (Cambridge, Mass.: MIT Press, 1989), pp. 13, 145.

In part a conservative response to the rise of the working class and the "dangers" it supposedly represented, especially those of contagious disease and political militancy, the welfare state also emerged from the variety of concerns articulated by experts pursuing such varied goals as workplace efficiency, psychological normalization, and healthy populations.[26] Industrialists, concerned about obtaining a reliable, docile supply of labor, and social reformers, crusading for what they took to be the best way to minimize social costs and maximize social benefits, shared a logic, even if their aims often appeared divergent. And because the welfare state rested on a certain social logic and a number of transferable social practices, it was viable in a variety of political settings, including Stalin's Russia.[27]

Rather than being viewed as a pathological case (deviating from the European norm because of the country's backwardness or agrarian social structure, the long history of Russian authoritarianism, the experience of the Civil War, Marxist ideology, the single-mindedness of Lenin, or the evilness of Stalin), the USSR in a narrative of the welfare state might appear as the standard whose uncanny success challenged the rest of the world to respond. More than in any other country, Stalinism seemed to bring together the elements of what was then the prevalent conception and experience of "progressive modernity": on the one hand, the deployment of a coordinated, purposeful economy, within which small, supposedly inefficient producers were replaced by larger and therefore mightier ones; and, on the other, the formation of a government of national unity that was above the seeming paralysis of parliamentary rule *and* unequivocally dedicated to the advancement of the commonweal.[28]

[26] For an excellent critical review of the explanations for the rise of the welfare state, see George Steinmetz, *Regulating the Social: The Welfare State and Local Politics in Imperial Germany* (Princeton: Princeton University Press, 1993), pp. 15–40.

[27] One study of pensions in Denmark, Sweden, Britain, France, and Germany that sought to demonstrate that welfare state practices normally attributed to labor movements originated in bourgeois politics took as its organizing principle the development of what the author called risk communities. In this way, the author demonstrated that the development and functioning of the welfare state were based on a way of looking at the world, or social calculus. Unfortunately, this and virtually all other comparative studies of the development of the welfare state invariably overlook the case of the USSR. Peter Baldwin, *The Politics of Social Solidarity: Class Bases of the European Welfare State, 1875–1975* (New York: Cambridge University Press, 1990). See also Francois Ewald, "Insurance and Risk," in Graham Burchell et al., eds., *The Foucault Effect: Studies in Governmentality* (Chicago: University of Chicago Press, 1991), pp. 197–210.

[28] The commitment of the Soviet state to social welfare was particularly dramatic given the prerevolutionary legacy. As one scholar has concluded, "welfare aid in Russia was never more than a palliative, and was rendered even more ineffective by the ravages of

Despite administrative and financial limitations, the Soviet social insurance system that came into being following the revolution specified benefits (in many cases equal to total earnings) in the event of death, disability, sickness, old age, pregnancy and childbirth, or unemployment, for working people and family members. In 1930, temporary unemployment benefits were abolished, but this was because, incredibly, unemployment itself was eliminated. By this time, moreover, the Soviet understanding of wellfare had come to include not only a guarantee of a job for everyone, but the payment of pensions upon retirement (a system that was made universal in 1937). The amount of benefits, particularly pensions, remained small, but there was no denying that the Soviet state had embraced a broad conception of social welfare – extending from employment and income to affordable housing, health care, and organized leisure – and had done so without prodding.

Not only could the USSR under Stalin plausibly assert that it had developed the programs and practices of state-guaranteed social welfare to a greater extent than had previously been the case anywhere, but it could do so in a way that contrasted with the fascist reaction: by embracing fully the illustrious European heritage known as the Enlightenment. For all these reasons, the Soviet example, as showcased at Magnitogorsk, could be said to have exerted a direct and profound influence on the rest of the world's industrialized countries. In a word, the USSR decisively shaped part of the bedrock of the world in which we live, a bedrock that today is coming apart everywhere.[29]

The Politics of Everyday Life

The Bolshevik leadership, with its grand designs for building socialism – along with the will and wherewithal to try to realize such a goal – set what might be called the broad agenda for what was meant to happen at Magnetic Mountain. Important as these intentions were, they constitute only the beginning of the story. For one thing, the policies and programs enacted contained irreconcilable aspects that surfaced during

World War I." Yet although the USSR had less of a base to work with than other nations, and had to overcome great calamities, it "achieved more comparatively than any other nation." Bernice Madison, *Social Welfare in the Soviet Union* (Stanford: Stanford University Press, 1968), pp. 3–76, 230.

[29] Few scholars have taken up, even in general terms, the influence of the USSR on Western Europe and the United States (as opposed to the third world). An important exception, although far too uncritical in its evaluation of Soviet realities, is E. H. Carr, *The Soviet Impact on the Western World* (New York: Macmillan, 1949).

the attempts to implement them; indeed, the methods of implementation themselves were often at odds with the stated goals of programs and policies. For another, these policies and programs formed part of the lives of people, ordinary and higher-ups alike, and their actions and reactions, initiatives and responses, in significant ways influenced how those programs were carried out, circumvented, and changed in unforeseen ways.

When we look closely at the USSR in the 1930s we see that the results of building socialism were not entirely what the Bolsheviks intended (that is, what the central party decrees said should happen). This does not mean, however, that the intentions can therefore be ignored or discounted. Although it is necessary to look beyond them, such intentions, programs, and policies were responsible for the fields of action within which the behavior of individuals took place. It is within these fields of action that we must look to see how the intentions were played, how the programs were implemented and what their consequences were – to see, in short, what kinds of lives people were able to lead, and how they understood their lives. To this end, there is no substitute for letting people speak as much as possible in their own words.[30]

As we shall see, the kinds of lives that the urban inhabitants came to lead and the identities they formed involved eager participation in, frequent circumvention of, and resourceful, albeit localized, resistance to the terms of daily life that developed within the crusade of building socialism. One resists, without necessarily rejecting, by assessing, making tolerable, and, in some cases, even turning to one's advantage the situation one is confronted with. An appropriate analogy is to the Japanese martial art of judo. Even when the weight of the force against one is seemingly overwhelming, as was the case with the Soviet state, the possibility remains to sidestep and thereby use that heavy force against itself.

Rather than the extension of Communist party control over more and more areas of life, therefore, it is possible to see – without denying the heavy coercive force of the Communist project – a two-way struggle, however unequal the terms, over the drawing of lines of authority, a struggle that involved continuous, if usually indirect, challenges to the perceived rules. It is not necessary to romanticize "the people" to argue

---

[30] Such a line of analysis, and its implications, have been set down in detail by Pierre Bourdieu, *Outline of a Theory of Praxis* (Cambridge, Mass.: Harvard University Press, 1977), esp. pp. 72–87; and ibid., "The Genesis of the Concepts of *Habitus* and *Field*," *Sociocriticism* 2, no. 2 (1985): 11–24. Bourdieu's imaginative approach to social action is ultimately embedded in a view of class domination achieved through successful manipulation of the state apparatus, a view whose adoption is not obligatory for those who seek to draw on his many insights.

that simply by living life, the urban inhabitants discovered that power was pliable. At the same time, their actions also demonstrated that power was productive: power relations created effects – of experience, identity, resistances. Concentrating on the rule articulation process in the encounters of daily life involves shifting the focus from what the party and its programs *prevented* to what they *made possible*, intentionally and unintentionally.

In sum, the analysis employed here begins with the party's noncapitalist agenda, follows the attempts to implement that agenda, recognizes ad hoc modifications in the agenda, particularly those occasioned by the actions of the citizenry (letting those citizens speak as much as possible in their own words), regards as resistances many actions normally seen as passive or "deviant," thereby adopting a widened view of the political, and is ultimately guided by the belief that the subject of inquiry should include not only what was repressed or prohibited but what was made possible or produced. Put another way, this study seeks to establish the varied and often unexpected effects of the identification of certain issues as problems, the attempts to introduce programs and practices to address these problems, and the struggles that ensued, especially the terms on which they were fought.

Such a methodology for doing social history is derived from the writings of Michel Foucault, who focused on what he called the problem of subjectivity, or the processes by which individuals are made, and also make themselves, into subjects under the aegis of the state.[31] Foucault singled out resistances as perhaps the most important element in the formation of modern subjectivity, yet he never gave resistances the empirical attention they deserved; nor did he spell out the kinds of compromises resistances forced on would-be social engineers at the top. By contrast, in this monograph the empirical investigation of resistances will occupy a central place, widening the analysis of subjectivity to include not only what Foucault designated as disciplinary techniques but also the politics of daily life.[32]

---

[31] Among Foucault's many works, the two that were most important for developing the approach adopted in this monograph are the essay "The Subject and Power," afterword to Hubert Dreyfus and Paul Rabinow, *Michel Foucault: Beyond Structuralism and Hermeneutics*, 2d ed. (Chicago: University of Chicago Press, 1982, 1983) and the lectures on Parrhesia (or the problem of truth telling in Ancient Greece), delivered at the University of California, Berkeley, in 1983, during and after which Foucault engaged in discussions of methodology. I also relied on the collections *Power–Knowledge: Selected Interviews and Other Writings, 1972–1977*, ed. Colin Gordon (New York: Pantheon, 1980) and *The Foucault Reader*, ed. Paul Rabinow (New York: Pantheon, 1984), including the valuable introductory essays by the editors.

[32] On the problem of daily life, I follow the Foucault-inspired analysis by Michel de Certeau. Whereas studies of culture as a material practice (as opposed to a representa-

As Foucault has argued, studying power relations at the micro-level hardly means ignoring the state. At the same time, however, he has repeatedly demonstrated that power is not localized in the central state apparatus.[33] This holds true even when there is thought to be no separation between the spheres "state" and "society," as was the case in the USSR, where everything was formally part of the state.[34] In the chapters ahead, mechanisms of power – such as mutual surveillance and self-identification – will be shown to exist alongside the state machinery, on a much more ordinary level, yet to sustain the state just as effectively as its primary institutions, including the police. In the USSR under Stalin, no less than in modern France, the state understood that its power rested on the characteristics and behavior of the people.

Applying Foucault's work to the USSR underscores yet again the contention made by the revolutionaries themselves that the enduring drama of the Russian revolution must not be sought in the supposed black-magic qualities of Marxism, the cunning opportunism and pitiless determination of the Bolshevik state-builders, or the evolution of the countryside in the 1920s, but in the historically conditioned merger of long-held geopolitical objectives with potent social concerns.

tion of underlying social forces) have usually been preoccupied with the producer (writer, city planner) and the product (book, city street), de Certeau focused his attention on the consumer (reader, pedestrian). Arguing that nothing exists until it is used, he viewed "consumption" as active, every bit a form of production, and argued that the result – achieved through "the art of doing" or "making do" – should be seen as "the invention of everyday life." Treating urban life as a kind of strategic engagement in which even the weak have recourse to many effective stratagems, he celebrated the inventiveness of people whose tactics of living are usually ignored. He also suggested that "resistance" in everyday life should be understood less as a bid for power than as calculated circumvention. De Certeau's perspective on "the appropriation of the urban milieu" provided a healthy corrective to analyses of largely immutable "structures" and "institutions," even if one cannot share the full extent of his unapologetic Romanticism. *The Practice of Everyday Life* (Berkeley: University of California Press, 1984; originally published in French, 1980).

[33] Foucault, *Power–Knowledge*, pp. 60, 122.

[34] In the literature on the rise of social welfare in France, much attention has been devoted to the conceptualization in the early nineteenth century of a realm called the social, which was said to lie between the state and civil society (the economy). This domain became the target of intervention and regulation, and thus the basis for the welfare state, in societies based on private property. In the USSR, however, no such separate domain of the social was postulated, for the obvious reason that there was thought to be no division between the state and society. Jacques Donzelot, *Policing of Families* (New York: Pantheon, 1979), including the foreword by Gilles Deleuze, "The Rise of the Social"); and Donzelot, *L'Invention du Social* (n.p., 1984). A different view of the social that emphasizes not its separateness but its role in enabling the interpenetration of state and society is offered by Jürgen Habermas, *The Structural Transformation of the Public Sphere* (Cambridge, Mass.; MIT Press, 1989), p. 231.

National power and social welfare drove the revolutionary process and culminated in the formation of an industrially based welfare state with an attendant consciousness. Stalinism was not just a political system, let alone the rule of an individual. It was a set of values, a social identity, a way of life.

When it comes to Stalinism, what needs to be explained and subjected to detailed scrutiny are the mechanisms by which the dreams of ordinary people and those of the individuals directing the state found common ground in this Soviet version of the welfare state. The aim of this book is to convey the nature of these partially intersecting dreams and to investigate at the level of the habitat the intricate encounters, conflicts, and negotiations that took place in and around the strategy of state-centered social welfare in its extreme, or socialist, incarnation. What follows, then, is an inquiry into the minutiae of urban life and how certain ways of thinking and accompanying social practices fit into the grand strategies of Soviet state building during the formative period of the 1930s, when the revolution came to Magnetic Mountain. The emphasis throughout is on experimentation and discovery.

Further Reading: Soviet State Welfare and Social Intervention

Mark B. Adams, "Eugenics as Social Medicine in Revolutionary Russia," in Susan Gross Solomon and John F. Hutchinson, eds., *Health and Society in Revolutionary Russia* (Bloomington, 1990).

David L. Hoffmann, "Mothers in the Motherland: Stalinist Pronatalism in its Pan-European Context," *Journal of Social History*, vol. 34 (2000).

Stephen Kotkin, "Modern Times: The Soviet Union and the Interwar Conjuncture," *Kritika*, vol. 2, no. 1 (2001).

Bernice Q. Madison, *Social Welfare in the Soviet Union* (Stanford, 1968).

Kenneth Pinnow, "Cutting and Counting: Forensic Medicine as a Science of Society in Bolshevik Russia, 1920–1929," in David L. Hoffmann and Yanni Kotsonis, eds., *Russian Modernity: Politics, Knowledge, Practices* (London, 2000).

Susan Gross Solomon, "Social Hygiene and Soviet Public Health, 1921–1930," in Solomon and Hutchinson, eds.

State Violence

6

State Violence as Technique: The Logic of Violence in Soviet Totalitarianism

Peter Holquist

Excerpted from Peter Holquist, "State Violence as Technique: The Logic of Violence in Soviet Totalitarianism," in Amir Weiner, ed., *Landscaping the Human Garden* (Stanford: Stanford University Press, 2003).

Editor's Introduction

A corollary to the Stalinist welfare state was the massive application of state violence under Stalin. Soviet leaders, in addition to enacting welfare programs to solve social problems and transform society, utilized excisionary violence – deportations and executions – to eliminate "socially harmful elements," and did so with the same goal of social transformation. They believed that the removal of social aliens would not only eradicate enemies of the Soviet regime but would purify society and move the country toward communism. Viewed from this perspective, Stalinist terror was not a consequence of Russian backwardness or Stalin's vindictiveness, but was instead an integral means by which Soviet leaders pursued their vision of an ideal society.

Soviet state violence reflected the same interventionist ethos that gave rise to the welfare state. It too was predicated on an allegedly scientific understanding of society and on technologies of social intervention. Social statistics and social cataloguing provided the Stalinist leadership with a statistical representation of Soviet society. Deportations and concentration camps offered them the means to remove entire categories of people deemed unfit due to their class background or political orientation. Of course it is important to maintain a sense of human agency and to acknowledge that social science and interventionist technologies did not in themselves cause Stalinist terror – Stalin and his fellow leaders clearly bear responsibility for the deportations and executions they ordered. But modern concepts and practices allowed Soviet leaders to conceive of and implement excisionary violence, and thus provided a necessary though not sufficient condition for Stalinist terror. In this sense, Stalinism cannot be understood apart from the modern conception of society as an artifact to be sculpted through state intervention.

On the surface it seems paradoxical that the Stalinist regime deployed welfare programs and state violence simultaneously. Why would a government extend health and welfare benefits, housing, education, and jobs to its citizens, yet at the same time arrest, deport, and execute millions of people? But when considered alongside one another, it becomes clear that state welfare and state violence were two dimensions of the same phenomenon – state intervention to refashion society according to an idealized vision of the social order. As discussed in the previous selection, this intervention was not unique to the Soviet Union and reflected broader European trends. In the twentieth century, state violence increased throughout Europe, as governments practiced forced sterilizations, deportations, internments, and exterminations on an enormous scale.

The First World War marked something of a watershed in the deployment of state violence. Wartime exigencies led to vastly increased state powers, including surveillance and internments designed to ensure the loyalty of the population. In most countries, these forms of state intervention were subordinated to the existing constitutional order once the war ended, but the Soviet system was formed at this moment of total war, and wartime practices became part of the new social and political order. The revolutionary origin of the Soviet state also meant fewer institutional and moral constraints on the ambitions of Communist Party leaders, who applied state violence to pursue their own ideological vision. A comparative examination of Stalinist state violence, then, allows one to highlight the distinctive as well as the common features of Soviet social practices. Similar social conceptions and state practices assumed very different forms when enacted in different political and ideological settings.[1]

In the following selection, Peter Holquist analyzes the origins of modern state violence. He notes that the very possibility of using coercion in ways the Soviet government did was predicated on a science of society and the definition of a social field to which this model of science could be applied. Such a conception of society as a realm for scientific study was widely held by government officials throughout nineteenth-century Europe, including in tsarist Russia. Tsarist bureaucrats compiled

[1] For further discussion, see David L. Hoffmann and Peter Holquist, *Cultivating the Masses: The Modern Social. State in Russia, 1914–1939* (Ithaca, forthcoming).

extensive statistics on the population of the Russian empire, and they came to express a preference for homogeneity, identifying ethnic minorities as potentially disloyal or harmful. During the First World War, the tsarist government acted upon this statistical representation of the population by deporting up to one million Jews, Germans, and other ethnic minorities from the western borderlands. Holquist thus highlights the First World War as a crucial watershed in the implementation of state excisionary violence.

Such violence continued during the Russian Civil War, when both sides – the Reds (Communists) and the Whites (anti-Communists) – sought to categorize the population, and carried out mass executions of those deemed harmful. Communists described their policy of de-Cossackization (the elimination of Cossacks) not as a defensive military action but rather as a measure to remove malignant social "elements" and ensure the health of society. For that reason Holquist characterizes Soviet state violence as based not only on social cataloguing but on an aesthetic vision of the ideal society. In that sense, social statistics and interventionist technologies were the means by which Soviet leaders pursued their ideological goal of building socialism.

Throughout the 1920s and 1930s the Soviet government compiled what Holquist calls a vast human archive. Through censuses, questionnaires, and an internal passport system, Soviet officials sought to know their society and every person in it. This archive of the population identified those individuals who, by virtue of their social origins or anti-Soviet activity, were slated for excision. Officials even categorized "anti-Soviet elements" as more or less harmful, with the more harmful targeted for execution and the less harmful for deportation to labor camps where they would be reformed. During the Great Terror, when Stalin and the Politburo ordered mass executions and deportations, the Soviet secret police relied upon these archival records of the population to know whom to arrest. The use of state violence to shape the population was thus predicated on a particular mapping of the politico-social body.[2]

Holquist concludes that the Great Terror under Stalin was an extension of the more general aspiration to sculpt society. He makes clear that all Soviet leaders, including but not limited to Stalin, envisioned violence as an essential means by which to progress toward communism. In the epigram of the original article from which this excerpt is taken, he quotes Nikolai Bukharin, a Communist Party leader and eventual purge victim of Stalin, as writing, "Proletarian compulsion in all its forms, beginning with execution by shooting and ending with the compulsory labor obligation,

---

[2] For more on Soviet state violence and the increasing importance of ethnic categories during and after the Second World War, see Weiner in this volume.

is – however paradoxical this might sound – the means for producing a Communist humanity from the human material of the capitalist epoch."[3] Stalinist terror, in this view, was not random violence, nor was it merely the repression of potential opposition. Soviet leaders employed state violence in an attempt to reshape society and indeed to refashion human nature itself.

Such a conclusion in no way endorses Stalinist terror. It does, however, demonstrate that the conceptual and technological prerequisites for Soviet state violence went far beyond Stalin, Soviet society, or socialist ideology. It suggests that our explanation of Stalinism must also take into account modern conceptions of the social field and modern state practices of social intervention. Holquist's article provides an excellent starting point for exploring these dimensions of Stalinism.[4]

---

[3] The italicized portion was underlined by Lenin, who noted in the margin "Precisely!" N. I. Bukharin, Problemy teorii i praktiki sotsializma (Moscow, 1989; original, 1920), pp. 168, 454.
[4] Holquist uses "totalitarianism" in his title, but his work is an example of post-revisionist scholarship, not the totalitarian model. See the full version of his article, where he distinguishes his use of the term from the Sovietological version of the totalitarian model.

State Violence as Technique: The Logic of Violence in Soviet Totalitarianism

Peter Holquist

With the outpouring of materials from the Soviet archives, there has been a tidal wave of literature on Soviet "repression."[1] Yet scholars continue to treat such violence as an unintended consequence of the Soviet project, as some unforeseen malfunctioning rather than the product of its working out. Other than the "Stalin as evil genius" thesis, there now exist two main schools on Soviet "Terror" among historians: it was either the product of tensions, be they social or political;[2] or it was the instrumental attempt to suppress opponents, real or imagined.[3] Regardless of differences, most approaches based on new archival materials share one common feature: they treat Soviet applications of violence as purely repressive, however manic or irrational. Indeed, violence is described as manic and irrational precisely because it so inexactly corresponds to its supposed repressive function.[4] As a result, actual instances of applied violence are treated as a rupture or deviation from a supposedly more normal Soviet policy.

Soviet applications of state violence upon the politico-social body were meticulously targeted and assiduously planned. To be sure, Soviet power simultaneously strove to cultivate society and each individual in it. But state violence was inextricably related to this desire to operate upon society as artifact. Dekulakization and the Great Terror were not inevitable products of either Marxism or even Bolshevism; but the Bolshevik aspiration to cultivate a socialist society, and as part of that,

---

[1] The best recent treatment is Oleg Khlevnyuk, "The Objectives of the Great Terror" in *Soviet History, 1917–1953: Essays in Honour of R. W. Davies*, eds. Julian Cooper, Maureen Perrie and E. A. Rees (New York, 1995); Alexander Solzhenitsyn, *The Gulag Archipelago*, 3 vols. (New York, 1974) is still valuable.

[2] J. Arch Getty, *The Origins of the Great Purges* (New York, 1985); Gabor Tamas Rittersporn, *Stalinist Simplifications and Soviet Complications: Social Tensions and Political Conflicts in the USSR* (Philadelphia, 1991); *Stalinist Terror: New Perspectives*, eds. J. Arch Getty and Roberta Manning (New York, 1993). For a critique of this approach, see Oleg Khlevniuk, "Les mécanismes de la 'Grand Terreur' des années 1937–1938 au Turkménistan," *Cahiers du Monde russe* 39, no. 1–2 (1998): 197–208, here at 197–98.

[3] Robert Thurston, *Life and Terror in Stalin's Russia, 1934–1941* (New Haven, 1995), esp. pp. 58, 227.

[4] Many years ago, Hannah Arendt concluded that totalitarian terror "has ceased to be a mere means for the suppression of opposition, though it is also used for such purposes" (*Origins of Totalitarianism* [New York, 1973], p. 464).

to cultivate each individual, envisioned violence. While its intensity varied, the use of violence in this way was not limited to the 1930s, but dates back to the founding of the regime.[5] That is, Soviet state violence was not simply repressive. It was employed as a tool for fashioning an idealized image of a better, purer society. After Shklovsky's seminal 1915–16 essay on formalist art, Soviet policies might best be described as "state violence as technique."[6] In the Soviet Union, as throughout Europe, technique – "the effective management of resources, both natural and human" – had become "a value and an aesthetic goal, not merely as a means to an end."[7]

To be sure, the Soviet state used violence to excise [*iz"iat'*] those individuals it had determined to be "socially harmful." It did so, however, not merely to ensure society's health and integrity, but equally to realize an idealized, fundamentally aesthetic image of society and each individual in it.[8] As Peter Fritzsche has noted for the Nazi project, National Socialism's "constructive program of national health was accompanied by a stern eugenics administration that sought progressively to weed out alleged biological dangers to the German Volk. From the very beginning, the regime applied measures to identify, segregate and eradicate debilitating or supposedly foreign matter." But one cannot appreciate the full nature of this project unless one also grasps "the fantastic vision of the National Socialists . . . A useful way of thinking about the links between the administration of modern reform and the extraordinary measures of National Socialism is to consider modernism in aesthetic terms."[9] To

[5] Along somewhat different lines, see Stefan Plaggenborg, "Gewalt und Militanz in Sowjetrussland, 1917–1930," *Jahrbücher für Geschichte Osteuropas* 44, no. 3 (1996): 409–30; for the Soviet postwar use of violence, see Amir Weiner's contribution to this volume.

[6] V. Shklovsky, "Iskusstvo kak priëm" in *Sbornik po teorii poeticheskogo iazyka* (St. Petersburg, 1917). See the excellent treatment in Katerina Clark, *Petersburg: Crucible of Cultural Revolution* (Cambridge, 1995), pp. 32–4.

[7] Modris Eksteins, *Rites of Spring* (New York, 1989), p. 70.

[8] Jochen Hellbeck, "Laboratories of the Soviet Self: Diaries from the Stalin Era" (Ph.D. dissertation, Columbia University, 1998) demonstrates this point; see also Katerina Clark, *Petersburg*; Eric Naiman, *Sex in Public: The Incarnation of Early Soviet Ideology* (Princeton, 1997); Boris Groys, *The Total Art of Stalinism* (Princeton, 1992); and Vladislav Todorov, *Red Square, Black Square* (Albany, 1995). For treatments of the simultaneity of the aesthetic and technical in the German context, see Modris Ekstein's *Rites of Spring* (Boston, 1989), esp. pp. 315–31; Klaus Theweleit, *Male Fantasies*, 2 vols., translated by Erica Carter, Stephen Conway and Chris Turner (Minneapolis, 1987–9), esp. 2: 197–206; David G. Horn, *Social Bodies: Science, Reproduction, and Italian Modernity* (Princeton, 1994).

[9] Peter Fritzsche, "Nazi Modern," *MODERNISM/Modernity* 3:1 (1996): 1–21, here 8–10. For other expressions of the fantastic and aesthetic as part of the National Socialist program, see Eksteins, *Rites of Spring*, pp. 303–4 and Saul Friedländer, *Nazi German and the Jews, 1933–1939* (New York, 1997), pp. 86–7.

emphasize this underlying aesthetic project in the Soviet case, I have chosen Shklovsky's term "technique" rather than a more technical term like "scalpel" for Soviet state violence.

The Emergence of State Violence as Technique

"A great many of the practices we associate with the Revolution had had precedents in the treatment of the people by the government during the last two centuries of the monarchy. The old régime provided the Revolution with many of its methods; all the Revolution added was a savagery peculiar to itself."[10] Alexis de Tocqueville of course was speaking of the French Revolution, yet his observation holds equally true for the new Soviet regime emerging out of 1917. There is now a tendency to displace all responsibility for the emergence of state violence onto Bolshevism as an ideology. But for its own ends, Bolshevism expanded upon existing practices. There were certainly specificities to Bolshevik applications of violence. Yet the very possibility of applying state violence to the politico-social body was predicated on two earlier developments: the emergence over the course of the nineteenth century of the "social" as a realm for state intervention; and, the fashioning of particular tools for operating on this realm, particularly in the course of the First World War.

To conceive of a politico-social body upon which to operate, one first has to conceive of a polity in social terms. This was new in the nineteenth century. The very term "social science" was not coined until the first years of the French Revolution. And this new way of seeing encompassed both a model of science (thus allowing for the conviction that the methods of science are applicable to human affairs) and a definition of the social field (providing a specific view of society and of the nature of social processes to which the scientific model can be applied).[11] This social field explicitly related the individual to the larger politico-social body. Emerging disciplines increasingly shifted from the traditional imagery of a metaphoric relation between the individual body and the social body, to an argument that there existed an actual correlation

[10] Alexis de Tocqueville, *The Old Regime and the French Revolution* (New York, 1983), p. 192; see also Keith Michael Baker, "Representation" in *The Political Culture of the Old Regime*, ed. Keith Baker (New York, 1986) and Roger Chartier, "The Chimera of Origins" in *Foucault and the Writing of History*, ed. Jan Goldstein (Cambridge, MA, 1994).

[11] Keith Baker, *Condorcet: from Natural Philosophy to Social Mathematics* (Chicago, 1975), p. x. On the rise of the social, see also Mary Poovey, *Making a Social Body: British Cultural Formation, 1830–1864* (Chicago, 1995); Jacques Donzelot, *The Policing of Families* (New York, 1979); and, on a later period, David Horn, *Social Bodies*.

between the two.[12] This binding of individuals to specific social categories contributed to the development of state measures to act on these individuals. The European state in the latter half of the nineteenth century devoted increasing attention to identifying and removing the social threat such individuals represented. Thus "a *scientific* approach that included careful and constant documentation – or scientific observation" was developed. "Evidently, the demands of bourgeois society for intellectual and moral 'hygiene' were inseparable from the practice of violent policing."[13]

As in the rest of Europe, the emergence of a social way of seeing affected how the Russian Imperial state came to view and treat its population. In particular, the discipline of military statistics emerged as one of the essential conceptual models for conceiving of Imperial society.[14] Military statistics originated among reforming bureaucrats in the mid-nineteenth century and were modeled upon similar European studies. Military statistics transformed the Empire's hitherto amorphous "people" [*narod*] into a well-defined "population" [*naselenie*] through an intensive statistical study of its inhabitants. And, of equal significance, military statistics came to express an aesthetic preference (registered in a scientific language) for homogeneity. Thus even prior to the First World War the Imperial state was mapping the population in accord with idealized images of the politico-social body. Military statistics constituted a particular social field upon which the state could act.

Nor were these studies of merely academic interest. In the course of the First World War the Imperial state translated these modelings of the population into actual policies. The forced deportation of Jews, Germans, Balts and other groups from the western borderlands during the war merely transcribed into practice what military statistics had been teaching for years.[15] Some estimates place the total number of

[12] Catherine Gallagher, "The Body Versus the Social Body in the Works of Thomas Malthus and Henry Mayhew," *Representations* 14 (1986): 83–106. See also Ian Hacking, "Biopower and the Avalanche of Printed Numbers," *Humanities in Society* 5, no. 3–4 (1982): 279–95 and Joan Scott, "Statistical Representations of Work" in *Work in France*, ed. Steven Kaplan and Cynthia Koepp (Ithaca, 1986).

[13] Alf Lüdtke, "The Permanence of Internal War," in *On the Road to Total War*, ed. Stig Förster and Jörg Nagler (Washington DC, 1997), here at 388–9; see also Robert Nye, *Crime, Madness and Politics* (Princeton, 1984).

[14] Alain Blum, "Oublier l'etat pour comprendre la Russie (XIXe–XXe siècles)," *Revue des Etudes slaves* 66, no. 1 (1994): 135–45; on the significance of military statistics, see Peter Holquist, "To Count, To Extract, To Exterminate: Population Statistics and Population Politics in Late Imperial and Soviet Russia" in *A State of Nations*, eds. Terry Martin and Ronald Grigor Suny (New York, 2001).

[15] On the deportations, see Eric Lohr, "Enemy Alien Politics in the Russian Empire during World War One" (Ph.D. Dissertation, Harvard University, 1999); S. Nelipovich, "V

deportees at one million. During the First World War, the deportation of unreliable elements simply became part of the conceptual landscape – a landscape that had been mapped by military statistics.

And the First World War practices of deportation prefigured many of those identified as somehow intrinsically "Bolshevik." Increasingly, threats to the state were described in prophylactic terms: the Jewish "element" in the Western borderlands was "pernicious" [*zlovrednyi*] and "harmful and dangerous for the Russian people."[16] (While different adjectival modifiers were employed, the expression "an . . . element dangerous to the . . . people" was the precise formula for later Soviet mass operations.) After the May 1915 anti-German pogrom in Moscow, when crowds had demanded the expulsion of all Imperial subjects of German background, the appointed head of the city expressed regret that there were simply too many German subjects to fit them in a concentration camp [*sic*] on an island in the Volga.[17] Punitive detachments, which were to become ubiquitous in all armies during the Russian Civil War, operated extensively during the 1916 Steppe uprising. The Imperial state in its total war manifestation thus elaborated an entire repertoire of practices for managing and operating upon the population, practices that were to be carried across the revolutionary divide.[18]

The First World War therefore represents a crucial watershed, as the Imperial state moved to fashion its vision of a body politic as much by excision as by acculturation. The First World War did not introduce such aspirations. Military statistics (and Russian colonial policy) had long suggested such "solutions" were possible. But total war was the context within which these practices emerged as a regular part of state policies.

poiskakh 'vnutrennego vraga': deportatsionnaia politika Rossii (1914–1917)" in *Pervaia mirovaia voina i uchastie v nei Rossii (1914–1918)*, 2 vols. (Moscow, 1994); Daniel Graf, "Military Rule behind the Russian Front," *Jahrbücher für Geschichte Osteuropas* 22, no. 3 (1974): 390–411; Mark von Hagen, "The Great War and the Mobilization of Ethnicity" in *Post-Soviet Political Order*, ed. Barnett Rubin and Jack Snyder (New York, 1998). For documents, see "Dokumenty o presledovanii evreev," *Arkhiv russkoi revoliutsii* 19 (1928): 245–84.

[16] On measures during the course of the First World War to protect Imperial forces from "harmful actions by the Jewish population," including the taking of hostages and mass deportations, see "Dokumenty o presledovanii evreev," pp. 248, 250–1, 256–8, 275 (Jews described as a "pernicious element"). See also *The Jews of the Eastern War Zone* (New York, 1916); and *Evakuatsiia i rekvizitsiia: spravochnik deistvuiushchikh uzakonenii i rasporazhenii* (Petrograd, 1916), pp. 99–102 for the 3 August 1914 instruction sanctioning hostage-taking in order to facilitate requisitioning in the war zone.

[17] Nikolai Kharlamov, "Izbienie v pervoprestolnoi: nemetskii pogrom v Moskve v mae 1915," *Rodina* 1993, no. 8/9: 127–32; also Iu. Kir'ianov, " 'Maiskie bezporiadki' 1915 g. v Moskve," *Voprosy istorii* 1994, no. 12: 137–50.

[18] Peter Holquist, " 'Information is the Alpha and Omega of Our Work,' " *Journal of Modern History* 69, no. 3 (1997): 415–50 and "To Count."

In this environment, the appeal of scientifistic solutions intertwined with an ethos of violence.[19]

In this light, the violence of the Russian Civil War appears not as something *sui generis* but rather as an expansion of state violence first massively employed in the Great War. Sharing a common conceptual matrix for population politics and emerging from the experience of total war, Whites just as much as Reds reflexively disaggregated the population into "elements" of varying reliability.[20] They then employed a prophylactics of violence on those elements deemed to be malignant or harmful. Whites termed Jews "microbes" or "bacilli"; Bolshevism was presented as "a social disease." And, *pace* many existing treatments, this violence was not 'wild' but very well-structured: White commanders sifted their POWs, selecting out the undesirables and having them executed in groups later, a process the Whites described as "filtering."[21] The Bolshevik application of state violence had its own specificities; but it was hardly unique.

Soviet State Violence as Prophylactics

So the preconditions for the application of violence to the politico-social body predated the Bolshevik regime. But the Soviets then employed violence as technique to fashion society in their own image. And the Soviet state did so as an explicitly ideological regime.[22] One can discern the Soviet state's constant devotion to the sculpting of its raw, human material, a project diligently pursued even in the years preceding the better known violence of the 1930s. Seen from this vantage point, the measures of the 1930s are not some anomaly or deviation, but only the largest and most ambitious effort in a project stretching back to 1917.

From the very first, the Soviet regime sought to rework the politico-social body. In 1919, in the midst of a Civil War for its very existence, the

---

[19] On the First World War as creating a culture of violence in Russia, see Gorky, *Untimely Thoughts*, pp. 9–12, 76–7, 128–30, 185, 195–9 (1917–18); Leon Trotsky, *Terrorism and Communism* (Ann Arbor, 1961; original, 1920), pp. 65–8; Plaggenborg, "Gewalt"; and Roger Pethybridge, *The Social Prelude to Stalinism* (New York, 1974), ch. 3.

[20] Peter Holquist, "Research Note: Anti-Soviet *Svodki* from the Civil War," *Russian Review* 56, no. 3 (1997): 445–50.

[21] Peter Kenez, "Pogroms and White Ideology in the Russian Civil War" in *Pogroms and Anti-Jewish Violence in Modern Russian History*, eds. John Klier and Shlomo Lambroza (New York, 1992); A. L. Litvin, "Krasnyi i belyi terror v Rossii, 1917–1922," *Otechestvennaia istoriia* 1993, no. 6: 46–62; E. I. Dostovalov, "O belykh i belom terrore," *Rossiiskii arkhiv*, vol. 6 (1995): 637–97, "filtering" at 678.

[22] David Hoffmann, "European Modernity and Soviet Socialism" in *Russian Modernity: Politics, Knowledge, Practices*, eds. David Hoffmann and Yanni Kotsonis (New York, 2000); Kotkin, *Magnetic Mountain*, excerpted in this volume.

Soviet state engaged in a policy of 'de-Cossackization."[23] This attempt to remove an entire segment of the population (the term employed again was "element") was not a defensive reaction to a hostile group but instead an attempt to foster an idealized image of the politico-social body by excising those 'elements' determined to be harmful. In a policy review, Reingol'd, a senior Party member, summed up the means and ends of de-Cossackization. Its goal had been "to make the Don healthy" [*Don ozdorovit'*]. To this end, Reingol'd suggested that the Soviet state "will sooner or later have to exterminate, simply physically destroy the vast portion of Cossacks."[24] The Party decree delineating this policy explicitly called for the instrumental use of "mass terror" and the outright and total "extermination" of the Cossack elite. As a direct consequence of this decree, upwards of ten thousand people were judicially executed.

Yet within several months de-Cossackization was abjured and the Cossacks became normalized as a component part of the Soviet population. This abrupt shift in policy has several lessons. First, while the essentialization of socio-political categories was a critical precondition for de-Cossackization, so too was the role played by political authorities who had sanctioned and pressed de-Cossackization. As Detlev Peukert has argued, the principle of selection and even elimination had long been present in scientific thought. But measures such as de-Cossackization became possible only when states – especially ones pursuing an explicitly ideological agenda – endorse one single branch of modern social thought, and grant it supreme state backing.[25] De-Cossackization was not so much the product of scientific models themselves, but the result of an ideological system extending scientistic reasoning as a universal template for dealing with perceived threats. The abrupt shift in policy towards Cossacks also demonstrates that what was important was not the category itself but a framework that sought to identify opposition in terms of malignancies to be removed in order to bring about the healthy, pristine and beautiful society. De-Cossackization was not an anomalous event but represented a Soviet propensity for fashioning visions of society by subtraction as much as by addition.[26] Periods when the regime resorted to such measures were not deviations but those conjunctures when it thought it possible or necessary to act

[23] Peter Holquist, " 'Conduct Merciless, Mass Terror': Decossackization on the Don, 1919," *Cahiers du Monde russe* 38, no. 1–2 (1997): 127–62.

[24] I. I. Reingol'd to the CC, "Dokladnaia zapiska" in *Bol'shevistkoe rukovodstvo: perepiska, 1912–1927* (Moscow, 1997), pp. 107–10.

[25] Peukert, "Genesis." Nye (*Crime*, pp. xi, 67–73) makes a similar observation about ideas of degeneracy in France.

[26] The Soviets were quite explicit about this: for a postwar recapitulation of this point, see G. Glezerman, "Likvidatsiia eksplutatorskikh klassov v SSSR" in *O sovetskom sotialisticheskom obshchestve*, eds. F. Konstantinov, M. Kammari, G. Glezerman (Moscow, 1948).

on a long-standing goal – to create a socialist society through managing and sculpting its human as well as its raw materials.

This project of politico-social fashioning even framed the conduct of military campaigns in the midst of the Civil War. Soviet anti-insurgency campaigns in the Don region in 1920–1 and against the Antonov movement in Tambov province in 1921 aimed as much at operating upon the politico-social body as at smashing military opposition.[27] Existing treatments merely portray Soviet anti-insurgent policies as repressive measures intended to eliminate political threats. In fact, the campaigns aimed at much more. Soviet forces did not seek to "pacify the people" [*usmirit' narod*] or "suppress the insurgency" [*podavit' vosstanie*]. Soviet measures sought instead "to remove and eliminate the bandit element" [*iz"iat' i istrebit' banditskii element*] and "to cleanse those regions infected by banditism" [*ochistit' raiony zarazhennye banditizmom*].[28] That is, they did not seek simply to pacify the countryside and enforce obedience. "Banditism" (described variously as "a dangerous epidemic" and "a psychological illness") was merely a symptom pointing to the presence of malignant and dangerous elements. The goal was to remove such tumors, whether they be active or benign: once the symptom of banditism revealed the presence of dangerous elements, cleansing was required whether the insurgency itself had continued or not.

Defining its task as excising malignant elements from the population led the Soviet state to apply different measures than if the goal had simply been to enforce obedience and order upon a territory. The goal was not just to secure obedience and order, but explicitly "to cleanse" [*ochishchenie, chistka, ochistit'*] the population of pernicious threats, to secure its full health and recovery [*polnoe ozdorovlenie*]. It is in this light that one must see Soviet orders insisting that "we must strive by all means at our disposal: (1) to capture all those individuals who have participated directly in bands and to capture those who have offered any aid to individual bands, and (2) then mercilessly eliminate a portion of them and settle the remainder beyond the boundaries of the territory"; or to

---

[27] This point is treated in greater-detail in Holquist "To Count." Such campaigns share some features of later Nazi 'cleansing operations' [*Säuberungsunternehmen*] in the Second World War: see Omer Bartov, *The Eastern Front: German Troops and the Barbarization of Warfare* (New York, 1986) and Mark Mazower, *Inside Hitler's Greece* (New Haven, 1993).

[28] For the Don in 1921, see Rossiiskii gosudarstvennyi voennyi arkhiv [RGVA], f. 25896, op. 1, d. 8, ll. 2–12, 15 (yearly report of Don Military assembly to combat banditism and report of local plenipotentiary); for the Soviet anti-insurgency campaign against Antonov, see *Antonovshchina: dokumenty i materialy*, ed. Viktor Danilov (Tambov, 1994).

execute all insurgents except the lowest rank and file, who were to be exiled from "infected" regions with their families.[29] Thus the goal of these anti-insurgency measures was not simply to pacify territories, but to secure the proper condition of the population either by physically removing or simply exterminating "harmful elements." And similar policies, albeit at a lower intensity, continued to be conducted throughout the supposedly benign NEP years of the 1920s.[30]

The drive to identify and then to remove "harmful elements" was not limited to anti-bandit operations. As Soviet forces prepared in 1920 to storm the last stronghold of the Whites in the Crimea, Stalin informed Trotsky that an order would soon be issued directing the "total extermination of the Wrangelite officer corps." After the Red Army had seized this last base of the White movement, Soviet authorities secretly awarded one Bolshevik 'hygienist' the Order of the Red Banner for (in the words of the commendation) "having cleansed the Crimean peninsula of White officers and counter-intelligence agents who had been left behind, removing up to thirty governors, fifty generals, more than three hundred colonels and as many counter-intelligence agents, for a total of up to twelve thousand of the White element."[31] This frantic search for the "officer element" within the Soviet population would continue for several decades.[32]

Nor was this process of "cleansing" limited to the fields of battle. Indeed, "questions of purity plagued the Party throughout the mid-1920s and the battles for power within it were fought along a discursive axis preoccupied with corruption," leading the Party to operate with a particular "inoculatory logic."[33] At the close of the Civil War, Soviet authorities pursued a systematic "filtering" of unreliable elements from the population. As the military threat receded and NEP was being introduced, the Bolsheviks had dispatched all potentially harmful elements to concentration camps. These camps cannot be understood merely as detention points for suspects or holding-pens for enemies. For an explicitly self-styled Marxist regime, they were a space where those who were redeemable could be reformed through labor.[34] But the camps served

---

[29] RGVA, f. 25896, op. 1, d. 8, l. 15; *Antonovshchina*, 165–6, 172, 182, 187.

[30] Holquist, "To Count."

[31] RTsKhIDNI, f. 17, op. 109, d. 117, l. 4 (Trotskii to Stalin); *Bol'shevitskoe rukovodstvo*, p. 150 (Stalin to Trotskii); commendation as cited in Litvin, "Krasnyi i belyi terror," pp. 55–6.

[32] Solzhenitsyn, *Gulag Archipelago*, 1: 39, 77.

[33] Naiman, *Sex in Public*, p. 263; similarly, Clark, *Petersburg*, p. 211.

[34] On the emergence of the system of concentration camps, see Michael Jakobson, *Origins of the Gulag: the Soviet Prison Camp System, 1917–1934* (Lexington, KY, 1993) and the documents in *Revelations from the Russian Archives*, eds. Diane Koenker and Ronald Bachman (Washington, 1997), pp. 132–40.

equally as a "filter," a space where those who could be redeemed through collective labor were separated out from those who were incorrigible and resistant to labor's ameliorative effects. Suspect elements were removed from the general population while their true nature was determined in the camps through a detailed hermeneutics of the self. Nor were these camps a minor affair. Orel province had four camps intended not only for compulsory labor but also for the filtration of suspects. In the course of four months, over thirty-five thousand individuals passed through Orel camp #1 alone.[35] The Moscow Cheka devoted itself to "the massive work in filtering out the enormous numbers of White Guard prisoners," processing twenty thousand White officers just in the summer of 1920.[36]

It is no exaggeration to describe the filtration process as a detailed hermeneutics of individual selves. All students at the (Soviet!) Petrograd Naval Academy were required to present themselves before a "filtration" commission in August 1921.[37] The commission interviewed each person individually and then divided the entire academy into groups of twenty-five. Andrei P. Belobrov was one of the elements to be filtered. After the initial interview, his group was transported by train to Moscow. (Given the dismal state of Soviet transport at the time, the use of a train for this purpose represented a major resource allocation.) From Moscow this group was then transferred (again, by train) to Vladimir-on-Kliazma, where the suspects were interred in a concentration camp. Three months later, after intermittent interrogations, Belobrov was taken individually to Moscow, where he was photographed and fingerprinted at the central secret police prison, the Lubianka. From there he was deposited in a "political isolator" in Moscow, where he remained until December. At that time he was again summoned to the Lubianka, where he was required to write a detailed autobiography, and again returned to the "isolator." He was summoned back to the Lubianka in February 1922, where he was issued a slip instructing him to present himself to Red Fleet headquarters for further assignment. Belobrov had

---

[35] "Lageria prinuditel'nykh rabot na Orlovshchine v nachale 1920-kh godov," *Rekviem* (Orel, 1995), vol. 2: 20–7.

[36] Dzerzhinsky to Lenin in *The Unknown Lenin*, ed. Richard Pipes (New Haven, 1996), pp. 119–21; on the Moscow camps, see also *Revelations from the Russian Archives*, pp. 134–8.

[37] This account based on A. P. Belobrov, "Kak bol'sheviki 'fil'trovali' flotskikh ofitserov," *Istochnik* 1996, no. 3: 64–81. On the place of autobiographies in Bolshevik hermeneutics, see Igal Halfin's "From Darkness to Light: Student Communist Autobiographies in the 1920s," *Jahrbücher für Geschichte Osteuropas* 45, no. 2 (1997): 210–36; and Igal Halfin, *Class, Consciousness, and Salvation in Revolutionary Russia* (Pittsburgh, 1999).

successfully passed through the "filtration." The entire process of hermeneutic probing so as to determine the true nature of this one man had required six months.

Belobrov was fortunate to emerge from the process of filtration. With the Civil War already won, the regime was busy discarding all that had been trapped by its politico-social filters. In early 1920, the Soviets captured and "filtered" Vasilii Khripunov and his two sons, all three of whom had served as officers in the anti-Soviet Don Army. The Soviets executed Vasilii but dispatched his two sons, via Ekaterinodar and Moscow, to a concentration camp in Tula, from whence they were soon released. (However, due to this blemish in their records, both Vasilii's sons were executed in 1937.)[38]

One of the most revealing accounts on "filtration" comes from comrade Rychkov, the head of the Tambov concentration camp, to a July 1921 closed gathering of Party members who had just participated in suppressing the Antonov insurgency.[39] Rychkov insisted that "we must reeducate [the former 'bandits'] so that we can release them as conscious individuals." Other Party members chided him for coddling his charges by setting up plays and choral societies, and demanded instead that "one should eliminate the enemy ... shoot them – period!" Rychkov responded:

> That is an entirely incorrect error, we've heard it repeatedly. It wouldn't take long to shoot them – unlike the bandits, we'd have enough cartridges. But to turn our recent, inveterate enemies into good, strong friends – that's what we need to do. Of course, if any barons or other wealthy sorts ended up there, they'd soon be a head shorter. Also, if a fervent, murdering bandit does not respond to political enlightenment, insists on his own way, his song won't last very long. But we must have an absolutely different approach for those who fell into error and deeply repent. Not for nothing did we, on orders from above, release an entire echelon back to their homes. . . . No, we destroy some, others – those who are able – we reeducate, turn to our side. Such are the conclusions we've come to in our camp.

---

[38] "Kazach'ia sem'ia Khripunovykh: vospominaniia E. V. Kalabinoi," *Voprosy istorii* 1996, no. 11–12: 73–86. For orders that captured officers are to be processed first by "special departments" and then dispatched to concentration camps, see *Rezoliutsii i postanovleniia vtorogo donskogo s"ezda sovetov* (Rostov, 1920), pp. 19–20; *Prikazy sovetskim voiskam 9-oi armii* (n.p., [1920]), p. 340; Gosudarstvennyi arkhiv rostovskoi oblasti [GARO], f. R-97, op. 1, d. 516, l. 36 (Don Cheka directive ordering all officers to be held in concentration camps in the far rear).

[39] " 'Sfotografirovannye rechi': govoriat uchastniki likvidatsii antonovshchiny," *Otechestvennye arkhivy* 1996, no. 2: 34–66.

Rychkov strenuously insisted on the camp's corrective rather than exclusively punitive functions before a closed Party gathering packed with those demanding merciless vengeance. Yet his account also reveals the obverse of this corrective policy: the camp was intended to winnow out those who were redeemable from those who were not. Those detainees determined to be incorrigible were slated for destruction ("we destroy some"). This policy was not limited to the Tambov camps. In March and April of 1921, just as the New Economic Policy was being introduced, over 540 officers were executed in the Arkhangel'sk concentration camp alone.[40] As a result of this assiduous filtering one scholar estimates that Soviet power executed over twenty-five thousand people in the eighteen months following the end of the Civil War.[41]

These examples from the Civil War and early 1920s demonstrate that the project of fashioning society by excising particular "elements" was an intrinsic aspect of Soviet power from the very first. To be sure, repression in the 1920s, during the New Economic Policy, was obviously much different than repression in the later paroxysms of interwar state violence, most notably those of 1929–33 and 1937–8. Violence in these "hot" periods was distinct both in its extent and in its lethality. However, the violence during these years was not so much an anomaly in Soviet history, as those conjunctures of perceived political and geo-strategic crisis when the Soviet state massively extended the logic of existing practices, overriding any previous constraints.[42] Indeed, violence during NEP, while not as extensive or lethal as earlier, during the Civil War, or in later instances, was nevertheless a prevalent feature of the time.[43]

The better known and more widely practiced applications of state violence of the late 1920s and 1930s operated within the same conceptual framework, that of excising malignant "elements" in order to safeguard the rest of society. Indeed, the arrests and executions in 1937–8 often proceeded according to lists drawn up during the 1920s, some as early as 1920–1. To be sure, in the later period the targeted "elements" comprised a much larger portion of the population and the proportion of

---

[40] Iu. V. Doinykh, "Predshestvenniki Solovkov: novye arkhivnye svidetel'stva," *Otechestvennye arkhivy*, 1994, no. 1: 76–80.

[41] This figure in Doinykh, p. 80.

[42] For the underlying logic of the terror of 1937–8, but with an analysis of the geopolitical conjuncture that made its particular unfolding possible, see Kotkin, *Magnetic Mountain*, chapter 7.

[43] Solzhenitsyn, *Gulag Archipelago*, vol. 1, chapter 2; Nicolas Werth, "De la trêve au grand tournant" in *Le livre noir du communisme*, ed. Stéphane Courtois et al. (Paris, 1997), esp. pp. 150–5; S. A. Krasil'nikov, "Ssylka v 1920-e gody," *Minuvshee*, vol. 21 (Moscow-St. Petersburg, 1997): 175–239.

those deemed incorrigible (and hence subject to execution) was incomparably higher, particularly in 1937–8.[44] But the later policies represented the extension and expansion of preexisting ways of viewing and acting upon the politico-social body.

Seen in this light, the 1929–30 dekulakization campaign represents no anomalous shift in Soviet policy, but rather the conjuncture when the regime sought to implement existing aspirations to practice "social prophylaxis" (Solzhenitsyn) and "prophylactic cleansing" (Molotov). Soviet directives on dekulakization proclaimed the campaign's goal to be "to cleanse the collective farms from kulak and other counterrevolutionary elements" and "to cleanse the farms of the elements that are infecting them."[45] The OGPU's 15 March 1931 "Memorandum on conducting the mass expulsion of dekulakized peasants" stated forthrightly that the goal of deportation from all regions was "*to totally cleanse [them] of kulaks*" [emphasis in original].[46] And the measures used to secure dekulakization replicated those employed earlier in de-Cossackization and especially in anti-bandit operations. Indeed, one can view dekulakization as an all-encompassing, Union-wide anti-bandit operation.[47] As with the earlier bandit and counterrevolutionary "elements," kulak elements were identified within the general population and then further disaggregated into the more and the less harmful. The February 2, 1930 OGPU directive #4421 on dekulakization identified two categories of kulak and sanctioned different measures for each group. As in earlier anti-bandit operations, the most harmful category was to be "immediately liquidated." Soviet activists declared that "We will exile the kulak by the thousands and when necessary – shoot the kulak breed"; "we will make soap of the kulaks"; and "Our class enemy must be wiped off the face of the earth." This was not mere rhetoric. More than 20,000 individuals were sentenced to death in 1930 alone, and this figure covers only those tried by the OGPU.[48] The remaining, "less harmful" category was deported from their home regions, whether

[44] See V. N. Zemskov, "Zakliuchennye v 30-e gody: demograficheskii aspekt," *Sotsiologicheskie issledovaniia* 1996, no. 7: 3–14.

[45] These examples from the Smolensk Archive, WKP 166, ll. 3–5, 30–8; for similar documents on the Poles'e and the Khar'kov regions, see *Revelations from the Russian Archives*, pp. 402, 416. On the dekulakization campaign, see Lynne Viola, *Peasant Rebels Under Stalin* (Oxford, 1997).

[46] N. Ia. Gushchin, '*Raskulachivanie' v Sibiri (1928–1934)* (Novosibirsk, 1996), pp. 111–12.

[47] Holquist, "To Count"; Viola, *Peasant Rebels*, pp. 175–9; and the language employed in the OGPU directive #4421 (see following note).

[48] OGPU directive #4421 in *Neizvestnaia Rossiia*, vol. 1 (Moscow, 1992), pp. 237–45; quotations from Viola, *Peasant Rebels*, p. 37; figure on sentences, O. V. Khlevniuk, *Politbiuro* (Moscow, 1996), p. 19.

merely from their districts or to distant "corrective-labor colonies" and "special settlements." And when they arrived at their places of detention, kulaks were again filtered. Immediately upon their arrival in Magnitogorsk, dekulakized peasants "were interviewed extensively for their biography, which was thought to be an indication of the degree of danger they posed."[49]

Thus the Soviet state's massive employment of violence in 1937–8, frequently termed the "Great Terror," can be viewed as expanding upon existing aspirations and even practices. The infamous Soviet "mass operations" of this period were again directed against "elements," this time "anti-Soviet," "counter-revolutionary" and "socially alien." As geopolitical tensions increased and Bolshevik eschatology pointed towards the "final, decisive struggle" promised by the *International* (sung ritualistically at Party gatherings), the February–March 1937 Party plenum devoted particular attention to the supposed presence of a great number of "anti-Soviet elements" in the politico-social body.[50] Consequently, the Politburo passed the 2 July 1937 resolution "Concerning Anti-Soviet Elements," a concern directly addressed by NKVD order #00447 of 30 July 1937.[51] This order, framing the most massive of the "mass operations," listed nine target populations (e.g., former kulaks, socially alien elements, former members of anti-Soviet parties, former priests, recidivist criminals) and divided them into two categories: "to the first category belong all of the most hostile of these elements. They are to be subject to immediate arrest and are to be shot upon examination. . . . to the second category belong the remaining less active but nevertheless hostile elements. They are subject to immediate arrest and detention in camps for a period of 8–10 years, and the most malicious and socially dangerous are to be held in prisons for that period." NKVD Order #00447 specified regional quotas for each category, decreeing 259,450 arrests, of whom 72,950 were to be shot, a total comprising well over

---

[49] Kotkin, *Magnetic Mountain*, p. 217; on the kulak "special settlers," see the documentary publication *Spetspereselentsy v zapadnoi sibiri*, 3 vols. (Novosibirsk, 1992–3).

[50] For the reports at this plenum, see *Voprosy istorii*, nos. 5–6 (1993). On how the geopolitical situation played into the Terror, see Kotkin, *Magnetic Mountain*, pp. 303, 310, 319–20, 334, 337; on how Bolshevik eschatology contributed to the dynamic, see Halfin, "From Darkness to Light" and *Class, Consciousness and Salvation*, as well as Stephen Hanson, *Time and Revolution* (Chapel Hill, 1997), pp. 166–70.

[51] For the Central Committee resolution and NKVD order #00447, see *Trud*, 4 June 1992; for increases in the arrest and execution target figures, see *Izvestiia*, 3 April 1996, p. 5. For the conduct of this operation in two regions, see Oleg Khlevniuk, "Les mécanismes de la 'Grand Terreur' des années 1937–1938 au Turkménistan," *Cahiers du Monde russe* 39, no. 1–2 (1998): 197–208, and *Leningradskii martirolog*, vol. 1 (Sankt-Peterburg, 1995), pp. 38–48.

ten percent of all those executed during 1937–8. And the regional list was incomplete, since the quotas omitted a number of regions. In any case, from late August to mid-December 1937 the Politburo, at the request of local authorities, sanctioned increases in the totals for execution by a further 16,800 people.[52]

As should now be clear, the oft-drawn distinction between "purges" [chistki] as a purely administrative practice limited to Party members and a "Terror" that swirled among the general populace only in 1937–8 is untenable.[53] Indeed, the very term "terror" seems not to have been employed by the historical actors at the time. (Not that Bolsheviks were opposed to the term: they employed it self-consciously and extensively in the Civil War). Instead, the Soviets proclaimed that they were "cleansing" society, protecting it through the use of the "supreme measure of social defense" – execution. Thus the various Party "purges" were only one aspect of the overarching drive to cleanse the entire politico-social body, both within the Party as well as outside it. Indeed, the vast majority of victims in the years 1937–8 were not Party members or state officials.[54]

The argument that Bolshevik applications of state violence sought to eliminate classes but not people is clearly wrong. Soviet attempts to eliminate classes meant the very real, intentional and physical elimination of individuals. While their category was primarily class, Marxists too spoke of degeneracy and the need to improve the population.[55] But the Soviet project was not simply to excise and eliminate; it was to do so in order to realize an idealized image of the politico-social body, of "the People-as-One."[56] How did the Soviets know what that was to be, and who did and did not belong?

[52] *Moskovskie novosti*, 21 June 1992; also *Izvestiia*, 3 April 1996. The number of victims of this operation certainly exceeded its official 'limits' (Khlevniuk, "Les mécanismes," pp. 202–4).

[53] E.g., J. Arch Getty, *The Origins of the Great Purge*; *contra* this, see Solzhenitsyn, *Gulag Archipelago*, 1: 70.

[54] For instance, 96% of the victims in the Tomsk region did not belong to the Party (V. N. Uimanov, *Repressii: kak eto bylo* [Tomsk, 1995], pp. 50–1). However Zemskov ("Zakliuchennye," p. 8) notes that such figures did not include those who had earlier been expelled from the Party. Undoubtedly, Party members suffered disproportionately in the Terror. The point, however, is that violence was not circumscribed to the Party.

[55] On German and Russian Marxists' fascination with eugenics, see Loren Graham, "Science and Values: the Eugenics Movement in Germany and Russia in the 1920s," *American Historical Review* 82, no. 5 (1977): 1133–64. Both Eric Naiman (*Sex in Public*) and Halfin (*Class, Consciousness and Salvation*) deal extensively with Soviet notions of degeneracy.

[56] See Claude Lefort, "The Image of the Body in Totalitarianism," in Lefort, *The Political Forms of Modern Society*, ed. John Thompson (Cambridge, 1986).

The Human Archive: Of Each and All

"Two new devices for political organization and rule over foreign peoples were discovered during the first decades of imperialism. One was race as a principle of the body politic, and the other bureaucracy as a principle of foreign domination. . . . Both discoveries were actually made on the dark continent."[57] Arendt's observation has been solidly demonstrated by a wealth of literature on colonial rule and domination.[58] Such "colonial" techniques then became embedded within the practices of the colonizing states and became increasingly deployed within Europe as well.[59]

Race, however, is not the only all-encompassing macro-category through which populations can be refracted. Class is another axis for aligning and explaining the social world, and it too purports to universal truth. Both nationalism and socialism can thus be seen to be the playing out of a more general tendency to homogenize polities, one on a national, the other on a class axis. If race and bureaucracy came powerfully together in the nineteenth century in the Dark Continent and India, in the twentieth century class and bureaucracy intertwined on the Eurasian land mass, in the Soviet Union.[60] The social field had emerged in the nineteenth century; in the early twentieth century, a state for the first time sought to catalogue and then act upon a specifically socialist vision of it.

Using the prism of Marxist analysis, the Soviet regime attempted to map its politico-social body *in toto* and situate every single individual component part of it. In so doing, the Soviet state sought not only to compile a vast human archive, but then to act upon its human material (again, in aggregate and individually).[61] These practices strove to make the individual and the collective politico-social body intersect –

[57] Hannah Arendt, *The Origins of Totalitarianism* (New York, 1951), p. 185.

[58] Among a vast literature, see Pradeep Barua, "Inventing Race: the British and India's Martial Races," *The Historian* 58, no. 1 (1995): 107–16; David Ludden, "Orientalist Empiricism: transformations of colonial knowledge" in *Orientalism and the Postcolonial Predicament*, ed. Carol Breckenridge and Peter van der Veer (Philadelphia, 1993); Benedict Anderson, *Imagined Communities*, expanded edition (New York, 1991); Bernard Cohn, "The Census, Social Stratification and Objectification in South Asia," in *An Anthropologist among the Historians* (New Delhi, 1987).

[59] Sven Lindqvist, *'Exterminate All the Brutes!'* (New York, 1996); Isabel Hull, "German Final Solutions in the Wilhelmine Period" (unpublished manuscript); Fran Hirsch, "An Empire of Nations" (Ph. D. thesis, Princeton University, 1998); Holquist, "To Count."

[60] Hirsch ("An Empire of Nations") presents Soviet measures as self-conscious attempt to implement "colonial models" of rule.

[61] *Programmy statisticheskikh kursov raionnykh i guberskikh* (Moscow, 1920), pp. 10–11; Kotkin, *Magnetic Mountain*, pp. 94–105.

here was the place where "People-as-One" was forged out of concrete individuals. But in this attempt to correlate an increasing individualization with the reinforcement of totality, the Soviet project is not some anomaly, but rather a particular playing out of the principles of modern political rationality.[62]

Through its censuses, through discriminatory legislation, through its ubiquitous detailed questionnaires, the Soviet state sought to know and order the world.[63] And this world was sculpted along the lines of Marxist analysis. From the very first years of the regime, authorities determined each and every person's "social background" and on this basis assigned them a place in their ordering of the politico-social body.[64] The censuses of 1926, 1937 and 1939 – each accompanied by a press campaign promoting it as an event of vital politico-social importance – delineated the boundaries and constitution of the socialist polity, a polity constituted by its individual component parts (hence the census).[65]

The "passportization" of the population was the most intrusive and effective device for cataloguing the population and impressing upon each and every individual their proper station within the newly-emerging socialist society. In the midst of the Civil War, Emmanuil Enchmen had (in a pamphlet published under Party auspices) proposed that "the communist society of the future will be founded on a system of 'physiological passports' for all human organisms," which were to serve simultaneously as a type of ration card for consumption and to determine the amount of joy its holder was to have.[66] While Enchmen's proposal for physiological passports now strikes us as bizarre, German

---

[62] Michel Foucault, "The Political Technology of Individuals" in *Technologies of the Self*, ed. Luther Martin, Huch Gutman and Partick Hutton (Amherst, 1988) and Keith Baker, "A Foucauldian French Revolution" in *Foucault and the Writing of History*, ed. Jan Goldstein. For how Nazi Germany and Fascist Italy situated the individuals within a politico-social matrix, see Götz Aly and Karl Heinz Roth, *Die restlose Erfassung: Volkzählen, Identifizieren und Aussondern im Nationalsozialismus* (Berlin, 1984); Horn, *Social Bodies*; and Carl Ipsen, *Dictating Demography: the Problem of Population in Fascist Italy* (New York, 1996).

[63] Sheila Fitzpatrick, "Ascribing Class: the Construction of Social Identity in Soviet Russia," *Journal of Modern History* 65, no. 4 (1993): 745–70.

[64] Fitzpatrick, "Ascrbing Class" and Elise Kimerling, "Civil Rights and Social Policy in Soviet Russia, 1918–1936," *Russian Review* 41, no. 1 (1982): 24–46.

[65] V. B. Zhiromskaia, "Vsesoiznye perepisi naseleniia 1926, 1937, 1939 godov," *Istoriia SSSR* 1990, no. 3: 84–104; Catherine Merridale, "The 1937 Census and the Limits of Stalinist Rule," *The Historical Journal* 39, no. 1 (1996): 225–40; and Francine Hirsch, "Ethnographers, Statisticians and the Making of the Soviet Union," *Slavic Review* 56, no. 2 (1997): 251–78. National Socialist censuses likewise had a constructivist agenda; Nazi statisticians described their task as *"deutsche Aufbauwerk"* (Aly and Roth, *Die restlose Erfassung*, p. 8).

[66] Cited in Naiman, *Sex in Public*, p. 76.

health officials in the early 1920s actually instituted a system of "health passports" and worked on "psycho-biograms" for relating the population's physical and mental qualities.[67] And while Bukharin criticized Enchman's proposal as excessively biologistic, Bukharin himself (elaborating on August Bebel and European socialist thought in general) entertained plans in the same period for statistical bureaus to regulate the work of everybody in the new socialist state.[68] In the course of the Civil War the Soviet state implemented a form of passport system – labor books – that encompassed aspects of both Enchmen's passport ideal and Bukharin's enthusiasm for work bureaus.[69]

Labor books passed with the end of the Civil War. It was not until 1932 that the Soviet state moved to realize a more total "passportization" of the population. Scholars have noted that a primary object of passportization was the regime's desire, in the wake of collectivization and the ensuing famine, to keep starving peasants on the land and out of the cities.[70] Alongside this task, the passport legislation was explicitly intended "to cleanse" the newly-emerging socialist spaces (new cities, constructions sites, worker dormitories) by distinguishing authentic citizens from those elements polluting the pristine new areas. The decree setting out the new passport system justified its introduction by invoking the need "to cleanse these populated points from kulak, criminal and other anti-Bolshevik elements who are hiding there." An accompanying editorial elaborated that a major goal was "to cleanse, to deport these parasitic elements from our cities, building areas, and workers' settlements" and that "the passport system is designed to help the immediate cleansing of these anti-Bolshevik elements from the cities."[71] And it was in precisely these terms that Soviet citizens understood passportization. As passports were introduced to Moscow, Stepan Podlubnyi, the son of a dekulakized peasant who had moved from Ukraine to Moscow under false documents, confided to his diary that only a miracle could save him from identification and expulsion. Yet he commented with evident approval that "not only institutions, but also the population follows this work with suspense . . . All in all, [passportization] is a sorting out, the

---

[67] Paul Weindling, *Health, Race and German Politics between Unification and Nazism, 1870–1945* (Cambridge, 1993), pp. 384–85.

[68] Naiman, *Sex in Public*, p. 77 for Bukharin's critique of Enchmen; Lars Lih, "The Mystery of the *ABC*," *Slavic Review* 56, no. 1 (1997): 50–72, Bukharin's enthusiasm for statistical bureaus at 53–4.

[69] Mervyn Matthews, *The Passport Society* (Boulder CO, 1993), pp. 16–19.

[70] Sheila Fitzpatrick, *Stalin's Peasants* (New York, 1994), pp. 92–5.

[71] *Pravda*, 28 December 1932. See also Kotkin, *Magnetic Mountain*, pp. 99–101 and V. P. Popov, "Pasportnaia sistema v SSSR (1932–1976)," *Sotsiologicheskie issledovaniia* 1995, nos. 8–9, who argues that the Soviet passport system differed fundamentally from its pre-revolutionary predecessor (no. 9, p. 5).

newest model of a human cleansing machine" [*v obshchem, sortirovka, liudechistil'ka noveishei konstruktsii*]. (Despite his reservations, Podlubnyi survived this round of "sorting," although the OGPU soon after revealed that it knew of his true background).[72]

As Podlubnyi himself suggested, passportization was intended to identify "socially harmful and socially dangerous elements" and to facilitate their surreptitious marking and excision. The government established secret bureaus, the purpose of which was to register "the kulak, criminal and all other anti-bolshevik elements" and aid in their removal.[73] According to records of the militia, more than 6.6 million passports had been issued in Moscow and ten other major cities through April 1933. Yet another 265,000 people had been denied passports, among whom the militia had identified over 67,000 "kulaks in flight and dekulakized individuals"; nearly 22,000 individuals whose civic rights had been revoked [*lishentsy*]; and 34,800 individuals "not occupied in socially useful labor" – all of whom were subsequently subject to expulsion.[74] By 1934, passportization had encompassed more than twenty-seven million people in the Russian Federation alone. Of these, Soviet authorities had refused passports to nearly 400,000 as "criminal and socially alien elements."[75] Thus compiling a human archive correlated individual bodies within the larger politico-social body and facilitated the application of violence as technique by identifying those "elements" against whom violence (as either forcible deportation or outright execution) was to be directed.

The cataloguing project enforced a new and powerful correlation between individual images and the imagined collective ideal. Photographic representations were inextricably intertwined with sociological profiles as individuals were catalogued into the People-as-One.[76] Carry-

[72] Stepan Podlubnyi, *Tagebuch aus Moskau*, ed. Jochen Hellbeck (Munich, 1996), pp. 109, 115, 122, 127 (original Russian text from personal communication, Jochen Hellbeck, October 14, 1997); also Jochen Hellbeck, "Fashioning the Stalinist Soul," *Jahrbücher für Geschichte Osteuropas* 44, no. 3 (1996), pp. 351–5.

[73] Popov, "Pasportnaia sistema," no. 8, pp. 11–13; also "Pasportnaia sistema Sovetskogo soiuza," Nicolaevsky collection, series 227, box 296, folder 18 (I thank Amir Weiner for help in obtaining this document).

[74] Popov, "Pasportnaia sistema," no. 8, p. 14, n. 4.

[75] *Rapports secrets soviétiques, 1921–1991*, ed. Nicolas Werth and Gaël Moullec (Paris, 1994), pp. 45–7.

[76] On photography and the emergence of the human archive, see Allen Sekula, "The Body and the Archive," *October* 39 (1986): 3–64. See also Susanne Regener, "Ausgegrenzt: die optische Inventarisierung des Menschen im Polizeiwesen und in der Psychiatric," *Fotogeschichte* 10 (38) (1990): 23–38; David Green, "Veins of Resemblance: photography and eugenics," *Photography/Politics: Two* (1986): 9–21; and Daniel Arasse, *The Guillotine and the Terror*, pp. 140–1. The Nazis later relied on passport photographs to amass an inventory of Jewish faces (Freidländer, *Nazi Germany and the Jews*, p. 245).

ing over the Bertillon cataloguing system from the Imperial regime, Soviet dossiers on "criminal elements" and "enemies of the people" integrated photographs and autobiographical expostulations alongside sociological data keyed to the master class grid.[77] For some, this linkage extended to their very last hour and even after death. Execution lists in Leningrad for 1937–8 instructed executioners that, upon taking possession of their charges at the prison, they were to interrogate each of the condemned, and to check each against his or her photo card, and only then to shoot them.[78] For their human archive, the Gulag administration supplemented the Bertillon system of photographs with the fingerprint system devised by Galton: the identity of some dead detainees was confirmed through post-mortem fingerprints.[79]

The link between the particular and the universal, the intertwining of an individual self and the politico-social body, was not reserved solely for criminals. The attempt to correlate individual life trajectories with that of the Soviet politico-social body explains the format of the ubiquitous questionnaires the Soviet state required its citizens to fill out. Such forms asked for one's social and economic standing at significant moments in Soviet society's trajectory: prior to February 1917; prior to October 1917; before and after collectivization.[80] In October 1937, the Soviet state introduced photographs to its internal passports (with a second photograph retained for the police's shadow archive), thereby adding the individual's image to the sociological profiles contained in their internal passports.[81] Here the macro-description of a healthy and beautiful society (recall the justification for introduc-

---

[77] For samples of Soviet criminal dossiers with their photographs, see " 'Troika posstanovila: rasstreliat'," *Volia* 1994, no. 2–3: 21–79; for other examples, see *Rekviem* (Orel, 1995), pp. 55–60; Vitaly Shentalinsky, *Arrested Voices* (New York, 1996).

[78] *Leningradskii martirolog*, photograph 23; for the use of photographs among Gulag inmates, see Peter Maggs, *The Mandelstam and "Der Nister" Files* (Armonk, NY, 1996), p. 20, M-6, K-25.

[79] Maggs, *The Mandelstam and "Der Nister" Files*, pp. 38–40, M-10, M-16.

[80] These questionnaires were virtually ubiquitous and invariably inquired after one's social and political standing at specific moments in Soviet history. For Red Army questionnaires for defectors (1919), see RGVA, f. 100, op. 2, d. 78, ll. 159–60; also RGVA, f. 1389, op. 1, d. 124, l. 160; for questionnaires for captured Antonov insurgents (1921), see *Antonovshchina*, pp. 283–92; for the forms of the Bureaus on Cooperation with the GPU on "suspicious and counterrevolutionary elements" (1922), see "Khoroshii kommunist v to zhe vremia khoroshii chekist," *Vestnik staroi ploshchadi* 1996, no. 1: 115–19; for questionnaires for arrestees from Moscow in 1937–8, see *Volia*, nos. 2–3 (1994): 23; for forms required of Party members in the Red Army in 1939–40, see V. Zenzinov, *Vstrecha s Rossiei* (New York, 1944), pp. 570–1. For how such "mythic" events came to structure frameworks of meaning for Soviet citizens, see Amir Weiner, "The Making of a Dominant Myth," *Russian Review* 55, no. 4 (1996): 638–60.

[81] Popov, "Pasportnaia sistema," no. 8, p. 13.

ing passports) intersected with individual likenesses. Passports, criminal dossiers, and workbooks simultaneously portrayed individuals while constituting them within the idealized projection of the socialist People-as-One.

This cataloguing of individuals was central not only to situating individuals within the idealized Bolshevik image of society, but also to the deletion of those who failed to correspond to this image. While the exact timing of arrest and the precise charges filed, depended on particular conjunctures, the individuals targeted for arrest and elimination had been identified long before through the cataloguing process. This process had already begun with the 1921 filtration campaign, and continued throughout the 1920s and 1930s.[82]

In the USSR, as throughout Europe, the human archive came to play a major role in identifying the specific individuals against whom state violence was to be directed.[83] In 1927, Mikhail N. Pokrovskii had proclaimed that "the archives' role is particularly great as a kind of arsenal, from which one can take those weapons that one uses until the moment one comes to use weapons of iron and steel."[84] One archival official elaborated upon this point in 1931, declaring proudly that one of the archives' functions was to cooperate with Soviet repressive organs. This task became nearly their sole pursuit in the 1930s.[85]

How could archivists help the Soviet state? By compiling card indexes. In 1927, a secret decree from the archival administration ordered employees in the Central State Archive to maintain card-files on individuals identified in the holdings of the tsarist police. Two years later, the Northern bureau of the Party's history section, in collaboration with the local state archival department, combed through the collections of the regional tsarist gendarme agency and the holdings of the regional

[82] Examples are legion. For the extensive documentation on a former Antonov leader, sentenced to exile in 1930 and executed in 1937, see *Antonovshchina*, pp. 283–92; the two Cossack brothers mentioned above, whose father was executed while they successfully passed through the Civil War's filtration, were rearrested and executed in 1937, in part for their participation in the White Army ("Kazach'ia sem'ia Khripunovykh," pp. 74–5).

[83] Sekula, "Body and the Archive"; Foucault, *Discipline and Punish*, p. 281; and n. 76 above. For how the compilation of a human archive facilitated the Nazi applications of violence against Jews, Gypsies, "the asocial" and the hereditarily and mentally ill, see Aly and Roth, *Die restlose Erfassung*; Michael Burleigh and Wolfgang Wipperman, *The Racial State* (New York, 1991); Saul Friedländer, *Nazi Germany and the Jews*, vol. 1, ch. 6; and Weindling, *Health, Race and German Politics*, pp. 384–5, 526–30. Weindling notes that "these surveys were a precondition for extermination" (528).

[84] V. E. Korneev and O. N. Kopylova, "Arkhivist v totalitarnom obshchestve: bor'ba za 'chistotu' arkhivnykh kadrov," *Otechestvennye arkhivy* 1993, no. 5: 29–43, here at 29.

[85] T. I. Khorkhordina, *Istoriia otechestva i arkhivy: 1917–1980* (Moscow, 1994), pp. 176–9. I thank Jan Plamper for bringing this work to my attention.

anti-Soviet government from the Civil War. From lists of commendations, transfer orders, and pay scales in the archive, they drew up a card file of twenty-five thousand individuals.[86]

And, as state violence intensified in the 1930s, archival information was in even greater demand. From the mid-1930s archives contained special sections that were staffed exclusively by OGPU employees. But the wave of requests for information that followed Kirov's death in 1934 was so great that it swamped the OGPU workers, requiring them to work twelve to fourteen hour shifts, prompting the party to mobilize student communists and communist pensioners for work in the archives. By 1937, archivists were instructed to respond only to the NKVD, to which the archival system was totally subordinated in 1938.[87] By the late 1930s, thirty archivists in the Central State Archive and forty in the State Military Archive were charged with the sole task of compiling card catalogues on people identified in the files of White military and civil institutions. By 1938, they had produced a card-file with 105,000 names; an expanded search the next year identified a further 500,000 people.[88]

Nor was this information of an antiquarian nature. The NKVD circular ordering the work explained that such searches were necessary to identify "anti-Soviet elements" still living on Soviet territory. In response, the Central State Archive drew up a list of 34,990 "active enemies of the people" and turned it over to the NKVD "for operational realization." Archivists identified 108,694 enemies of the people in 1939. Due to frantic combing through the newly-acquired Baltic and Ukrainian archives, and in part also to the archivists at the Central State archive who over-fulfilled by 100,000 their quota of card-files, archivists identified a further 1,399,217 enemies in the following year.[89]

It was these preexisting card indexes and lists that served as the reservoir for arrests and executions upon demand from the Center. Local organs of the NKVD had files encompassing ten to fifteen percent of the total adult population, usually broken down into three categories of perniciousness. (Both the 1930 OGPU dekulakization directive and the 1937 NKVD order on "anti-Soviet elements" divided their target populations into two categories of "more" and "less harmful," with the more harmful slated for execution). When local officials received orders from the Center for arrests and executions, they simply worked off such lists.

[86] V. E. Korneev and O. N. Kopylova, "Arkhivy na sluzhbe totalitarnogo gosudarstva," *Otechestvennye arkhivy* 1992, no. 3: 13–24.

[87] Khorkhordina, *Istoriia otechestva i arkhivy*, pp. 177–8.

[88] Korneev and Kopyleva, "Arkhivy na sluzhbe," pp. 19–20.

[89] Korneev and Kopylova, "Arkhivy na sluzhbe," pp. 20–2.

If the quota exhausted the first list, they simply moved onto the second list, and then the third.[90]

For its campaign against anti-Soviet elements (as per NKVD order #00447), the most massive of the mass operations, the Soviet state relied upon its human archive. Two weeks before the operation commenced, local NKVD branches received an order "to register and classify all hostile and anti-Soviet elements according to their degree of activity and social danger," whom were then further sub-divided into two categories: those to be executed and those to be exiled.[91] State security organs then proceeded with this operation on the basis of the NKVD's card files. Only after these files had been exhausted did the NKVD resort to sweeps of market-places and the fabrication of counterrevolutionary organizations.[92]

The Soviet cataloguing venture was inextricably linked to the larger project of sculpting an aestheticized politico-social ideal. Violence-as-technique required a mapping of the politico-social body, to indicate what was to be preserved and what was to be eliminated; the cataloguing of society did precisely this. In doing so, it united the images of the individual (both visual and narrative) with that of the politico-social body. This linkage forged in a dossier often outlasted the actual individual. The Soviet regime retained its mountains of documentation on those it had excised from the politico-social body for decades after the individuals so documented had been executed.

This article has sketched a number of points. First, it has proposed that, while Bolshevism as ideology was critical for determining how state violence was to be applied, state violence did not originate with the Bolsheviks. In significant ways, the Bolsheviks expanded upon state practices developed in the late Imperial period and massively implemented in the First World War. Second, it has argued that the Soviet regime's application of state violence is better understood as a fundamentally aesthetic project to sculpt an idealized image of the politico-social body rather than as a narrowly understood medico-prophylactic pursuit. Third, this endeavor of sculpting society was essential to Soviet policy from the very first; the Great Terror of the 1930s was an extension and expansion of this aspiration, the conjuncture when the regime sought to act on long-standing goals to sculpt society's human as much as its raw material. Fourth, the regime's drive to order and classify its population was central to its larger endeavor of creating a beautiful and

[90] Zemskov, "Demografische aspekty," p. 7; also Uimanov, *Repressii*, 25, 27, 47; Solzhenitsyn, *Gulag Archipelago*, 1: 34–35; Khlevniuk, *Politbiuro*, p. 196.

[91] *Leningradskii martirolog*, pp. 38–48, esp. p. 39.

[92] Oleg Khlevniuk, , "Les mécanismes," p. 203.

pure society by enforcing criteria of excision as well as inclusion. While sanctioning mass violence, the Soviet regime never set the extermination of people as an objective in itself.

Further Reading: Stalinist State Violence

Paul M. Hagenloh, " 'Socially Harmful Elements' and the Great Terror," in Sheila Fitzpatrick, ed., *Stalinism: New Directions* (London, 2000).

Peter Holquist, " 'Conduct Merciless, Mass Terror': Decossackization on the Don, 1919," *Cahiers du Monde russe*, vol. 38, no. 1–2 (1997).

Galina Mikhailovna Ivanova, *Labor Camp Socialism: The Gulag in the Soviet Totalitarian System*, trans. Carol Flath (Armonk, NY, 2000).

Michael Jakobson, *Origins of the Gulag: The Soviet Prison Camp System, 1917–1934* (Lexington, 1993).

David R. Shearer, "Social Disorder, Mass Repression, and the NKVD during the 1930s," *Cahiers du Monde Russe*, vol. 42, no. 2-3-4 (2001).

Amir Weiner, ed., *Landscaping the Human Garden* (Stanford, 2003).

Part II   The Consequences of Stalinism

Resistance and Conformity

7

Everyday Stalinism: Ordinary Life in Extraordinary Times

Sheila Fitzpatrick

Excerpted from Sheila Fitzpatrick, *Everyday Stalinism: Ordinary Life in Extraordinary Times: Soviet Russia in the 1930s* (New York: Oxford University Press, 1999).

Editor's Introduction

Stalinism had devastating consequences for the Soviet population. Collectivization entailed the dispossession and deportation of millions of peasants, many of whom subsequently died of hunger, exposure, or disease.[1] Millions more starved to death in the 1932–3 famine caused by collectivization and state grain requisitions.[2] During the Great Terror in the late 1930s the Soviet secret police executed and incarcerated several million more victims.[3] After the Second World War, Stalin had entire national minorities deported from their homelands to Siberia or Central Asia.[4] While scholars disagree on the total number of deaths caused by Stalinism, there is no doubt that Stalin and his policies killed millions of

---

[1] V. P. Danilov, R. T. Manning, L. Viola, eds., *Tragediia Sovetskoi derevni: Kollektivizatsiia i raskulachivanie. Dokumenty i materialy v 5 tomakh, 1927–1939* (Moscow, 1999); Lynne Viola, "The Other Archipelago: Kulak Deportations to the North in 1930," *Slavic Review*, vol. 60, no. 4 (2001).

[2] Robert Conquest, *Harvest of Sorrow: Soviet Collectivization and the Terror-Famine* (London, 1986); M. Ellman, "A Note on the Number of 1933 Famine Victims," *Soviet Studies* 1991, no. 2.

[3] Robert Conquest, *The Great Terror: A Reassessment* (New York, 1990); in this volume, see Khlevnyuk. On the Gulag prison camp system, see Aleksandr I. Solzhenitsyn, *The Gulag Archipelago*, trans. Thomas P. Whitney and Harry Willetts, 3 vols. (New York, 1973–1978); Galina Mikhailovna Ivanova, *Labor Camp Socialism: The Gulag in the Soviet Totalitarian System*, trans. Carol Flath (Armonk, NY, 2000).

[4] A. M. Nekrich, *The Punished Peoples: The Deportation and Tragic Fate of Soviet Minorities at the End of the Second World War* (New York, 1978); in this volume, see Weiner.

people.[5] In addition to those directly shot, imprisoned, or starved, many other Soviet citizens suffered enormous deprivation and hardship under Stalinism.

How did the population react to Stalinist policies? Totalitarian theorists believed that the extreme brutality and terror of the Soviet system cowed people into complete subservience, leaving them atomized and unable to resist. But revisionists challenged this assumption and argued that Soviet citizens continued to think and act for themselves. Newly opened archives have now allowed scholars to confirm that Soviet people not only pursued their own interests, but that they actively or passively resisted Stalinist policies. Historians have shown that peasants fought back against collectivization, workers engaged in strikes, and Soviet citizens privately denounced Stalin and other Communist Party leaders.[6] Scholars have also demonstrated the multiple ways that people tried to operate within the Stalinist system, and to turn Soviet policies to their advantage.[7] Studies of resistance, then, represent an important new area of research.

Among those who have written on resistance to Stalinism is Sheila Fitzpatrick, the most eminent scholar in the field of Soviet history. For the past three decades she has conducted pathbreaking research on the social and cultural history of the Stalin era. In the following selection, Fitzpatrick describes the lives and attitudes of average citizens under the Stalinist regime. She portrays the despotism and upheavals of Stalinism as giving people a sense that their lives were unpredictable and precarious. While this unpredictability imparted a sense of fatalism, it also encouraged a certain amount of risk-taking to acquire material goods in this time of extreme shortage. Soviet citizens took risks both within the system, striving for promotions and perks, and outside the system, stealing food or bartering on the blackmarket.

---

[5] Stephen G. Wheatcroft, "New Demographic Evidence on Excess Collectivization Deaths," and S. Rosefielde, "New Demographic Evidence on Collectivization Deaths: A Rejoinder to Stephen Wheatcroft," *Slavic Review*, vol. 44, no. 3 (1985); Alec Nove, "How Many Victims in the 1930s," *Soviet Studies* 1990 no. 2; J. Arch Getty, Gabor T. Rittersporn, Viktor N. Zemskov, "Victims of the Soviet Penal System in the Pre-war Years: A First Approach on the Basis of Archival Evidence," *The American Historical Review*, vol. 98, no. 4 (1993).

[6] Jeffrey J. Rossman, "The Teikovo Cotton Workers' Strike of April 1932: Class, Gender and Identity Politics in Stalin's Russia," *The Russian Review*, vol. 56, no. 1 (1997); Lynne Viola, *Peasant Rebels Under Stalin: Collectivization and the Culture of Peasant Resistance* (New York, 1996); Sarah Davies, *Popular Opinion in Stalin's Russia: Terror, Propaganda and Dissent, 1934–1941* (New York, 1997).

[7] Sheila Fitzpatrick, *Stalin's Peasants: Resistance and Survival in the Russian Village after Collectivization* (New York, 1994); Golfo Alexopoulos, "Portrait of a Con Artist as a Soviet Man," *Slavic Review*, vol. 57, no. 4 (1998); A. K. Sokolov, ed., *Obshchestvo i vlast': 1930-e gody: Povestvovanie v dokumentakh* (Moscow, 1998); N. B. Lebina, *Povsednevnaia zhizn' sovetskogo goroda, 1920/1930 gody* (St. Petersburg, 1999).

In public, the Soviet population conformed to official laws and doctrine, and even mouthed slogans of support for Stalin and socialism. But this outward conformity did not mean people respected Soviet officials and leaders. As Fitzpatrick argues, most people remained skeptical of official proclamations and passively antagonistic toward Communist Party authorities. In conversations and anonymous letters, people expressed their resentment of Party power and privileges – resentments exacerbated by the desperate shortages of food, clothing, and housing that characterized the Stalin era. Average Soviet citizens complained that Party officials lived well while everyone else went hungry, and thus expressed an "us-versus-them" mentality. Contrary to Soviet propaganda, then, much of the population did not stand united behind Stalin and the Communist Party.

On the other hand, there were some people who actively or tacitly supported the Stalinist system. Fitzpatrick writes that active support came primarily from those who benefited from the system, including newly promoted Party officials and Stakhanovites (hero workers).[8] Some young people also identified with the Soviet cause and worked hard to help build socialism. Fitzpatrick notes that the Soviet government was associated with progress in the minds of most citizens, especially young enthusiasts but even those opposed to the Soviet regime. Moreover, the Stalinist state was virtually the sole provider of goods and services within the system, and as such people came to depend on it for food, clothing, housing, jobs, health care, and pensions. Soviet citizens who wished to receive these benefits adopted a posture of supplication, not resistance.

In most cases, then, resistance to Stalinism remained passive. Average Soviet citizens resented the Party elite and complained about food shortages, but they did not rise up against the Stalinist regime. Confronting the fierce repression and economic hardship of the Soviet system, people sought to get by as best they could. This meant outward conformity and even supplication to Soviet authorities in order to receive benefits of the expanding Soviet welfare state. It also required using personal connections and illegal means to obtain the food and clothing necessary to survive. As Fitzpatrick concludes, Soviet Man (Homo Sovieticus) assumed many different guises, from operator to conformist, but above all he was a survivor.

---

[8] On Stakhanovites, see Lewis Siegelbaum, Stakhanovism and the Politics of Productivity in the Soviet Union, 1935–1941 (New York, 1988).

Everyday Stalinism: Ordinary Life in Extraordinary Times

Sheila Fitzpatrick

A popular joke of the 1920s and 1930s concerns a group of rabbits that appear at the Soviet–Polish frontier, applying for admission to Poland. When asked why they wish to leave, they reply: "The GPU has given orders to arrest every camel in the Soviet Union." "But you are not camels!" "Just try telling that to the GPU."[1] This is one of many rueful jokes of the period that emphasize the arbitrariness of terror. But terror was not the only thing that was arbitrary in Stalin's Russia. Rewards – for example, those that fell in the laps of celebrity Stakhanovites and other famous ordinary people – were also arbitrary. The whole bureaucracy acted in a arbitrary manner, minimally guided by law and only sometimes manipulable via personal connections. Political leaders made abrupt switches in state policy, often discarding without explanation a course that had been ruthlessly pursued for years and substituting something completely different, even contradictory. Every time this happened, some arbitrarily chosen scapegoats were punished for overzealousness in carrying out the old policy.

These were circumstances that encouraged fatalism and passivity in the population, instilling a sense that the individual was not and could not be in control of his own fate. These attitudes were often evident in Harvard Project (HP) interviews, notably with respect to questions about how Soviet citizens could protect themselves or advance their interests in a variety of hypothetical situations. "They could do nothing" was the favorite response – even though this was often contradicted when, under further questioning, the respondents suggested things the hypothetical citizen *could* do.[2] In the real world, of course, Soviet citizens were by no means totally without strategies of self-protection, however rooted their sense of dependency and lack of agency. Indeed, to assure the authorities of one's own powerlessness – as the Harvard Project respondents were doing to their American interviewers – was exactly such a strategy.

---

[1] Paraphrased from W. H. Chamberlin, "The 'Anecdote': Unrationed Soviet Humor," *Russian Review* 16: 1 (1957), 31. Another version of the joke is in Iurii Borev, *Istoriia gosudarstva sovetskogo v predaniiakh i anekdotakh* (Moscow, 1995), 40.

[2] Janos Kornai, *Economics of Shortage* (Amsterdam, 1980), 567; idem, *The Socialist System: The Political Economy of Communism* (Princeton, 1992), 56; HP, #357 (XIX), 6; #394 (XX), 11; #399 (XX), 12.

"I feel I've lived someone else's life," said one woman interviewed in the post-Soviet period, referring to the disruptions that propelled her out of the village at the time of collectivization. This was part of the complex of feelings that led Harvard Project respondents to say that life in the Soviet Union in the 1930s was not "normal," that one could not "make a normal life." Respondents never accepted individual or collective responsibility for this; the situation was squarely blamed on "them," on the government, on all those external forces that put one's own life out of one's control. Abnormality had many aspects, including unpredictability, dislocation, and state violence against citizens, but one motif was constant: it was an abnormal life because of the privations and hardships. Some respondents even used the phrase "living normally" to mean living a comfortable, privileged life – the life to which everyone was entitled, not the life that most people had. "Normal life" was an ideal, not a statistical concept.[3]

The sense of unpredictability was heightened by the sharp breaks, relocations, and deracinations that were part of Soviet lives. The pattern started with the First World War and Civil War, when huge numbers of people were uprooted geographically and socially, losing touch with family and friends, working in occupations different from the ones that had seemed marked out for them. The Revolution opened doors for advancement to some people, closed them for others. Then, at the end of the 1920s, came the new upheavals of Stalin's revolution, shattering routines and expectations once again. Peasants stigmatized as kulaks were deported or ran away to the cities, often with little sense of what they wanted out of their new lives. Their sense of dislocation is conveyed in the response of one Harvard Project interviewee, son of a kulak expropriated in 1930, who had difficulty answering a question about what his father had wanted him to be. "When we lived on the land he wanted me to become a peasant," he said finally. "When we were chased from the land we lost all orientation of what we wanted to become. *I was left up to my fate.*"[4]

Life could seem just as unpredictable to those who were beneficiaries of Soviet opportunities. All those dazzling success stories (related in Chapter 3 of the original publication) of Cinderella-like ascents from the

[3] Barbara Alpern Engel and Anastasia Posadskaya-Vanderbeck, *A Revolution of their Own: Voices of Women in Soviet History* (Boulder, Co., 1997), 46; HP, #511 (XXVI), 6; #420 (XXI), 10; #4 (1), 36. Note that the complaint about being deprived of the possibility of living "normally" was heard once again in the 1980s when it was linked to the perception that the Soviet Union was not a "civilized" country. In its *perestroika* incarnation, the substance of the complaint was that educated professionals were unable to secure a Western lifestyle and living standards.

[4] HP #92 (VU), 39 (my emphasis).

humblest position to the heights express a sense of astonishment as well as satisfaction and self-congratulation. In addition, rising to the heights had its own risks. It could happen that the same person experienced both a sharp ascent and a sudden fall, as was the case with a young man selected by the Komsomol for training as an aviator, whose good fortune was abruptly cut short when his father was arrested and the family exiled. There was a recognized trade-off between the benefits of a career and its disadvantages: as one Harvard respondent put it, "Veterinary work in general in the Soviet Union is good. A veterinarian has the possibility of getting products [i.e., food]. On the other hand it is like work of every employee and specialist. It is dangerous. There is planning; the plan is high, and a man can be brought to court at any moment." Some people refused to accept promotion because of the greater responsibilities and dangers. "To raise one's position means more responsibility. The greater the responsibility, the nearer the unmasking. To sit at the bottom was safer."[5]

In one of the few peasant diaries we have from the Stalin era, the writer's main subject was the weather, which in his world was the primary arbitrary determinant of good and bad fortune; the government was virtually ignored. Urban diarists, by contrast, carefully recorded the government's major initiatives, presumably for the same reason the peasant diarist noted changes in the weather. These Stalin-era diaries are particularly interesting for the amount of time and thought their writers gave to public affairs, especially if one defines that concept broadly to include the economy and the availability or otherwise of consumer goods. Private life and personal emotions are of course present in the diaries, but they seem confined and crowded by public events and pressures, always liable to be thrust from center stage by some external crisis.[6]

Stepan Podlubnyi wanted to find friends, but they should be friends who could help his project of becoming a good Soviet citizen, free of the taint of his kulak past. Liubov Shaporina, former wife of the composer Iurii Shaporin, wrote obsessively of the loss of her young daughter, but conflated that loss and the destruction of her personal happiness with the intelligentsia's and Russia's sufferings at the hands of state during the Great Purges. In Arkadii Mankov's diary, public affairs, viewed with a deeply jaundiced eye, were the main topics, and even when he men-

---

[5] L. Sigel'baum [Siegelbaum] and A. Sokolov, eds., "1930-e gody: Obshchestvo i vlast'. Povestvovanie v dokumentakh," ms., 199; HP #531. (XXVII), 14 and 28–9; Harvard Project respondent, quoted H. Kent Geiger, *The Family in Soviet Russia* (Cambridge, Mass., 1968), 172.

[6] The peasant diarist is Fyodor Shirnov in *Intimacy and Terror: Soviet Diaries of the 1930s,* ed. Veronique Garros, Natalia Korenevskaya, and Thomas Lahusen (New York, 1995).

tioned family matters, discussion of the state often intruded. For Galina Shtange, an activist in the wives' movement, a major theme for her diary reflections was the conflict of family obligations and public ones. For the schoolgirl Nina Kosterina, a dedicated chronicler of first love and friendship in the early part of her diary, private life became hopelessly compromised and entangled with public issues after the arrest of her father as an "enemy of the people."[7]

Little wonder that Russians looking back on their lives in the Stalin period often use public events, not private ones, as markers and framing devices. When an American scholar interviewed old Russian peasant women about their lives at the beginning of the 1990s, his interviews "were designed to capture their experiences with childbirth and child care, on the assumption that the birth and nurture of children are defining events of a woman's life." He found, however, that public events dominated both the lives and the women's way of remembering them. "The life of virtually every woman I interviewed was . . . shaped more powerfully by the events of the early 1930s. Nearly every woman had a broken life, with the break dating to that time (although for some the war played an even bigger role). Their children were important to them, but their identity and the places they ended up in life were defined much more by the upheavals of the 1930s."[8]

When respondents in the Harvard Project were asked how to get ahead in Soviet society, some said education and proletarian origins, some said time-serving and informing, many said connections, and a few said luck.[9] Luck was indeed extremely important. For this reason, Stalinist citizens, although generally passive, were also intermittent risk-takers – people who bought lottery tickets and played the potentially dangerous game of denouncing their bosses; people who were liable to tell anti-Soviet jokes, and who sometimes, when drunk, made obscene gestures at sacred images in public places. They were by no means as cautious as one might expect of persons living under a highly repressive regime, perhaps because they had no confidence that caution would ensure survival.

---

[7] Jochen Hellbeck, ed., *Tagebuch aus Moskau 1931–1939* (Munich, 1996); diaries of Shrange, and Shaporina in *Intimacy and Terror*; A. G. Man'kov, "Iz dnevnika riadovogo cheloveka (1933–1934 gg.)," *Zvezda*, 1994 no. 5, and "Iz dnevnika 1938–1941 gg.," ibid., 1995 no. 11; Nina Kosterina, *Dnevnik Niny Kosterinoi* (Moscow, 1964).

[8] David L. Ransel, "Summer Nurseries under the Soviets as Device for Mobilizing Peasant Women and Diminishing Infant Mortality," paper delivered to First Midwest Russian History Workshop, Ann Arbor, March 1991, and private communications to the author, 14 and 23 January 1998. See also responses in Engel, *Revolution*, using revolution, collectivization, and war as markers: e.g. 83, 114, 128–9, 173.

[9] See, for example, HP #3 (1), II; #4 (1), 9; #8 (1), 9.

Risk-taking was sometimes a necessity for effective functioning. Industrial managers, for example, could not get the raw materials, spare parts, and labor they needed without breaking rules and taking risks, despite the ever-present possibility that they would be punished. The economic historian Joseph Berliner pointed out that in the Soviet Union "the successful manager, the one who climbs swiftly to the top and makes a brilliant career, is the one who is willing to hazard arrest and prison sentence. There is a selective process at work which raises the risktaker to the top, and causes the timid to fall by the wayside."[10]

Risk-taking (as opposed to prudent calculation) was held in high popular esteem. Even the literary intelligentsia, one of the most intimidated and risk-averse groups in Soviet society, made heroes of its risktakers as well as its martyrs. Writers like Mikhail Bulgakov who sailed right up to (or beyond) the limits of the permissible in their writings were admired for doing so; journal editors and theater directors won prestige with their peers, as well as risking punishment, when they tried to publish or stage such works.

The gambling mentality, it should be noted, was a direct antithesis of the rational planning mentality that the regime in principle approved and tried to inculcate in its citizens. In official discourse, there was nothing more glorious than the Five-Year Plan and the regularity and predictability suggested by the phrase "according to the plan." Spontaneity or happenstance, the opposite of predictability, was something that had to be overcome; accident (in the sense of unpredicted occurrence) was not only deplorable but epistemologically trivial; the term "accidental elements" was used for people who had no right to be there, or simply no rights. Yet all this stood in a dialectical relationship to the mentality of most Soviet citizens, who looked to "spontaneity" (an agentless concept in Russian) to deliver them when they were headed for trouble with the regime's plans, and knew that what "planned distribution" of goods really meant was shortages.[11]

A propensity for occasional or even regular risk-taking did not mean that people were not frightened of the regime. Of course they were frightened given the regime's proven willingness to punish, the strength of its punitive arm, its long and vengeful memory, and the unpredictability of its outbursts. Hence, the normal posture of a Soviet citizen was passive conformity and outward obedience. This did not mean, however, that Soviet citizens necessarily had a high respect for authority. On the contrary, a degree of skepticism, even a refusal to take the

[10] Joseph Berliner, "Blat is Higher than Stalin," *Problems of Communism* 3:1 (1954), 31.
[11] The Russian terms are *po planu, planomernost', planovoe nachalo, planovoe raspredelenie; stikhiinost'* (spontaneity) and *sluchainost'* (accident), both antonyms of *zakonomernost'; sluchainye elementy.*

regime's most serious pronouncements fully seriously, was the norm. Of all the Soviet citizen's repertoire of everyday resistance, the popular phrase "This too will pass," said with a shrug in response to some new policy initiative from above, was one of the most devastating from the regime's standpoint. Although the literature of socialist realism did its best to provide exemplars of purposeful, dedicated, effective leadership, other images of authority proved at least as durable.[12]

In two of the most widely read and best-loved literary classics of the prewar Stalin period, Ilf and Petrov's *Twelve Chairs* and *The Golden Calf*, the hero is a confidence man whose stock in trade is his ability to out-talk and out-think slow-witted local officials. In the film *Lieutenant Kizhe* (1934), now best remembered for its score by Prokofiev, the authorities (from the time of Emperor Paul) are so stupid that they appoint a man to the Guards, disgrace him and sentence him to Siberia, pardon him, and promote him once again to the rank of general – all without notic-ing that he never existed. In the great popular literary success of the Second World War, Aleksandr Tvardovskii's *Vasilii Terkin*, the eponymous protagonist is an anti-hero who possesses all the foraging and survival skills needed by *Homo Sovieticus* and has the same good-humored con-tempt for authority as Jaroslav Hasek's *Good Soldier Schweik*.[13]

The antithesis of "us" and "them" was basic to Soviet subaltern men-tality in the 1930s. "They" were the people who ran things, the people at the top, the ones with power and privilege. "We" were the ones at the bottom, little people without power or privilege whom "they" pushed around, exploited, deceived, and betrayed. Of course, the dividing line shifted according to the speaker's own position. Just as no Soviet pro-fessional of the Brezhnev period ever admitted to being a "bureau-crat,"[14] so no Soviet citizen of the 1930s was likely to identify himself as one of "them," either with respect to power or privilege. "They" – the ones with *real* power and privilege – always existed in a higher sphere than the speaker.[15]

For one kolkhoznik, writing to express his views on the Constitution, there were two classes in society: "[white-collar] employees and the

---

[12] "This too will pass" = *Proidet*. On the Soviet positive hero, see Katerina Clark, *The Soviet Novel: History as Ritual* (Chicago, 1985), 167–71 and passim.

[13] I. Il'f and L. Petrov, *Dvenadtsat' stul'ev* (1918) and *Zolotoi telenok* (1930–31); Harlow Robinson, *Sergei Prokofiev* (New York, 1988), 277; (*Kizhe*); Aleksandr Tvardovskii, *Vasilii Terkin* (1941–45). Note also the equally popular samizdat sequel of the post-Stalin period, *Terkin na tom svete* (1954–63) [in Aleksandr Tvardovskii, *Vasilii Terkin* (Moscow, 1995)] was an explicit mockery of Soviet bureaucracy.

[14] See Jerry F. Hough, *Democratization and Revolution in the USSR, 1985–1991* (Washington, D.C., 1997), 52.

[15] For an interesting discussion, see Sarah Davies, " 'Us Against Them': Social Identities in Soviet Russia, 1934–41," *Russian Review* 56:1 (1997).

workers are one class, and the second class is kolkhozniks [who] bear all the burdens, all the hard work and all the taxes, and the employees have no [burden], as the ruling class." But workers who addressed this topic always saw their own class as the one that was exploited. "Comrade Zhdanov, at all the meetings they talk about the classless society, but in fact it isn't like this, you have a handful of people who live and forget about Communism. It is time to stop feeding [senior officials], it is time to close the 'Torgsins,'" wrote one aggrieved group anonymously. Administrators "live in the best conditions and live at the expense of the labour of the working class," complained another worker, noting that "new classes have developed here, with the only difference being that they are not called classes."[16]

For many Soviet citizens, it seems, privilege and political power became so closely linked in the 1930s that there was little room for other kinds of class hostilities. Resentment of privilege was very strong, but it seems to have been directed almost solely against the privileges of office-holders, that is, against the state and the Communist Party, not against the privileges of the intelligentsia. When Harvard Project interviewers, looking for data on class antagonisms within the society, asked which of the basic social groups (intelligentsia, employees, workers, peasants) received "less than they deserved," they received a remarkable response – in effect, ironically, a rousing endorsement for Stalin's claim that class antagonism had been eliminated in the Soviet Union. *All* social classes, even the intelligentsia, were considered to receive "less than they deserved" – by a majority of respondents of all classes, although admittedly only about half the working-class and peasant respondents had this opinion of the intelligentsia. In addition, many respondents hastened to remind the interviewers that there was another relevant group that had been omitted from the question, namely "party people": they were the ones who got *more* than they deserved.[17]

This tenderness toward the intelligentsia on the part of workers and peasants is surprising, since anti-intelligentsia feeling had apparently run strong in the working class in the revolution and throughout the 1920s, when "bourgeois specialists" were frequently attacked as survivors of the Tsarist privileged classes who had managed to hang on to their privileges despite the Revolution. During the 1928 Shakhty trial, workers not only accepted the state prosecutor's view that the engineers

---

[16] GARF, f. 3316, op. 40, d. 14, 1. 80 (1936); TsGAIPD f. 24, op. 2v, d. 1518, 1. 32 (letter signed "Workers of the Kirov plant," 1935); worker's comment (1934), quoted in Sarah Davies, *Popular Opinion in Stalin's Russia: Terror, Propaganda and Dissent, 1934–1941* (Cambridge, 1997), 139.

[17] Alex Inkeles, *The Soviet Citizen: Daily Life in a Totalitarian Society* (New York, 1968), 300–1.

charged were guilty of sabotage and treason, but even tended to go further ("Ripping their heads off would be soft treatment"; "We must shoot all of them or else we'll have no peace."[18]).

If these attitudes went into remission in the 1930s, this may have been because the regime's "war against the nation," as Adam Ulam has called it, focused popular anger exclusively on the party and its leaders, or it may have been a response to the fact that the intelligentsia had been substantially renewed through state-sponsored and other upward mobility from the lower classes since 1928.[19] It should also be noted, however, that the Harvard Project respondents probably understood the "less than they deserved" question as an inquiry about victimization rather than about privilege. The notion of collective victimization was much favored by Soviet citizens, and they were not exclusionary in their application of it. There was more satisfaction in pointing out that virtually everyone suffered than in quibbling about degrees.

So far, I have been describing popular attitudes to the regime that fall mainly in the range between passive acceptance and cautious hostility. Lack of personal security, suppression of religion, the emergence of a new privileged class, and police surveillance and terror no doubt contributed to this broadly based popular criticism of the regime in the 1930s. But the primary cause of it was surely economic: people were living badly, worse than they had done ten or twenty years earlier. "We were better off before" (during NEP, under the Tsars) was probably the most frequently reported of all critical comments in the NKVD's summaries of popular opinion. Under such circumstances, it would have been extraordinary if people had not blamed the government, all the more in that the privation ordinary citizens experienced was so clearly related to government policies like collectivization and crash industrialization.

Despite its promises of future abundance and massive propaganda of its current achievements, the Stalinist regime did little to improve the life of its people in the 1930s. Judging by the NKVD's soundings of public opinion, a problematic source but the only one available to us, the Stalinist regime was relatively though not desperately unpopular in Russian towns. (In Russian villages, especially in the first half of the 1930s, its unpopularity was much greater.) Overall, as the NKVD regularly reported and official statements repeated, the ordinary "little man" in Soviet towns, who thought only of his own and his family's welfare,

[18] Quoted in Matthew E. Lenoe, "Soviet Mass Journalism and the Transformation of Soviet Newspapers, 1926–1932," (Ph.D. diss., University of Chicago, 1997), 313.

[19] Adam B. Ulam, *Stalin* (New York, 1973) (ch. 8: "The War against the Nation"). On renewal of elites, see Sheila Fitzpatrick, *Education and Social Mobility in the Soviet Union, 1921–1934* (Cambridge, 1979), ch. 9.

was "dissatisfied with Soviet power," though in a somewhat fatalistic and passive manner.[20] The post-NEP situation was compared unfavorably with NEP, and Stalin – despite the officially fostered Stalin cult – was compared unfavorably with Lenin, sometimes because he was more repressive but more often because he let the people go hungry.

This is not to say that Stalin's regime was without support from its citizens. Active support came from the young, the privileged, office-holders and party members, beneficiaries of affirmative action policies, and favored groups like Stakhanovites. Of these, the young are perhaps the most interesting category. Less inclined than their elders to react to economic hardship, urban youth, or at least an impressive proportion of that group, as well as many young peasants with some schooling, seem to have assimilated Soviet values, associating them with a rejection of all that was boring, corrupt, unprincipled, old, and routine, and identi-fied, often passionately and enthusiastically, with Soviet ideals. They were ready to go adventuring in the Soviet cause: they grew up wanting to go on polar expeditions and volunteer to build Komsomolsk in the Far East. This was the cohort that, as Solzhenitsyn put it, had grown up under Soviet power and regarded the revolution as "ours." Even young people who had experienced stigmatization on the grounds of their social origin often shared this "Soviet" orientation of their more fortu-nate peers. "I didn't join the party, but I was a Communist at heart," said a teacher, who suffered much in the 1930s for being a priest's daugh-ter, in a recent interview.[21]

The attitudes of the majority of urban citizens who were not active supporters of the regime are much harder to get at than those of the activists and youthful enthusiasts. The working class, to which the regime had looked for support in the 1920s, had changed so much as a result of peasant influx and the upward mobility of "old" workers that both its coherence as a class and the workers' sense of a special con-nection with the regime must be called into question. A number of labor historians see the dominant motif of the 1930s as state exploitation and worker resistance. It is likely, nevertheless, that many workers retained a residual feeling of connection with the Soviet cause, especially in cities with a strong revolutionary tradition like Leningrad, and that this con-stituted passive support for the regime.[22]

---

[20] Although passivity was the rule, there were exceptions: see Jeffrey J. Rossman, "The Teikovo Cotton Workers' Strike of April 1932: Class, Gender and Identity Politics in Stalin's Russia," *Russian Review* 56:1 (1997).

[21] Aleksandr I. Solzhenitsyn, *The Gulag Archipelago*, trans. Thomas P. Whitney (New York, 1974), 160; Geiger, *Family*, 300; Engel, *Revolution*, 97.

[22] On labor in the 1930s, see Lewis Siegelbaum and Ronald Grigor Suny, eds., *Making Workers Soviet: Power, Class, and Identity* (Ithaca, 1994), and the excellent summary of

It has recently been argued that it makes no more sense to ask whether Soviet citizens did or did not accept the Soviet worldview than to ask whether medieval people accepted the Christian worldview: there was simply no other available.[23] The analogy has obvious weaknesses since in the Soviet case everyone over thirty in 1937 could perfectly well remember a pre-Soviet world, and in the census of that year more than half the population identified themselves as religious believers, thus rejecting a basic tenet of the Soviet worldview. Nevertheless, the argument is useful in reminding us that most people most of the time do accept their governments, and the chances are that the Russian urban population in the 1930s was no exception.[24]

In the first place, the Soviet government had positioned itself as the repository of national sentiment and patriotism; its nation-building and national-strengthening projects could appeal even to citizens who complained about shortages and resented the privileges of the office-holding elite. In addition, in the course of the 1930s the Russian element in Soviet patriotism came increasingly to the fore, with the return of Russian history to the school curriculum, of uniforms and insignia for the Soviet Army that resembled those of the former Russian Imperial Army, and so on.[25] This was likely to raise passive-approval rates as far as the Russian population was concerned, though it may have had other consequences in the non-Russian republics.

In the second place, this was a regime that had apparently successfully associated itself with progress in the minds of many of its citizens. If the Soviet worldview was not literally the only one available to Russians in the 1930s, it was the only available worldview linked to modernity. Whether or not the Soviet regime had broad legitimacy with the population, its modernizing (civilizing) mission appears to have done so. As far as we can tell, most people accepted the dichotomy of "backwardness" and "culture" and the proposition that the regime was

the current state of knowledge in Ronald Grigor Suny, *The Soviet Experiment* (New York, 1998), 240–49. For the exploitation position, see Donald Filtzer, *Soviet Workers and Stalinist Industrialization: The Formation of Modern Soviet Production Relations, 1928–1941* (Armonk, N.Y., 1986), 8–9; on resistance, see Rossman, "Teikovo."

[23] Jochen Hellbeck, "Fashioning the Stalinist Soul: The Diary of Stepan Podliubnyi (1931–1939)," *Jahrbucher fur Geschichte Osteuropas*, Bd. 44, Heft 3 (1996), 365; see also Stephen Kotkin, *Magnetic Mountain: Stalinism as a Civilization* (Berkeley, 1995), 225–30.

[24] The rural population is another matter for, as I argued in *Stalin's Peasants: Resistance and Survival in the Russian Village after Collectivization* (New York, 1994), the trauma of collectivization left the peasantry angry and alienated throughout the decade. For census data, see Iu. A. Poliakov, et al., "Polveka molchaniia (Vsesoiuznaia perepis' naseleniia 1937 g.)," *Sotsiologicheskie issledovaniia*, 1990 no. 7, 65–6.

[25] See ch. 4 [of the original publication], and N. S. Timasheff, *The Great Retreat: The Growth and Decline of Communism in Russia* (New York, 1946).

helping the population to become less backward and more cultured that lay at the heart of the Soviet message. They may personally have cherished some aspects of their own backwardness (e.g., getting drunk and beating their wives), but this was quite compatible with accepting that drunkenness and wife-beating were bad and signs of an uncultured, undeveloped human being. It could even be that the same person who grumbled one day about the disappearance of fish from the market was capable the next day of telling his neighbor that grumbling about shortages was a sign of backwardness and lack of political development.

In the third place, the Soviet state was becoming a welfare state, however incomplete and spasmodic its delivery of benefits in the 1930s. The state was the monopoly distributor of goods and services, which meant that allocation – the power to decide who got what – was one of its most important functions. As Janos Kornai puts it, in Soviet-type systems the population is under the "paternalistic tutelage" and care of the party and state. "The bureaucracy stands in *loco parentis*," he writes, "all other strata, groups, or individuals in society are children, wards whose minds must be made up for them by their adult guardians." The citizen's natural posture toward a state that controls distribution of goods and benefits is one of supplication, not resistance. It may also be one of passive dependence; indeed Soviet officials frequently complained about the "dependent" habits of *Homo Sovieticus*, his lack of initiative and his stubborn expectation that the state would and should provide.[26]

The Soviet state, with which citizens' everyday lives were so entangled, was a peculiar hybrid. On the one hand, it remained revolutionary, committed to changing the world and shaking up the lives of its citizens, and retaining all the violence, intolerance, and suspicion that pertain to those aims. On the other hand, it was moving toward the welfare-state paternalism that would characterize Soviet-type systems in the postwar period, and was already perceived by its citizens in these terms. These two facets of the state seem very different, but they had important elements in common. First, both the revolutionary and the paternalist states disdained law and bureaucratic legalism, preferring voluntarist solutions in the first case and personalistic ones in the second. Second, both had a very strong sense of the responsibilities of leadership. In revolutionary terminology, this was the vanguard concept. In the paternalist state, the vanguard concept became, in effect, "Father knows best."

---

[26] Kornai, *Socialist System*, 315, 56. On the allocative function of the state, see Katherine Verdery, *National Ideology under Socialism: Identity and Cultural Politics in Ceausescu's Romania* (Berkeley, 1991), 74–83. "Dependent" = *izhdivencheskii*.

If we consider what models or metaphors of the Soviet state might help us understand the practices of *Homo Sovieticus*, several possibilities present themselves. In the first place, Soviet society may be conceptualized as a prison or a conscript army. This catches the elements of regimentation, strict discipline, and confinement within a closed institution with its own strict codes of behavior, often bewildering to outsiders. The behavior of prisoners and conscripts reflects their fear of punishment, which may be incurred by failing to follow orders or random mischance. A sharp dividing line separates guards and officers in such institutions from inmates and recruits: these are "us" and "them" situations. Bullying by guards/officers produces resentment, though it is also seen as part of the natural order of things. There are informers among the inmates, but "ratting" to the authorities on other inmates is nevertheless strongly condemned in the inmate community. Desertion/attempting to escape is severely punished. In the case of the army, patriotism and the spirit of patriotic duty are strongly inculcated.

Another way of conceptualizing Soviet society is as a school of the strict type, probably a boarding school. The school is also a closed institution with its own conventions and discipline. School spirit, the local form of patriotism, is inculcated. A social gulf separates teachers and pupils; tattling to the teachers is prevalent, but disapproved of in the pupil community. Teachers often speak in homilies, recommending virtues such as cleanliness, quietness, politeness, and respect for elders and school property that pupils may or may not inwardly accept but in any case regard as suitable only for the teacher-dominated public sphere, not for private intercourse with fellow pupils. Many activities in the school that are described as voluntary are in fact compulsory, and in general pupils often observe and privately ridicule the hypocrisy of the school's public discourse and the divergence from it of the teachers' conduct.

There is, however, an important difference between schools and other closed institutions – schools have the function of education. The school is a civilizing institution: its raison d'être is to impart the learning and behavioral skills appropriate to the adult (cultured) society that the children will eventually have to join. Most pupils accept the premise that, however unpleasant the educational process may be, it is ultimately for their own good. This model undoubtedly comes closest to the Soviet regime's self-conception as an enlightened vanguard carrying out a civilizing mission. Education was one of the regime's core values; school – as in the epithet "school for socialism," applied to a variety of Soviet institutions from the trade unions to the Red Army – was a key metaphor.

Finally, there is another less exalted model of the Soviet state that may help illuminate Soviet everyday practices: the soup kitchen or the relief agency. Soviet citizens were masters of self-representation as the deserving poor; they regarded it as the state's obligation to provide them with food, clothing, and shelter. Very likely, being deserving poor, they also feel an obligation to work, but the relationship of work to welfare is not seen as reciprocal. The whole range of supplicatory and dependent behaviors characteristic of Soviet citizens outlined above fits the soup kitchen model better than any of the others. The client of a soup kitchen does not feel that he or she is involved in a self-improvement project, in contrast to the school pupil, nor has he the strong fear of punishment and sense of loss of freedom characteristic of prisoners and army recruits. He may or may not feel grateful to the organizers of the soup kitchen, although periodically he is likely to reproach them for not providing enough soup or saving the best meals for favorite clients. But basically he sees the soup kitchen just as a source of goods he needs, and judges it primarily by the quantity and quality of the goods and the convenience of obtaining them.

This book has described a wide range of practices of everyday life in Stalin's Russia: "getting" goods legally and illegally, using patrons and connections, counting living space in square meters, quarreling in communal apartments, "free" marriage, petitioning, denouncing, informing, complaining about officials, complaining about privilege, enjoying privilege, studying, volunteering, moving up, tumbling down, confusing the future and the present, mutual protection, self-criticism, scapegoating, purging, bullying subordinates, deferring to officials, lying about social origin, unmasking enemies, hunting spies, and many others. It was a life in which outward conformity to ideology and ritual mattered, but personal ties mattered even more. It was a life of random disasters and of manifold daily irritations and inconveniences, from the hours wasted in queues and lack of privacy in communal apartments to the endless bureaucratic rudeness and red tape and the abolition, in the cause of productivity and atheism, of a common day of rest. There were fearful things that affected Soviet life and visions that uplifted it, but mostly it was a hard grind, full of shortages and discomfort. *Homo Sovieticus* was a string-puller, an operator, a time-server, a freeloader, a mouther of slogans, and much more. But above all, he was a survivor.

Furthering Reading: Resistance and Conformity under Stalin

Golfo Alexopoulos, *Stalin's Outcasts: Aliens, Citizens, and the Soviet State, 1926–1936* (Ithaca, 2002).

Sarah Davies, *Popular Opinion in Stalin's Russia: Terror, Propaganda and Dissent, 1934–1941* (New York, 1997).

Sheila Fitzpatrick, *Stalin's Peasants: Resistance and Survival in the Russian Village after Collectivization* (New York, 1994).

Lesley A. Rimmel, "*Svodki* and Popular Opinion in Stalinist Leningrad," *Cahiers du Monde russe*, vol. 40 (1999).

Jeffrey J. Rossman, "The Teikovo Cotton Workers' Strike of April 1932: Class, Gender and Identity Politics in Stalin's Russia," *The Russian Review*, vol. 56, no. 1 (1997).

Lewis Siegelbaum and Andrei Sokolov, *Stalinism as a Way of Life: A Narrative in Documents* (New Haven, 2000).

Lynne Viola, *Peasant Rebels Under Stalin: Collectivization and the Culture of Peasant Resistance* (New York, 1996).

Lynne Viola, ed., *Contending with Stalinism: Soviet Power and Popular Resistance in the 1930s* (Ithaca, 2002).

Stalinist Subjectivity

8

Working, Struggling, Becoming: Stalin-Era Autobiographical Texts

Jochen Hellbeck

Originally appeared as Jochen Hellbeck, "Working, Struggling, Becoming: Stalin-Era Autobiographical Texts," *The Russian Review*, vol. 60, no. 3 (2001).

Editor's Introduction

While research on resistance emphasizes the population's rejection of Stalinist policies and ideology, other new research suggests that at least some people accepted and internalized the official Soviet worldview. In order to gauge citizens' internalization of official values, it is necessary to gain access to their inner thoughts, and to analyze how the Stalinist system shaped their sense of self. Because individuals think and act according to their understanding of themselves and their place in the world, their sense of self determines their ability to become subjects, or actors, in everyday life. Subjectivity – the capacity to think and act based on a coherent sense of self – is therefore a crucial area of inquiry for historians studying how people were affected by Stalinism.

As already discussed, the totalitarian model presented Stalinism as terrorizing the population into complete subservience, forcing people to hide their true selves or eliminating their sense of self altogether. Revisionists and historians of resistance countered that individuals in Soviet society did have a sense of themselves and their interests, and that they supported or opposed policies based on self-interest. But some post-revisionist thinkers have argued that people's sense of themselves and their interests did not arise independently of the system in which they lived. These scholars have criticized the tendency to assume that people had a pre-existing sense of self-interest which transcended the historical specificities of their time and place.[1] According to this view, historical agency exists, but it is

---

[1] See, for example, Anna Krylova, "The Tenacious Liberal Subject in Soviet Studies," *Kritika*, vol. 1, no. 1 (2000).

not the agency of free-thinking, self-made individuals, as depicted in liberal thought. Instead, state power and official discourse play a role in constituting individuals as subjects.[2]

In the following article, Jochen Hellbeck explains that Soviet authorities purposefully set out to make people into revolutionary subjects. Rather than seeking to repress or obliterate people's sense of self, Stalinist institutions and propaganda were intended to foster conscious citizens, who would voluntarily participate in the building of socialism and derive their sense of self from doing so. In this way, Stalinist state power was productive as well as repressive, for it offered people a coherent sense of self and purpose. The objective of Soviet authorities was to make citizens understand their lives as part of the larger revolutionary project. For those who accepted their place in this project, Soviet power offered an opportunity to contribute to something of world historical importance, the creation of socialism which heralded a new era for humankind.

Hellbeck highlights Soviet practices of subjectivization – the process by which individuals were inculcated with a sense of themselves as participants in the grand crusade of building socialism. Political agitation, education, and even gulag prison camps (where "bourgeois elements" were supposedly reformed through hard labor) all provided means to instill in people a new consciousness – an awareness of themselves as historical agents in the process of revolutionary transformation. Soviet authorities also required people to engage in autobiographical writing and speaking to make them reflect on their lives. Collective autobiographies such as the factory history project enlisted thousands of workers to write the story of Stalinist industrialization. The theme of these officially sponsored autobiographies was not only how workers built a new world, but also how building it transformed them into new people – fully conscious subjects who had realized their human potential.[3]

To conduct his inquiry into Stalinist subjectivity, Hellbeck utilizes the personal diaries of people who lived in the Stalin era. These diaries reveal that some people did internalize Soviet categories and ideology. Diarists sought to chronicle the building of socialism and described their own lives as part of this larger collective struggle. In this way they represented

---

[2] Even in liberal democracies the state plays a role in shaping people as self-interested subjects. Through private property rights and a discourse on individualism, the state helps give citizens an understanding of themselves and their world. One might add that in Western societies, microscopic networks of power and non-state institutional practices, from religious confession to psychoanalysis, also constituted individuals as subjects. See Michel Foucault, "The Subject and Power," in Foucault, *Beyond Structuralism and Hermeneutics*, ed. by Hubert Dreyfus and Paul Rabinow (Chicago, 1982).

[3] See also Igal Halfin, "From Darkness to Light: Student Communist Autobiography during NEP," *Jahrbucher fur Geschichte Osteuropas*, vol. 45, no. 2 (1997).

ideal Soviet subjects, who achieved self realization by understanding their lives in terms of the overall revolutionary project. Even a worker who in his diary denounced the Stalinist regime for capitalist exploitation did so using official terminology and with the hope that real socialism might ultimately be achieved. Other diarists described material hardship under Stalinism, but did so in order to emphasize their heroic sacrifice in building socialism.

People also used their diaries as instruments of self reflection and self improvement. Hellbeck quotes one diarist who chastised himself for petty thoughts and vowed instead to focus on the heroic tasks of socialist construction. He and other diarists thereby sought to imbue their lives with larger ideological meaning and to rise above selfish individual concerns. For those who adopted the official Soviet worldview, the life of the individual and the life of the collective were supposed to merge into one. Private life was to disappear under socialism, as people found individual fulfillment by joining the collective. At least some Soviet citizens came to think in these terms, as shown by Hellbeck's important work.

Working, Struggling, Becoming: Stalin-Era Autobiographical Texts

Jochen Hellbeck

One of the assumptions most deeply ingrained in the Western imagination of the Stalinist regime is that at their core, members of Soviet society resided externally to state policies and Bolshevik ideology. Though the "system" was successful, through a combination of propaganda and coercion, in enforcing a degree of outward popular conformity, individuals were able to mitigate these pressures by retreating into private spheres unaffected by "official" ideology. In search of Soviet citizens' concealed or repressed selves, scholars have placed high hopes on the newly available "hidden transcripts" (James Scott) of Soviet society: secret NKVD reports and interrogations, unpublished correspondence, diaries. It is in this body of unofficial or secret sources that the authentic scripts of individual selfhood, the essence of their subjectivity, is expected to be uncovered. In the Stalinist context subjectivity, which I define as a capacity for thought and action derived from a coherent sense of self, is thus regarded as a quality that manifests itself against, and in spite of, the policies of the Soviet state.[1]

A related, but more pessimistic view casts doubt on Soviet citizens' ability to develop any notion of individual subjectivity at all. According to this view, all political initiative was monopolized by the revolutionary state, and revolutionary politics by their very nature undercut the production of stable identities. As a consequence, Soviet citizens were jolted

I am grateful to Igal Halfin, David Hoffmann, Peter Holquist, and the workshop and conference participants at the University of Michigan, Michigan State University, University of California at Berkeley, University of California at Riverside, Stanford University, and the Maison des Sciences de l'Homme, Paris, for their comments and suggestions. I also want to thank Véronique Garros, Natalya Korenevskaya, and Thomas Lahusen for generously sharing with me a great number of diaries from the Stalin period. Support for the writing of this article was provided by the Michigan Society of Fellows.

[1] See Jochen Hellbeck, "Speaking Out: Languages of Affirmation and Dissent in Stalinist Russia," *Kritika* I/1 (Winter 2000): 71–96. The latest to invoke James Scott's dichotomy of official and hidden transcripts are J. Arch Getty and Oleg V. Naumov, *The Road to Terror: Stalin and the Self-Destruction of the Bolsheviks, 1932–1939* (New Haven, 1999). For a critique of this essentially liberal conceptualization of the self see Anna Krylova, "The Tenacious Liberal Subject in Soviet Studies," *Kritika* I/1 (Winter 2000): 119–46.

out of traditional frames of self-definition and kept suspended in a climate of recurrent rupture, insecurity, and disorientation.[2]

What links these two interpretations is the notion that the Soviet regime sought to subjugate individuals' sense of selfhood, forcing them to conceal their subjectivities or obliterating them altogether. My article highlights an opposite dynamic: it argues that the primary effect on individuals' sense of self of the Revolution of 1917 and of Soviet revolutionary practice was not repressive, but productive. To a large extent revolutionary politics centered on creating revolutionary selves, on making Soviet citizens think of themselves and act as conscious historical subjects.[3] The activities of autobiographical reflection, writing, and speech formed an important medium through which revolutionary subjectivities were to be attained. Soviet citizens living through the first decades of Soviet power were intensely aware of their duty to possess a distinct individual biography, to present it publicly, and to work on themselves in search of self-perfection. Most important, they were forced to acknowledge the political weight of their biography. The intense politicization of acts of talking and writing about oneself also influenced the writing of diaries in the 1930s – the actual source body investigated in this essay.

As a textual genre, the diary, along with other autobiographical narratives, was markedly shaped by the Soviet Revolution. In prerevolutionary times, writing an account of one's life or keeping a journal was limited to a relatively small segment of educated Russian society. Following the Revolution of 1917, the autobiographical domain expanded dramatically, both in absolute numbers and in sociological terms. It was not just that many more individuals became engaged in writing and talking about themselves but that the autobiographical domain reached entirely new layers of the population, thereby creating a new, specifically Soviet, subgenre of sorts: of authors groping for a language of self-

[2] Stefan Plaggenborg recently formulated this view from a cultural anthropological standpoint in "Grundprobleme der Kulturgeschichte der sowjetischen Zwischenkriegszeit," *Jahrbücher für Geschichte Osteuropas* 48 (2000), no. 1:109–18, esp. 115–16. See also Moshe Lewin's earlier notion of the Stalinist " 'quicksand' society" (*The Making of the Soviet System: Essays in the Social History of Interwar Russia* [New York, 1985], 221). The loss of the self is also a central theme in Hannah Arendt's analysis of totalitarian regimes, *The Origins of Totalitarianism* (1951, rev. edn., New York, 1973).

[3] When talking about the self-creating effects of the Russian Revolution, I certainly do not want to imply that selves, as self-conscious beings, did not exist prior to the Revolution. My argument is rather that the Revolution deployed on a massive scale a new thinking about the self as both a problem and a political project. For a model of this approach to the self as a problem see Michel Foucault, *The History of Sexuality*, vol. 1, *An Introduction* (New York, 1978), chap. 1; ibid., vol. 2, *The Use of Pleasure* (New York, 1985), introduction.

expression at the same time as they learned to read and write.[4] The Civil War accounts by Isaak Babel and Andrei Platonov indulge in recording the awkward, earnest, and intense attempts by barely literate peasant-soldiers to cast themselves as revolutionary subjects.[5]

In part this obsessive talk about the self was a direct offshoot of the Revolution, an immediate articulation of the revolutionary ideas of human liberation, social emancipation, and the dignity of the person-ality, all of which had made an explosive appearance in 1917.[6] But it is important to consider how this humanistic discourse was from the beginning appropriated by the Soviet regime and thus integrated into an agenda of individual activation and mobilization in the service of strengthening the revolutionary state. With its stress on subjective involvement in the revolutionary cause, the Bolshevik regime was pursuing a quintessentially modern agenda of *subjectivization*, of foster-ing conscious citizens who would become engaged in the program of building socialism of their own will.[7] Soviet revolutionaries sought to remove all mediation between the individual citizen and the larger community, so that the consciousness of the individual and the revo-lutionary goals of the state would merge. In the process, individuals were expected to refashion their very selves, by enacting revolutions

[4] Bibliographic evidence as well as what is known on state-sponsored efforts at autobio-graphical writing suggest that – both numerically and in terms of sociological breadth – the early Soviet regime engendered the largest collective autobiographical project under-taken in modern history. Only the Chinese Communist case may have rivalled the Soviet autobiographical project in terms of the sheer number of individual autobiographies sponsored by the regime. For a bibliography of published autobiographical material relat-ing to the Soviet period see the ongoing publication project, *Sovetskoe obshchestvo v vospominaniiakh i dnevnikakh: Annotirovannyi bibliograficheskii ukazatel' knig, publikatsii v sbornikakh i zhurnalakh*, ed. V. Z. Drobizhev, 4 vols. (Moscow, 1987–95). The production of autobiographical literature increased significantly after 1917 ("Memuarnaia liter-atura," in *Literaturnaia entsiklopediia*, vol. 7 [Moscow, 1934], cols. 131–49). The popu-larity of the diary genre in Soviet Russia is underscored by a bibliography of recent journal publications of archival documentations, which lists more than two hundred diaries or diary excerpts. See *Otkrytyi arkhiv: Spravochnik opublikovannykh dokumentov po istorii Rossii XX-go veka iz gosudarstvennykh i semeinykh arkhivov (po otechestvennoi peri-odike 1985–1995 gg.)*, ed. I. A. Kondakova (Moscow, 1997).

[5] See Isaak Babel, *Red Cavalry* (New York, 1929); and Andrei Platonov, *Chevengur* (Paris, 1972).

[6] Mark Steinberg, "The Language of Popular Revolution," in *Voices of Revolution, 1917* (New Haven, 2001). The humanist theme is strongly expressed in Maxim Gorky's serial-ized commentary in *Untimely Thoughts: Essays on Revolution, Culture, and the Bolsheviks, 1917–1918* (New York, 1968).

[7] The ethos of social activation associated here with the Soviet regime was in fact already implemented in the course of World War I. But the Bolsheviks' approach was distinct in that they transposed the spirit of total wartime mobilization to postwar conditions and introduced a much broader set of practices to realize this goal. See Peter Holquist, " 'Infor-mation is the Alpha and Omega of Our Work': Bolshevik Surveillance in Its Pan-European Context," *Journal of Modern History* 69 (September 1997): 415–50.

of their souls, paralleling the revolutions of the social and political landscapes.

What made this discourse of rearing conscious revolutionary subjects so potent was the fact that it was actualized through a host of *subjectivizing practices*, including political agitation, educational policies, and reeducational measures aiming at "reforging" class aliens. Even Gulag camps, staffed with large libraries and other educational facilities, were conceived of as construction sites of the New Man. Within this transformative framework, the Soviet state attached particular significance to the practice of autobiographical writing and speaking, both as a manifestation of the state of consciousness a given individual had achieved, and as a tool of raising this consciousness further. The most widespread type of formalized self-presentation in the Soviet system was the *avtobiografiia* – a short account of an individual's life, submitted in prose and presented orally, listing this person's educational and professional achievements, but in its core focusing on the formation of his or her personality. This form of self-presentation originated in the Communist party milieu as a means of assessing a given candidate's level of political consciousness. Yet, it was practiced also in the Komsomol and in nonparty institutions, such as universities and organs of state administration. In applying for membership in one of these institutions, any applicant had to compose and recite such an autobiography.[8] Significantly, Soviet citizens were required to resubmit their autobiography at recurrent intervals throughout their lives. It is therefore safe to assume that individuals were familiar not only with this genre of self-presentation and its attendant rules but also with the underlying assumption that their biographies were subject to rewriting, in accordance with the progression of the Revolution along with the development of their own, subjective political consciousness.

During the first decades of Soviet power, state and party agencies also poured considerable energy into the production of large-scale autobiographical projects involving thousands of Soviet citizens.[9] Workers and

---

[8] On the poetics of self-fashioning in Soviet autobiographies see Igal Halfin, "From Darkness to Light: Student Communist Autobiography During NEP," *Jahrbücher für Geschichte Osteuropas* 45 (1997), no. 2:210–36. The genre of the Soviet autobiography bears striking parallels to the Puritan mode of self-constitution, as at least once in their lives all Puritan converts were required to write and publicly recite their own spiritual histories. These autobiographical texts were shaped against the texts of predecessors and fellow believers ("To be a pilgrim was to travel in the 'Way' of such texts within the Puritan culture"; Kathleen M. Swaim, *Pilgrim's Progess, Puritan Progress: Discourses and Contexts* [Urbana, 1993], 137).

[9] S. V. Zhuravlev, *Fenomen "Istorii fabrik i zavodov": Gor'kovskoe nachinanie v kontekste epokhi 1930-kh godov* (Moscow, 1997); Frederick Corney, "History, Memory, Identity and the Construction of the Bolshevik Revolution, 1917–1927" (Ph.D. diss., Columbia University, 1997), esp. 273–8, 316–20.

soldiers wrote their recollections of the Revolution of 1917, and labor collectives in various branches of Soviet industry narrated the epic tale of their construction campaign at the Stalinist "industrialization front." In all of these cases the plot operated on two levels, relating how individuals *made* the Revolution, *constructed* a factory, *built* the Metro, and so on, and at the same time, how they themselves *were made* by the Revolution and how they *were forged* as subjects in the course of the Stalinist industrialization drive. This twofold theme was especially pronounced in the case of class enemies, criminals, and social outcasts, who were to be reforged into conscious and socially useful citizens through the combined tools of labor and autobiographical writing. Their accounts of their lives describe the full trajectory of self-transformation, from "human weed" or "bad raw material," living in a similarly unformed or polluted social environment, to conscious, self-disciplined beings residing in the well-ordered socialist garden created to an extent by themselves.[10]

Alongside other autobiographical genres, Soviet revolutionaries also promoted the diary as a subjectivizing technique. Consider the case of the "Red Army notebook" (*knizhka krasnoarmeitsa*) of the Civil War period, a booklet designed for each individual Red Army soldier, for the sake of recording the ammunition, food, and clothing supplies distributed to him. The booklet contains a blank page at the end bearing the heading "for personal notes." A caption below reads: "If possible, keep a diary of your service in the Workers' and Peasants' Red Army."[11] Yet notwithstanding this glaring case, the diary never received the same official support as the production of complete autobiographical narratives.[12] Soviet activists were deeply ambivalent about how suitable the diary was as a catalyst of socialist self-transformation. They acknowl-

---

[10] See the final chapter, "Gorky sums up," in *Belomor: An Account of the Construction of the New Canal between the White Sea and the Baltic Sea* (New York, 1935); and A. S. Makarenko, *The Road to Life: an Epic of Education* (Moscow, 1951). The highest form of subjectivity, however, the role of progenitor of the New Soviet Man, was reserved for Stalin himself, who was likened to "a gardener rearing his beloved fruit tree." See "Otchetnyi doklad tov. Molotova o rabote pravitel'stva VII S″ezdu Sovetov SSSR," *Pravda*, 29 January 1935. On the "gardener" and the "gardening state" see also Zygmunt Bauman, *Modernity and the Holocaust* (Ithaca, 1989), 13, 71, 91–92.

[11] *Knizhka krasnoarmeitsa* (Ekaterinoslav, 1919). I thank Peter Holquist for pointing out this source to me.

[12] Compare the case of seventeenth-century New England, where prescriptions on diary-keeping were central to the production and dissemination of the revolutionary, Puritan self (Charles E. Hambrick-Stowe, *The Practice of Piety: Puritan Devotional Disciplines in Seventeenth-Century New England* [Chapel Hill, 1982]). For the scattered initiatives of Soviet pedagogues, psychologists, and literary activists to mobilize the introspective and self-transformative powers of the diary in their efforts to create the New Man, see chapter two of my forthcoming *Revolution of the Soul: Diaries from the Stalin Era*.

edged that the diary had traditionally served as an inherently bourgeois medium that tended to further individuals' selfish, narcissistic drives, or at best produced "empty talk." There was also the suspicion that a diary, if written on one's own and concealed from the gaze of the collective, could undermine a Communist's socialist consciousness and become a breeding ground of counterrevolutionary sentiment.[13] This suspicion was poignantly expressed in the fact that diaries were among the materials most coveted by NKVD officers during searches of apartments belonging to "enemies of the people." Some literary specialists expressed not so much suspicion, but rather disdain toward the diary medium: they expressly favored the production and publication of memoirs over diaries because the memoir had the educational advantage of presenting a cohesive. unified narrative of self-development. The diary narrative, by contrast, was choppy and resonated with competing voices in the process of self-constitution. The memoir represented a finished piece of work – it was a monument of the completed self, whereas the diary functioned as a mere construction site of the self, conceived of as a work-in-progress.[14] As a disillusioned literary editor in charge of publishing a collection of workers' self-narratives put it: "[Diaries] can give great results, yet these results won't come overnight. The diary demands time, but we need material now."[15]

It is important to bear official ambiguities toward the diary in mind when studying the existing diary literature of the 1930s, since such a perspective allows us to understand these diaries as far more than an unmediated product of Soviet state policies of subjectivization. Only in a few cases did diaries originate as clear assignments prescribed by Soviet officials; for the most part, they were kept on the initiative of their authors, who in fact often deplored the absence of official precepts of

[13] Oleg Kharkhordin, "Reveal and Dissimulate: A Genealogy of Private Life in Soviet Russia," in *Public and Private in Thought and Practice*, ed. Jeff Weintraub and Krishan Kumar (Chicago, 1994). In Ilia Erenburg's novel, *Second Day (Den' vtoroi)*, it is the chief villain, Vasia Safonov, who keeps a diary shielded from the collective, to which he confides his counterrevolutionary thoughts. Transposed to real life, the same scenario could be observed in the case of Kirov's murderer, Leonid Nikolaev, whose diary the state prosecution used to provide evidence for his anti-Soviet disposition (Robert Conquest, *The Great Terror*, 56). To counter possible individualistic effects of diary-keeping and foster the development of a collectivist consciousness, Soviet pedagogues also assigned collectively kept "brigade diaries" in factories and schools. The Nazi regime in Germany produced a racialized version of the collective diary, with Nazi ideologues calling for the writing of "clan diaries" (*Tagebuch der Sippe*), from which future generations were to "draw power and knowledge and obtain insights into the character and fate of their blood relatives (*Blutsverbundenen*)" (Peter Boemer, *Tagebuch* [Stuttgart 1969]).

[14] "Memuarnaia literatura," 132.

[15] Josette Bouvard, "Le moi au miroir de la société nouvelle: Les formes autobiographiques de l'histoire" (unpublished ms.), 85.

self-transformation according to which they could pattern their lives. An investigation of this diary literature thus highlights the extent to which individuals, acting on their own, creatively wove themselves into a loose matrix of subjectivization produced by the Revolution, and how these individuals themselves supplied some of the core categories and mechanisms of self-realization in a Soviet vein.

The following discussion presents a sample from a large pool of diaries from the 1930s, most of which have become available to researchers following the opening of the Soviet archives. The diarists cover a broad occupational and sociological spectrum, and they include both urban and rural residents, members of all generations, men and women.[16] The discussion is broken down into three parts. I begin by focusing on diaries as chronicles of socialist construction, before moving to an investigation of the introspective and self-transformative functions of Stalin-era diaries. The third section places Soviet diaries and notions of Soviet subjectivity in relationship to the binary concept of the public and the private sphere.[17]

Excluded from the present investigation are diaries lacking an auto-biographical orientation. This essay thus does not explore the diaristic

---

[16] The sociological breadth and variegated textual nature of the corpus of diaries on which this study is based (totalling about one hundred) defies simple classification. It is safe to say, though, that the majority of the diaries were written by members of a younger generation (authors born between 1895 and 1920). In terms of the provenance of these diaries, a good number of them, authored by members of the state bureaucracy, or the technical and artistic intelligentsia, had been deposited in Soviet state archives and been accessible to researchers already before the collapse of the Soviet Union. Others, belonging to the same group of people, had been locked away in *spetskhrany* until the late 1980s. A third group of diaries is derived from nonstate archives established during the perestroika period (for example, Memorial and the Narodnyi arkhiv) or from private archives. Numerically, diaries from the latter two groups prevail strongly. Although impressive in number, these diaries scratch only the surface of the total of surviving diaries from the early Stalin period. The greatest as of yet untapped repositories of diaries from the 1930s are the central and regional archives of the KGB, to which foreign researchers still have virtually no access. Innumerable other diaries are preserved in private households throughout the post-Soviet territory. There is reason to fear that many diaries from the early Soviet period might get lost or never be made available to researchers, for the simple reason that their current owners are unaware of the historical significance of this genre. For a detailed survey of diaries from the 1930s see Hellbeck, *Revolution of the Soul*, chap. 3. Several of these previously unknown diaries from the 1930s have already been published in the West. See especially Véronique Garros et al., eds., *Intimacy and Terror: Soviet Diaries of the 1930s* (New York, 1995); and Jochen Hellbeck, ed., *Tagebuch aus Moskau 1931–1939* (Munich, 1996).

[17] Given space constraints, the important themes of critical opinion, repression, and self-censorship in diaries from the 1930s, as well as the relationship between autobiographical writing and Stalinist terror cannot be dealt with in the present article. These issues are discussed in Hellbeck, *Revolution of the Soul*.

genre as a whole, nor does it set itself the goal of deducing from diaristic texts how their authors actually experienced the Stalin period. This latter point needs to be stressed, in view of the intuitive popular tendency to view the diary as an experiential sanctuary of sorts, as a repository of individuals' innermost thoughts and feelings. Yet no autobiographical text, however intimate and confessional it claims to be, is able to provide an immediate answer to the question of experience. Self-narratives can be fully understood only if situated in the context of historically specific conventions of how to conceive of oneself and present oneself. With respect to the Stalin era, this context was shaped by the language of the Russian Revolution, the rise of a new mode of universal self-expression, the politicization of the self in the wake of 1917, and the totalizing insistence on universal self-transformation and self-disclosure on the part of the Soviet regime. This frame goes a long way to explaining why the self is such a prominent theme in Stalin-era diaries and why there is a remarkable scarcity of non-Soviet modes of self-realization in these texts. Not all diaries from the 1930s are autobiographical in character, but to the extent that they invoke the self, most of them move within distinctly Soviet parameters of selfhood, by stressing the themes of work on the self, social utility and integration, and historical orientation.

Chronicles of Socialist Construction

Soviet diaries from the 1930s bespeak an extraordinary involvement of their authors in the development of the Soviet system. Diarists were often aware of participating in an exceptional, historic period, which it was their obligation to record. "When will I finally write my memoirs about the 1930s?" one of them asked.[18] The fact that this author posed the question in 1932, when the actual "1930s" had barely begun, illustrates how much there existed at the time a notion of the Stalinist industrialization campaign as a distinct epoch in the making. Another diarist, a party activist involved in the collectivization campaign, wrote his autobiographical record as a chronicle of class struggle. He began to keep the diary following his appointment as chairman of a village Soviet. The first entry summarizes his achievements at his former workplace, which had also been at the collectivization "front": "There were many victories and defeats. The class enemy, the kulak, did not sleep, organizing the backward mass of the *bedniaki* (poor peasants) and *seredniaki* (peasants of average means) against the kolkhozes. . . . Thus, in a

---

[18] Diary of Stepan Podlubnyi, entry of 2 September 1932, in *Tagebuch aus Moskau*, 92.

bitter skirmish with the obsolete and dying capitalist elements, our kolkhozes have been born, reared, and strengthened. A lot of struggle still lies ahead, especially at the new location, the Pirogov village Soviet, where I have been transferred by the district committee of the party."[19] Tellingly the narrator begins by setting up a macro frame, the collectivization campaign in the Soviet countryside, in which he then places events from his own personal life. The same strategy is visible in the diary of Masha Scott, who expands the ideological frame structuring the narration of her personal life to its utmost extent – the epic of international class struggle. Masha Scott, one of the builders of the city of Magnitogorsk, related in her diary her first encounter with John Scott, a visiting American engineer, whom she would later marry. She described how disappointed she felt upon seeing this fabled American visitor in person – an emaciated young man, dressed in rags and covered with blast-furnace dust:

> The first American I had ever seen, he looked like a homeless boy (*bezprizornik*). I saw in him the product of capitalist oppression. I saw in my mind's eye his sad childhood; I imagined the long hours of inhuman labor which he had been forced to perform in some capitalist factory while still a boy; I imagined the shamefully low wages he received, only sufficient to buy enough bread so that he could to go work the next day; I imagined his fear of losing even this pittance and being thrown on the streets unemployed in case he was unable to do his work to the satisfaction and profit of his parasitic bosses.[20]

Ideological tenets, in the sense of projections of a world to be realized, also informed diaries that were produced explicitly as chronicles of everyday life (*byt*). Nikolai Zhuravlev, an archivist from Kalinin, began his diary with the following introductory remark:

> I am a local historian (*kraeved*) and an archivist. I know the significance for the historian of a document which deals with the everyday. I understand that a document, an ordinary document filed in an office, narrates primarily about extraordinary facts and remains silent about all that has firmly become an attainment of everyday life (*byt*). Which office will describe for you a normal day in the life of a normal person? ... This is why, in support of the historian of the city of Kalinin (the future will tell whether this will be myself or someone else), I have decided to begin these

---

[19] "1933–1936 gg. v griazovetskoi derevne (Dnevnik A. I. Zhelezniakova)," *Vologda: Istoriko-kraevedcheskii al'manakh*, vyp. 1 (Vologda, 1994), 455, entry of 30 May 1933.

[20] John Scott, *Behind the Urals. An American Worker in Russia's City of Steel* (1942; enlarged ed., prepared by Stephen Kotkin [Bloomington, 1989]), 118–19.

notes in which I will try, as far as possible, not to talk about the turns of my heart, but will concentrate more on facts.[21]

Tellingly, the author's purported desire to write a chronicle of everyday life was motivated by an extraordinary event – the eight hundredth anniversary of the founding of Kalinin (Tver'): "The day on which my notes begin is an extraordinary one in the chronicles of the city. . . . It is a big holiday. . . . You feel this when you look at the faces of the people walking by. Among them are many kolkhoz workers who have come to the regional center to celebrate yet another victory of socialist agriculture." The following day, Zhuravlev summarized his impressions about the city festival: "Celebrations like this can take place only in the land of socialism! I remember these official 'festivities' under Tsarism. . . . But our holiday is a genuine mass holiday, a genuine holiday of the people."[22]

Zhuravlev's diary project illustrates the political significance of the category of everyday life in the Soviet system. In view of the stated goal of the Bolshevik regime to revolutionize all aspects of the traditional everyday, a diarist's description of living conditions under Stalinism was a profoundly ideological gesture.[23] It is in this light that the following diary, of the Leningrad worker and student Arkadii Man'kov, should be read. Man'kov's account also focused on the *byt* of the Stalin era, but it emphasized solely the misery and despondency suffered by the working population. Man'kov's express purpose in keeping his diary of the 1930s was diametrically opposed to Zhuravlev's, as he sought to denounce the achievements claimed by the Stalinist regime. The contemporary social structure in the Soviet Union, Man'kov wrote, was "purely capitalist"; to refer to it as a Marxist state was blasphemous. All the while, however, Man'kov called for the realization of Marx's revolutionary goals – the end of exploitation and the arrival of material plenty. Like Zhuravlev, he referred to his diary as raw material for a history of the everyday life of the Stalin period that historians would have to write one day, and as was also the case with Zhuravlev, Man'kov's account of the everyday was embedded in a vision of the

---

[21] Diary of Nikolai Zhuravlev, entry of 6 January 1936, in Gosudarstvennyi arkhiv Kalininskoi oblasti, f. r-652, op. 1. ed. khr. 2.

[22] Ibid., entry of 7 January 1936. In spite of Zhuravlev's intention to keep an impersonal diary of everyday life in Kalinin, his chronicle did turn largely into a confessional genre, recording intrigues at the workplace and problems with his adulterous wife at home.

[23] On Soviet designs to revolutionize byt see Naiman, *Sex in Public: The Incarnation of Early Soviet Ideology* (Princeton, 1997), 185–8; Katerina Clark, *Petersburg, Crucible of Cultural Revolution* (Cambridge, MA, 1995), 242–60; Michael David-Fox, *Revolution of the Mind: Higher Learning among the Bolsheviks, 1918–1929* (Ithaca, 1997); and Christina Kiaer, "Boris Arvatov's Socialist Objects," *October* 81 (Summer 1997): 105–18.

socialist society of the future.[24] In spite of their radically different diagnoses, these two authors thus expressed themselves within a shared horizon of meaning defined by the campaign of building socialism.[25]

A diarist's mention of extreme material hardship by itself did not have to stand in the way of his or her ideological commitment. On the contrary, Galina Shtange, a fifty-year-old housewife married to a leading Soviet engineer, deliberately mentioned the adverse conditions of contemporary life in order to underscore the heroic sacrifice assumed by herself and her generation in the building of socialism.

> It's just horrible when you think about how people live these days, and engineers in particular. I heard about one engineer, who lives with his wife in a nine-[square-] meter room. When his mother came to visit, there was absolutely no place for him to do his work. So he put the lamp on the floor and lay down (on his stomach under the table) and worked that way, he couldn't put it off, he had a deadline. I wrote down this example so that those who come after us will read it and get a sense of what we went through.[26]

The unstated assumption motivating this entry was that future generations of Soviet citizens, living in a materially plentiful Communist world, would have difficulty imagining the hardships borne by those who sacrificed themselves for the building of this future.

The sense that a diary kept in the 1930s, to be legitimate, had to be ideological in character, is also reflected in the laments of two diarists that their chronicles failed to reach such a level of interpretation. Repeatedly the Komsomol activist Anatolii Ul'ianov voiced his frustration at his own writings in his diary:

> 4/12/1933 I've just read through a couple of pages. How much emptiness, and how little reflection of life. The life about which people write

---

[24] A. G. Man'kov, "Dnevnik riadovogo cheloveka (1933–1934)," *Zvezda*, 1994, no. 6: entries of 30 January and 24 July 1933. Man'kov later became a well-known historian of pre-Petrine Russia. He published, among other things, an acclaimed edition of the 1649 Ulozhenie, *Sobornoe ulozhenie 1649 goda: Tekst kommentarii*, ed. A. G. Man'kov (Leningrad, 1987).

[25] In his diary, Ivan Sich, a retired schoolteacher of French, also focused on the hardships of everyday life, contrasting them to the ideological proclamations of the Soviet regime. Sich especially made a point of recording the critical views of workers toward Soviet power, to discredit the latter's claims for legitimacy. Unlike Man'kov, however, Sich did not seem to be motivated by a personal vision of a better socialist world. See I. I. Sich, "Fragments du journal inédit d'Ivan Ivanovič Sitč," *Cahiers du monde russe et soviétique* 28 (1987), no. 1:75–94; esp. entries of 7 November 1929 and "First days of June (1930)."

[26] Diary of Galina Shtange, in *Intimacy and Terror*, 167–218, entry of 1 January 1937.

books. . . . They rear heroes. But what do I have? I will try to be more detailed and more prosaic in writing about myself at home and at work.

5/7/1933 The end of the [diary] notebook is approaching. This notebook spans almost eight months, i.e., two thirds of a year. But life is very incompletely illuminated. It is even very, very slightly illuminated. There are a lot of thoughts in there, but little on the essence of existence.

Firmly intent on devoting his diary to the essence of life, Ul'ianov intermittently produced a series of entries exclusively on his labor activities, summarizing production targets and results of the factory at which he worked, Komsomol meetings, and his work as a social activist.[27] But he soon fell back into his habitual diaristic mode again. As late as in 1937 he complained:

1/15/1937 About the diary. What kind of stupid trumpery I have been writing over the last days (no, all the time!) in my diary. There is no life in it, only nonsense about womenfolk. From today on, I have decided to write only about what is real, what has happened as an accomplished fact, and I'll discard the rest. Yeah, and my life is somehow petty; in my twenty-three years, I haven't done anything intelligent, anything heroic; I'm only groping around like an idiot. A diary should reflect only the truth – live, heroic truth – but everything that I have written to date is some kind of nonsense. Under no circumstances will I keep writing like this.

Especially intriguing in this entry is how Ul'ianov's observation on the trivial character of his diary notes brings him to conclude that he is leading a petty life. There seems to be hardly any difference in the author's mind between "writing like this" and "living like this." The boundary between writing and actual life is blurred, and there is a palpable sense of the diary's power to literally write its author's life: the more disciplined and consistently heroicizing his autobiographical narrative unfolds, Ul'ianov implies, the more real and heroic his actual life will become.

Another diarist, the writer A. V. Peregudov, realized only from the distance of a quarter century that his diary project had failed. In an entry of 1961 he remarked:

It's been almost twenty-five years that I haven't opened this diary. I reread my notes and was amazed about how petty they are. But where are all the great things (*to velikoe*) that took place in our country, changing its face and strengthening its might? My explanation for this is that the diary

---

[27] Diary of Anatolii Ul'ianov, in Otdel rukopisei Rossiiskoi gosudarstvennoi biblioteki (OR RGB), f. 442, op. 1, ed. khr. 10, entries of 20 May and 13 July 1933.

was not destined for such a high purpose, but was kept for small, "intimate and lyrical" notes which revolved only around my family life and nature and were of great interest only to myself and Mariia. How I regret now that I did not keep a different, a great diary, devoted to the great events. I tried frequently, but I never wrote it.[28]

How widely the diaristic genre was deployed for chronicles of socialist construction is also illustrated in the case of the numerous travel diaries left behind by foreign visitors to the Soviet Union in the 1920s and 1930s. Whether enthusiastic or sceptical in their responses, these authors invariably shared an impulse to witness and record in their personal chronicles the building of the New World.[29]

Beyond their ideological nature, another remarkable feature of many diaries from the 1930s is their emphasis on the narrator's personal involvement in the development of the Soviet system. Vsevolod Vishnevskii, the playwright, wanted his diaristic record to serve as historical testimony, to be consulted by future generations to judge his own and his contemporaries' actions: "Our task is to preserve for history our observations, our present point of view – the point of view of the participant. You see, a year from now, or ten years from now, from the perspective of time, everything will become clearer. Possibly, there will be another point of view, another judgment. Therefore let us leave for the grandsons and great-grandsons our story. Our mistakes and victories will be the lessons for tomorrow."[30]

The urge to write oneself into the Soviet revolutionary trajectory can even be observed on the part of a potential victim of socialist construction, notably the campaign to collectivize agriculture. The diarist, Tikhon Puzanov, was a peasant youth from the Don region, who was still living in his parents' uncollectivized household in early 1933. The family could not meet the grain delivery quotas mandated by the local Soviet and was threatened with expropriation and exile. While narrat-

---

[28] Diary of A. V. Peregudov, in Rossiiskii gosudarstvennyi arkhiv literatury i iskusstva (RGALI), f. 2211, op. 3, ed. khr. 18, entry of 8 April 1961. Peregudov's diary notes of the 1930s are indeed redundant and shallow, consisting for the most part of weather reports and minute descriptions of the author's activities, particularly the types of food and drinks consumed on a given day ("I slept . . . got up . . . drank two cups of tea . . . went to . . .").

[29] For references to the extensive body of Western travellers' descriptions of the emerging Soviet state see Paul Hollander, *Political Pilgrims: Western Intellectuals in Search of the Good Society* (New Brunswick, 1998), and Christiane Uhlig, *Utopie oder Alptraum? Schweizer Reiseberichte über die Sowjetunion, 1917–1941* (Zurich, 1992).

[30] Vsevolod Vishnevskii, *Sobranie sochinenii v 5 tomakh, vol. 6, (Dopolnitel'nyi): Vystupleniia i radiorechi. Zapisnye knizhki. Pis'ma* (Moscow, 1961), entry of 22 January 1942.

ing in the diary his and his family's harsh "struggle for existence" under the conditions of spreading famine, Puzanov also dreamt about the happy future promised by collectivization, emphasizing his active personal involvement in the realization of this future:

> All that I think about is how we will attain the happy future. Others think in a contrary way – they wait for it to happen (*zhdut gotovogo*). And they are the majority, they are not a bit interested in their work. They don't care about how they work, as if they were serving a sentence. They aren't involved in the present world (*Oni ne zhivut nastoiashchim*). For them it is all difficult and torturous, since collective labor has not yet entered the consciousness, the blood of the young; and the people are dreaming about a smallholder's existence (*mechtaiut o edinolichnoi zhizni*).[31]

Although himself a member of a kulak family, Puzanov took part in the collectivization campaign, joining activists' raids on uncollectivized peasant households. On the pages of his diary he emphasized his "genuine loyalty to the kolkhoz system," taking issue with those who suspected that he was working in the kolkhoz only to "save [his] skin."[32]

Most tangibly the subjectivizing effect of revolutionary ideology – the sense of the self coming to fruition through joining the socialist campaign – is evoked in case of the kolkhoz activist Aleksandr Zhelezniakov. On the occasion of the sixteenth anniversary of the October Revolution, he noted:

> How good it is to feel, live, and win in struggle! There is not, there was not, and there will not be in world history a generation more happy than ours. We are the participants in the creation of a new epoch! Do you remember, enemies, you who are encircling us from all sides, that only twenty years ago we were puny insects, crawling on the masters' floors, and then this paltry person, strangled by capitalism, comprehended himself as a class and shattered the whole world to its foundations on 7 November, sixteen years ago. . . . There is nothing greater than to be a member, a citizen of the Soviet land and to belong to Lenin's Communist party, hardened in battles and led in our times by the beloved leader,

---

[31] Tikhon Puzanov, " 'Zhatva'33-go goda," *Molodaia gvardiia*, 1991, no. 5:207–8, entry of 2 April 1933; see also entry of 1 January 1933).

[32] Ibid., entry of 6 January 1933 "Friday." The notion of the diary as a work record and expressive medium of self-realization is also present in the journal of the coal miner Vladimir Molodtsov: "11/29/1930 The highest feeling that I could experience in my short life, this is the feeling of being conscious of the fact that I am a part of the miners' collective. What a great thing not to notice, not to count the hours of the working day, not to wait for the end of the shift, but instead to strive to prolong it . . . and after the shift, to leave as a victor in the fulfillment of the plan! How joyful it is to see oneself ahead of the others" (*Chelovek sredi liudei: Rasskazy, dnevniki, ocherki* [Moscow, 1964], 161–91).

Comrade Stalin, with whom we are celebrating together *today the day of
the great victories* of technical progress. Had the October Revolution not
happened, could I have conceivably understood life in this way, and could
I have conceivably forgone my personal life for the struggle for common
goals? No! I would have remained a half-animal, but now I am happy. I
was raised by Lenin's party, and I have become ideologically hardened! I
am prepared to confront any difficulties and to bear any sacrifice in the
name of the great goals of the building of the Communist society.[33]

Logbooks of the Soviet Self

To be sure, passages like the one just quoted, celebrating the merging of
the self with the collective, appear to have been rare moments of rapture
erupting from the generally less spectacular flow of the diary narrative.
More typical of Soviet diaries was a mode of doubt, insecurity, and
intense self-criticism, coupled with admonishments not to give up work
on oneself. In these cases the diary acted as a normalizing technique, a
medium through which the mind observed and controlled psychic and
bodily processes. The inward gaze provided by the diary enabled its
author to embark on an extended struggle in battling weaknesses and
impurities of the self.

A large number of diaries from the 1930s functioned as both records
and tools of psycho-physical training. They worked as an introspective,
controlling, and regulating device, enabling their authors to monitor
the physiological and intellectual processes at work in them, in the
service of controlling and perfecting them. To document this self-
transformative project, diarists repeatedly invoked the concepts of
"planning," "struggle," and "consciousness," core Communist values
of the period, highlighted especially during the first Five-Year Plans.[34]

In her diary the young schoolteacher Vera Shtrom repeatedly voiced
the need to control and rationalize her life. She sought to achieve this
by analyzing her soul and bringing to light the realm of her "subconscious feelings."[35] Shtrom also confided her dreams and fantasies, all
her "crazy" thoughts, to the diary, but expressly in a desire to "system-
atize [her] impressions" and, ultimately, to live her life in "plan-like" and
"systematic" fashion.[36] Similarly, Anatolii Ul'ianov, a Moscow worker

[33] "1933–1936 gg. v griazovetskoi derevne," 454–521, entry of 11 October 1933.
[34] Katerina Clark, *The Soviet Novel: History as Ritual* (Chicago, 1981); Nathan Leites, *A
Study of Bolshevism* (Glencoe, IL, 1953).
[35] Diary of Vera Shtrom, in Tsentr dokumentatsii "Narodnyi arkhiv" (TsDNA), f. 336, op.
1, ed. khr. 32, entries of 31 July and 14 August 1930.
[36] Ibid., entries of 14 August 1930, and 5 May and 9 July 1931.

and Komsomol activist, mobilized the diaristic medium to bring order in his life and increase his work performance:

> I want to establish exact regulations of my money spending and daily planning. I already did this today (it will be difficult, but I'll succeed). But I want to introduce a planliness of work (*planovost' raboty*) into my daily life, for both my mental-physical and leisure [activities]. I will try to make my work more manageable this way. Fewer of the usual tricks (walks with the "perfidious" Katia, etc, etc.)[37]

To fight the "disorder in [her] soul," which she repeatedly diagnosed in her diary, the writer Vera Inber advocated what she called "'techniciz-ing the soul' . . . in other words, constructivism." In keeping with this mechanistic imagery she remarked elsewhere: "Man is a factory. And his mind is the director of this factory."[38]

Diarists established a variety of related dichotomies to describe the composition of their self and the work attendant to change it. These binaries included the opposition between the mind and the body, individ-uals' "ideology" and their "psychology," or, in the words of one diarist, his "will" and his "heart."[39] In all oppositional pairs the will played a central role in the project to raise or remake the self. The will appeared as coterminous with an individual's subjectivity. It was described as an autonomous power residing within the self that, once activated, raised the self to the level of a historical agent. In this context the diary func-tioned as a catalyst shaping and strengthening the diarist's will.

Leonid Potemkin, a student at the Sverdlovsk Mining Institute, repeatedly reflected in his diary on the duality of mind and body. He described how his mind, or conscious will, challenged and eventually overcame the sluggishness of the body, which hitherto was controlled by physiological, natural, and hence unconscious forces, thus enabling him to merge with the laboring collective.[40]

Vladimir Molodtsov, a coal miner, observed that his will (or ideology – he used the two terms interchangeably) was engaged in a battle with his "psychology":

> It is interesting how there is a lack of accordance between psychology and ideology. Ideologically, I myself mobilized myself [sic] to catch up with the

---

[37] Diary of Anatolii Ul'ianov, entry of 23 March 1930. See also entries of 7 March 1936 and 4 May 1938.
[38] Vera Inber, *Stranitsy dnei perebiraia . . . : Iz dnevnikov i zapisnykh knizhek*, rev. ed. (Moscow, 1977), entry of 9 July 1933.
[39] *Chelovek sredi liudei*, 161–91 (entry of 29 November 1930).
[40] Diary of Leonid Potemkin, in *Intimacy and Terror*, 251–92 (undated entry following 31 July 1935; see also entry marked "July 1936").

plan, and although I am working actively, my psychology still draws me back home, to my hearth. This is evidenced by the increasing numbers of dreams over the past two days, in which I saw my mother. But ideology will raise psychology, this has to occur.[41]

In the pages of his diary, Stepan Podlubnyi, a young Moscow worker of kulak origins, elevated willpower to a moral ideal: "For a long time already, I have liked people with a strong will. No matter who this person is, but if he or she has great willpower, this is a good person."[42] Podlubnyi assiduously recorded all the instances when he felt that his own willpower had increased,[43] but for the most part, his diary was a record of his failures – both at the work place and in his personal life – which Podlubnyi perceived to be rooted in his weak will.[44] But for Podlubnyi, his diary amounted to more than a bulletin of the "sickness of [his] will" (31 October 1935); writing in the diary was also a cure, since he reasoned that by forcing himself to write regularly he would also increase his willpower (29 January 1933).

Willpower was attained through struggle. Diaries of the 1930s abound in references to life as a continuous struggle. Aleksandr Zhelezniakov, the Vologda kolkhoz activist, described a hey harvesting campaign conducted under his initiative. To take advantage of a brief spell of dry weather, he coerced the recalcitrant kolkhoz women workers into staying in the field until all work was finished:

> We mowed until eleven at night, and the field was mown. The moon played a big role and helped me resolve this difficult task. Thanks to the party. It reared in me firmness and resolve in struggle, to win in the most difficult conditions. What great happiness! Great, limitless happiness! I remember the words of Marx and Engels: "Struggle is happiness!" The next morning it rained again.[45]

In their journals, diarists waged struggle not just against an Other – recalcitrant kolkhoz workers, or the forces of nature – but also against themselves. Ul'ianov once noted in his diary that he had already improved somewhat in terms of his manners and his education. But he remained critical about certain aspects of his personality: "In spite of my literacy, sometimes it is scandalous how coarse I am. Of course I don't want to turn into a sickly-sweet intellectual (*slashchaven'kii*

---

[41] *Chelovek sredi liudei*, 171 (entry from 17 November 1930).
[42] *Tagebuch aus Moskau*, 147 (entry from 5 January 1938).
[43] Ibid., 122–3, 125–6, 154 (entries of 10 March and 1 April 1933, and 16 April 1934).
[44] Ibid., 95–6, 118, 182, 198, 203–4 (entries of 6 October 1932, 8 February 1933, 27 December 1934, and 28 March and 30 September 1935).
[45] "1933–6 gg. v griazovetskoi derevne" (entry of 12 October 1935).

intelligent). But what I want to be is not to be an animal." The entry concluded with the resolution: "Struggle against coarseness, inconstancy, and lies" (9 December 1932). Or, to cite from Podlubnyi's diary: "I don't know where, I think it was Gorky who said that 'life is a struggle.' A very apt observation. A life without struggle – that is not the life of a human being, it's an animal's life. As far as I can remember about myself, all of my life has evolved as an inner, emotional struggle" (2 May 1933).

So far our discussion has focused on the role of the diary as a self-disciplining technique. Yet, some of these diary narratives also evolve in a spiritual register. They describe a movement directed toward self-renewal, a movement proceeding rarely in a straight line, and more often as an uneven process marked by intense struggle. The specific role of the diary in staging this journey of self-becoming is expressed in the case of the playwright Aleksandr Afinogenov, who referred to the daily entries of his journal as "strict roadmarks of every single day that I have lived" (7 October 1937). One of Afinogenov's principal goals in keeping a diary was the production of a visible trace of self-development. Interrupting this journey was tantamount for him to a retraction into his present, imperfect self. To this extent, reviewing past diary entries enabled Afinogenov to monitor and sustain his journey toward salvation:

> *11/16/1937* Right now, today . . . I got up with the desire to somehow move on: not to stop THINKING and ACCUMULATE what I've already begun to accumulate, always LOOKING BACK and EXAMINING MYSELF, NOT ALLOWING MYSELF TO BECOME MY FORMER SELF, if even only a tiny bit.

Elsewhere Afinogenov vowed never to

> rest content with myself and my road. LOOK UP YOUR NOTES MORE OFTEN, look up the pages written on days of expectation and reevaluation of yourself. May what you wrote back then serve you as a PERMANENT REMINDER. Never depart from these notes (always collate them and and check: what you wrote comes from the very depths of your heart's sensitivity) (*11/6/1937*).[46]

The sense that life for a citizen living in the Soviet system evolved as a journey is also graphically expressed in the autobiography of Heinrich Vogeler, a German Communist who emigrated to the Soviet Union in the 1930s and wrote a memoir, titled "Becoming" (*Werden*), shortly before his death in 1942. In a diary note of that period, Vogeler explained his

[46] RGALI, f. 2172, op. 3. ed. khr. 5.

principal purpose in writing this autobiography: "Perhaps this book will be read by people who are looking for paths to reach the new life. My story will allow them to recognize wanderings which they can avoid for themselves."[47]

As these last examples illustrate especially well, Soviet diaries from the 1930s were characterized not just by an agenda of self-transformation but also more basically, by a quest for self-expression. Expression, not repression, appears to be the principal theme of diary self-narratives from the period. The desire to fuse with the collective, to secure integration in Communist, collectivist values, was not a self-effacing dynamic, it did not diminish the private self, but on the contrary, allowed it to grow.

Public and Private

Historians of the Soviet system often assume that only privately voiced statements are reliable indicators of individuals' "real" beliefs. They therefore endow the diary, understood as a private record par excellence, with a unique potential to express the individual self in undistorted fashion. Accordingly, diaries originating in the public realm – such as production or brigade diaries, or records written for the public eye – are dismissed as inauthentic records, especially in view of the pressures applied by the Soviet state which forced diarists to practice self-censorship. Yet, this exclusive correlation of the authentic self with the private sphere would leave researchers with preciously few "real" diaries to work with. Moreover, such a rigorous selection would risk missing the essential meaning of the diary in the context of the Stalinist order.

Our discussion thus far has shown that many diaries from the 1930s were kept as work projects of the self. Particularly in the case of class aliens, the desire was great to eventually publish their individual accounts of self-transformation, as visible proof, to others and to themselves, that they had successfully reworked themselves. Stepan Podlubnyi, the son of a kulak who lived in Moscow and tried to become a New Soviet Man, already knew the title of the autobiographical novel, which he was to produce from his diary notes: "The Life of an Outlived Class, its Spiritual Rebirth and Adaptation to New Conditions."[48] The writers Marietta Shaginian and Vera Inber, both of impure, non-Soviet origins and therefore threatened with social marginalization, published

---

[47] Werner Hohmann, *Heinrich Vogeler in der Sowjetunion 1931–1942: Daten-Fakten-Dokumente* (Fischerhude, 1987), 97.
[48] Stepan Podlubnyi, diary entry of 25 September 1934, in *Tagebuch aus Moskau*, 92.

their diaristic accounts of self-transformation during their lifetimes.[49] Although the published versions of the diaries were censored, this does not mean that the diary manuscripts themselves were kept as publishable records. Quite to the contrary, Podlubnyi was painfully aware that many passages in his diary would cost him dearly if they were to be revealed to state organs, but he still believed that one day censorship would be eased and his memoir would see the light of day (25 September 1934). His diary was at the same time an account of self-transformation addressed to the public, as well a secret "soulmate," to whom he confided the problems encountered while seeking to transform himself. A number of other diarists kept their self-records secretly, while simultaneously entertaining thoughts of literary publications to be based on the diary material. Thus, multiple diverging impulses appear to be at work in these diaries, making it extremely difficult to categorize them as private, semiprivate, or public records.

It is standard practice among literary theorists to treat the private literary voice as a fictional device. Even the most privately conceived self is staged, using available discursive conventions, as soon as it enters the literary realm.[50] Rather than inferring a private, and by implication, authentic, self from a given diary, it would more fruitful to define the diary in terms of a genre of private discourse, as a medium through which diarists could cultivate – rather than simply express – a private self. But complicating the issue further is the problem of employing the notion of the private for analytical purposes in the context of the Soviet state which regarded it as one of its principal tasks to eliminate all traces of the bourgeois order, chief among them the public-private division. In the eyes of Soviet Marxists, bourgeois privacy was a beguiling yet utterly disingenious concept which promised individual self-realization, but in fact only deceived the working class over the state of its social alienation. Once the illusory fusion of the individual with the partial private sphere propagated by the bourgeois order was broken up, the formerly oppressed subjects would regain their nature as social beings. Their inner being and outer function would become one.[51]

Keeping in mind the particular status of the private realm in a Marxist state, it may be useful to consider the categories employed by Soviet diarists themselves to conceptualize their social existence, rather than to distinguish *a priori* between private or public spheres and

[49] Marietta Shaginian, *Dnevniki 1917–1931* (Leningrad, 1932); Inber, *Stranitsy dnei perebiraia.*

[50] Manfred Jurgensen, *Das fiktionale Ich: Untersuchungen zum Tagebuch* (Bern, 1979), 7–8; Andrew Hassam, *Writing and Reality: A Study of Modern British Diary Fiction* (Westport, 1993), 4, 8, 51.

[51] Henry J. Koren, *Marx and the Authentic Man* (Pittsburgh, 1967), 114.

purposes of diary-writing. To begin with the case of Galina Shtange, a fifty-year-old housewife who joined the newly founded movement of housewife activists, "Obshchestvennitsa," in 1936, her diary shows an inversion of the hierarchy of the public and private spheres found in liberal thought.[52] Liberal discourse represents family life as the principal domain of the private. It is the realm of the individual's unfettered self-realization, outside of the encroachments of market relations and state authority. While also contrasting her family existence to the public sphere, Shtange, however, sought individual fulfillment in the latter. Torn between her duties as a housewife and a social activist, between the exigencies of her family and the Revolution, she subordinated the former to the latter.[53] This is how she described her first enrollment in the Soviet women's movement: "*5/13/1936* I was sitting at home, preoccupied with my own narrow little family affairs, when Zabelina came over and invited me to take part in an informal meeting with several other ladies from the Commissariat of Communication and Transportation who wanted to join the movement. Naturally I agreed." A few months later, already an activist, she complained that her family prevented her from realizing herself: "*8/27/1936* So much for my community work! . . . I was completely engrossed in my work for two months. I found my element and felt wonderful, in spite of being so tired. . . . So I decided to give up the work that I love so much, and take up cooking, dishwashing, and diapers again." And in her summary of that year she decried her need for a "personal life":

> *12/27/1936* The year is drawing to a close. It was a painful one for me. The family is upset that I spend so little time at home. I'm sorry for them, but what can I do? I'm not old yet, I still want to have a personal life. Now that I've fulfilled my obligations to my family, in the few years that remain to me *I want to live for myself*, I will always be sincerely glad to help them (emphasis added).

Shtange represented the private–public divide in the form of two different self-trajectories. Her narrow, petty household duties stood in the way of the self-realization she hoped to achieve by serving the Revolution. Seen in his light, Shtange's diary, which is almost exclusively a record of her public activities, emerges as a catalyst of her Soviet self. In 1938, forced to give up her work as an activist and return to the household, she observed that she had "suddenly aged by many years."[54]

---

[52] Diary of Galina Shtange, in *Intimacy and Terror*, 167–218.

[53] On the reversal of gender roles in and following the Soviet Revolution see Elizabeth Wood, *The Baba and the Comrade* (Bloomington, 1997).

[54] Diary of Galina Shtange, in *Intimacy and Terror*, entry of 2 April 1938.

The implication was that working for the Revolution had a rejuvenating effect. "Our work should be joyful, it's only natural," Shtange noted elsewhere in her diary. "Man is a social animal. He can be happy and joyful only in a collective. Leave a man alone, even in a golden palace, and his joy for living will just fade and die. Only an awareness of his usefulness to society can bring joy and satisfaction."[55] The statement Shtange makes about herself applies to her diary as well: precisely because she cannot remain alone cut off from the collective, her diary, in so far as it is to reflect her sense of self, cannot possibly remain a fully private record. It has to be devoted to public life to be significant and satisfying. In this light it appears only logical that Shtange pasted her diaries with numerous newsclippings, other documents from the public world, as if to underscore that her personal voice could come to fruition only in the frame of the Soviet collective.[56] Shtange's case thus illustrates once more that self-expression in the Soviet context does not stand in the way of, but on the contrary thrives on, public deeds and texts.

Stepan Podlubnyi conceptualized the relation between the private and the public realm in terms of an inner and an outer self. In his diary he often mentioned the feelings of his "inside" (*vnutrennost'*), using this expression synonymously with his "soul" (*dusha*). His goal was to activate the inner self so that it would merge with the revolutionary agenda of the Soviet state. As he understood it, the soul of a Soviet citizen was to be filled with a distinctly political spirit and should form a realm of enthusiasm. He was dissatisfied when noticing that "all the inside (was) asleep" or when he felt himself to be in an "idiotic and nonpolitical mood" (7 June 1932).

To be sure, Podlubnyi did develop a distinct notion of the private, and he identified this sphere with parts of his diary. The diary represented his "only friend," the only partner to whom he confided those thoughts that he knew would be dangerous to voice to anybody else, even to close friends. But he regarded these thoughts to be illegitimate. He possessed no positive notion of a private sphere in which to anchor a sense of self and personal values diverging from the public norms. He

---

[55] This passage, from a speech given by Shtange to the wives of commanders in the Transport Sector, follows her diary entry of 27 December 1936.

[56] My view of this diary as a coherent agenda of self-expression departs from the interpretation made by the editors of Shtange's diary, who stress the disparate nature of the various sources – diary entries, newspaper clippings, letters, photographs, and the like – making up this "diary-herbarium," and who view the actual diary as a composite of interwoven "codes in which the subject moves forward and unravels, like a spider that dissolves itself in its own web" (*Intimacy and Terror*, 168–9). In my view, this interpretation overstates the formal differences between the various textual and visual genres involved in the diary, and by the same token it underrates the existential meaning at stake for authors like Shtange in the production of these self-records.

therefore did not conceive of his diary as a record of a private sphere to be remembered. Rather, it served him as a "rubbish heap" onto which he could discard all the "garbage" accumulating in his mind (23 January 1933). He envisioned writing as a struggle from which he would ultimately emerge cleansed, fully identical with public values and thereby unencumbered of any alternative selfish, and hence impure, private sphere.

Stalin-era journals are replete with private thoughts – private in the sense of being confidential and certainly not written for the public eye – but more often than not their authors viewed them as expressions of weakness, as tokens of their lack of willpower, yet not as a source of pride or a kernel of their selfhood. The public–private binary is thus not very helpful for an understanding of Soviet subjectivities if we assume the private realm to be the exclusive locus of positive identity. As such, privacy has no obvious meaning. It aquires positive or negative valence depending on the discourse in which the self articulates itself. In the Soviet case, given the radically public and collectivist ethos promoted by the revolutionary state, it may be not so surprising after all that practically none of the 1930s diaries known to me were kept to cultivate a private existence in distinction from the public sphere. The type of self-realization pursued by diarists was to be reached through techniques of purification and remaking the self. Rather than using the dichotomy of private and public, diarists situated their personal, and particular, existence with respect to the general public interest. These descriptions evoke two trajectories – the life of the individual and the life of the collective – which were ideally to merge into a single whole. Time and again, diarists wrote of their efforts to merge their personal lives with the "general stream of life" of the Soviet collective.[57] A private existence in distinction or even opposition to the life of the collective, however, was considered inferior and unfulfilled.

Iuliia Piatnitskaia described in her diary a sense of personal regression arising from her inability to participate in the forward-thrusting life of the Soviet people. An engineer by background, she had lost her job following her husband's arrest in 1937, and now spent much time at a public library, leafing through technical journals:

I looked through *Mechanical Engineering*. Every day that I live through pushes me further back. New machines are being built: lathes, agricultural tools, machines for the Metro, for bridges, etc. Work has been organized in new ways. . . . Engineers are raising in new ways questions of

[57] See, for example, the diary of A. Afinogenov, entry of 29 July 1937 (RGALI, f. 2172, op. 3, ed. 5).

organization and or the technology of tool production. All in all, there is no doubt that life is moving forward, regardless of any "sticks in the wheel." The wonderful Palace of Culture for the Zisovets plant. I'm getting really jealous: why am I not in their collective?[58]

One of the strategies employed by Piatnitskaia to deal with the calamity of her husband's arrest, a strategy also suggested by the state procurator to whom she turned for help, was to "stand above [her] personal life" (9 April 1938). Piatnitskaia was "tortured" that she could not bring herself to hate her husband, an enemy of the people. She urged herself to "prove, not for others, but for myself," that she could overcome her personal doubts and distance herself from him: "You will prove with this that you stand higher than a wife, and higher than a mother. You will prove with this that you are a citizen of the Great Soviet Union. And if you don't have the strength to do this, then to the devil with you."[59]

This article has sought to introduce a historically contextualized notion of subjectivity for the early Soviet period (1917–41). Contrary to a widespread popular habit to cast the Soviet regime solely as an oppressive power that strove to subjugate Soviet citizens' sense of their selves, the essay has pointed to the Revolution as a tremendous subjectivizing force. This was on account not only of the language of individual and social emancipation which burst on the scene in 1917 and provided people with entirely new registers of self-expression. More important was the fact that subjectivity became an intensely political and, indeed, redeeming category practically from the outset of the Revolution. The questions of who one was, for or against the Revolution, whether one could change, and how one could demonstrably transform oneself into a revolutionary subject, were central, arguably the most pressing, questions of the period of early Soviet rule – questions that the Soviet regime pursued in the name of the Revolution, but of course also for the purpose of molding a loyal popular following. As a consequence, Soviet citizens had no choice but to be aware of their "selves" as a distinct political category, as a personal identity subject to public scrutiny, and as an entity to be molded and perfected through work on oneself. The Revolution thus underscored – or in many cases actually created – the sense that one possessed, and had to be able to present, a distinct personal biography. Without any doubt the uninterrupted chain of

---

[58] Iuliia Piatnitskaia, *Dnevnik zheny bol'shevika* (Benson, VT, 1987), 149 (entry of 26 March 1938).
[59] Ibid., entry of 27 May 1938.

social and personal ruptures caused by war, revolution, and intense Soviet social engineering had a shattering effect on individuals' preexisting sense of selves, but it would be wrong to infer from this a social landscape of fractured, atomized individuals, as has been suggested,[60] because at the same time (and as never before) Soviet citizens were urged to comprehend themselves in terms of coherent self-narratives and thus to sculpt themselves as autobiographical subjects. From the outset, Soviet revolutionary policies had a strong subjective corollary, whereby individuals were to weave their subjective voices into the collective project of building a socialist society. This subjective stance, which gained even more political weight in the 1930s as compared to the preceding decade, has to be taken into account when studying autobiographical statements of the age.[61]

Conceivably one of the most lasting effects of the prewar Soviet regime was the creation of coherent and purposeful individual biographies on a mass scale. In any event one can observe a recurrent desire on the part of surviving Soviet citizens to emphasize a sense of historic purpose and personal fulfillment when recounting their experience of the prewar Stalin period. Antonina Berezhnaia, formerly an engineer from Sverdlovsk, surprised her Western interviewers who kept asking her about the shortages and difficulties of her youth. Instead, all she wanted to do was talk about "production and work for the public good over personal life and private satisfaction."[62] And Leonid Potemkin, author of a remarkable self-expressivist Stalin era diary, was adamant in his old age to combat the notion that Stalinism meant just sacrifice, just evil, and just repression. In his own words: "I categorically reject the slanderous claim that our generation allegedly lived its life in vain."[63]

---

[60] See especially Plaggenborg, "Grundprobleme der Kulturgeschichte."

[61] On the turn toward individuating practices in the 1930s see Vadim Volkov, "The Concept of *Kul'tumost'*: Notes on the Stalinist Civilizing Process," in *Everyday Revolution: Subjects in Formation in Early Soviet Culture*, ed. C. Kiaer and E. Naiman (forthcoming); Oleg Kharkhordin, *The Collective and the Individual in Russia* (Berkeley, 1999); Vladimir Papernyi, *Kul'tura "Dva"* (Ann Arbor, 1985); and Raymond A. Bauer, *The New Man in Soviet Psychology* (1952; reprint ed. Cambridge, MA, 1968).

[62] Barbara Engel and A. Posadskaya-Vanderbeck, eds., *A Revolution of Their Own: Voices of Women in Soviet History* (Boulder, 1998), 101–16, esp. 102–3. Berezhnaia also remembered how as a worker forewoman she tried to raise the morale of her fellow workers by going through the shop and singing them the song, "All Our Life Is a Struggle." A portrait photograph of hers from 1932, which she showed to her Western interlocutors, bore the dedication on the back: "A few words to my friend: Only by means of persistent struggle and lengthy work on the self can a person reach the heights of science. It is essential to value life and to know how to extract from it only what is good, uniting that with one's ideals. Then life will be interesting and full of happiness" (ibid., 107–8).

[63] Author's interview with L. A. Potemkin, 29 March 1995.

Further Reading: Stalinist Subjectivity

Veronique Garros et al., eds., *Intimacy and Terror: Soviet Diaries of the 1930s* (New York, 1995).

Igal Halfin, *From Darkness to Light: Class, Consciousness, and Salvation in Revolutionary Russia* (Pittsburgh, 2000).

Igal Halfin, ed., *Language, Revolution, and the Poetics of Revolutionary Identity* (London, 2002).

Jochen Hellbeck, "Fashioning the Stalinist Soul: The Diary of Stepan Podlubnyi, 1931–1939," *Jahrbucher fur Geschichte Osteuropas*, vol. 44, no. 3 (1996).

Oleg Kharkhordin, *The Collective and the Individual in Russia: A Study of Practices* (Berkeley, 1999).

Anna Krylova, "The Tenacious Liberal Subject in Soviet Studies," *Kritika*, vol. 1, no. 1 (2000).

Eric Naiman, *Sex in Public: The Incarnation of Early Soviet Ideology* (Princeton, 1997).

Women and Gender

9

Women in Soviet Society: Equality, Development, and Social Change

Gail Warshofsky Lapidus

Excerpted from Gail Warshofsky Lapidus, *Women in Soviet Society: Equality, Development, and Social Change* (Berkeley: University of California Press, 1978).

Editor's Introduction

Stalinism had a particularly strong impact on women's lives and gender roles in Soviet society. In addition to the repression and hardship suffered by the entire population, women experienced both new opportunities and new burdens under Stalin. Stalinist industrialization required the recruitment of large numbers of women into the industrial workforce, thereby granting them new employment opportunities and restructuring the gendered division of labor. At the same time, the Soviet government sought to increase the birthrate by emphasizing women's reproductive obligations and their "natural roles" as mothers. Women under Stalinism ended up with the double burden of work outside the home combined with uncompensated domestic labor and responsibility for childraising.

To explain how Stalinism restructured the gender order and yet nonetheless perpetuated women's inequality is an important historical problem. There were members of the Bolshevik Party who already before the Revolution called for women's liberation and equality.[1] Bolshevik feminists, such as Aleksandra Kollontai, sought to abolish the family and establish collective responsibility for childraising, so as to free women for equal participation in public life.[2] Early Soviet legislation weakened the family and official propaganda heralded equal opportunities for women under

[1] Richard Stites, *The Women's Liberation Movement in Russia: Feminism, Nihilism, and Bolshevism, 1860–1930* (Princeton, 1977).

[2] Barbara Evans Clements, *Bolshevik Feminist: The Life of Aleksandra Kollontai* (Bloomington, 1979).

socialism. But women's equality was not a priority for most Party leaders, and many, including Lenin and Stalin, were not prepared to abolish the family. Moreover, a myriad of social problems, from prostitution to homeless children, prompted calls to reinforce traditional family and gender roles.[3]

In the selection below, Gail Lapidus explains that when the Stalinist leadership did recruit women into the industrial labor force, it was not to provide them with equal opportunity but rather to fill a desperate need for labor during the industrialization drive.[4] Literally millions of women were recruited into Soviet industry in the 1930s, and during the Second World War this recruitment intensified, so that women constituted a majority of all workers by 1945. Industrial employment offered women new wage-earning possibilities, but it did not lead to equality. Women faced substantial hostility and discrimination from male managers and workers, and often they received the low-status, low-paying jobs in factories. Simultaneously women continued to bear the brunt of childcare and domestic chores. Despite official promises to provide childcare and communal dining facilities, these services remained badly underfunded throughout the Stalin era, so women had to fulfill their traditional household functions in addition to working outside the home.

Lapidus also discusses the Stalinist regime's family policy and its impact on women. In the mid-1930s, the Soviet government reversed its legislation weakening the family and began to promote the importance of marriage and family. In addition to reflecting a more general move toward social stabilization, this policy was enacted by Stalin and his fellow leaders in order to raise the country's birthrate. Soviet legislation in 1936 banned abortion, and a concurrent propaganda campaign stressed women's obligation to have children. This campaign defined women's identities less as independent wage earners and more as wives and mothers. Whereas feminist ideas of the early Soviet period had stressed similar and equal roles for men and women in public life, Stalinist policy tended to promote differentiation in gender roles.

Legislation and propaganda during the Second World War and postwar period further differentiated women from men. The mobilization of men for military service, while it created even greater employment opportunities for women on the homefront, reinforced the difference in gender roles. Family legislation in 1944 further strengthened the family and offered increased material rewards to women who had many children, thereby tying women's identity even more closely to motherhood. Pro-

---

[3] Wendy Goldman, *Women, the State and Revolution: Soviet Family Policy and Social Life, 1917–1936* (New York, 1993).
[4] See also Melanie Ilic, *Women Workers in the Soviet Interwar Economy: From 'Protection' to 'Equality'* (New York, 1999).

paganda and fiction of the postwar period reinforced traditional gender roles by portraying women in a subordinate position to their husbands within the family. Thus, as Lapidus shows, Stalinism provided women with new opportunities, but it did not grant them equality. The Stalinist leadership was guided not by feminist principles but rather by an instrumental desire to mobilize women's manual and reproductive labor. For women the result was a dual role as both workers and mothers, and the double burden of uncompensated domestic labor and full-time work outside the home.

Women in Soviet Society: Equality, Development, and Social Change

Gail Warshofsky Lapidus

By the end of the first decade of Soviet rule, a gradual shift had occurred in the assumptions and orientations that guided Soviet policy. The egalitarian and libertarian strains of Bolshevism, limited and contradictory from the start, had been temporarily reinforced by the imperatives of insurgency. With the consolidation of the new regime, they were overwhelmed by new economic and political priorities.[1] Acute tensions arising from the rule of a modernizing, authoritarian elite over a largely peasant society compelled further adaptations of revolutionary aspirations to the realities of Russian life. Moreover, while the revolutionary generation of Old Bolsheviks steeped in the cosmopolitan intellectual traditions of European social democracy still dominated the Party's central organs, the vast expansion of the Party's membership in the 1920s altered its composition, center of gravity, and outlook. Lower levels of the Party apparatus were increasingly staffed by a new generation of Party recruits, who were of very different social origins and political orientations and who brought more traditional attitudes and patterns of behavior to political life.[2] Under these circumstances, a libertarian concern with the requisites of female emancipation receded still further into the background, and more instrumental preoccupations came increasingly to the forefront of political life.

It was not, then, a revolutionary program of emancipation that brought about the profound changes in women's roles of subsequent decades. Nor was it the slow but cumulative effect of broader economic and social changes. The transformation of women's roles was, to a considerable degree, the indirect result of the inauguration of the

---

[1] For a suggestive treatment of the broader transformation of Soviet ideology see Barrington Moore, *Soviet Politics: The Dilemma of Power* (Cambridge, Mass., 1959).

[2] The rapid growth of the Party from a prerevolutionary membership of 8,500 in 1905 to 24,000 in early 1917 and to over 1,000,000 by 1925 offers some indication of the shrinking weight of the Old Bolshevik contingent. By the end of 1927 more than 60 percent of the secretaries of Party cells were persons who had joined the Party after 1921 (Leonard Schapiro, *The Communist Party of the Soviet Union* [New York, 1959], p. 311). See also Merle Fainsod, *How Russia is Ruled*, 2nd ed. (Cambridge, Mass., 1963), pp. 248–59. and T. H. Rigby, *The Communist Party Membership in the USSR* (Princeton, 1968), p. 52. Roger Pethybridge examines the political consequences of backwardness in *The Social Prelude to Stalinism* (London, 1974).

First Five Year Plan in 1928, the collectivization of agriculture that accompanied it, and the emergence of new patterns of authority under Stalin.

The forced collectivization of agriculture, with its stunning impact on authority structures and social relationships in the rural milieu, and the massive entry of women into the industrial labor force during the 1930s, a process given still further impetus by the outbreak of World War II, were the central features of this social transformation. With them came a vast expansion of educational opportunities for women, the spread of a network of institutions for the education and care of children, and the enactment of protective labor legislation and social programs designed to ensure the compatibility of women's domestic responsibilities with industrial employment. These changes reverberated across the whole range of social institutions including, most importantly, the family itself.

Yet the context in which these changes occurred bore little resemblance to the visions surrounding initial discussions of the woman question. Where earlier advocates of drawing women into paid employment had seen it as a way of enhancing female status and independence, rising rates of female employment during the 1930s were a largely unplanned expression of a sustained economic and social crisis. The emergence of new institutional arrangements to support these new economic roles – communal child care facilities, communal dining, communal housing – occurred in a chaotic atmosphere, as a hastily improvised response to the pressures of rapid urbanization and rising female employment.

Nevertheless, the new roles assumed by women were neither accidental nor random. They were intimately linked to a strategy of industrial development in which women were not merely the beneficiaries but also the instruments and shock absorbers of a particular pattern of political, economic, and social modernization. Broadly speaking, the Stalinist strategy of industrialization – with its consequences for employment, urbanization, stratification, consumption, the supply of services, and the reproduction and socialization of children – necessarily entailed the performance of particular economic and social roles by women. Some aspects of these roles were dramatically new, and all involved an intensification of societal demands. In other respects, however, Stalinism perpetuated or even strengthened traditional norms and patterns of behavior and extended them to new contexts.

Indeed, it was the extraordinary scope and pace of social transformation and the unexpected emergence of what Moshe Lewin has aptly labeled a "quicksand society" that called forth Draconian measures to limit the scope of social dislocation and to create islands of stability in a sea of social chaos.[3] The family policies of the revolutionary era fell victim to new needs. Efforts to halt the further fragmentation of family life and to stem the alarming decline of birth rates occasioned by material hardship and social instability resulted in a partial reversal of earlier legislation. Measures originally designed to enhance the freedom and autonomy of women and to complement potential new economic roles were whittled away or abandoned in a desperate attempt to enhance the stability of the family and give greater official recogniton to its procreative and socializing functions.

A distinctive new social order gradually took shape under the force of these often contradictory pressures. New obligations, roles, and opportunities for women were assimilated into older values and patterns of behavior to create an amalgam of tradition and transformation that was the essence of the Stalin era.

Social Production: Female Employment and Industrialization

The inauguration of the First Five Year Plan in 1928 and the forcible collectivization of agriculture that accompanied it brought profound changes in the economic and social roles of Soviet women. For rural Russia, Stalinism brought intense economic pressures and a new locus of authority while leaving intact many basic features of economic and social life. The extensive involvement of women in agricultural labor continued under collectivization; the intimate connection between household and productive activity in the rural milieu limited the direct impact of new economic and political conditions on patterns of female employment. The migration of large numbers of women to urban and industrial regions, where the separation of household from employment was sharp, had, by contrast, profound structural consequences.

Throughout the 1920s the conviction that women should be drawn into social production on a vast scale had remained a largely theoretical concern. The general contraction of the economy and the influx of rural migrants resulted in high rates of urban unemployment, which affected women with particular severity.[4] Similarly, the commitment to

---

[3] Moshe Lewin, "Class, State and Ideology in the Piatiletka," in *Cultural Revolution in Russia, 1928–1933,* ed. Sheila Fitzpatrick (Bloomington, 1978).

[4] The rise in unemployment between 1922 and 1929 and the particularly high incidence of female unemployment are documented in Solomon Schwarz, *Labor in the Soviet Union* (New York, 1931), pp. 38–9. The First Five Year Plan anticipated a gradual decline in unemployment between 1929 and 1933, not yet understanding the transformation of the entire labor market that was already under way and that would shortly result in acute labor shortages.

the creation of a network of public child-care institutions and communal services and to an expansion of educational opportunities for women was not translated into reality on any substantial scale during this first decade.

The rapid expansion of the economy after 1928 transformed a politically desirable objective into a pressing economic need. As late as 1929 the authors of the First Five Year Plan still looked at female labor primarily as it affected women's economic and political status. They recommended an intensified enrollment of women in new industrial areas, fearing that the planned expansion of basic industries, in which few women were employed, would lead to a decline in the overall ratio of women workers.[5] The Plan envisioned only a modest increase in the proportion of women employed in the public sector, from 27 percent of the socialized labor force in 1927–8 to 32.5 percent in 1932–3.[6]

These expectations were rapidly overtaken by the momentum of economic changes. In the winter of 1929–30 unemployment began to decline, and by 1930 a combination of demographic and economic factors had created an acute manpower shortage. Party and governmental efforts to regulate the labor force were supplanted by measures to assure its supply and to allocate manpower to individual industries and plants. Growing concern with the fuller utilization of urban manpower resources focused increasingly on the need to draw women into industrial employment. A new perspective emerged in official documents, one that viewed the increased employment of women not in terms of its effects on women but as essential to the fulfillment of the economic plans.

A resolution of the Party Central Committee in September 1930 stated that, "to insure the fulfillment of the production program for the third year of the five-year period," it was necessary to "draw more juvenile workers as well as wives of workers and other toilers into production."[7] This Party directive was followed shortly by a government decree spelling out concrete measures to increase the employment of women. Quotas were established for the various industries, and educational institutions were required to admit fixed proportions of women for

[5] "If the proportion of women employed in various occupational divisions remained unchanged, the different pace of developing the several sections of the national economy would result in a decline of the percentage of women among the total of wage earners. ... This would be quite unsound; we must make it our task to widen the scope of women's work everywhere." *Five Year Plan of Economic Construction of the USSR* (Moscow, 1929), Vol. 2, p. 180.

[6] Ibid. In the spring of 1930 the target was raised to 34 or 35 percent.

[7] *Pravda*, September 3, 1930.

training in different fields.[8] In January of 1931 the People's Commissariat of Labor issued two listings of occupations, one enumerating those to be reserved exclusively for women and one listing those to be reserved predominantly for women, a striking example of the tendency for traditional conceptions of "women's work" to be extended to a new context. While this particular measure was later superseded, the notion that certain occupations were particularly suitable for an expansion of female labor persisted and served both to enhance and to channel the entry of women into the modern sector of the labor force.

The years between 1930 and 1937 saw a massive influx of women into industry. By 1932 the number of women employed had risen from three million to six million, far exceeding all estimates, yet so dramatic was the increase in total employment during these years that the proportion of women remained at 27.4 percent, virtually unchanged from 1927–1928. The greatest gains were made in industry, and particularly in industries such as construction, where women had previously played a negligible role.

The reception of women workers in traditionally male fields was frequently hostile, according to many accounts, although this was less often the case in the eastern regions of the USSR, where the demand for new labor was particularly great and where the absence of entrenched male traditions permitted more flexible hiring practices. Most of these new women workers were young and unskilled, and lower levels of qualifications and experience combined with employers' discrimination to channel them into lower levels of the occupational hierarchy.

During the Second Five Year Plan period, between 1933 and 1937, an even more substantial rise took place in female industrial employment. A total of 3,350,000 women entered the labor force during these years, constituting some 82 percent of all newly employed workers. In 1937 almost 9.4 million women were employed, raising their proportion of the labor force to 34 percent.[9] By November 1939 the proportion of women in industry in general had reached 41.6 percent, and women constituted an even higher proportion of manual workers. Whole industries were now utilizing women on an unprecedented scale; women formed one-fourth of the manual workers in iron ore mining, coal mining, and the iron and steel industry. The First and Second Five Year Plans paved the way for the even greater reliance on women workers during World War II, when the massive mobilization of males for military service would otherwise have had adverse effects on productive capacity. As the war finally drew to a close in 1945, the pro-

---

[8] V. N. Tolkunova, *Pravo zhenshchin na trud i ego garantii* (Moscow, 1967), pp. 87–97.
[9] Schwarz, *Labor in the Soviet Union*, pp. 71–2.

portion of women in the modern sector had reached an all-time high of 56 percent.

The massive entry of women into industrial production was interpreted by many in the language of an earlier epoch. The First Five Year Plan period had evoked a revival of civil war militance and utopianism. In the enthusiasm of cultural revolution, the new role of women in economic life was seized on as additional evidence of the imminence of full socialism. A vast and vivid literature extolled the industrial millennium and linked the new economic role of women to sweeping plans for the communal reorganization of life. Elaborate economic calculations rationalized and buttressed visionary schemes.[10]

In the face of a growing labor shortage, the social costs of private household production appeared particularly wasteful. S. G. Strumilin, a prolific theorist of the future socialist society, and a key figure in the formulation of the First Five Year Plan, had computed that for every unit of population some seven hundred hours of precious time were lost in cooking, laundry, and the care of children. As a consequence, he estimated, some thirty million potential workers were required to devote full time to unproductive household labor.[11] Strumilin's concern was echoed in a study by the Workers and Peasants Inspection of the RSFSR:

> Every day 36 million hours are expended in the RSFSR for cooking alone. This means that on the basis of the eight-hour working day, four and one-half million workers or double the number that are employed in heavy industry are occupied in cooking. At the same time, collective cooking of the same amount of food would require one-sixth of this time, and would release over four million housewives for productive labor.[12]

The development of a wide network of communal institutions for child care, laundry, and cooking was now urged not merely to free women

[10] For a fascinating discussion of these utopian visions, see S. Frederick Starr, "The Anti-Urban utopias of Early Stalinist Russia," in Fitzpatrick, *Cultural Revolution*. A collection of proposals is included in B. Lunin, ed., *Goroda sotsializma i sotsialisticheskaia rekonstruktsiia byta* (Moscow, 1930). One approach called for the manufacture of portable dwellings in modular units to house one person each, encouraging geographical and social mobility for the "liberated" members of former households. Proposals for communal housing and services, utopian in appearance, were plausible in the context of the First Five Year Plan. As Starr points out, "collectivization was a fact wherever factories were built without first constructing adequate housing," while the shrinking allotment of space in both Moscow and in the newer cities meant that "communalization by necessity was already in practice."

[11] S. G. Strumilin, *Rabochii byt v tsifrakh* (Moscow, 1926).

[12] Susan Kingsbury and Mildred Fairchild, *Factory, Family, and Women in the Soviet Union* (New York, 1935), p. 202.

from the drudgery of household work but to release a vast pool of labor for the expanding Soviet economy.

The wider utilization of female labor offered still further advantages. The increased employment of urban women could substitute for an additional influx of labor from rural areas, thus substantially reducing the cost of the urban infrastructure needed to support a larger labor force. As another economist calculated:

> During the third and fourth year of the Five Year Plan we shall need at least one and a half million new employees in industry alone, and about four million for the economic system as a whole. If we count even two members to a family, and if each family must have its own housewife engaged exclusively in unproductive labor, it would mean that we should have to bring in eight million people from the villages, in order to get four million workers – and this in turn would mean a building program quite beyond our means.[13]

Other Soviet writers were quick to point out that female employment would also facilitate a more efficient organization of urban life. The savings resulting from the reduction of the number of dependents per wage earner would become available for investment in communal facilities. This argument recurred frequently in the wave of pamphlets and books decribing the future socialist city that was inspired by the revival of utopian leftism between 1928 and 1932. As one prominent theorist suggested:

> In individual households from 10 to 15 percent of the general cost of the establishment is spent on separate kitchens, laundries, and storerooms. When building centralized houses, all these auxiliary rooms will be unnecessary and our communal kitchens, dining-rooms, and laundries will not require so much expenditure. Construction of special buildings for the education and boarding of children may not be considered as an extra expense for this eliminates the need for living quarters for children in the adults' houses. We should also remember that the communal house emancipates women and thus decreases the number of dependents in the family. If, for instance, we need 10,000 workers for a new factory, we have to build a town for at least 40,000 people if we are going to have houses with individual apartments; but *if we build a socialist city, we shall need to accommodate only from 20,000 to 24,000 people, since the women will have free time for the factory and the only dependents will be children.* (Italics added.)[14]

---

[13] Ibid.
[14] Ibid., p. 203.

Economic rationality appeared to buttress utopian fervor in the view that the employment of women would not only finance the development of new services but would result in higher levels of family income and therefore a real improvement in welfare: "It has already been planned to raise the workers' budget about 100 percent by the end of the five-year period, and the productive labor of the adult women members of the family will raise the income to a figure at least two and a half times greater than it is at present."[15]

To what extent these were conscious and explicit objectives directly affecting the planning process itself is difficult to answer on the basis of the available evidence. Influential economists and political figures were prominent among the authors of these proposals, and supported them with elaborate economic calculations. Yet the political conflicts surrounding the planning process, the atmosphere in which the First Five Year Plan was launched, and the chaotic conditions that followed suggest that events far outran the capacity of the leadership to direct and control them. It is, therefore, more likely that the rising participation of women in the labor force was a secondary consequence of labor shortages and falling real wages, retrospectively rationalized as a step toward liberaton.

Soviet planners clearly sought to limit the furious pace of urbanization.[16] Severe restrictions were placed on migration, internal passports were reintroduced in 1932, and *kolkhoz* (collective farm) members were required to obtain formal permission to leave the countryside. Still, the actual rate of migration vastly exceeded the planned rate. Also unplanned, but the inevitable outcome of economic decisions, was a sharp decline in real wages. An acute inflation was responsible for a dramatic increase in nominal wage levels, but this rise concealed a serious decline in purchasing power and living standards.

The decline in real wages made it virtually impossible to support an urban family with several dependents on the income of a single breadwinner. Large numbers of women were therefore obliged to seek employment to supplement family income. Indeed, the very fact that the decline in real wages did not preclude a rise in per capita urban consumption during these years was largely due to the entry of urban women into the labor force in large numbers.[17] As official statistics

[15] Ibid., p. 204.
[16] The argument that socialist industrialization strategy involves an effort to economize on urbanization costs is developed in more general terms in Gur Ofer, "Industrial Structure, Urbanization, and Growth Strategy of Socialist Countries," Hebrew University of Jerusalem Research Report No. 53 (Jerusalem, 1974).
[17] Janet Chapman, *Real Wages in Soviet Russia* (Cambridge, Mass., 1963), p. 137.

reveal, a steady decline occurred in the number of dependents per wage earner, from 2.46 in 1928 to 2.05 in 1930, 1.59 in 1935, and 1.28 in 1940.[18] While part of this decline was a consequence of falling urban birthrates, the figures also reflect the fact that rising female employment reduced the number of dependents supported by the income of the household head.

The massive entry of women into the labor force was given additional impetus by other features of Stalinist policy. The devastating impact of collectivization on rural economic and social life brought large numbers of women to cities in search of employment. The purges brought with them not merely political insecurity but deportations and deaths, which in turn obliged additional numbers of women to become self-supporting. Finally, the massive mobilization of men for military service during World War II required a vast influx of female replacements. The enormous loss of males transformed millions of widows into heads of households, and deprived a whole generation of women of the opportunity to marry at all. Throughout the Stalin era, then, an expanding demand for labor in the modern sector interacted with demographic imbalances and economic insecurity to increase the availability of women for such employment.

Whether the rise in female employment was anticipated or intended at the start of the First Five Year Plan or was initially an explicit feature of a larger strategy of industrial development, it was a consequence of both specific economic policies and of larger social changes associated with Stalinism. Moreover, the terms on which it occurred profoundly altered the definition of women's liberation. In earlier discussions, the entry of women into the labor force was viewed in political terms, as a dimension of emancipation. Economic independence was viewed as a prerequisite of genuine equality. Now, the employment of women in the industrial labor force was integral to a strategy of development that utilized female labor as a major economic resource, facilitating a rapid expansion of the labor force at relatively low cost.

Whether the massive entry of women into social production would in fact prove liberating depended on the wider social context in which it occurred. Educational opportunities and vocational training were essential if women were to occupy anything but the least skilled positions. Moreover, if the new economic roles of women were to place them on an equal footing with men, massive investments in public services were essential. An extensive network of preschool institutions and after-school programs was needed for the care of children of working mothers, while the development of communal laundries, dining rooms,

---

[18] Ibid., p. 167.

and other social services to free women from household chores was vital if their employment was to constitute a form of liberation rather than an additional burden.

The development of these services, however, failed to keep pace with the entry of women into industry. Indeed, the whole pattern of Soviet industrialization explicitly depended on the low priority assigned to precisely those economic sectors that might have lightened the burdens of working women. Soviet development priorities not only failed to relieve the pressures on the individual household to any substantial degree; it actually increased them in ways that prevented women from profiting fully from new opportunities. Economic policies resting on the underdevelopment of the service sector and social policies designed to strengthen the family as a reproductive and socializing institution assigned a set of functions and roles to women that in some respects intensified the sexual division of labor both in public arenas and within the family itself.

Family Policy and the Redefinition of Female Roles

The economic pressures on the household associated with Stalinist industrialization were accompanied by new political demands as well. Since they contradicted the central assumptions on which early Soviet orientations toward the family rested, it is not surprising that a reassessment of family policy followed.

The new family legislation of the Stalin era was marked by certain conservative, even authoritarian, features that constituted a significant departure from earlier precedents. In the face of such massive social transformations as those brought about by industrialization and collectivization, and the new opportunities for social mobility these changes created for women, a focus on the conservative features of Stalinism may appear puzzling. Yet the central feature of Stalinism – the feature that distinguished it most sharply from the preceding regime – was precisely its amalgam of radical transformation and social conservatism. Massive social dislocation called forth efforts at stabilization and integration that drew heavily on the values, behavioral patterns, and organizational mechanisms of traditional Russian society while adapting them to new purposes.

The "revolution from above" of 1928–32, which marked the first phase of Stalinism, was characterized by a militance and radicalism evocative of the civil war period.[19] Rapid industrialization and agricul-

---

[19] For a collection of studies dealing with the effects of these events in different areas of Soviet politics and society, see Fitzpatrick, *Cultural Revolution in Russia*.

tural collectivization were its central features, but these were also years that saw a dramatic increase in the availability of institutional child care and in the scope of women's industrial employment, educational opportunities, and political participation. The first stage of Stalinism was, in short, a period of rapid social change that left its imprint on a very wide range of social indicators.

The campaign for industrialization and collectivization absorbed the energies and enthusiasm of Party militants, temporarily eclipsing the burning social and sexual controversies of the 1920s. It simultaneously undermined the institutional and political bases of support of an older generation of revolutionary leaders and cultural authorities. By late 1931, in reaction to the social disorganization and breakdown that these radical changes had precipitated, a process of retrenchment was visible, and the contours of a new stage of development with new priorities began to emerge. By the mid-1930s – in education, law, and culture, as well as in family policy – a new orientation had taken shape.[20]

Interpretations of Stalinism that see only its archaic and Thermidorean features, on the one hand, or those that stress its functional necessity to the creation of a modern industrial society, on the other, overlook its adaptive and integrative aspects. A complex interplay of historical and cultural traditions, the socioeconomic environment, the emerging political system, and the personality and attitudes of Stalin himself shaped the transformation of Soviet political culture in the 1930s.

This transformation involved the final repudiation of the libertarian and egalitarian strains that had stamped the economic and social legislation as well as the political values of the 1920s. Stalin's attack on "petty-bourgeois egalitarianism" in 1931 signaled the reintroduction of substantial wage differentials as an incentive to economic productivity and an increasing differentiation of status and prestige to reinforce new authority relations. These broader changes in social and political values, which were themselves significant for the definition of women's roles, had particular ramifications for the role of the family.

The shift in Soviet policy toward the family in the mid-1930s was neither a conclusive demonstration of the family's functional necessity nor a complete reversion to the status quo ante. It occurred in the context of political and economic changes that transformed the environment in which the family was embedded. The nationalization of industry and the collectivization of agriculture had shattered the

---

[20] These shifts are reviewed in N. Timasheff, *The Great Retreat* (New York, 1946); Leon Trotskii, *The Revolution Betrayed*, trans. Max Eastman (New York, 1937); and Fainsod, *How Russia is Ruled*, pp. 104–16.

family's control over productive resources, while the expansion of public education reduced its influence over the socialization and placement of children. Moreover, as refugee interviews made clear, the conviction that the Soviet state controlled the future made the majority of families unwilling to jeopardize the future access of their children to education and employment by communicating their own hostility to the younger generation. In the light of these circumstances, a change in official policy could be based on the reasonable assurance that the new recognition now granted the family would not seriously compromise the new social order.

The actual substance of the family legislation enacted in the mid-1930s was relatively moderate in its provisions.[21] In a broader sense, however, such legislation expressed a new orientation toward the family that constituted a dramatic departure from the values and expectations of elite culture in the earlier decade. No longer was the "withering away" of the family or, for that matter, of the state itself viewed as the inevitable and desirable consequence of economic and political change; like the state, it was argued, the family grows stronger as full socialism approaches. The family was now said to be the bulwark of the social system, a microcosm of the new socialist society. It was required to reproduce in miniature the authoritarian and hierarchical features of the emerging political Leviathan. In *The Revolution Betrayed* (1936), Trotskii pointed to the shift in family policy as an especially telling expression of a Thermidorean reaction, explaining that "the most compelling motive of the present cult of the family is undoubtedly the need of the bureaucracy for a stable hierarchy of relations and for the disciplining of youth by means of 40 million points of support for authority and power."[22]

The new orientation, far from devaluing the role of the family, now treated it as a pivotal social institution performing vital functions. It was to serve above all as a model of social order, and for this purpose marital stability was essential. The independence, autonomy, and mobility encouraged by earlier legislation were henceforth to be restricted in the interests of preserving a stable and monogamous partnership. As *Pravda* proclaimed, "so-called 'free love' and all disorderly sex life are bourgeois through and through, and have nothing to do with either socialist

---

[21] For a translation of the text of such legislation, as well as some of the accompanying official explanations of the new family policy, see Rudolf Schlesinger, comp., *Changing Attitudes in Soviet Russia – The Family in the USSR* (London, 1949), pp. 251–347. See also Alex Inkeles, *Social Change in Soviet Russia* (Cambridge, Mass., 1968), Ch. 11; Kent Geiger, *The Family in Soviet Russia* (Cambridge, Mass., 1968), Ch. 4; and Wilhelm Reich, *The Sexual Revolution*, trans. Theodore P. Wolfe, 4th ed. rev. (New York, 1969), Pt. II.

[22] Trotskii, *The Revolution Betrayed*, p. 153.

principles or the ethics and standards of conduct of the Soviet citizen.
. . . The elite of our country . . . are as a rule also excellent family men
who dearly love their children. And vice versa: the man who does not
take marriage seriously . . . is usually also a bad worker and a poor
member of society."[23]

The effort to promote the stabilization of the family was also linked
to a serious concern with the declining birthrate. A massive press campaign linked the joys of motherhood with the benefits of Soviet power.
"A woman without children merits our pity, for she does not know the
full joy of life. Our Soviet women, full-blooded citizens of the freest
country in the world, have been given the bliss of motherhood."[24] The
idealization of the family and of marital stability and the close association of femininity with maternity had as a counterpart the repression
of sexual deviance as a social crime. Harsh measures were directed for
the first time against both prostitution and homosexuality in the effort
to extend order and discipline to personal life.

Yet the attempt to encourage reproduction by portraying motherhood as the supreme obligation of Soviet women cast some doubt on the
simultaneous claim that it was the supreme joy. Indeed, the enormous
hardships faced by women workers in the forced industrialization of the
times were reflected in the decline of birthrates and in the large numbers
of abortions. These conditions motivated the effort to offer enhanced
protection and increased material incentives to potential mothers.[25]
Special state allowances were granted to mothers of large families.
Single-child families, insisted one distinguished educator, breed egotism
and unhappiness, while large families – seven was his favorite number
– make it possible to rear children in a proper collective spirit.[26]

But the effort to encourage reproduction did not rely on moral
suasion and material incentives alone. The abolition of legal abortions
was the most dramatic feature of the new family legislation of 1936.
Abortions could henceforth be performed only when pregnancy endan-
gered the life or health of the potential mother; criminal penalties were
attached to violations.

This particular provision of the draft legislation did not go unchallenged. A number of critical letters were published in the press, along

---

[23] Schlesinger, *Changing Attitudes*, p. 252.

[24] Ibid., p. 254.

[25] The annual total fertility rate dropped from 4,826.1 in 1930 to 4,255 in 1931 and
3,575 in 1932; a low of 2,904.9 was reached in 1934. See D. Peter Mazur, "Reconstruction of Fertility Trends for the Female Population of the USSR," *Population Studies*
21 (July 1967): 38.

[26] Anton Makarenko, *The Collective Family: A Handbook for Russian Parents*, trans. Robert
Daglish (New York, 1967), pp. 43–47.

with elaborate justifications for the changes. Its objectionable features were spelled out in a letter from a young engineer, who wrote:

> The prohibition of abortion means the compulsory birth of a child to a woman who does not want children ... The birth of a child ties married people to each other. ... Where a child comes into the family against the will of the parents, a grim personal drama will be enacted which will undoubtedly lower the social value of the parents and leave its mark on the child. A categorical prohibition of abortion will confront young people with a dilemma: either complete sexual abstinence or the risk of jeopardizing their studies and disrupting their life. To my mind any prohibition of abortion is bound to mutilate many a young life. Apart from this, the result of such a prohibition might be an increase in the death rate from abortions because they will then be performed illegally.[27]

Her anxieties, in retrospect, appear to have been well-founded. In evaluating the effects of Stalin's legislation, perhaps with an eye to current controversies, the author of a recent study concluded that its impact on birthrates was short-lived, and its larger consequences harmful: "The 1936 resolution forbidding abortion in point of fact did not and could not be any serious stimulant to raising the birth rate ... it merely led many women having unwanted pregnancies to have illegal abortions, risking their health and sometimes their lives."[28]

If the stabilizing and reproductive functions of the Soviet family were reinforced by new legislation, the economic role of the household in providing a wide array of services was recognized in new attitudes. Even housework, once so harshly stigmatized by Lenin, was now considered "socially useful labor," while Soviet wives were assured that achieving a comfortable home life was a desirable goal. The ranks of proletarian heroines were now joined by the wives of the new Soviet elite of managers and engineers, praised not for heroic feats of production but for introducing civilization into the lives of their men by planting flowers outside power stations, sewing linen, and opening fashion studios.[29] The status and identity of a woman were no longer to be derived exclusively from her independent role in production but at least in part defined ascriptively, as functions of her performance in the roles of wife and mother. The full implications of this redefinition of femininity for the stratification system remained to be worked out.

---

[27] Schlesinger, *Changing Attitudes*, p. 257.

[28] E. A. Sadvokasova, *Sotsial'no-gigienicheskie aspekty regulirovaniia razmerov sem'i* (Moscow, 1969), p. 210.

[29] Schlesinger, *Changing Attitudes*, pp. 235–50.

The socializing functions of the family received particular emphasis in the new orientation of the Stalin period. Marital stability was itself a condition of the proper upbringing of children. But the view of the family as a central socializing agency represented a major shift of perspective. No longer was upbringing treated as properly a communal responsibility; the burden was shifted back to the family. But the function itself was redefined in the process, so that upbringing within the home was not merely a private matter but involved parental responsibility to the larger community. In the words of Anton Makarenko, a leading educational authority of the period: "In our country the duty of a father toward his children is a particular form of his duty toward society. . . . In handing over to you a certain measure of social authority, the Soviet state demands from you correct upbringing of future citizens."[30]

Taken together, these aspects of Stalinism represent an effort to mobilize women intensively on behalf of a widening array of economic, social, and political objectives. Increasing demands on women were the accompaniment of expanding opportunities. Pressures toward female employment in industry, the demands on the household, and the treatment of marriage, reproduction, and socialization – all effectively broadened the definition of women's obligations to the larger community. The new image of feminine virtue incorporated wifely and maternal duties in addition to a contribution to the building of socialism.

The tension of contradictory norms and expectations in the new definition of femininity is splendidly conveyed in the speech of a Soviet fictional heroine on a visit to the Kremlin in 1937:

> "Our feminine hearts are overflowing with emotions," she said, "and of these love is paramount. Yet a wife should also be a happy mother and create a serene home atmosphere, without, however, abandoning work for the common welfare. She should know how to combine all these things while also matching her husband's performance on the job."
> "Right!" said Stalin.[31]

The new Soviet heroine was to join a highly competitive participation in the economic arena with nurturing family roles of a rather traditional kind. This portrait, however, offers striking contrast to the female political activists of revolutionary literature. In the first decade of Soviet development, the entry of women into public roles was inextricably associated with their liberation from family roles, and emancipation was

---

[30] Makarenko, *Collective Family*, p. xii.
[31] F. Panferov, *Bruski*, cited in Xenia Gasiorowska, *Women in Soviet Fiction* (Madison, 1968), p. 53.

defined as the opportunity for women to enter as fully into public roles – political and economic – as men. With the shift in policy toward the family, this unity was ruptured. It was now argued not only that women's public roles, largely confined to participation in production, were compatible with extensive family roles but also that the two reinforced each other and were both necessary to real womanhood. Where revolutionary feminism had anticipated the increasing identity of male and female roles, the values of the Stalin era stressed differentiation and complementarity.

The Stalin era was marked by a sharpening differentiation of male and female roles in political life as well. The growth of female political participation did not produce a corresponding increase in the role of women at the apex of the political hierarchy. In the increasingly hierarchical, elitist, authoritarian, and competitive political climate of Stalinism, women were virtually excluded from positions of real importance and were utilized – like Kollontai, Krupskaia, and Stasova – for largely symbolic purposes.

All these trends were further intensified by World War II. The massive mobilization of men for military service created extraordinary opportunities for women to rise to positions of real authority in economic and political life. Communal facilities were rapidly expanded to enable increasing numbers of mothers to join the labor force, while the higher educational institutions became almost entirely female. The heroic performance of Soviet women in wartime – whether on the military front or behind the lines – received elaborate recognition in wartime fiction and seemed to promise more genuine equality in the postwar era.

But the war years brought still further pressures, which sharpened the normative differentiation of masculinity and femininity, even as women took on previously male roles.[32] This differentiation extended even to the labor camps, where the sexual segregation of prisoners was introduced in 1944. It received its ultimate expression in the abolition of coeducation in many Soviet schools in 1943. While the separate education of boys and girls proved temporary, its justification went beyond the military needs that precipitated it. Underlying the measure was a definition of masculine and feminine roles of far wider significance, which survived the abolition of separate education to persist in more

---

[32] Jean Lipman-Blumen's treatment of role de-differentiation as a system response to crisis offers a useful perspective for interpreting the patterns of female employment in the USSR. When the specific crisis involves a major war, however, the result may be a sharpening of normative definitions of masculinity and femininity, as the Soviet experience suggests; "Role de-Differentiation as a System Response to Crisis: Occupational and Political Roles of Women," *Sociological Inquiry* 43 (April 1973): 105–30.

limited form to this day. A leading educational authority explained its underlying rationale:

> It is essential to introduce into girls' schools such additional subjects as pedagogics, needlework, courses in domestic science, personal hygiene and the care of children. . . . Those who attend boys' schools . . . must be able to cope with simple repairs to electrical installations and heating systems, and with the repair of household objects. . . . It is necessary that the future warrior and commander should be able to use a map. . . . In boy's schools the principal should as a rule be a man, and in girls' schools a woman.[33]

The trend toward increased differentiation of males and females in both family law and educational policy thus offers support for the hypothesis of Philip Slater that the sharper the differentiation of conjugal roles in a society, the greater the reliance that will be placed on sex segregation in the training of children for these roles.[34]

The Family Edict of July 1944 represented the capstone of this trend.[35] It introduced even more severe restrictions on divorce, requiring a two-stage legal proceeding and the payment of high fees. It went still further in protecting the sanctity of marriage by ending all recognition of unregistered marriages. The new edict thus recreated for the first time in post-revolutionary Russian history the distinction between legitimate and illegitimate children. Not only would a blank space now appear on the birth certificates of all children born outside registered marriages, but suits to establish paternity in such cases were also banned. At the same time, honorary titles and increased material incentives to motherhood, married or unmarried, offered additional protection and security to mothers as compensation for new burdens.

In its effort to encourage the postwar reestablishment of family life by protecting men from paternity suits, the new legislation obliged women to bear alone the consequences of extramarital relationships. But the official encouragement of a double standard of sexual morality and the sacrifice of women's and children's rights to the desire for a high birthrate further undermined the commitment to sexual equality enshrined in early Soviet legislation. In essence, in the words of a recent Soviet critic, it "encouraged a frivolous attitude toward women."[36]

---

[33] Schlesinger, *Changing Attitudes*, pp. 364–5.
[34] Philip Slater, "Parental Role Differentiation," in *The Family: Its Structure and Functions*, ed. Rose Laub Coser (New York, 1964), p. 362.
[35] For its text, see Schlesinger, *Changing Attitudes*, pp. 367–76.
[36] E. Z. Danilova, *Sotsial'nye problemy truda zhenshchiny-rabotnitsy* (Moscow, 1968), p. 64.

In the aftermath of World War II, the high priority assigned to marital stability and the need to replenish the severe population losses of wartime further sharpened the tension between the political and economic priorities of the Stalin period and the commitment to female equality and independence. As demobilized veterans returned to reclaim positions of authority now occupied by women or to rebuild shattered families with the expectation of female support, comfort, and self-sacrifice as reward for wartime hardships, conflicting needs and contradictory norms emerged acutely. Bare statistics document the fall of women from positions of economic and political authority without conveying the extent of regret or relief. But the human strains and ambiguities that accompanied the difficult transition of a war-torn society to the new priorities of the post-war era and the tensions involved in the readjustment of male-female relationships to postwar life are best captured in the fiction of the postwar period.

In a poignant tale of rural life, a woman widowed by war who drowns her sorrows in work and rises to the chairmanship of the collective farm is suddenly confronted, after years of separation, by the unexpected return of her husband. The adjustment to new realities proves difficult for both. The husband, vacillating between pride and humiliation, muses:

> He was used to being boss in his house. He used to walk along the village with an unhurried step, holding his head high and proud. When he was on his way home from the army, he thought he would turn mountains over. But there are no mountains. . . . And Marya, she moves about, gives orders. And the more she gives orders, the more she grows even in his eyes. And the more she grows, the smaller he gets. . . . And it seems she needs her husband and then again it seems she does not.[37]

A struggle over power leads to growing estrangement, ended by the intervention of the local Party secretary, who, far from encouraging Marya's aspirations, criticizes her misuse of power.

In countless similar tales, postwar authors chide their too ambitious heroines for clinging to newly won independence and neglecting the psychic needs of their men. The dilemmas created for women by the conflict of public commitments and personal life are a recurrent theme of postwar literature, and the sacrifice of ambition to family life is the prescribed solution. The potential conflict over status and mobility that

---

[37] Georgii Medynsky, "Marya," translated in Vera Dunham, *In Stalin's Time* (Cambridge, England, 1976), p. 216. For a suggestive general treatment of this issue, see Chapter 14 of Dunham.

equality might create is conveniently forestalled, and domestic happiness is offered as a surrogate for competitive achievement.

A similar lesson emerges from the story of another marriage in which the heroine occupied a position of greater authority than her husband. Affirming her determination to compartmentalize roles, she announces: "'At work, I am your boss. Watch out and don't resent it. But at home, if you want to, I'll submit to you.' Having, however, thought it over, she refined her statement: 'But at home, we'll be equals.' "[38] But even this solution is insufficient to resolve the tension felt to be inherent in the reversal of traditional statuses. The heroine therefore urges her husband to continue his studies so that a more fitting balance can be restored, and as if further explanation is necessary, the author firmly drives the point home: "'Come on, do me the favor, catch up. . . . I can't be the boss forever. I'll be having children. . . .' In her speaks no longer a stubborn agronomist but a woman's ambition. That ambition consists not of a drive to surpass one's beloved, but, rather, in being able to consider him superior to anybody else, including herself."[39]

The submissive heroines of postwar Soviet fiction represent a response to strains resulting from the structural changes of the Stalin era as well as the social effects of the war years. The increasing education and employment of women, juxtaposed to pressures for the maintenance of stable family relationships, created disequilibrium and tension in male–female relationships based on relatively traditional cultural assumptions. Parsonian sociology has suggested that the precarious balance between family and occupational structure in industrial societies has generally been maintained by inhibiting dual linkages between the two, which would create tension and competition between husband and wife and which would undermine the complementarity of roles it assumes to be essential to family stability.[40] By excluding married women from labor-force participation or confining them to secondary and residual occupational roles and by treating marriage as a mechanism for the economic support of women, equilibrium is maintained at the cost of full equality.

Because it was committed to and dependent on the participation of women in the labor force, Soviet policy rejected the use of marriage for the support of women and emphasized measures that would make it

---

[38] Yu. Kapusto, "Khleboroby," translated in Dunham, *In Stalin's Time*, p. 223.

[39] Ibid.

[40] Talcott Parsons, "The Social Structure of the Family," in *The Family: Its Function and Destiny*, ed. Ruth Anshen (New York, 1940), pp. 173–201; see also Constantina Safilios-Rothschild, "Dual Linkages Between the Occupational and Family System: A Macrosociological Analysis," in *Women and the Workplace*, eds. Martha Blaxall and Barbara Reagan (Chicago, 1976), pp. 51–60.

possible for women to combine work and family responsibilities. But, in the absence of an elaborate network of supporting services, and without a redefinition of cultural norms to support new roles within the family, some curtailment of female professional aspirations and mobility was necessary to preserve the equilibrium of the two-worker family. If the family was not to be sacrificed to the professional equality of women, equality itself would have to give way.

For the new Soviet heroine, therefore, economic independence had altered but not destroyed the traditional foundations of marriage. While productivity in economic life was valued and achievement rewarded, female occupational mobility was limited by the competing requirements of family life. The proud independence of the revolutionary heroine had faded from literature, along with images of the political activist whose dedication to building the new society overrode all other commitments and priorities. Male prerogatives in economic and political life received emphasis, while women were assigned as a high priority the task of producing citizens.

Thus, the acute role strain that was the legacy of the Stalin era was managed by women through the limitation of family size, on the one hand, or the limitation of professional commitments, on the other. The official insistence that Soviet policy had created optimal conditions for combining professional and family responsibilities could not be challenged, nor the problems it created directly confronted, so long as Stalinist priorities dominated Soviet life.

Further Reading: Women and Gender in Soviet Society

Lynne Attwood, *Creating the New Soviet Woman: Women's Magazines as Engineers of Female Identity, 1922–1953* (New York, 1999).

Frances L. Bernstein, "'The Dictatorship of Sex': Science, Glands, and the Medical Construction of Gender Difference in Revolutionary Russia," in David L. Hoffmann and Yanni Kotsonis, eds., *Russian Modernity: Politics, Knowledge, Practices* (London, 2000).

Mary Buckley, "The Untold Story of *Obshchestvennitsa* in the 1930s," *Europe–Asia Studies*, vol. 48, no. 4 (1996).

Choi Chatterjee, *Celebrating Women: Gender, Festival Culture, and Bolshevik Ideology, 1910–1939* (Pittsburgh, 2002).

Barbara Evans Clements, Barbara Alpern Engel, Christine D. Worobec, eds., *Russia's Women: Accommodation, Resistance, Transformation* (Berkeley, 1991).

Wendy Z. Goldman, *Women, the State and Revolution: Soviet Family Policy and Social Life, 1917–1936* (New York, 1993).

Anne E. Gorsuch, "'A Woman is not a Man': The Culture of Gender and Generation in Soviet Russia, 1921–1928," *Slavic Review*, vol. 55 (1996).

Melanie Ilic, *Women Workers in the Soviet Interwar Economy: From 'Protection' to 'Equality'* (New York, 1999).

Melanie Ilic, ed., *Women in the Stalin Era* (New York, 2001).

Rosalind Marsh, ed., *Women in Russia and Ukraine* (New York, 1996).

Rebecca Balmas Neary, "Mothering Socialist Society: The Wife-Activists' Movement and the Soviet Culture of Daily Life," *The Russian Review*, vol. 58, no. 3 (1999).

Susan Reid, "All Stalin's Women: Gender and Power in the Soviet Art of the 1930s," *Slavic Review*, vol. 57(1998).

Elizabeth A. Wood, *The Baba and the Comrade: Gender and Politics in Revolutionary Russia* (Bloomington, 1997).

Ethnicity and Nationality

10

Nature and Nurture in a Socialist Utopia: Delineating the Soviet Socio-Ethnic Body in the Age of Socialism

Amir Weiner

Excerpted from Amir Weiner, "Nature, Nurture, and Memory in a Socialist Utopia: Delineating the Soviet Socio-Ethnic Body in the Age of Socialism," *The American Historical Review*, vol. 104, no. 4 (1999).

Editor's Introduction

Stalinism also had strong impact on ethnic and national minorities in the Soviet Union. According to Marxist theory, nationalism and national identity were bourgeois phenomena which would fade under socialism. But Soviet authorities in many ways fostered the very national consciousness they presumed to supercede. Rather than replacing national identity with an allegiance to socialism, Soviet nationality policy made ethnic and national minorities more aware of their distinctiveness. This national consciousness subsequently fueled separatist feelings among national minorities, and ultimately contributed to the breakup of the Soviet Union in 1991.

The Soviet government's promotion of national identity has been the subject of important new scholarship in Soviet nationality studies, one of the most vibrant subfields in Soviet history over the past decade. Research on Soviet nationality policy has shown that both the structure and policies of the Soviet government encouraged national consciousness among ethnic minorities. Proceeding from the assumption that repression of nationalism would only worsen it, Lenin and Stalin granted national institutions to ethnic minorities to try to disarm nationalism and allow these minorities to evolve beyond national attachments to class consciousness and socialism. The structure of the Soviet Union therefore included national republics and territories, each with their own governing bodies and national symbols. Moreover, national minority languages were permitted to flourish and national elites were recruited into the Communist Party.[1]

In addition to promoting national identity among ethnic minorities deliberately, the Soviet government engaged in practices of classification and categorization which inadvertently fostered national consciousness. These practices included the drawing of territorial boundaries for republics corresponding to each major nationality, though the delineation of geographically based nationalities involved assigning national identities even to people who did not identify themselves in national terms. Soviet officials' desire to know and manage the population prompted them to conduct censuses, in which they categorized people by their nationality. The internal passports introduced by the Soviet government in 1932 specified people's nationality in their passports, so that all citizens had to identify themselves in terms of their nationality. All of these practices encouraged or even required people to think of themselves in national terms.[2]

Over time, Soviet authorities themselves came to see national and ethnic categories in increasingly absolute terms. Despite the ideas of Marxism, which viewed nationality as constructed, Stalinist nationality policy increasingly came to treat ethnicity and nationality as primordial and essential.[3] Stalinism also entailed extremely coercive policies toward national minorities, including mass ethnic deportations in the late 1930s, and deportations of entire nationalities after the Second World War. Soviet nationality policy, then, underwent a dramatic and coercive evolution under Stalin. From seeing nationality as a mutable consciousness, the Stalinist leadership came to view certain national minorities as undifferentiated, irredeemable groups.

Amir Weiner has produced pioneering scholarship both on the origins of Stalinist excisionary violence, and on the application of state violence

[1] Ronald Grigor Suny, The Revenge of the Past: Nationalism, Revolution, and the Collapse of the Soviet Union (Stanford, 1993); Terry Martin, The Affirmative Action Empire: Nations and Nationalism in the Soviet Union, 1923–1939 (Ithaca, 2001).

[2] Yuri Slezkine, "The USSR as a Communal Apartment, or How a Socialist State Promoted Ethnic Particularism," Slavic Review, vol. 53, no. 3 (1994); Francine Hirsch, "The Soviet Union as a Work-in-Progress: Ethnographers and the Category of Nationality in the 1926, 1937, and 1939 Censuses," Slavic Review, vol. 56, no. 2 (1997); Jorg Baberowski, "Stalinismus als imperials Phanomen: die islamischen Regionen der Sowjetunion, 1921–1941," in Stefan Plaggenborg, ed., Stalinismus: neue Forshungen und Konzepte (Berlin, 1998).

[3] Terry Martin, "Modernization or Neo-traditionalism? Ascribed Nationality and Soviet Primodialism," in David L. Hoffmann and Yanni Kotsonis, eds., Russian Modernity: Politics, Knowledge, Practices (New York, 2000).

to ethnic and national minorities. In the selection below, he describes the tension within Soviet ideology between nurture and nature. According to Marxism, enemies of socialism were products of their capitalist environment, so they could be reformed and incorporated into the socialist collective. But over time, Soviet authorities increasingly came to see enemies as inveterate "anti-Soviet elements," and this perspective left no room for re-education or redemption. With the cultivation of ethnic particularism (through the mechanisms described above), Stalin and his fellow leaders increasingly targeted certain national minorities as enemies – what Weiner calls the ethnicization of the Soviet purification drive.

Weiner demonstrates that the Second World War intensified the Stalinist leadership's drive to purify Soviet society by removing enemies, including national minorities deemed wartime collaborators. Drawing comparisons with other countries in Europe, he highlights the distinctive Soviet treatment of those who collaborated with the Nazis during the war. For Soviet authorities, collaborators were not by-products of wartime occupation but socialism's eternal enemies which the war had uncovered. Amnesty was out of the question for these enemies; they had to be removed from society altogether. In cases where collaboration was seen in ethnic terms, the Stalinist leadership ordered the deportation of entire peoples, such as the Crimean Tatars. Ukrainian nationalists, who during and after the war fought for independence from the Soviet Union, were summarily shot, with no opportunity for re-education or rehabilitation.

In the wake of the war, Soviet leaders also began to view Jews as an alien group in society. Jews were described as immune to assimilation, and hence an exception to the Marxist principle of nurture over nature. Persecution of Jews soon followed and official Soviet anti-semitism reached its peak in 1953 during the so-called Doctors' Plot, when prominent Jewish doctors were arrested and accused of plotting to murder Stalin and other leaders. But as Weiner argues, the Jewish case underscored a crucial distinction between the Soviet and Nazi regimes. The Soviets consistently rejected the biological determinism and virulent racism of the Nazis. Even at the height of the Soviet anti-semitic campaign, hundreds of thousands of Jews remained Communist Party members, including Lazar Kaganovich, one of Stalin's closest lieutenants. Moreover, Soviet excisionary practices, even as they assumed the form of ethnic deportations, never included industrial killing and genocide, as was true of Nazi state violence.

The Second World War, then, accelerated the Stalinist purification drive, and led to the totalization of ethnic categories. Indeed, as Weiner shows, this acceleration was linked with the Soviet concept of historical time and the postwar belief that the final stage of history was fast approaching. To prepare for the communist utopia, Stalin and his fellow leaders strove all the more relentlessly to eliminate those who violated the country's "moral-political unity," including national minorities accused of wartime collaboration. But despite Soviet authorities' increasing tendency to view enemies as irredeemable, Marxist ideology and the privileging of nurture over nature continued to inform Soviet policies. Stalinist excisionary practices, even when totalized, never derived from a genocidal ideology and never introduced exterminatory institutions.

Nature and Nurture in a Socialist Utopia: Delineating the Soviet Socio-Ethnic Body in the Age of Socialism

Amir Weiner

In the wake of the disintegration of the Soviet polity, scholars have thoroughly reevaluated basic categories in Soviet history such as class, ethnicity, and nationality, as well as the policies associated with them. Amazingly enough, however, with rare exceptions, these categories and policies have been treated as the context for evaluating Soviet practices rather than being contextualized themselves. This essay seeks to advance the current discussion by situating these concepts within the overarching Soviet enterprise: the unfolding revolutionary transformation of society from an antagonistically divided entity into a conflict-free, harmonious body. The view of society as a malleable construct went hand in hand with a continuous purification campaign seeking to eliminate divisive and obstructing elements. Exclusion and violence, in this light, were not random or merely preventive police measures that delineated the boundaries of the legitimate and the permissible but, rather, integral parts of the ongoing community-structuring enterprise. I trace the rationale of the Soviet Marxist quest for purity by focusing on three crucial components: the correlation between the progression of the revolutionary time line and the measures taken to realize the socialist utopia, the impact of Nazism and capitalism on the Soviet political and social calculus, and the sites of excision. The marked emphasis on ideology does not deny nor diminish the impact of circumstances, especially those of the magnitude experienced during World War II, or the role of institutions such as the political police, the NKVD, which had a vested interest in a permanent purge. It does explain, however, why the Soviets reacted in the unique way they did to the same circumstances experienced by other polities, why their unique punitive institutions were created in the first place, and why the regime pursued its purification campaigns well after the conditions that initiated them had dissipated.

Marxist regimes struggled with assigning primacy to either the "objective" category of class origin or to the "subjective" criteria of conduct and experience. In polities founded on the Marxist premise of the primacy of acculturation, but simultaneously engaged in the constant eradication of social strata presumed to be illegitimate, the tension between nurture and nature was constant. It intensified as the Soviet polity advanced along the road to socialism and communism and radicalized its purification policies both qualitatively and quantitatively. Following the establishment of socialism and especially in the wake of World War II, social and ethnic categories and practices were totalized in a marked shift: enemy groups previously considered to be differentiated, reformable, and redeemable were now viewed as undifferentiated, unreformable, and irredeemable collectives. This totalization of the Marxist sociological paradigm challenged the commitment to the primacy of nurture over nature in the ongoing social engineering project, inviting comparison with contemporary biological-racial paradigms, most notably, that of Nazi Germany – a comparison the Soviets were well aware of yet wanted to avoid at all costs. The absence of genocidal ideology and institutions allowed for different modes and sites of total excision from the socio-ethnic body within the socialist utopia. Still, Soviet contemporaries continued to confront the ever-present shadow of the biological-racial ethos.

The Soviet purification drive operated on a universal–particularistic axis, combining the modern European ethos of social engineering with Bolshevik Marxist eschatology. Their fusion created a stable menu of categories and practices and a dynamic mode of applying them. The Soviet state emerged and operated within an ethos aptly named by Zygmunt Bauman as the "gardening state," which appeared ever more universal in the wake of the Great War. This cataclysmic event brought to fruition the desires for a comprehensive plan for the transformation and management of society, one that would create a better, purer, and more beautiful community through the removal of unfit human weeds. It was, in a word, an aesthetic enterprise. The unprecedented increase in the capacities and aspirations of the state went hand in hand with the view of society as raw material to be molded into an ideal image. The transformation – or removal – of the individual and the community became the accepted goal of the state both in its welfare and its punitive policies. . . .

Whatever its ideological coloring, social engineering possessed a tremendous capacity for violence. The mobilization of the legal and medical professions for the goal of perfecting society shifted the political discourse to new realms. The pretense of scientific criteria and measures to study and work on the population meant that the state would employ the most advanced and radical tools in its quest for a purer, better society. The urge to maximize the management of society gave birth to a myriad of institutions for activities such as passport control, surveillance, and physical and mental cataloguing, without which the radical transformation of populations could not have taken place. And it was perfectly logical that the most radical forms of mass extermination were preceded by smaller scale destruction of groups categorized as incompatible and irredeemable both medically and legally, then supplemented by military-industrial methods of operation.

Where the paradigm of modernity falls short is by not providing a satisfactory explanation for the *evolution* of purification drives in totalitarian systems. If the urge to perfect societies stemmed from the universal axis of modernity, its implementation acted on clearly particularistic urges. First, the "gardening state" blossomed throughout Europe no less than in the Soviet Union. In the wake of the Great War, the European political landscape was marked by planned economies, elaborate surveillance systems, and thoroughly politicized eugenics research. Yet it was the Soviet polity that ended up with teleology as its economic modus operandi alongside a system of concentration camps, mass deportations, and killings. Indeed, the Soviets went out of their way to underline this difference. Unlike the Philistines who constantly lament brutality and the loss of lives and preach reconciliation, the ultimate goal of the social engineering project – a genuine moral-political unity of society – could be reached only through an irreconcilable and violent struggle, declared Soviet ideologues. Second, the campaign to eradicate internal enemies within the totalitarian state intensified *after* all residues of political opposition had been crushed and, in the Soviet case, following the declaration that Socialism had been built. Terror becomes total, Hannah Arendt observed, when it becomes independent of all opposition.

The key to the distinctive development of the Soviets' purification drive lay in the volatile fusion of historical time and its ultimate goal. It was an eschatological worldview in the sense of belief in an end to History; it was apocalyptic in its belief in the imminence of the End and that, in the wake of reaching socialism, Soviet people were living at the final stages of History; it was millenarian in its belief that the final cataclysm would be followed by the kingdom of communism, namely a conflict-free and harmonious society, the very feature that set it apart from other totalitarian enterprises, which espoused a cyclical conception of time and envisioned an endless struggle for domination and survival. The quest for purity was neatly tied to *the* distinguishing aspect of the Bolshevik utopia: from the moment of its establishment in power, the Soviet regime imposed a time line marking concrete stations on the road to realization of the communist utopia. Thus in 1947, the draft of the party program set the goal of "building of a communist society in the USSR in the course of the next twenty to thirty years," and in 1948, a leading political theoretician could declare confidently that,

> if it was possible to organize a socialist society on the whole within twenty years from the moment of the triumph of Soviet power under the most difficult circumstances, then it is entirely possible to assume that after the triumphant conclusion of the Patriotic War and the restoration of the ruined people's economy, two more decades will be enough to roughly erect the highest stage of communism. *Therefore, the generation which in 1920 was fifteen to twenty years old will live in a communist society.*[1]

A year later, communism was said to be around the corner, with each day bringing forward more evidence of the triumphant march to communism, including the markers of communist harmony – liquidation of the great schisms between mental and physical labor and between town and village – as the first secretary of the All-Union Leninist Communist League of Youth (Komsomol) assured the delegates to the Eleventh Congress of the organization in March–April 1949. The "overwhelming majority" of Soviet youth, noted another secretary, already possessed "all the elements of the character of the man of Communist society."[2] On the eve of the Nineteenth Party Congress in October 1952, Stalin threw his personal weight behind the matter when he sought in his last major work on *Economic Problems of Socialism in the USSR* to rush the march toward the higher stage of communism by creating a central barter system that would replace collective farm property and commodity exchange in the countryside, which he viewed as the last existing obstacles to a full-blown communist economy. And with the addition of the new socialist "shock brigades" – the People's Democracies in East Asia and Europe – which altered the pre-war isolation, "the mighty motherland" was said to be in the flower of its strength, possessing "everything necessary for building of a complete communist society."[3]

These time markers had a direct impact on the definition of the "weeds" intruding on the harmonious garden and the measures taken to uproot them. Groups and individuals perceived to be hostile were continuously referred to in biological-hygienic terms, whether vermin

[1] Indeed, this confident prediction was presented as a "scientific answer to the question on the historical epochs of building communism [that] we find in the writings of Lenin and Stalin." Tsolak Stepanian, "Usloviia i puti perekhoda ot sotsializma k kommunizmu," in F. Konstantinov, et al., *O sovetskom obshchestve: Sbornik statei* (Moscow, 1948), 539, 540, 542, italics in the original.

[2] *Komsomol'skaia pravda*, March 30 and April 2, 1949.

[3] See the speeches by Georgii Malenkov and Stalin at the Nineteenth Party Congress, *Pravda*, October 6 and 15, 1952.

(*parazity, vrediteli*), pollution (*zasorenost'*), or filth (*griaz'*), and were subjected to ongoing purification. Yet the implications of this biological-hygienic rhetoric were not static. With the declaration of Socialism built, the victorious outcome of the Great Patriotic War, and communism in sight, the eradication of "this debris of the old world, a weed that somehow grew up between the stones of our radiant building,"[4] assumed even more urgency. In his well-known speech at the February–March 1937 plenary session of the Central Committee, Stalin explicitly identified the new type of internal enemy in the age of socialism, the elusive one, a theme that he had already begun to develop in 1933 at the completion of collectivization. Since official ideology and its institutional implementation were infallible, errors and failures could be attributed only to the ill-will of individuals. After several decades of socialism in power and constant purges, the continued existence of such human weeds must be a result of their devious and elusive nature. Like a cancer, they mutated themselves in different forms and various locations. And since this vermin could not repent, it had to be removed from the body in its entirety. The question was only how. The former brand of internal enemies, argued Stalin, was openly hostile to the Soviet cause by virtue of social origin and professional orientation and could not be mistaken for anything other than that. The new saboteurs, on the other hand, were "mostly party people, with a party card in the pocket, i.e., people who formally are not alien. Whereas the old vermin turned against our people, the new vermin, on the contrary, cringe before our people, extol our people, bow before them in order to win their trust."[5] Such enemies, reasoned Stalin, would resort to the most extreme measures in their struggle against the Soviet state. The latter must guarantee the excision of this vermin from its midst.

Stalin's warning was repeatedly invoked in the postwar purge campaigns but with an additional edge. The moral-political unity gained by the relentless and thorough purge was posited against the proliferation of "fifth columns" in the rest of Europe, which, in the Soviet view, was a major factor in its quick collapse before the Nazi onslaught. With the announcement in mid-January 1953 of the uncovering of the "Doctors' Plot," a group of physicians, the majority of whom were Jews, accused of plotting to murder Soviet leaders, *Komsomol'skaia pravda* reminded Soviet youth that even when defeated the enemy does not rest. "Having

[4] *Komsomol'skaia pravda*, February 12, 1953.
[5] I. Stalin, "O nedostatkakh partiinoi raboty i merakh likvidatsii trotskistskikh i inykh dvurushnikov: Doklad na Plenume TsK VKP (b) 3 Marta 1937," *Bol'shevik* 7 (1937): 7. See Hiroaki Kuromiya's examination of the January 1933 speech in his *Freedom and Terror in the Donbas: A Ukrainian-Russian Borderland, 1870s–1990s* (Cambridge, 1998), 184–5.

won the war we turned to construction again because we love life and youth, because we want to make our land a flourishing garden. But while we build we must remember that the enemy will continue to send spies onto our home front, to recruit all kinds of scum in order to undermine our strength, to poison our joyous, happy life . . . the greater the successes in building communism in the USSR, the more active and vile the operations of the imperialists and their myrmidons," concluded the call for vigilance. Like the biblical serpent, these enemies were the most elusive imaginable. "The spies and saboteurs sent to us by the imperialist intelligence services or recruited by them within the country from among incompletely routed anti-Soviet scum do not operate openly. They operate 'on the sly,' they mask themselves in the guise of Soviet persons to penetrate our institutions and organizations, to worm their way into confidence and conduct their foul work," was *Izvestiia*'s editorial from the same day. An unwaivering vigilance was required in order to "ensure the cleansing of people's minds from the survivals of capitalism, from the prejudices and harmful traditions of the old society," concluded the editorial.[6]

The arrival of socialism ordained new sites of excision. First, with the destruction of antagonistic classes, internal enemies became enemies of the people and were to be sought in new realms. By then, it was the nationality question that harbored the clearest and most present danger to the moral-political unity of all the people, declared Stalin in the Seventeenth Party Congress of 1934, underlining the increasing ethnicization of the Soviet social body and the shift in the search for the enemy within. The fight against recurrences of nationalist views had become the most critical task in the struggle against the last vestiges of capitalism in the consciousness of people, echoed Dmitrii Chesnokov, a prominent party ideologue, in 1952. The residue of "zoological" chauvinism, especially in regions that were temporarily exposed to fascist propaganda during the German occupation, represented a stubborn intrusion on Soviet harmony and called for the most severe measures if harmony was to be maintained, Chesnokov concluded.[7]

Second, Soviet relations to the parallel modern politics across the European continent were not merely phenomenological. Rather, the Soviets were constantly checking their methods in the European mirror. The anxiety of potential degeneration into a zoological ethos was strongly present in the minds of Soviet contemporaries. Throughout the 1930s, Soviet leaders, notably Stalin himself, reacted vehemently

---

[6] *Komsomol'skaia pravda*, January 15, 1953; *Izvestiia*, January 15, 1953.

[7] Dmitrii Chesnokov, *Sovetskoe sotsialisticheskoe gosudarstvo* (Moscow, 1952), 209. The necessity for coercion in the age of harmony and socialist democracy was hammered out by Chesnokov throughout the entire exhaustive text. See 246, 556.

against any suggestion that their sociologically based model of the human subject could be equated with any biologically based, genetically coded enterprise, whether the racial Nazi polity or eugenics and euthanasia policies, which enjoyed widespread acceptance during that decade. When the totalization of categories and practices in the wake of the war drove home the inevitable comparison with the Nazi racial-biological code, the Soviets went out of their way to emphasize that their destruction of internal enemies was not genocidal and that, unlike the death camps, their own penal system remained true to its corrective mandate.

The specific sites of purification derived from this anxiety. The acute Soviet awareness of being equated with the Nazi racial-biological enterprise and the fact that total excision did not necessarily imply physical elimination pointed to other sites of purification in addition to deportations or executions. Memory was a key political arena where the body social was delineated. Inclusion and exclusion within the Soviet body were defined to a large degree through both the commemoration of cataclysmic events and the simultaneous erasure of the counter-memories of groups and events deemed incompatible with communist harmony. In the highly stylized Soviet polity, hierarchies of commemoration reflected the political status of groups. World War II played a central role in this process, especially as the experience of the war turned into the core legitimizing myth of the Soviet polity, along with the denunciation and removal of some key elements of the Stalinist regime and the routinization of other fundamentals of the revolutionary ethos. The exclusion of certain groups from official representations of the wartime Soviet fighting family and the denial of particularistic suffering destined groups to political invisibility, depriving them of official recognition of their distinct, collective identities.

This essay examines the varieties of the Soviet purification drives as they evolved in relation to two groups that came to epitomize the obstacles to harmony from the late 1930s on: the Ukrainian nationalist movement (a political-ideological effort identified with its place of origin, Western Ukraine, but often substituted for the entire Ukrainian nation) and the Jewish minority. The sites of the Soviet drive explored here are the central-western regions of Ukraine, which served as a laboratory for social-ethnic engineering for every political movement that gained the upper hand there, beginning with the deportations of Germans, Poles, and Jews by the czarist government in 1915, and followed by the upheavals of the civil war, collectivization drive, and famine. From the early 1930s, the population in these regions was subjected to consecutive deportations of ethnic minorities and mass executions during the Terror, followed by Nazi population policies and

Ukrainian nationalist ethnocentric policies, and finally by the resumption of the Soviet purification drive in the wake of World War II. The history of these regions offers a unique insight into the evolution of Soviet population policies.

As the Nazi war machine began to roll back across the European continent, nations appeared determined to exact revenge on those deemed collaborators with the Nazi occupiers. Following humiliating defeats and years of occupation, the purge of the national body became the order of the day. On the surface, the European purification enterprise appeared universal and grappled with common core dilemmas regarding its form, extent, limits, and categories.

In their search for solutions to these dilemmas, nations referred primarily to familiar paradigms. Indeed, most European countries had had prior experience in mass exclusionary and reintegrative social operations. In the wake of the Great War, during which many of these nations had been occupied, European countries acquired rich experience in the use of amnesty legislation and the resocialization of political opponents and criminal offenders, albeit with different degrees of success and popular approval. For instance, bitter debates over the reintegration of World War I collaborators took place in Belgium, which delayed amnesty legislation until 1937, while in the Netherlands the resocialization policy of criminal offenders was enacted methodically through an extensive network of prison and aftercare associations, including churches and trade unions. It came as no surprise that the relapse of some of the rehabilitated collaborators in Belgium into similar criminal behavior during the Second World War worked to toughen attitudes toward amnesty and rehabilitation, while in the Netherlands the resocialization programs and facilities for criminals were easily converted to reintegrate their World War II black sheep.

Less expected was the early realization that the prosecution of collaborators was not a challenge to the pre-war order but, rather, a manifestation of its continued power. A full investigation of collaboration – and not merely of those who served in the German punitive and propaganda institutions – threatened to open a Pandora's box of de facto accommodation by many of the sitting bureaucratic, judicial, and economic elites. In essence, the entire existing order. And since the latter showed no signs of acquiescence, the debate soon devolved into partisan politics. Public life under Nazi occupation was left out of the investigation, as were numerous high officials who fit well into the renewed conservative order. While the postwar European state was busily extending its domain into practically every sphere of society, the temptation to recall strayed, yet seasoned, bureaucrats was easily rationalized. The impact of the unfolding Cold War could not be ignored, either. In Hungary, a tiny communist party vying for more members opted for mass recruitment of none other than the rank-and-file of the Arrow Cross, the fascist organization now in disgrace whose class orientation was deemed more important than its political past. On both sides of the European divide, the developing conflict dictated a facade of national unity. Unpleasant and painful reminders were shelved, or rather erased from the official memory of the war.

Wartime experience, however, defied a universal definition of collaboration. In the vengeful atmosphere of devastated Poland, attending concerts at which German music was performed was deemed a collaborative act by the secret courts. At the same time, in so many countries from France to Norway to Hungary, the very same people both collaborated and resisted in accordance with their perceptions and expectations of German policies and the changing tide of the war. Neither martyrs nor evildoers were in the majority in Nazi-occupied Europe. And it was precisely this gray mosaic that stood in the way of national reconstruction.

At its core, the purge of collaborators was not merely about retribution or restoration. Deep down, it was about the shaping of postwar society. Purification was a transitional, medium between the imperfect past and the improved – if possible, perfect – society of the present and future. If the European experience is taken as a whole, it appears that a precondition for the success of purification was an ideal representation of the people as a positive, undifferentiated entity. "The People" as one mythic group had to be exonerated from charges of collaboration. The charge of collaboration was assigned to isolated patches of weeds. In a concrete, tactical calculus, the blame for the initial humiliating defeats and atrocities would be shifted from segments of one's own society to an alien element. A dignified future required a heroic past. And if the past was to be a guide to the future, it had to be painted in crisp colors. No shades of gray would interfere with the heroic tale of the struggle between good and evil. And so, as quickly as the vengeful spirits arose, so, too, did they abate. All over Europe, retribution against alleged collaboration faded away at a truly amazing pace, and arguments in favor of the reintegration of convicted collaborators surfaced shortly after the end of the hostilities.

The Soviet experience, too, pointed to an earlier paradigm, but one that accentuated the sharp distinctions between totalitarian and other political enterprises. The Soviet policy of purge was not merely reactive. Nor was it conditioned by tactical requirements. Rather, purification and reintegration were complementary components of the colossal project of building a new socialist polity. Specific developments in the domestic and international arena affected the choices of targets, but the goals and methods of dealing with these targeted groups and individuals were subjected to an ongoing endeavor of restructuring. If the study of the horrifying wartime losses and destruction helps to explain the harsh retaliation of the Soviets, then the reading of the war into the progressing revolutionary narrative elucidates the unique choices of methods.

The war was not merely an unpleasant accident, nor was it a customary clash between two major powers. It was the realization of a historical nightmare, one that Soviet power expected from the moment of its inception. Throughout the 1930s, Soviet citizens were constantly warned against the evils of German fascism and its implications for the USSR. The dominant theme of the Terror in 1937–8 was the excision of fascist agents from the Soviet body politic. If the alleged crimes of the sinners in the late 1930s were presumed to anticipate the forthcoming catastrophe of the capitalist encirclement, then the alleged crimes in the 1940s were perceived as the full-blown actualization of the worst fears of the preceding decade. In the postwar official narrative, the war was perceived as the inevitable outcome of historical forces. "It would be wrong," declared Stalin in his election speech on February 9, 1946, "to think that the Second World War was a casual occurrence or the result of the errors of any particular statesmen, though mistakes were made. Actually, the war was the inevitable result of the development of world economic and political forces on the basis of modern monopoly capitalism."[8]

In this light, collaborators were not the by-products of the war but eternal enemies whom the war and occupation helped uncover. Their destruction was therefore not merely an act of defense but the execution of the Will of History. The passage of time did not work to moderate the punitive policies against those accused of collaboration. Whereas French politicians were quick to interpret public opinion surveys supporting a reconciliation bill as a mandate for enacting amnesty, Valentin Ovechkin's pleas for compassion toward those who went through the hell of occupation remained unheeded. "Solicitude for the welfare of traitors who helped the Nazis lacerate France shows up the present-day collaborationists in their true colors. Birds of a feather," was the bitter reaction of Soviet newspapers when the French National Assembly launched the debate over the final legislation of mass amnesty for convicted collaborators in December 1952.[9] As Europe was moving fast on

[8] I. V. Stalin, "Rech na predvybornom sobranii izbiratelei Stalinskogo Izbiratel'nogo okruga goroda Moskvy," in Stalin, *Sochineniia*, 3 (16): 2.
[9] "Amnesty for Traitors," *New Times* (Moscow) 49 (December 3, 1952): 19–20; "Krestovyi pokhod frantsuzskoi reaktsii," *Izvestiia*, December 7, 1952.

the road to amnesty and rehabilitation, the Soviet Union in contrast intensified its campaign of retribution.

Ultimately, Soviet purification drives were never restrained by circumstances. The purge of the party – the vanguard of the Soviet polity – was not subject to administrative-managerial requirements, nor did the admission that many communists had not risen to the occasion form an obstacle to the purged. When the population at large was purged, entire ethnic groups were stigmatized as collaborationist and deported into the Soviet interior. Within the grand scheme of social engineering, even the loss of face was not a weighty factor. And no external pressure, such as the European Court exerted on Belgium in 1961, was allowed to interfere with the pursuit of purity.

However, the Soviet purification drive was not entirely different from the European purge. If the postwar experience of Belgium, Czechoslovakia, and Yugoslavia is any indication, it appears that multi-ethnic formations in many ways comprised a distinct effort at purification. Wherever collaboration was presumed to have had an ethnic face, the process of the purge continued well beyond that of the more homogenous polities and assumed a more vindictive character. Indeed, here lay the gravest challenge to the ideal representation of the "Good People," a challenge that resonated most clearly in the Soviet Union. One could think, and with considerable justification, that the uninhibited savagery of the German occupation of the Soviet territories would perpetuate the myth of the "Good People" and make the purge of the collaborationist weeds a common national enterprise. Finding themselves at the bottom of the Nazi racial hierarchy, the Slavic populations soon discovered that the various distinctions the Nazis applied to each of them mattered little in the New Order. But the harmonious representation of the People collided with the unintended legacy of Soviet pre-war nationality policy. The racially based Nazi ethos had fallen on fertile ground. The principled cultivation of ethnic particularism by the Soviets, be it the creation of ethno-national territories or the ethnicization of the enemy-within category, rendered critical segments of society susceptible to ethnically based visions and practices. In such a milieu, the occupation of the non-Russian Slavic republics for most of the war, and the slightest preferential treatment by the Germans, triggered contemporaries' reflection on the consequences of the ethnicized Soviet world. In many regions, the Soviet nation-building project had to be reconciled with the ethnic legacy of collectivization, famine, and deportations. Similarly, the postwar translation of ethnically based hierarchies of heroism into hierarchies of loyalty was a powerful challenge to the myth of the "Good People." This leads us to consider briefly the nature of the Soviet purification drive as it evolved prior to the cataclysm of World War II, against which background the magnitude of the postwar cleansing must be measured.

In a polity built on the premise of "national in form, socialist in content," ethnicity was not expected to become the primary category in social engineering. Early on, however, the brutal experience of the Don Cossacks during the Russian civil war and the suspicion cast on the Polish and German minorities throughout the 1920s made it clear that this neat distinction between form and content was difficult to maintain. As the Soviet crusade approached the realm of socialism, the tenuous balance between social and ethnic origins increasingly tilted in the direction of the latter. True, class would continue to be the *raison d'être* of the revolutionary enterprise to the very end, a concept written into the structure of each and every Soviet institution. It was not for nothing that Stalin, the very person who renounced class heredity as a detrimental factor in determining political legitimacy, went out of his way to scorn party members in the Seventeenth Party Congress who "dropped into a state of foolish rapture in the expectation that soon there will be no classes and therefore no class struggle."[10] But over-shadowed by Stalin's often-quoted remark was the addendum that the survivals of capitalism were "much more tenacious in the sphere of the national problem . . . because they are able to disguise themselves in national costume."[11] The threats to the aspired harmony assumed an ethnic face.

The conflation of class and ethnic categorization resurfaced with a vengeance once collectivization began. Soviet power forcefully drove home the ethnicization of class-enemy categories, especially when applied to the ethnic mosaic of the border regions. Already at the onset of the assault on the well-off peasants, or kulaks, in January 1930, local party organizations were ordered by the Ukrainian Central Committee to "devise special perspectives with regard to the national minorities districts (Germans, Bulgarians, and others)."[12] And since Poles – as well as Germans and Jews – were perceived as kulaks by nature, they were marked for collectivization regardless of socioeconomic status.

The ascendance of ethnicity within the excision enterprise was further accentuated when deportations commenced in March 1930. The Politburo's order specifically targeted ethnic Poles irrespective of the stage of collectivization and regardless of their material position. Indeed, only half of those deportees from the border belt of the

[10] I. V. Stalin, "Otchetnyi doklad XVII s"ezdu partii," in *Sochineniia,* 13 (Moscow, 1951), 351.
[11] Stalin, "Otchetnyi doklad XVII s"ezdu partii," 361.
[12] PAVO, f. 29, op. 1, d. 577, l. 133.

Ukrainian Republic in 1930 were classified as kulaks. With socialism built, ethnic hostility replaced class antagonism as the primary category intruding on harmony, a shift that was underscored when the purification drive accelerated in the mid-1930s. Well before deportations resumed in early 1935, every ethnic German living in the Soviet Union was "individually registered to the fullest extent" and his or her personal data transmitted to the Central Committee.[13] On November 5, 1934, the Central Committee in Moscow ordered local authorities throughout the Soviet Union to "remove the hostile anti-Soviet element from the German villages and deport them out of the region and to apply the harshest methods against the most active ones." The decree was implemented despite awareness of a steep decline in the absolute number of ethnic Germans in the border regions during the preceding period.[14]

The ethnicization of categories intensified the drive to homogenize the Soviet body social. Those marked for deportation were classified as "undesirable elements," and the enterprise was officially characterized as a "cleansing of the mass pollution of the [Polish] national village Soviets."[15] Hand in hand, scores of national soviets and schools were declared artificial and counterrevolutionary institutions. On the path to communism, the reference to any structure as an artificial creation by a foreign organization marked it as a weed to be uprooted from the Soviet garden. It seemed no accident that district authorities were ordered to explain to parents that children should be instructed in their "mother tongue," and consequently several hundred schools were converted to Ukrainian language schools.[16] The same rationale was offered in late 1937 when the Organizational Bureau of the Central Committee (Orgburo) decreed the liquidation of a large number of national districts and village Soviets (German, Polish, Estonian, Finnish, Koreans, Bulgarians, and others) throughout the entire union. The Orgburo declared them to be artificial creations that did not correspond to their national composition and, even worse, the creations of "enemies of the people led by bourgeois nationalists and spies."[17] Simultaneously, the Far East region was cleared of all ethnic Koreans, and large numbers of

[13] Ingeborg Fleischhauer and Benjamin Pinkus, *The Soviet Germans: Past and Present* (London, 1986), 90.

[14] PAVO, f. 136, op. 3, d. 225, ll. 23–31.

[15] Tsentral'nyi derzhavnyi arkhiv hromads'kykh ob"iednan' Ukrainy (hereafter, TsDAHOU), f. 1, op. 16, d. 12, ll. 39, 280; GARF, f. 5446, op. 16a, d. 265, l. 14.

[16] PAVO, f. 136, op. 3, d. 371, l. 5; PAVO, f. 136, op. 6, d. 591, ll. 1–3, 11.

[17] The Central Committee approved the resolution on December 17. Tsentr Khraneniia Sovremennykh Dokumentov (hereafter, TsKhSD), f. 89, op. 62, d. 6, l. 14; d. 4, l. 1; RTsKhIDNI, f. 17, op. 114, d. 829, ll. 119, 121, 123–6.

Germans, Poles, and Latvians were arrested or executed regardless of their social class, occupation, or geographical location. In some Ukrainian regions, arrests and executions eliminated almost all Germans and Poles.

Finally, the Terror delivered a brutal message regarding the limits of redemption in the wake of triumphalistic socialism. In his canonization of the history of the Communist Party, the *Short Course*, Stalin celebrated the physical annihilation of the elusive enemies who managed to survive previous cycles of purification. With Socialism built, extermination was the only way to cope with those who had not yet redeemed themselves. It seemed no accident that the first salvo of the ensuing terror was directed at the punished and pardoned. Indeed, the latter figured prominently in the Politburo resolution of July 2, 1937, "Concerning Anti-Soviet Elements." Having been punished and stripped of their hostile class identity, these individuals and groups appeared to have redeemed themselves through productive labor, which won them not only the restoration of voting rights but also the release of some from the special settlements. Indeed, only two years earlier, the rehabilitation of former kulaks was trumpeted as the triumph of nurture over nature. Celebrating the completion of the White Sea Canal, the authors of the special commemorative volume noted that "on the whole kulaks were the hardest to educate ... but even in these *half-animals*, the idolaters of private property, the truth of collective labor at last *undermined a zoological individualism.*"[18] Accordingly, on January 25, 1935, all former kulaks regained their voting rights. But two and a half years later, the Central Committee identified recently rehabilitated former kulaks as the principal anti-Soviet element, responsible for a barrage of diversionary acts in the countryside. In spite of regaining their civil rights and permission to return from exile to their homes, they had allegedly resumed hostilities against the socialist state. In essence, they proved to be immune to socialist corrective measures and were consequently irredeemable. They were marked for immediate arrest and execution. In the era of socialism, redemption was not offered twice.

Still, the pre-war cleansing policies maintained several key features that set them apart from those of the postwar era. First, they aimed largely at cleansing specific territorial space – mainly border regions populated by minorities with an external active homelands – or politically suspicious segments of these communities, but not entire peoples, which meant that targeted groups were treated as differentiated entities.

---

[18] *Belomor: An Account of The Construction of the New Canal between the White Sea and the Baltic Sea*, Maxim Gorky, L. Auerbach and S. G. Firin, eds. (New York, 1935), 341, italics added.

The lists of deportees from villages with "concentrated Polish and German populations" were to include "independent peasants who did not fulfill their obligations to the government and unreliable collective farmers [*kolkhozniki*]," just as the arrest and execution lists for these nationalities at the height of the Terror consisted of mainly political émigrés, alleged spies, and people working in sensitive industries. Equally important, deportees often remained within the boundaries of the Ukrainian Republic. Hence, even after the conclusion of repetitive waves of deportations, border regions were still populated by tens of thousands of members of the deported groups, just as members of the marked groups residing outside the targeted region were left unharmed, notably including Koreans.

Second, differentiation often left the door open for possible redemption. The GULAG doors kept revolving, with 20 to 40 percent of the inmates released annually. Rehabilitation of deported kulaks continued throughout the second half of the 1930s. The Council of People's Commissars Resolution on October 22, 1938, provided children of former kulaks with internal passports and the right to move to their place of choice (with the exception of closed districts), a right that elevated them not only above their previous status but also above the rest of the Soviet peasantry, which was deprived of passports and hence the right of free movement. Surveillance reports on deportees divided them into subgroups corresponding to their potential for redemption. Hence the 15,000 ethnic Germans deported in the spring of 1936 were split into a first group composed mostly of demobilized Red Army servicemen, who responded to the resettlement with optimism; a second group that felt cheated but could be redeemed with the right dose of propaganda; and a third, whose expectations of a German invasion and unification with their German brethren marked them as hopeless. Consequently, ethnic Germans throughout the Soviet Union were still regarded as reliable enough to be drafted into the Red Army, a policy that was bound to change only after this minority (and others) was targeted in its entirety with the outbreak of the war. Even Koreans residing outside the Far East were inducted into the Red Army, and their wartime exploits would be recognized and rewarded by the Soviet state.

Notably, the war itself soon became a redemptive vehicle for pre-war outcasts. On April 11, 1942, the State Defense Committee (GKO) passed a resolution that allowed the drafting of former kulaks into military service. The spouses and children of the draftees were released from the special settlements and received passports. In 1943 alone, this cohort amounted to 102,520 people. As the head of the GULAG administration noted with unconcealed satisfaction, many of those released served with distinction, including five who had received the nation's highest award, Hero of the Soviet Union. Inmates, including "politicals" of the Terror era, were encouraged to follow these examples and win their way back into society. Nor should the release of some 43,000 Poles categorized as members of an "enemy nation" merely two years before be ignored. In 1944, the NKVD and the USSR Procuracy agreed not to prosecute former kulaks who left the special settlements for various wartime services and failed to return. Mass rehabilitation intensified in the postwar years. In 1946, the regime removed all limitations imposed on the families of former kulaks who had children in the Soviet Army, were participants in the Great Patriotic War, or received governmental awards, and on women who married local residents.

With World War II, the ethnicization of categories of the enemy within came full circle. An apparent consequence of the wartime redemption was the substitution of ethnicity for class as the dominant inmate category in the Soviet penal system. On the eve of the war, 90.9 percent of the 977,000 people recorded living in the special settlements were classified as kulaks or family members of kulaks. But on the eve of the final wave of releases in early 1954, members of the 1929–33 generation numbered only 17,348 people. By then, the vacuum created by the release of 975,000 camp inmates to the front between 1941 and 1944 was filled with inmates from the nationalities deported during the war, the newly annexed Baltics, western Ukraine, and Belorussia.

The war saw a stark shift in the purge policies from cleansing certain spaces to cleansing peoples in toto. The pre-war focus on specific border regions was replaced by the targeting of each and every member of a stigmatized group regardless of geographical location or service rendered to the Soviet state. Whatever anxieties and inhibitions that had brought to a halt excision campaigns like that against the Cossacks in 1919 were now removed. Excision was intended to be total, irreversible, and pursued relentlessly. The treatment of ethnic Germans served as a model for this new stage. Hence the decree on the resettlement of the Volga Germans on August 28, 1941, was followed by decrees that extended resettlement to all ethnic Germans in the Soviet Union and that ordered the removal of all ethnic Germans from the ranks of the fighting Red Army. Remarkably, the decrees followed an earlier official recognition of the voluntary enrollment of the community for the Soviet cause and the heroic fight of some of its members against the Nazi invaders. Moreover, as one scholar aptly observed, the deportation resolution was framed as a prophylactic measure rather than a punitive one, where the Germans were accused of harboring scores of diversionist and hostile attitudes to Soviet power as opposed to performing concrete anti-Soviet acts. The same applied to all other ethnic groups marked for excision in the wake of the war. Whereas during the pre-war era the presence of relatives who had served in the Red Army or partisan detachments was enough to protect kulak families from being deported, by the end of World War II, officers and soldiers of the deported nationalities were severed from their units, often to be sent to the newly established special regime camps or work battalions while the war was still being waged. As indicated by the assault on the communal structure of the above communities as well as the Jewish community, the postwar calculus was indifferent to the security of the borders and the existence of hostile external homelands of stigmatized nationalities. The enemy within was ostracized and acted on as a totality. Those convicted of political crimes were exiled indefinitely upon completion of their sentences. With the building of communism set as a political goal and with a time line in place, the belief in the malleability of the human subject in general and of internal enemies in particular eroded.

Wartime conditions, especially in the occupied territories, furthered ethnonational divisions, for example, German differentiation of POWs (such as the release of ethnic Ukrainians), the passivity of the majority of the population, and the fact that the partisan movement was disproportionally populated by ethnic Russians. Already during the war, the Soviet criminalization of passivity (directed against the "hubbies" hiding behind women's skirts, as one partisan leader referred to those who claimed to be terrorized by the prospects of Nazi retaliation) assumed a clear ethnic face. Finally, the ferocious clashes with nationalist separatist movements significantly contributed to the hardening of Soviet attitudes toward domestic enemies. But wartime circumstances alone cannot account for the qualitative shift in the Soviet purification drive. Their meaning for and impact on contemporaries could not be detached from the preceding Soviet experience and treated as universal. The endurance and institutionalization of state revenge against those identified as internal enemies set the Soviet Union apart from other European countries and the United States, and points to another explanation. Wartime circumstances were read into the progressing narrative of the revolution, which was itself undergoing change at the time.

Reflecting on his wartime experience in Yugoslavia, Milovan Djilas, then a communist partisan leader, rationalized the execution of the leaders of a certain clan, whose members were friendly to the communist partisans, as the failure of some of its members to subject their "primeval clan ties" and loyalties to that of their political organization. The agitated members of the Tadic clan were executed together with royal officers, "not merely for economy but to associate the fate of party enemies with that of outside enemies." This ideological commitment, noted Djilas, allowed for opponents, whoever they were, to be dealt with in summary fashion.[19] Djilas would later conceptualize the role of ideology in the practice of violence. "No matter what your ideology may be," said Djilas, "once you believe that you are in the possession of some infallible truth, you become a combatant in a religious war. There is nothing to prevent you from robbing, burning and slaughtering in the name of your truth, for you are doing it with a perfectly clear conscience – indeed the truth in your possession makes it your duty to pursue it with an iron logic and unwavering will . . . [I]deology demands the liquidation of your enemies, real or imagined."[20] With the inspiration of revolutionary idealism, neither mass brutality in general nor the killing of individuals in particular was considered regrettable or detrimental. Indeed, while the Soviet practice of violence could be and was triggered by specific circumstances such as military necessity, its logic was anchored in ideology. Violence was applied within a well-defined ideological framework, which earmarked certain groups based on preconceived biases and was incorporated into an all-encompassing drive to purify the socio-national body. Any potential restraint on the exterminatory campaign against the Ukrainian nationalists was neutralized by an appeal to higher loyalties. Brutalities were committed as the ultimate expression of loyalty to the socialist drive and its administrative embodiments: the Communist Party and the Soviet Ukrainian nation.

In this light, the very existence of the Ukrainian nationalists was a violation of the natural order, and hence no mitigating circumstances could be allowed in assessing their crimes. Nor would utilitarian considerations play a role in the fight against them. They would have to be excised from the Soviet Ukrainian body. Soviet intelligence reports reveal that the Soviets were aware of the nationalists' clashes with the Germans. Knowledge, however, did not imply recognition. Notably, the reports carefully emphasized that the shift in the nationalists' policy resulted not from a change of heart or convictions but merely from disappointment at their treatment by the Germans. For the Soviets, the very existence of the nationalists was the bone of contention, not their tactics or alliances.

The total alienation of the nationalist cause was captured in a colorful passage by Dmitrii Medvedev, a partisan leader-turned-writer. Refer-

[19] Milovan Djilas, *Wartime* (New York, 1977), 164–5; and Djilas, "Christ and the Commissar," in George Urban, ed., *Stalinism: Its Impact on Russia and the World* (London, 1982), 203–8.
[20] Djilas, "Christ and the Commissar," 207.

ring to his own contacts with the nationalist leader "Bul'ba" (Borovets) and his entourage, Medvedev explained the national and linguistic alienation of the latter:

> The speech of the "hetman" was incomprehensible, a barbarian mixture of Ukrainian and German words. It was a language, as we later realized, broadly used by those Ukrainian nationalists brought up in the pubs of Berlin and in the taverns of Ottawa and Chicago, persons without a passport, without a homeland, subjects of the international black market, rascals, ready to sell themselves to the Gestapo or the Intelligence Service or the Federal Bureau of Investigation or any other bourgeois espionage organization.

National ostracization was augmented by a touch of class alienation. "Whereas the [Bul'ba] wore a *zaporozhtsa* [a Ukrainian national shirt], the [others] preferred a European suit, a colorful tie and manicured fingernails, which were considered a sign of special refinement among the bandits," noted Medvedev.[21]

The nationalists were de-individualized, portrayed as an undifferentiated collective, detached from any specific domestic intimate environment, and often referred to as animals. Killing them was not to involve any sense of guilt. Thus members of the Soviet polity should engage in systematic elimination of the "snake-like, slavish dogs of the Nazi hangmen," the "Ukrainian–German fascists" or the "agents of foreign intelligence services," rather than mere "Ukrainian nationalists." Nikita Khrushchev told a plenum of the Central Committee, "They [the Ukrainian nationalists] killed themselves trying to please their master – Hitler, and to get only a small portion of the loot for their doggish service. The German invaders shed the blood of Soviet Ukraine, shot hundreds of thousands of Soviet people – women, the elderly and children. *The Ukrainian–German Nationalists* assisted and at present [continue to] assist the Germans in these bloody crimes, fulfilling the role of hangmen.[22] To make things worse, while the German component of the evil duo was beaten and driven out of the homeland, its Ukrainian counterpart continued the destructive mission. The efforts to sabotage the restoration of the economy were seen as the fulfillment of German instructions. Hence the internal enemy remained foreign even when its foreign ally invader was expelled from Soviet territory. The nationalists' efforts to disassociate themselves from their alliance with the Germans were dismissed by Khrushchev as a play in the face of inevitable defeat.

[21] Dmitrii Medvedev, *Sil'nye Dukhom* (Moscow, 1951), 84, 86.
[22] TsDAHOU, f. 1, op. 1, d. 664, ll. 262–3.

On the battlefield, therefore, the campaign against the nationalists was deliberately launched as a war without prisoners. Between February 1944 and May 1946, 110,825 nationalists were killed within a territory inhabited by less than 9 million ethnic Ukrainians. NKVD reports on individual clashes with nationalist detachments repeatedly failed to mention prisoners taken alive, emphasizing almost total annihilation. Deportations reached their climax between 1939 and 1953, when some 570,826 people were deported from Ukraine without permission to return. A close look at the deportation figures, however, highlights the exterminatory character of the anti-nationalism campaign in the field. Between February 1944 and January 1946, the NKVD claimed to have detained 110,785 bandits (50,058 were convicted), but only 8,370 people were arrested as members of the Organization of Ukrainian Nationalists and 15,959 as active insurgents. The 182,543 nationalists deported from the seven western regions between 1944 and 1952 included family members of OUN or the Ukrainian Insurgent Army (UPA) and their supporters, non-adults, and families of those killed in clashes. Simply put, most of the active nationalist guerrillas were killed on the battlefield. On the battlefield, "We did not take prisoners as a rule. If we did take prisoners, we shot them after a preliminary interrogation," a commissar of a partisan detachment casually told members of the Commission for the Compilation of the Chronicles of the Great Patriotic War.[23]

Accordingly, the execution of captured nationalist guerrillas became a didactic public spectacle, with party officials presiding over summary trials and hangings in the village square. Quite likely, the ritual of hanging, which had already been practiced against convicted collaborators, was intended to add an element of humiliation and terror, since the Soviet Criminal Code spoke only of shooting (*rasstrel*) as the exceptional measure of punishment for extremely serious crimes. Once again, a comparison with other countries is telling. Estimates for the Netherlands were three or four deaths on the occasion of arrests and forty deaths in the internment camps caused by resistance members acting as guards. In the significantly more violent Belgium, there were about forty extra-judicial executions. In the USSR, public executions of alleged collaborators with the Germans were something to brag about when party officials recounted their recent experience in the partisans' ranks. The Special Department of the Lenin Mounted Brigade, which operated for a short time in the Vinnytsia region, was reported to have executed, often in public, no fewer than 825 collaborators. If the figures provided by the brigade's leaders are taken at face value, then the

---

[23] Institut Istorii Rossii, Otdel rukopisnykh fondov, f. 2, op. 9, d. 3, l. 5.

number of people executed by a single partisan brigade, not necessarily the largest one and operating within a rather small region in Ukraine, amounted to 13.7 percent of the total number of summary executions before and during the liberation of France, and 233 percent of those in Belgium. Finally, violence was exercised primarily for political rather than military reasons. The Soviet authorities made extensive use of the Destruction Battalions (*istrebitel'nye bataliony*) – auxiliary detachments of armed civilians charged with hunting down German and nationalist stragglers – while professing their negligible military value in the pre-1939 Soviet territories. The value of these formations, noted the deputy head of the Ukrainian NKVD, was the radicalization and proliferation of violence among the population at large, a key consideration in the Soviet Manichean worldview.

As summary executions of presumed collaborators proliferated in the initial stage of liberation, the returning Soviet powers moved quickly to curtail them. Immediately upon liberation, Red Army officers were said to prosecute, and in some cases execute, partisans who exacted arbitrary revenge after the liberation. Random retributions, which often bordered on anarchy, were not merely a threat to state authority; for the latter, revenge was not necessarily the main motivation. The exercise of retribution only by Soviet authorities integrated it into the overall purification drive, which by now engulfed every layer of the polity. The return of the regime as the sole arbiter and executor of revenge meant that the purge would be conducted along lines that could hardly be imagined in a random, popularly initiated purge. Extrajudicial justice operated as a cathartic moment, after which exhaustion, the desire to forget the imperfect past, and the impulse to reinstate a certain equilibrium would combine to extinguish the flames of arbitrary acts. This, however, was not to happen. The transfer of the prosecution of alleged wartime collaborators and bystanders to the jurisdiction of the NKVD Military Tribunals signaled that purges would become a permanent component in the political and social life of the liberated regions.

The irreversibility of any form of collaboration was further underlined by the absolute denial of political or social rehabilitation, even given the dire need for experienced personnel, a policy that set the Soviet Union further apart from other European countries that had been occupied by the Germans. In France, the willingness of large segments of the population to accept certain acts of collaboration as legitimate, albeit undesirable, acts of survival was taken by the authorities as a mandate for mass amnesty. In the Soviet Union, by contrast, the presence of similar sentiments worked to solidify the regime's resolve to excise collaborators, regardless of circumstances and the need for their services.

And unlike France, there was no political or social redemption for people known to have served under the occupation authorities. There, noted Soviet commentators, the replenishment of the state and military apparatus with former Vichyites amounted to a conscious blurring of the distinction between victims and victimizers. Nor could the stain of collaboration be removed by postwar performance. Soviet authorities continued to exact revenge on those suspected of collaboration down to the bottom of the social ladder. Professional and bureaucratic skills counted for nothing even in the face of severe shortages. Time and again, successful rural experts and *kolkhozniki* were denied governmental awards based on their spotty wartime records. Tellingly, crimes appeared as a biological trait when the definition of irredeemable sins was extended to include blood relatives of collaborators. Scores of individuals were denied awards merely for being related to people who served as policemen or in the Vlasov army. Sons, after all, could be responsible for their fathers.

Along with the revival of capital punishment for political crimes, the irredeemability of the Ukrainian nationalists was codified on April 6, 1950, by order of the Council of Ministers of the USSR. This directive replaced shorter deportation terms for those exiled from Ukraine between 1944 and 1949 with permanent exile (*navechno*), most notably the 182,543 members and supporters of the OUN-UPA and their families. By 1950, Ukrainian nationalists appeared beyond hope, and their exclusion from the Ukrainian body national was meant to be permanent. Accordingly, families of both arrested and slain nationalist activists were deported. The death of the latter was not necessarily redemptive.

Purification continued relentlessly. As European legislators were feverishly passing amnesty laws for convicted wartime collaborators, in the Soviet Union the search for and prosecution of alleged collaborators intensified. Between September 20 and October 10, 1947, alone, 326 people were arrested in the eastern regions of Ukraine on charges of collaboration with the German occupation authorities, making them the single largest group of the 668 people charged with "anti-Soviet activity." The 1955 amnesty decree of wartime collaborators excluded those convicted of murder and torture of Soviet citizens, a rather fatal exception. Whereas by 1958 in France, all those convicted of participating in the massacre at Oradour-sur-Glane, the single largest wartime massacre of a non-Jewish population, were released from prison, the Soviet regime continued to prosecute and execute similar cases well into the 1980s. As late as December 1984, military tribunals sentenced to death individuals guilty of killing Soviet POWs, activists, Jews, and communist partisans.

Nor did the post-Stalin amnesty signal rehabilitation. Individuals associated with nationalist forces in Ukraine were released from the camps in early 1954, but it was only in mid-1991, with the looming demise of the Soviet system, that they were granted complete rehabilitation, on the grounds that "their hands were not stained with blood." The same logic was applied to the national arena, where the decaying regime mobilized all its resources in a vain effort to block the rehabilitation of OUN-UPA in western Ukraine. Damning information from the KGB archives about UPA atrocities was circulated in press conferences and published in the popular press. Graphic data on massacres of peaceful citizens, ethnic Poles, and Soviet activists, and the close collaboration with the Nazis, were used to underline the essence of the nationalist movement as alien to the national body. In response to pleas by the L'viv regional party committee secretary, the Central Committee in Moscow addressed the issue in a specific decree. The Central Committee went out of its way to prevent the "justification of the crimes of the OUN bands under the guise of criticism of Stalinism." To counter the rehabilitation efforts by a variety of opposition groups in western Ukraine, it ordered the release of archival documentaries on the nationalist atrocities during and after the war, arranged for young people to meet victims of the nationalists, and organized a scholarly conference on the "anti-people" deeds of the OUN-UPA. With the approach of the fiftieth anniversary of the Great Patriotic War, the treacherous nationalists were to be exposed. As long as the Myth of the War was the pillar of the polity's legitimacy, the excision of the nationalist cause was non-negotiable.

It comes as no surprise that the totalization of Soviet practices in the quest for purity brought to the fore the inherent tension between the biological and the sociological categorization of the enemy within, and consequently the inevitable comparison to Nazi Germany, the other totalitarian enterprise. Nowhere else was this issue exposed more clearly than in the Soviet policy toward its Jewish minority. In the wake of the war and the trauma of the Holocaust, conducted extensively on Soviet soil with the implicit and often explicit approval of the local populace, as well as a wave of popular and official anti-Semitism that swept the immediate postwar era, ordinary Jewish citizens and activists began to ponder the unthinkable: was there a logical affinity between the two ideologies? Already in the summer of 1944, a group of disgruntled, demobilized Jewish servicemen protested in a letter to Stalin that the Ukrainian Communist Party had "a lot in common with the course that originated earlier from the chancery of Goebbels, whose worthy transmitters turned out in the Central Committee and the Council of People's

Commissars of *Ukraine*."[24] This point was also laid out bluntly by Vasilii Grossman in his epic *Life and Fate*, which he started writing at this time. Grossman chose none other than the triumphant moment and site of Stalingrad to underline the common ethos of the Nazi and Soviet enterprises:

> Suddenly, probably because of the war, he began to doubt whether there really was such a gulf between the legitimate Soviet question about social origin and the bloody, fateful question of nationality as posed by the Germans . . . To me, a distinction based on social origin seems legitimate and moral. One thing I am certain of: it's terrible to kill someone simply because he's a Jew. They're people like any others – good, bad, gifted, stupid, stolid, cheerful, kind, sensitive, greedy . . . Hitler says none of that matters – all that matters is that they're Jewish. And I protest with my whole being. But then we have the same principle: what matters is whether or not you're the son of an aristocrat, the son of a merchant, the son of a kulak; and whether you're good-natured, wicked, gifted, kind, stupid, happy, is neither here nor there. And we're not talking about the merchants, priests and aristocrats themselves – but about their children and grandchildren. Does noble blood run in one's veins like Jewishness? Is one a priest or a merchant by heredity?[25]

Indeed, in the wake of the war, Soviet public representations increasingly identified Jews as inherently resistant to Soviet acculturation and, even more threateningly, as an undifferentiated entity. As early as December 1941, during a conversation with a visiting Polish delegation, Stalin found time to reflect on the martial qualities of the warring sides. The Slavs, observed the Soviet leader, are "the finest and bravest of all airmen. They react very quickly, for they are a young race which hasn't yet been worn out . . . The Germans are strong, but the Slavs will defeat them." Jews, on the other hand, were repeatedly referred to as "poor and rotten soldiers."[26]

A core message of the anti-cosmopolitan campaign in the late 1940s was that the Jew remained a Jew, an eternal alien to the body national, no matter what the circumstances. As such, he had to be stripped of the false layers within which he deceptively wrapped himself. In early 1949, the Soviet press violated one of the taboos of Bolshevik revolutionary culture when it started disclosing pseudonyms. The birth names of assimilated Jewish figures in the arts were regularly attached to their

---

[24] TsDAHOU, f. 1, op. 23, d. 2366, l. 25.
[25] Vasilii Grossman, *Zhizn' i sud'ba* (Moscow, 1988), 542–3.
[26] Stanislaw Kot, *Conversations with the Kremlin and Dispatches from Russia* (Oxford, 1963), 153.

assumed ones. And so the literary critic Ilia Isaakovich Stebun learned, along with the readers of the republic's main newspaper, that at the end of the day, after honorable service at the front and a career of writing in the Ukrainian language, he was still Katsenelson. Similarly, the poet Lazar Samilovich Sanov found out that his own work in the Ukrainian language and service as a war correspondent did not change the fact that he was still Smulson, just as Zhadanov was still Livshits and Gan remained Kagan.

When the anti-Semitic campaign was reaching its climax in early 1953, the alleged Jewish resistance to Soviet acculturation called for uncompromising methods by the authorities. While exposing an accused Jewish embezzler in the small town of Zhmerynka who, needless to say, had managed to avoid the front during the Great Patriotic War ("he fell ill precisely at the end of June 1941"), the satirical magazine *Krokodil* posed a rhetorical question: "To tell you the truth, we became tired of reading your decisions scattered there: 'to reprimand, to point out, to suggest,' etc. *Doesn't it seem to you, comrades, that you overestimate the educational significance of these resolutions of yours? And, anyway, who are you trying to reeducate? With such touching forbearance, too?*"[27] The Jew, simply put, proved to be the anomaly in the Marxist premise of the primacy of nurture over nature. He was immune to reeducation. In early 1953, with the recent executions of the Jewish Anti-Fascist Committee leadership, the unfolding Doctors' Plot, and rumors about the inevitable mass deportation of Jews dominating the day, the recommendation to transfer the case to the regional prosecutor (an office famed for meting out swift and harsh punishments) sent the unequivocal message that there was only one way to deal with such types. As the living antithesis to the core Soviet myths of hard and honest socialist labor and the martyrdom of the recent war, the Jew was beyond redemption. His nature was immune even to the powerful acculturation of nearly four decades of Soviet life.

Uncovering the *real* Jew, however, was not confined to the Stalin era. Several years later, it was the turn of the de-Stalinizing Khrushchev to warn other communists against false hopes of acculturating the Jew. While attending a session of the Central Committee of the Polish Communist Party, Khrushchev urged the Poles to correct the "abnormal composition of the leading cadres" as the Soviets successfully had done. Staring hard at the chairman of the meeting, Roman Zambrowski, who was born Zukerman, Khrushchev exclaimed: "Yes, you have many leaders with names ending in 'ski,' but an Abramovich remains an

[27] Vasilii Ardamatskii, "Pinia iz Zhmerinki," *Krokodil* 8 (March 20, 1953): 13.

Abramovich. And you have too many Abramoviches in your leading cadres."[28] Sometime later, while reflecting on the evident failure of the Jewish Autonomous Region of Birobidzhan to establish itself as a national homeland for Soviet Jewry, Khrushchev concluded that it was the result of historical conditions. Yet his description of the sociological was practically biological. "They [the Jews] do not like collective work, group discipline. They have always preferred to be dispersed. They are individualists," Khrushchev told *Le figaro* in an interview in March 1958. Finally, in the crudest officially ordained anti-Semitic publication to emerge from the Soviet system, Trohym Kychko's *Iudaizm bez prikras*, Nazi-like vocabulary and illustrations drove home the message of alienation of everything distinctively Jewish from the tradition of progressive humanity in general, the Soviet family in particular, and even more specifically, from the Ukrainian nation. Portrayed as speculators and hostile to manual labor, collaborators with the Nazis, and murderers of Symon Petliura, Jews were entirely excluded from the October Revolution, the Great Patriotic War, and Ukrainian aspirations for independence – all subjects of core myths within the Soviet milieu.

But this complete exclusion concealed a crucial difference between the Nazi and Soviet enterprises. The class-based Soviet theory and practices of structuring society seemed to present an ominous obstacle to the application of uniform social targeting. Classes, strata, and layers were neither faceless nor homogeneous. Rather, they were variegated and arranged in a hierarchical order based on the services their members had rendered to the communist drive. Responsibility and accountability were assessed on the individual's merit, even though this principle was often compromised in the course of exercising the structuring acts. Maxim Gorky was not off the mark when he stated in his celebratory volume of the construction of the White Sea Canal that "the dictatorship of the proletariat has once more earned the right to declare: 'I do not fight to kill as does the bourgeoisie: I fight to resurrect toiling humanity to a new life. I kill only when it is not possible to eradicate the ancient habit of feeding on human flesh and blood.'"[29] Moreover, individuals maintained the right to appeal and often did so successfully. No one could articulate this principle better than Stalin, and for good reason. In a series of speeches delivered as the Terror approached its climax, Stalin explained its guidelines. Concluding his remarks to the plenary session of the Central Committee on March 5, 1937, Stalin warned the delegates not to confuse sworn and irredeemable enemies with those who recanted and redeemed themselves

---

[28] Joseph B. Schechtman, *Star in Eclipse* (New York, 1961), 81.
[29] *Belomor*, 338.

when they joined forces with the Bolsheviks in the anti-Trotskyite campaign or those "who, at one point happened to be walking along the street where this or that Trotskyite happened to be walking, too." "In this question, as in all other questions, *an individual, differentiated approach* is required. We must not treat all alike," concluded Stalin.[30] Three months later in a speech before the Military Council of the Defense Ministry on June 2, 1937, in the wake of the liquidation of the military leadership, Stalin reflected on the tension arising from the Soviet search for the enemy within. Reminding his audience of Lenin's noble and Friedrich Engels's bourgeois origins on the one hand, and of the proletarian origins of Leonid Serebriakov and Iakov Livshits (former Central Committee Secretary and Deputy People's Commissar of Communications, respectively) who turned out to be bad apples on the other, Stalin concluded:

> Not every person of a given class is capable of doing harm. Individual people among the nobles and the bourgeoisie worked for the working class and not badly. Out of a stratum such as the lawyers came many revolutionaries. Marx was the son of a lawyer, not a son of *a batrak* [agricultural laborer] or of a worker. Among these strata can always be found people who can serve the cause of the working class, no worse, [but] rather better, than pure-blooded proletarians. That is why the general standard, that this is not a *batrak*'s son, is an outdated one, not applicable to individual people. *This is not a Marxist approach . . . This, I would say, is a biological approach, not a Marxist. We consider Marxism not a biological science, but a sociological science. Hence this general standard is absolutely correct with regard to estates, groups, strata, [but] it is not applicable to every individual who is not of proletarian or peasant origins.*[31]

Indeed, the Soviets persistently rejected the primacy of the biological over the sociological. The principle of human heredity and its potential practices, whether exterminatory euthanasia or constructive eugenics, were officially repudiated in the Soviet Union from the early 1930s on. What is more, the Soviet Union was practically alone among the major countries in the 1930s in its rejection of euthanasia or sterilization of the mentally retarded, a practice that was embraced, often enthusiastically, on both sides of the Atlantic. In such an atmosphere, Nobel Prize-winning doctor Alexis Carrel could call on modern societies to do away with the mentally retarded and criminals who cost a fortune to maintain in asylums and prisons. "Why do we preserve these useless and

---

[30] "Zakliuchitel'noe slovo tovarishcha Stalina na plenume TsK VKP (b) 5 marta 1937 g.," *Bol'shevik* 7 (1937): 19.

[31] "Rech' I. V. Stalina v Narkomate oborony, 2 iiunia 1937 g.," *Istochnik* 3 (1994): 73–4, italics added.

harmful beings? Why should society not dispose of the criminals and the insane in a more economical manner?" asked Carrel. The worst criminals (including the insane and people who misled the public in important matters), he concluded, "should be humanely and economically disposed of in small euthanasic institutions supplied with proper gases ... Modern society should not hesitate to organize itself with reference to the normal individual. Philosophical systems and sentimental prejudices must give way before such a necessity."[32] In Nazi Germany, as several scholars have recently reminded us, euthanasia was a key element in ideology and practice, and the forerunner of the persecution of the Jews, gypsies, and homosexuals, in sharp contrast to the Soviet purification drive, which at no point was anchored in genocidal ideology. Without it, the operation of industrialized killing – the aspect that set the Holocaust apart from other genocides – was inconceivable.

The same logic applied to eugenics, the constructive twin of euthanasia. In his 1935 *Out of the Night: A Biologist's View of the Future*, Hermann Muller, the chief advocate of eugenics in the Soviet Union, argued that with artificial insemination technology, "in the course of a paltry century or two ... it would be possible for the majority of the population to become of the innate quality of such men as Lenin, Newton, Leonardo, Pasteur, Beethoven, Omar Khayyam, Pushkin, Sun Yat Sen, Marx ... or even to possess their varied faculties combined ... which would offset the American prospects of a maximum number of Billy Sundays, Valentinos, Jack Dempseys, Babe Ruths, even Al Capones."[33] But when Muller forwarded a copy of his book to Stalin in May 1936 and assured him that "it is quite possible, by means of the technique of artificial insemination which has been developed in this country, to use for such purposes the reproductive material of the most transcendently superior individuals, of the one in 50,000, or one in 100,000, since this technique makes possible a multiplication of more than 50,000 times," he practically sealed his fate and the fate of eugenics in the Soviet Union for the next three decades. Stalin read the book, and although he did not respond in writing or verbally until June 1937, his actions spoke for themselves. Muller escaped the Soviet Union by the skin of his teeth, but his cohort was shot to a man. The Institute of Medical Genetics was disbanded, and the era of Lysenkoism and its doctrine of acquired characteristics was ushered in. In the long process of constructing a socialist society, acculturation prevailed over biology as the means of both the expansion and purification of the polity.

[32] Alexis Carell, *Man, the Unknown* (London, 1935), 318–19.
[33] Mark B. Adams, "Eugenics in Russia, 1900–1940," in Adams, ed., *The Wellborn Science: Eugenics in Germany, France, Brazil, and Russia* (New York, 1990), 194–5.

And indeed, there was not, nor could there be, a highly placed Jew such as Lazar Kaganovich in the Nazi leadership; nearly half a million Jews could neither serve in the Wehrmacht nor become members of the National Socialist Party. It did not matter if they had excelled in the ranks of the German army in the Great War. There was one Jew, and he could not be Nazified. The Jew was an enemy not because of a role he played or a position he represented. He was evil incarnate, irredeemable, and unreconstructed, and as such, had to be exterminated. The basis on which the extermination of the Jewish "lice" took place was neither that of religion nor law but the racial biopolitics of genetic heredity. That was not the case in the Soviet Union. True, enacting the motto "sons are not responsible for their fathers" proved difficult. Just two years after Stalin's famous dictum, NKVD and party investigators were busily plunging into the records of members of the Communist Party, resurrecting from oblivion the original sin of the wrong social origin to destroy scores of true believers and their families. In the wake of the Terror, it appeared as if the stain of bad social origin was unremovable and incurable. It took the war to realize and institutionalize Stalin's dictum in Soviet political life. Nevertheless, even at the height of the officially endorsed anti-Semitic campaign, there were hundreds of thousands of Jews in the ranks of the party, the army, and scores of other political institutions. Restrictions on the number of Jews in state institutions (*numerus clausus*) could and did coexist side by side with Jewish high officers, Heroes of the Soviet Union, and party activists. The Nazi antithesis was still a powerful deterrent, especially regarding the Jews. The United Nations draft resolution of the Genocide Convention on November 21, 1947, provided the Soviets with the opportunity to elaborate their own definition of excisionary and exterminatory ideologies and practices. In his comments on the treaty, Aron Trainin, then the leading Soviet authority in international law, agreed with the prevailing notion of genocide as extermination of national or racial collectives. His points of disagreement, however, were telling. First, argued Trainin, however extreme the persecution of political opponents based on political motives may be, it does not constitute genocide. Second, the definition of genocide should not be confined to physical extermination but applied to the curtailment of collective national-cultural rights as well. "Of course, in the land of the Soviets, where the Leninist–Stalinist national politics triumphs and the cooperation of nations is a political reality, there is no problem of national rights and national minorities," wrote Trainin. It was, however, the case in the capitalist world, where class exploitation could be identified with national oppression. Not only lynch trials but also a dense net of national-cultural barriers separate Negroes in the United States from the white population, Trainin continued.

Accordingly, international law should struggle against both lynch trials, as tools of physical extermination of Negroes, and the politics of national cultural oppression. Therefore, along with physical and biological genocide, the notion of national-cultural genocide must be advanced, a genocide that sets for itself the goal of undermining the existence and development of national and racial groups.[34]

In essence, these were the twin pillars of Soviet population policies: the application of state violence anchored in political rationale and the simultaneous cultivation of ethno-national particularism. Without them, one could hardly understand the simultaneous eradication of entire national elites and intelligentsias along with the persistent delineation of particularistic identities. In this light, total excision in the Soviet polity was not necessarily exterminatory, nor did it operate by a racial-biological code. And this, in turn, shifts the focus of our discussion to another political arena within which the Soviet socio-ethnic body was delineated, that of commemorative politics of cataclysmic events. . . .

Reflecting on the horrific slaughter consuming Europe at the time, Sigmund Freud observed in April 1915 that war was merely an instrument that stripped away illusions and layers of civility, "laying bare the primal man in each of us." The key, then, to the total barbarization of warfare lay not with the states but with the community and its individual components, which "no longer raise objections . . . to the suppression of evil passions, and men perpetrate deeds of cruelty, fraud, treachery and barbarity so incompatible with their level of civilization that one would have thought them impossible."[35] One could hardly deny the brutalization of public life triggered by the cataclysmic experience of the Great War, or any other mass, violent conflict for that matter. Categorization and treatment of enemies as undifferentiated, unreformable, irredeemable, and hence exterminable appear as a logical consequence from which even Marxist regimes, armed with a sociological paradigm premised on differentiation, reform, and redemption, could not escape.

Nor were the origins and technologies of Soviet violence divorced from those of other modern "gardening states." The refusal of the Soviet party-state to recognize any self-imposed restrictions on its aspirations

[34] Aron Naumovich Trainin, "Bor'ba s genotsidom kak mezhdunarodnym prestupleniem," *Sovetskoe gosudarstvo i pravo* 5 (May 1948): 4, 6.
[35] Sigmund Freud, "Thoughts for the Times on War and Death," in James Strachey, ed., *The Standard Edition of the Complete Psychological Works of Sigmund Freud* (London, 1957), 14: 275–300. Here, 280, 299.

and practices certainly set it apart from liberal democracies. Yet this very refusal was rooted in the modern secular state's assumption of responsibility for the spiritual, social, and physical well-being of its subjects. With the diminishing power of divine doctrines and their institutional incarnations, such as the Catholic church in the pre-modern era, which had often contained its violent schemes, the modern state was restrained by and accountable to none in its drive to remold society and individuals.

Yet the endurance of Marxist state violence and its constant acceleration in peacetime pointed to an additional source. As communist regimes shifted gears in their pursuit of homogenized and harmonious societies, their belief in the malleability of human nature seemed to wane. In the Soviet Union, those marked by the party-state as internal enemies after the establishment of socialism were deemed irreducible, unreformable, and irredeemable elements; and in the heyday of the Cultural Revolution in China, the "blood pedigree theory" was practiced under the slogan: "If the father's a hero, the son's a good chap; If the father's a reactionary, the son's a bad egg." Did nurture finally succumb to nature? Not necessarily. Excision, even when totalized, did not emanate from a genocidal ideology and was not practiced through exterminatory institutions. Hence communists repeatedly turned their attention to groups and individuals they had already engaged previously, an inconceivable practice had these entities been stigmatized a priori as racially or biologically unfit. Purification did not engage collectives as such but rather the individuals who comprised them. As the ticking of the Soviet eschatological clock grew louder, they bore the brunt of an increasingly urgent quest for purity.

Further Reading: Soviet Nationality Policy

Peter Blitstein, "Nation-building or Russification? Obligatory Russian instruction in the Soviet non-Russian School, 1938–1953," in Ronald Grigor Suny and Terry Martin, eds., *A State of Nations: Empire and Nation-making in the Age of Lenin and Stalin* (New York, 2001).

Rogers Brubaker, "Nationhood and the National Question in the Soviet Union and Post-Soviet Eurasia," *Theory and Society*, vol. 23, no. 1 (1994).

Francine Hirsch, "Toward an Empire of Nations: Border-Making and the Formation of Soviet National Identities," *The Russian Review*, vol. 59, no. 2 (2000).

Adeeb Khalid, *The Politics of Muslim Cultural Reform: Jadidism in Central Asia* (Berkeley, 1998).

Terry Martin, *The Affirmative Action Empire: Nations and Nationalism in the Soviet Union, 1923–1939* (Ithaca, 2001).

Paula Michaels, "Medical Propaganda and Cultural Revolution in Soviet Kazakhstan, 1928–1941," *The Russian Review*, vol. 59, no. 2 (2000).

Douglas Northrop, "Languages of Loyalty: Gender, Politics, and Party Supervision in Uzbekistan, 1927–1941," *The Russian Review*, vol. 59, no. 2 (2000).

Matt Payne, "Forge of the Kazakh Proletariat? The Turksib, Nativization, and Industrialization during Stalins's First Five-Year Plan," in Suny and Martin, eds.

Yuri Slezkine, "The USSR as a Communal Apartment, or How a Socialist State Promoted Ethnic Particularism," *Slavic Review*, vol. 53, no. 3 (1994).

Ronald Grigor Suny, *The Revenge of the Past: Nationalism, Revolution, and the Collapse of the Soviet Union* (Stanford, 1993).

The Postwar Years

11

Russia after the War: Hopes, Illusions, and Disappointments

Elena Zubkova

Excerpted from *Russia after the War: Hopes, Illusions, and Disappointments, 1945–1957*, trans. and ed. by Hugh Ragsdale (Armonk, NY: M. E. Sharpe, 1998).

Editor's Introduction

The Second World War affected far more than just Stalinist policy toward ethnic and national minorities. It touched the lives of all Soviet citizens, usually in very tragic ways. Some 27 million people in the Soviet Union died as a result of the war.[1] Virtually every family in the country lost at least one close relative. Entire cities and towns were destroyed, leaving millions of people homeless. The scale of death and destruction was due in part to huge territorial losses at the beginning of the war coupled with brutal Nazi occupation policies. When Hitler invaded the Soviet Union in June 1941, he took Stalin by surprise, and the German army drove all the way to the outskirts of Moscow in a matter of months. Only after the decisive victory at Stalingrad in 1942–3 was the Soviet army able, at tremendous cost, to begin expelling the Nazis from the country. The Nazis employed a scorched earth strategy as they retreated, burning crops and demolishing cities.

In addition to causing widespread death and destruction, the war reshaped the Soviet Union in fundamental ways. Soviet citizens' lives and mentalities were entirely transformed by the war. Millions of people volunteered for or were drafted into the military, and those who survived to the end of the war marched through eastern Europe all the way to Berlin. On the homefront, millions of women took over factory jobs and collective farm positions vacated by men who had joined the army. Huge

---

[1] As discussed in Zubkova's selection below, historians still debate the total number of Soviet casualties during the war.

numbers of people and entire factories from the western part of the country were evacuated to cities in the Urals, Siberia, and Central Asia. Victory in the war required enormous resourcefulness and sacrifice on the part of soldiers, partisans, and civilians, and at the end of the war many people had developed a new-found sense of initiative and entitlement. But most of all, victory in the war raised to unprecedented heights the power and prestige of Stalin and the Stalinist system.

Despite the importance of the war, historians are only now beginning to study its effect on Soviet society and on the Stalinist system more generally. In addition to Weiner's pioneering work, Elena Zubkova's book *Russia after the War* makes a major contribution to our understanding of Soviet society in the postwar years. In the excerpt below, Zubkova describes the impact of the war, not only regarding the death and destruction it caused, but in terms of its lasting psychological effect on Soviet citizens. As such a cataclysmic event, the war could not but shape people's thinking and perceptions for years to come. The war thus influenced political and social developments for the remainder of the Stalin era (up to his death in 1953) and even beyond.

Zubkova begins by analyzing the demographic and social implications of wartime casualties. Because three-quarters of the nearly 27 million killed in the war were men, a severe gender imbalance emerged in the postwar years. Especially among young adults, women far outnumbered men, so many women had little prospect of getting married, or of remarrying if they had lost their husbands in the war. Some unmarried women had children anyway, though these children grew up without fathers. Of course many children lost fathers during the war, or were orphaned altogether. Moreover, children and teenagers often suffered long-term health problems as a result of malnourishment, disease, and overwork during the war.

Zubkova attaches special significance to the place of veterans in postwar society. A total of 8.5 million men had been demobilized from the Red Army by 1948, and these veterans had difficulty adjusting to civilian life. Compounding their readjustment problems was the fact that many of them could not find employment or worked in jobs for which they had no training. Two million veterans were left with permanent disabilities as a result of wartime injuries and could not work at all. Those veterans who returned home to areas formerly under Nazi occupation often lacked adequate housing as their homes had been destroyed in the war. Veterans, then, made up an important new social group which enjoyed substantial prestige but also faced enormous obstacles in postwar life.

Zubkova asks whether these veterans constituted a potential force for political change after the war. She makes an analogy with veterans of the War of 1812 who, having defeated Napoleon and marched all the way to

Paris, later revolted against the tsarist autocracy and demanded a constitution. Soviet veterans of the Second World War also derived a sense of prerogative from their victory, and they too had their horizons expanded by fighting abroad. The fact that they maintained informal networks among themselves seemed to offer the chance to organize for political change. More generally some veterans and civilians hoped that Stalin and his regime would reward them for their great sacrifices in the war by granting some sort of political liberalization. But such liberalization was not forthcoming – on the contrary, the Stalinist regime became more rigid and repressive than ever.

Zubkova explains that several countervailing factors precluded demands for political change. First, the wartime victory elevated Stalin's prestige and seemed to vindicate all aspects of the Stalinist system. Despite the enormous human costs of collectivization, rapid industrialization, and the Great Terror, even these policies could be justified as necessary measures to prepare for war. Second, the war created a sense of unity between the population and the Soviet government, so it was difficult for people to break that unity by opposing the Stalinist regime in the postwar era. Third, after years of fighting, death, and destruction, the Soviet people above all wanted peace. Most of them were not prepared to engage in a struggle with their own government to force political change.

The lack of a coherent political challenge to Stalinism did not mean that all Soviet citizens were complacent. Workers evacuated during the war to factories in Siberia voiced their sense of betrayal when, after victory, the government did not allow them to return to their homes. Other workers organized demonstrations to demand better living and working conditions. The postwar economic situation was so impoverished that much of the population lived without basic items of food and clothing. Hunger and suffering were widespread and people also feared a rise in crime due to extreme shortages. But despite incredible hardship, no broad-based challenge to Stalinist regime emerged. The Soviet people learned to accept continued suffering, as they put aside their hopes for a better life after the war.

Russia after the War: Hopes, Illusions, and Disappointments

Elena Zubkova

The Victory and the Victors

The war naturally left a dreadful legacy across the country. An extraordinary state commission, charged with calculating the material losses resulting from combat operations and defense expenditures more generally, assessed the cost at 2,569 billion rubles.[1] This figure took into account the destruction of cities and towns, industrial enterprises, and railroad bridges; the loss of output of pig iron and steel; the contraction of the motor vehicle fleet and the livestock population; and so on. Nowhere, however, was there mention of the number of lives lost (if we ignore the figure of 7 million announced by Stalin in 1946).

The magnitude of human losses in the Soviet Union during the Second World War is still disputed among historians. One reason for the disagreement is the lack of a complete statistical base and authoritative figures on birth and death rates, the natural rate of growth of the population, and other demographic indicators.[2] Research based on the methodology of demographic balance[3] indicates total human losses in the USSR during the war of 26.6 million people.[4] Approximately 76

This chapter was translated and edited by Hugh Ragsdale.

[1] B. N. Ponomarev, *Istoriia SSSR s drevneishikh vremen do nashikh dnei*, 11 vols. (Moscow, 1966–80), 11: 47. [As the ruble of the time was a controlled currency not traded in world financial markets, its real value is impossible to determine, and hence it hardly makes sense to try to give an equivalent dollar value for the sum cited here. – H.R.]

[2] Not even the formerly secret information recently put at the disposal of historians on the demographic composition of the population during and after the war has clarified the situation fully. The indices of the birth and death rates of the population held in different offices of the government (for example, the Central Statistical Administration of the USSR and the Ministry of Health) often not only fail to coincide but contradict each other. The most detailed examination of the problem is in V. P. Popov, "Prichiny sokrashcheniia chislennosti naseleniia RSFSR posle Velikoi otechestvennoi voiny," *Sotsiologicheskie issledovaniia*, 1994, No. 10, 76–9.

[3] The human losses evaluated here to determine the demographic balance include: (a) those dying as a consequence of the military or other action of the enemy; (b) those dying as a result of the higher level of mortality during the war in the rear, in the regions abutting the front, and in the occupied territory; (c) those people from the population of the USSR on 22 June 1941 who left the territory of the country during the war and did not return before its conclusion (not including POWs and displaced persons).

[4] E. M. Andreev et al., *Naselenie Sovetskogo Soiuza, 1922–1991 gg.* (Moscow, 1993), 73.

percent, that is, about 20 million, were men, the greater part of whom had been born between 1901 and 1931 – the most capable contingent of the male population.[5] This circumstance alone suggests the seriousness of the demographic problems of postwar society. In 1940 the Soviet population numbered 100.3 million females and 92.3 million males. The primary source of the imbalance was the superior life expectancy of women, especially after age 60. In 1946 the Soviet population numbered 96.2 million females and 74.4 million males; and in comparison with the prewar situation, the substantially greater number of women was already conspicuous in the age cohort of 20- to 44-year-olds. In 1940, there were 37.6 million women and 34.8 million men between the ages of 20 and 44, whereas in 1946 there were an equal number of women and 10 million fewer men of the same age cohort.[6] In the countryside the situation was even worse. Whereas in 1940 the ratio of women to men on collective farms was approximately 1.1 : 1, in 1945 it was 2.7 : 1![7]

Women thus constituted the great majority of the postwar Soviet population. This situation brought on serious problems, not only demographic but psychological as well, eventuating in social pathology and the lonely solitude of women. The postwar fatherlessness of so many children engendered a striking vogue of adolescent vagabondage and crime. Nevertheless, all the losses and deprivations notwithstanding, it was precisely the initiative of women that made postwar society so prolific. Bereft of husbands, left without the hope of having a conventional family, and in the most difficult of material conditions, many women continued to bear children. In 1946, for example, 752,000 children were born to unmarried mothers; in 1947, 747,000; in 1948, 665,000; in 1949, 985,000; in 1950, 944,000; in 1951, 930,000; in 1952, 849,000.[8]

The children of wartime were a special problem, the least secure part of the population. During the war, children suffered side by side with adults and sometimes more than adults. They died in bombing raids, of hunger and disease, or they were forcibly deported abroad. The war years depressed the birth rate of the population palpably. In 1946 there were 53 million children below age 14 – 14 million fewer than in 1940.[9] Many teenagers had to go into industrial production during the war, both in order to take the place of adult workers leaving for the front and

---

[5] Ibid., 77.

[6] Ibid., 121–34.

[7] Iu.V. Argutiunian, *Sovetskoe krest'ianstvo v gody Velikoi otechestvennoi voiny* (Moscow, 1963), 318.

[8] Popov, "Prichiny sokrashcheniia chislennosti naseleniia RSFSR posle Velikoi otechestvennoi voiny," 91.

[9] Andreev et al., *Naselenie Sovetskogo Soiuza, 1922–1991*, 53, 70.

in order to secure the means of subsistence for themselves and their families. Teenagers worked as if they were adults, sometimes ten to twelve hours a day. Stressful work and constant undernourishment unavoidably damaged the health of the younger generation.

In June 1945 the party Central Committee ordered an official inspection of the industrial enterprises of Gorkii Oblast (province) for the purpose of evaluating teenagers' working conditions and the state of their health. The commission's conclusions were disturbing: "In the majority of the industries examined, normal living conditions for teenagers were not available, and these circumstances lead to sickliness and retardation of their physical development."[10] In the Molotov Factory a medical examination of 1,070 teenagers was carried out. It found 379 (35 percent) of them clinically ill: sixty-four suffered from diseases of the digestive tract; fifty-one, skin rashes and other dermatological disorders; six, tuberculosis; and four, muscular dystrophy. Of 670 youths between ages 15 and 17, 340 (50.6 percent) suffered from a retardation of growth (height) of one to two years, and 413 (61.6 percent) were underweight. The majority were anemic.[11]

Psychologists observed that the children of wartime matured early – that is, they developed an outlook on life more sophisticated than that of their peers growing up in peaceful conditions. Such precocity exacted an inevitable psychological price. The child's psyche suffered aggravated trauma from the loss of loved ones, the fear of death, and the dread of being orphaned. A whole generation of children grew up without fathers in Russia, children without a home in the full sense of the word. They grew up in a truncated family or without any family, in schools, kindergartens, or urban shelters designed to ameliorate this deprivation. And the postwar shelter was a special world with its own norms of behavior and forms of social control. It was an institution that in many respects formed the psyche of a whole generation. Its children learned to live by the unwritten rules of shelter society, and it was no accident that in their subsequent adult life the social relations formed in the shelter played no less a role than those of blood relations. These people were team players, disdaining individualism; and yet, ironically, it was especially in their midst that striking forms of individualism took root.

The society emerging from the war differed from conventional society not only in its demographic structure but also in its social composition. It was no longer made up of the traditional categories – the urban and rural, industrial workers and civil servants, youth and pensioners – but

[10] Dokladnaia zapiska upolnomochenogo Komissii partiinogo kontrola pri TsK VKP(b) po Gor'kovskoi oblasti "O neudovletvoritel'nom kul'turno-bytovom obsluzhivanii i proizvodstvennykh usloviakh rabochikh-podrostkov na riade predpriiatii Gor'kovskoi oblasti, 11 June 1945; RTsKhIDNI, f. 17, op. 122, d. 103, l. 77.
[11] Ibid.

rather of a mentality born of the war. In this sense the most prominent face of postwar society was that of the man in uniform, the veteran. Toward the end of the war, the Soviet army numbered 11 million people.[12] According to the law of 23 June 1945 on demobilization, the first to be discharged from the army were the thirteen most senior age-groups, and by 1948 the process of demobilization was fundamentally complete. A total of 8.5 million men were demobilized.[13]

In various ways, everybody faced the problem of transition from war to peace, economically, socially, and psychologically. Of course, the process affected most the interests of those now completely alienated from civilian society, those who had lived four years in a different environment, the soldiers. The gravity of the losses, the material deprivations experienced with minor exceptions by everyone, were aggravated for the veterans by the additional psychological problems inherent in the transition to civilian life. For many, therefore, the mobilization that had been so much anticipated at the front turned into a serious problem in itself – specially for the youngest soldiers, those born in the years 1923–7, who had gone to the front straight from the schoolroom without the chance to acquire any occupational experience at all. War was their only profession, their only competence the capacity to wield weapons and fight. Moreover, this generation had suffered losses greater than any other, especially in the first year of combat. The war to a remarkable degree washed away the boundaries between age-groups. The various generations, their human losses mounting, virtually merged into one – the generation of victors – forming thereby a new mentality that united them in a shared community of problems, attitudes, wishes, and aspirations. Of course, this community of concerns was relative – even in the war there was no perfect unity among soldiers – but the spirit of front-line brotherhood continued for a long time to influence the postwar atmosphere.

The majority of demobilized veterans sought work almost at once. Thus, according to the figures of some forty regional party committees, of 2.7 million recently demobilized persons in January 1946, 2.1 million (71.1 percent) were employed. Of the number of veterans employed at that time, more than half (55 percent) worked on collective farms or state farms.[14] The figures on veterans' employment varied significantly by different regions. In Irkutsk Province, for example, in January 1946 more than half of the able-bodied returning veterans had

---

[12] *Istoriia SSSR s drevneishikh vremen*, 11:53.

[13] Ibid., 56.

[14] Informatsiia Organizatsionno-instruktorskogo otdela TsK VKP(b) o vypolnenii postanovleniia TsK VKP(b) ot 25 avgusta 1945 g. "O rabote mestnykh partiinykh organizatsii i sovetskikh organov po ustroistvu demobilizovannykh iz deistvuiushchei armii," 11 March 1946; RTsKhIDNI, f. 17, op. 122, d. 145, l. 193.

not found work; in the city of Tiumen, 59 percent were unemployed; in Astrakhan Province, 64 percent.[15] The reasons for this situation varied. Sometimes there was no work for the particular specialty in which the demobilized were qualified; sometimes they were offered unskilled work and pay not commensurate with their qualifications. Thus of forty-seven demobilized veterans returning to the factory Red Chemist in Vladimir Province, only sixteen received work in their field of qualification, while the remainder were directed to wood-cutting.[16] This state of affairs was similar in other regions.

In addition to the problem of finding work was the problem of finding living space, a matter especially acute in areas that had suffered heavy combat damage. In such places many families of the demobilized had to live in dugouts or in other poor substitutes for homes. It was not only the demobilized who lived in such conditions, however, and the mastery of primitive circumstances was only one of the strategies of survival in postwar society.

The war, it seemed, had exhausted the last reserves of human strength. The Soviet army, alone among those engaged in the war, did not follow the practice of granting rest-and-recreation furloughs (with the exception of short-term leaves for the wounded). Czech historian Boguslav Shnaider [Czech Bohuslav Šnajder – H.R.] observed that human losses in the Soviet army could have been fewer had it not suffered unremitting psychological overload. "Soldiers of the Red Army were under constant psychological pressure, which was unprecedented in the history of warfare. Fatigue and psychic exhaustion exceeded all imaginable limits."[17] This fatigue made itself felt after the war as well. The veterans noticed with surprise that during the war, constantly shuttling between life and death, people did not suffer from conventional "peacetime" illnesses. When the war ended, on the other hand, such illnesses quickly reappeared: their reserves of physical resistance had run out. By no means everyone returned from the front in good health. While we have statistics, however imprecise, on the wartime losses, until this day we lack figures on those who died of wounds and illnesses after the war. Toward the end, among those demobilized on grounds of health, there were 2 million invalids; and among them, around 450,000 with one amputated limb and around 350,000 with a diagnosis of osteomyelitis (inflammation of bone marrow).[18] The

[15] Ibid., l. 194.

[16] Ibid.

[17] Boguslav Shnaider, "Neizvestnaia voina," *Voprosy istorii*, 1995, No. 1: 110.

[18] Dokladnaia zapiska zaveduiushchego otdelom Upravleniia Kadrov TsK VKP(b) Petrova "O neobkhodimosti perestroiki dela lechebnoi pomoshchi invalidam Otechestvennoi voiny," 25 April 1945; RTsKhIDNI, f. 17, op. 117, d. 511, l. 107.

invalids, more even than the other veterans, were in need not only of surgery or medication but of psychological treatment as well. Toward the end of the war, however, only a third of the infirmaries for invalids had a physician attached, not to speak of full medical services.[19] Much more complicated for the invalids than for the other veterans was the search for work, and the situation of those who had lost their sight was practically hopeless. Without supplementary income, it was very difficult, almost impossible, to live on a single invalid's pension. The begging of cripples around bazaars and railroad stations became a characteristic feature of the time. Invalids were required to undergo an annual medical examination – to confirm the continuation of their disability – a procedure exacted even of those who had lost a limb at the front ("as if it would grow back," in the grim joke of the veterans). The majority of invalids left thus on the sidelines of life were young people; and their consciousness of not being needed, their superfluousness in the new postwar life, for the sake of which they had sacrificed themselves, was especially painful.

Other veterans were able to get good work or prestigious duties and to enter institutes of higher education or continue studies interrupted by the war. Their acquisition of a higher social status, however much it was deserved, nevertheless introduced a notorious difference of interest into this social community formerly so closely knit. It prompted a process that Mikhail Gefter denominated "the fracturing of the generation of victors,"[20] and it was not in the least spontaneous but was deliberately orchestrated from above.[21]

The veterans returning from the war were sometimes considered potential neo-Decembrists, suggesting an analogy with the developments in Russia after the War of 1812, in particular the uprising of several regiments in St. Petersburg in December 1825.[22] This potential

---

[19] Ibid., 108.

[20] Mikhail Gefter, "Stalin umer vchera. . . . ," in A. A. Protashchik, ed., *Inogo ne dano* (Moscow, 1988), 305.

[21] One of the first problems of the deliberate division of Soviet society into different interest groups after the war was described by Vera S. Dunham, *In Stalin's Time: Middleclass Values in Soviet Fiction* (Cambridge, MA, 1976), 12.

[22] For all of the differences in the historical conditions of the two wars, that of 1812 and that of 1941–5, they had similar sociopsychological consequences: the awakening of the spirit of freedom, the aspirations of the people for a better life as a reward for the victory, the birth of progressive political ideas among the intelligentsia and others. There was also some parallel in the moods of the peasantry in favor of the abolition of serfdom in the earlier case and of the abolition of the collective farm in the second. Both wars also provided an impetus for reevaluation of political values in the minds of social groups participating in the power structure, some representatives of which gradually formed conservative and reformist wings. [That is, they were opposed to the radical storm and stress approach to economic planning and expansion, in favor of emphasizing consumer

was not, of course, realized, in any event not directly, in the early postwar years, as it was suppressed by the regime. Thus the question is almost never raised: were the veterans capable of forming an active force for political (*obshchestvennyi*) change immediately after the war? I pose this question quite seriously, not merely to assess the potential strength of the forces committed to freedom but in order to identify a moment when progressive reforms might have found sufficiently broad social support. If we continue the analogy with the Decembrists, then the factor of timing appears to be a key consideration: the Decembrist uprising occurred more than twelve years after the end of the war of 1812 – again, not accidentally. The war alone did not engender political positions, not to speak of forming organizations for the pursuit of political activity, because war assigns other duties. But war also modifies the bases of cultural life, stimulates a reexamination of conventional assumptions, and forms a moral-psychological foundation for the future. What comes of it all depends on the particular conditions of the postwar years. It must be obvious, however, that the first years after the end of a successful war are not the most favorable time to engage in a struggle with the victorious government. The poor prospects of such an open confrontation in the Soviet Union in 1945 may be explained by the influence of several factors.

First, the very character of the war – patriotic, liberating, just – presupposes the unity of the society – people and government – in the commitment to a national cause, the expulsion of the enemy. Victory in such a war was envisioned as a triumph of the entire nation. Linked by a common interest, the common challenge of survival, the community of government and people was gradually forged as they jointly laid aside the assumptions of civilian life and brought together the deceived hopes below and the crisis of command above.

Second, we must consider the psychological factor of the overload of stress on the people, of four years spent in the trenches and the consequent need for emotional release, for liberation from the endurance test. The people, having long borne the burdens of demolition, naturally grasped the opportunity for peaceful construction. At this juncture, the enjoyment of peace was of premium value and excluded any consideration of violence. "The massive homelessness of millions of people, which is to say, the war, is sickening," Emmanuil Kazakevich wrote from the front; "more than the danger and the risk, it is really the homeless-

industry rather than the capital goods industries – in Soviet parlance, Group B and Group A respectively – and committed to economic concessions for the peasantry. – H.R.] This wing of the administration was characterized by a wish to turn from the idea of autocratic power – the *vozhd'*, leader, Stalin – to power limited to some degree by the influence of democratic institutions.

ness. . . ."[23] Speaking in May 1945 to a group of writers, her colleagues, Vera Ketlinskaia summoned them to envision in all of its complexity "not only the pride of the victors but the enormous grief of the long-suffering people."[24]

A period of convalescence, both physical and emotional, was inevitable after the war, a complex and painful period of restoration of civilian life in which conventional problems, such as housing, might have to remain unresolved for a time. The problem of housing was not only one of living space: one of the most serious problems after the war was the establishment of a family life. The leading challenge for the veterans of the time was to readjust to such a life, to enroll themselves in it, to learn to live in such an unaccustomed way. "Everybody wanted to organize some kind of life," Viacheslav Kondratiev recalls. "We had to live. Some married. Others entered the party. . . . We had to adjust to a new life. There was no alternative."[25] Perhaps some people had alternatives, but for the majority of veterans the problem of reintegrating into civilian life was depressingly simple. They had to take life as they found it.

Third, loyal to the Soviet order though they were, not all veterans looked upon it as ideal, or even as just. The facts of the prewar years, the experience of the war, and observations during the campaign in Europe forced them to reflect, to wonder about the justice of elements of the regime, if not of the regime as a whole. There was not necessarily a direct link, however, between dissatisfaction with the structure of life at home and action aimed at changing it. The establishment of such a link depended upon the evolution of a concrete program of future action, a conception of goals and a mechanism for their realization; but no such instrument existed. "There was much in the system that we did not accept, but we could not imagine any other kind," Viacheslav Kondratiev admitted.[26] This statement may seem surprising, but it reflects a contradiction characteristic of people's thinking in the postwar years. The regime was perceived as an inflexible given, irremediable and independent of human will, of one's own aspirations and wishes.

All of these factors allow us to affirm the impossibility during the first days after the victory of open popular opposition to authority. Such was the peculiarity of the moment. Yet the potential for the development of a mature and dynamic political opposition was present. That is, there was a fully possible prospect that the veterans themselves – the liberal

---

[23] Emmanuil Kazakevich, *Slushaia vremia: Dnevniki, zapisnye knizhki, pis'ma* (Moscow, 1990), 259.

[24] RGALI, f. 631, op. 15, d. 737, l. 86.

[25] Interview with V. L. Kondrat'ev; author's personal archive.

[26] Viacheslav Kondrat'ev, "Ne tol'ko o svoem pokolenii," *Kommunist*, 1990, No. 7: 115.

fraction of them – could become a potential support and one of the principal moving forces of a future process of reform. Reform is usually preceded by an emotionally critical stage characterized by a mental ferment and the consolidation of active political forces. The war initiated this stage, which continued long after the war had ended. Although its development proceeded by increments, obscured by the many mundane problems, the process produced distinct forms of expression.

It was sustained particularly by the channels of communications among the veterans, who after the war remained in contact with each other, destined to be a part of an invisible network, a combat community with its attendant legacy of common postwar problems. Life in the communal huts and apartments so typical of the time was an awkward medium for this kind of intercourse. Therefore it took place as a rule away from home, either in the student dormitories to which many veterans returned, or, more typically, in newly opened cafés, snack bars, and beer halls – "blue Danubes," as they were called. These latter places became the refuges of veterans' social life and gave rise to an altogether peculiar phenomenon of the time, "tavern" (*shalmannaia*) democracy.

> How many of these holes-in-the-wall, snack bars, pavilions, and taverns (*shalmany*), these blue Danubes, were opened by the wrecked and half-destitute country in order to comfort and warm the returning soldiers, in order to provide them the glow of an evening's uninhibited company, to help them speak out, to soften their hardened souls, to enable them to look one another in the eye unhurriedly and to realize that a seemingly unimaginable peace and quiet had really come? In the inconceivably close spaces between shell-scarred houses, in the open fields, among huts and fences, in rustic groves these evening retreats sprang up, and here popular parlance, ignoring the street address, fixed to each establishment a distinct and indelible name, which is not to be found in the guidebooks.[27]

This modest portrait from Viktor Smirnov's story "Zaulki" (Back Streets) tells us what the blue Danubes were in the life of people returning from the war. They were merely everyday life, yet they were so much more.

Led by their own problems in separate ways, the veterans came together again where the nostalgia of the front reigned. And the more commonplace or desperate postwar life became, the more sharply and distinctly were the values of the warrior imprinted in their consciousness, especially those making him "indispensably necessary." The peaceful life was already structured on other principles: the soldier who experienced during wartime the feeling that "he alone held the fate of

[27] Viktor Smirnov, "Zaulki: Povest'," *Roman-gazeta*, 1989, No. 3–4: 8.

the country in his hands" was driven after the war to the sad admission that "with me, without me, everything goes on anyway."[28] The former values persisted only among a narrow circle of friends, really only in the little retreats of blue Danubes. "9 May, 1950," Emmanuil Kazakevich noted in his diary, "the Day of Victory . . . I went to a beer bar. Two invalids and a plumber . . . were drinking beer and reminiscing about the war. One of them wept and said: If there were another war, I would go. . . ."[29]

Nostalgia for the front inspired the tone of camaraderie in the blue Danubes, where candor in conversation and sentiment was habitual, notwithstanding the presence of spies. There society was constituted as formerly by the laws of war, and the openness with which people shared their experience contrasted with the completely different spirit saturating the atmosphere outside. Whatever we may think of these blue Danubes, they came to embody by force of circumstance the last refuge of the spirit of freedom brought from the front. All the other channels were simply closed; and it was not the fault of the veterans that, in place of genuine freedom, all that was left them was the freedom to talk over a glass of beer, or that this freedom, too, was soon taken away, putting the finishing touches on a deliberate campaign to wipe out the potential benefits inherent in the victory.

This campaign began in fact on the day after the victory, the credit for which was immediately divided and apportioned. On the day when the war ended, *Pravda* distributed the credit for the victory in the following fashion: "The victory did not come of itself. *It was won* by the self-sacrifice, the heroism, the military mastery of the Red Army and of the whole Soviet people. *It was organized* by our invincible Bolshevik Party, the party of Lenin and Stalin, *it was led* by our great Stalin. . . . Long live *our great Stalinist* victory!"[30] [Author's emphasis – E.Z.] And so the victory was called "ours" and "Stalin's" simultaneously, but the subtext was obvious: "our" victory occurred only because it was primordially "Stalin's." In the same issue of *Pravda*, in the column entitled "News from Abroad," the victory was characterized as "a day forecast by Comrade Stalin."[31]

In his "Address to the People" Stalin himself distributed the emphasis somewhat differently. The *vozhd'* (leader) addressed himself to "compatriots, fellow countrymen and countrywomen," giving the obligatory credit to the victorious people: "The great sacrifices that we have borne

[28] Viacheslav Kondrat'ev, "Paradoksy frontovoi nostal'gii," *Literaturnaia gazeta*, 9 May 1990, 9.

[29] Kazakevich, *Slushaia vremia*, 28.

[30] *Pravda*, 9 May 1945.

[31] Ibid.

in the name of the freedom and independence of our Fatherland, the innumerable deprivations and losses suffered by our people in the course of the war, the intensive labor in the rear and at the front, offered on the altar of the country, have not been made in vain and eventuated in the complete victory over the enemy."[32] The address contained not a word of the party and its role in the organization of victory. Stalin simply excluded this intermediary link between himself and the people.

On 24 May Stalin pronounced his famous toast "to the health of the Russian people," naming the Russian people "the leading force of the Soviet Union among all the people of our country." Speaking of it as the "leading people," he again remained silent on the "leading party."[33] A month later, on 25 June, at a reception in the Kremlin in honor of the participants in the victory parade, a fresh nuance appeared in Stalin's interpretation, the so-called "proposition of the screws." In spite of the frequency of the citation of this toast, taken out of context it offers only a limited opportunity for analysis. In any event, the context of the occasion is no less important than the content of the toast. Stalin spoke toward the end of the reception, after the tributes in honor of the military commanders, the scientific and technical advisers, and the industrial leaders had already been made. The keynote of his speech was clear. He proposed a toast "to the health of the people of modest rank and obscure station. To the people who may be considered the screws in the great machine of state, without whom we, the marshals and commanders of the front armies, to put it crudely, are not worth a farthing. These are the people who sustain us, as a foundation supports a summit."[34] Stalin thus revised his former thesis on the union of leader and people, sketching their relationship as one of summit and base, thereby necessarily diminishing the status of the latter from that of "great people" to people as screws – cogs – in the machine. The toast contained an additional thought: Stalin not only established the hierarchical principle in the community of leader and people; he also set the simple people against their superiors, their bosses – beneath his own level, of course – preserving for himself the function of supreme arbiter at the nexus where the lines of the management of the masses and the management of the bosses came together.

Even before the importation from the war of the grim dichotomy of *us* and *them* began to change the nature of personal relations, Stalin tried consciously or unconsciously to direct the process into the channel that he needed. He removed himself from the society of *we*,

---

[32] Ibid., 10 May 1945.
[33] Ibid., 25 May 1945.
[34] Ibid., 27 June 1945.

moved into a kind of solitude, preserving for himself the right of orchestrating the process of marking sociopolitical boundaries, among which was the definition of "ours," "not ours," "theirs," and "the enemies'." This was in reality a return to the prewar system of power relations, reestablishing the absolute power of the leader and ignoring those who genuinely deserved the credit for the victory. It was not surprising that many veterans felt offended and bitter to be assigned to the ranks of mere "screws." And although propaganda affirmed that the words of the leader about the screws were affectionate and fatherly and that they "exalt all our people," these illusions did not prevail. Life itself left few hopes and illusions. The veterans, by their own admissions, felt less and less needed, and some of them, the invalids, felt entirely superfluous.

"How to Live After the War?": The Conflict of Expectation and Reality

The war changed the face of world politics. The common threat brought nations together, postponed their usual quarrels, and turned national pride and ethnic antagonisms into unwanted handicaps. The worldwide cataclysm diverted the nations from the usual posturing about the superiority of one political system or another and encouraged them to embrace the priority of common human values and the idea of global unity. At the end of the war this idea seemed about to materialize, conciliating the conflicts among recent allies and damping the ardor of the diehard revanchists. Even the genesis of the Cold War, followed by the atomic psychosis, could not entirely scotch the idea of a Common European Home. Of course, merely beginning to turn this idea into political reality required the passage of several decades and the change of several political generations. The postwar leaders continued to think in terms of the old categories of confrontation: one side feared the spread of communist contagion, and the other guarded itself against bourgeois influence. The iron curtain descended between East and West Europe. Thereafter Soviet citizens could only guess at what was going on in the world, until they realized with bitter surprise that the defeated enemy had quickly regained his feet and laid the foundations of a new and vigorous life, while they themselves were subsisting on meager rations and blaming their misery on the consequences of the war.

But it did not have to be so. The victory offered Russia the opportunity to choose whether to develop itself together with the civilized world or to go its own way as formerly in the tradition of socialist messianism. There was without doubt an alternative to the policy of isolation.

The victory raised to an unprecedented height not only the international prestige of the Soviet Union but the authority of the regime inside the country as well. "Drunk with the conceit of victory," wrote the veteran Fedor Abramov, "we decided that our system was ideal, . . . and we not only neglected to improve it, but, on the contrary, we grew ever more dogmatic about it."[35] The Russian philosopher Georgii Fedotov, reflecting on the influence of Stalin's soaring authority on the development of internal political processes, also came to a disturbing conclusion: "Our forebears, in the company of foreigners, felt compelled to blush for Russian autocracy and serfdom. If they had observed such worldwide servility before the tsar as Europe and America exhibited before Stalin, it would not have occurred to them to feel embarrassed about the behavior of their countrymen."[36]

The saying "victors are not to be judged" is not an acquittal but a cause for reflection, as illustrated by Viktor Nekrasov's comments:

> Alas! We excused Stalin for everything! Collectivization, the purges, the execution of his colleagues, the defeats of 1941. And he, of course, then understood all the power of the people believing in his genius, understood that there could no longer be any mistake about that, that only throwing the harsh truth [he was indispensable! – H.R.] in their face would unite them, that there could be no return to the rivers of blood, not of the war, but of the prewar period. And we, callow intelliligentsia, having become soldiers, believed in this myth with our whole heart and entered the party of Lenin and Stalin.[37]

May 1945 was the high point of the authority of Stalin. His name was linked in the mind of the masses with the victory, and he was perceived as being virtually the bearer of divine providence. The war correspondent Alexander Avdeenko recalls going to the victory parade with his young son.

> I take my son in my arms, raise him up. The Lenin Mausoleum is ten meters or a little more away. The reviewing stand and everybody on it is as if in the palm of our hands.
> "Do you see him?"
> "Aha. Standing in the rain. The old man. Is he getting wet?"
> "Tempered steel does not fear rain."
> "Is he a man of steel? Is that why he is called Stalin?"

[35] Fedor Abramov, "A liudi zhdut, zhdut peremen: Iz dnevnikovykh i rabochikh zapisei," *Izvestia*, 3 February 1990.

[36] Georgii Fedotov, "Rossiia i svoboda," *Znamia*, 1989, No. 12: 214.

[37] Viktor Nekrasov, "Tragediia moego pokoleniia. *V okopakh Stalingrada*: Do i posle," *Literaturnaia gazeta*, 12 September 1990, 15.

"An ordinary man, but a will of steel."
"Papa, why is he not happy, is he mad at somebody?"
"At God, probably, who didn't send us good weather."
"So why didn't Stalin order God to send us good weather . . . ?"[38]

Stalin the man had by this time been so transformed into the idol of the *vozhd'* that he virtually acquired the image of a living icon. The mass consciousness, attributing mystical power to the icon, as it was supposed to do, canonized all that was identified with it, be it the authority of the system or the authority of the ideas on which the system was based. Such was the contradictory role of the victory, which brought both the spirit of freedom and the psychological instruments thwarting the further development of that spirit, the instruments that perpetuated the supremacy of the alleged architect of victory. The euphoria of victory was not the most receptive atmosphere for discussing social problems, and this fact constitutes an obstacle to our analysis of the situation, though it does not entirely spoil it.

Otherwise, Georgii Fedotov, imagining all the obstacles to a progressive transformation of the Soviet regime, could scarcely have written in 1945 that "there is now no more agonizing issue in Russia than that of freedom. Not in the sense, of course, of the question whether it exists in the USSR, something that only foreigners, the most ignorant of them, can contemplate. But rather whether its rebirth is possible after a victorious war. That is what we are all thinking now, we genuine democrats and semifascist fellow travelers alike."[39] As for the question whether it was possible, neither Fedotov nor other soberly thinking people inside or outside the country gave a single uniform answer. Certainly they did not imagine a sudden metamorphosis into democracy in the USSR. They simply evaluated the postwar situation as a chance for the development of freedom, although they did not consider it to be promising.

The democratic traditions in the internal life of the country were very weak. The structures of political and cultural life gravitated distinctly toward authoritarian forms and were not receptive to innovations of an alien kind. But the war, in opening a window onto the world at large, permitted a view of the democratic experience of Europe and America. Not by chance, Mikhail Gefter, considering the evolution of attitudes of people during the war, wrote that "we are, of course, Russian and Soviet, but we have seen the world, too."[40] The war expanded the scope of the Russian outlook and the perspective in which

---

[38] Cited in "Dnevniki vesti ne razreshalos'," *Sovetskaia kul'tura*, 25 April 1990.
[39] Fedotov, "Rossiia i svoboda," 198.
[40] Mikhail Gefter, "Stalin umer vchera. . . . ," in A. A. Protashchik, ed., *Inogo ne dano* (Moscow, 1988), 305.

the individual could imagine his own potential. In spring 1945 "people not without grounds considered themselves giants," as Emmanuil Kazakevich expressed it.[41]

The veterans entered an atmosphere of peacetime life without forgetting the most terrible and dreadful war. The reality of peacetime was more complex, however, than they had imagined, not at all what it had appeared from the vantage point of the trenches. "In the army we often spoke of what life would be like after the war," recalled the journalist Boris Galin, "how we would live on the day after the victory; and the nearer the end of the war came, the more we thought of it, and we pictured things in rainbow colors. We never imagined the scale of destruction or the scope of reconstruction required to heal the wounds inflicted by the Germans."[42] Konstantin Simonov largely agreed: "We imagined life after the war as a holiday that would begin when the last shot was fired."[43] It was difficult for people to entertain other expectations after four years of the extraordinary stress of combat. It was altogether understandable that a normal life, a simple life in which one was not subjected to constant danger, seemed during wartime to be a providential promise. The war led people, those at the front and those in the rear, to romanticize the prewar period and to a certain extent to idealize it. Enduring the deprivations of the war years, people often subconsciously revised their recollections of peacetime, remembering the good and forgetting the bad. The wish to restore time past prompted the simplest answer to the question, "How to live after the war?" "As before the war," of course.

Life as holiday, life as fairy tale: with the help of this image in the mass mind a special conception of postwar life was formed – without contradictions, without pressure – a tendency stimulated in reality by one factor, hope. Such a life existed, however, only in books and the theater. It is a fascinating fact that during the war the libraries experienced an increased demand for the literature of adventure and fairy tales.[44] On the one hand, this interest is explained in part by the change in the age of the people working in the libraries and using them. During the war 50 to 70 percent of teenagers went into industrial production. After the war the reading rooms of libraries were filled by young veterans whose intellectual growth had been interrupted by the war and who consequently returned from the front to the reading tastes of their youth. But

[41] Emmanuil Kazakevich, *Slushaia vremia: Dnevniki, zapisnye knizhki, pis'ma* (Moscow, 1990), 316.

[42] Boris Galin, "V odnom naselennom punkte: Rasskaz propagandista," *Novyi mir*, 1947, No. 11: 162–3.

[43] K. M. Simonov, *Sobranie sochinenii*, 6 vols. (Moscow, 1966–70), 3: 124.

[44] RGALI, f. 631, op. 15, d. 737, ll. 86–7.

there is another side of the question: the growth of interest in this genre of literature and films was a choice to reject the cruel reality of the war. It was a demand for compensation for psychic overload. Thus it was possible to observe during the war, as for example Mansur Abdulin tells us, "the enormous appetite for all that was not related to the war, for films with dancing and merrymaking, for performing artists and comedians."[45] The faith that life after the war would quickly improve continued for several years after it ended.

Kubanskie kazaki (Kuban Cossacks) was the most popular of all postwar films. It depicted the life of a village in the north Caucasus after the war as contented, abundant, and joyful. Reality was utterly different, of course, and the film was consequently subjected to severe and appropriate criticism. But the critics did not consider one circumstance: there was an element of truth in this film-fable that conveyed the spirit of the time. The journalist Tatiana Arkhangelskaia remembers an interview with one of the participants in the making of the film, who told how hungry the well-dressed boys and girls were, while in the film they happily gazed on a surfeit of fruits made of plaster and papier-mâché. "But we believed," she added, "that it would be that way and there would be plenty of everything . . . all one could wish. And we needed to think so in order to sing songs and make everything seem all right."[46]

Hope for the better and the optimism that it nourished imparted a kind of shock tempo to the first stages of postwar life, generating a special, victorious public atmosphere. "My whole generation, with the exception of just a few, experienced the difficulties," remembers the builder V. P. Serikov. "But our spirits didn't fall. The chief thing was that the war was behind us. There was the joy of work, of victory, a spirit of competition."[47] The emotional élan of the people, the aspiration actually to realize through work a peaceful life, enabled them quickly enough to resolve the basic tasks of reconstruction. This outlook, however, notwithstanding its great creative force, bore within itself a tendency of another kind: the need for a relatively painless transition to peace ("the worst is behind us") and the perception of this process as generally untroubled. The farther it proceeded, the greater was the intrusion of reality, which was in no hurry to turn into life as fairy tale.

The difficulties of life, unavoidable after such a destructive war, were accepted as normal by the majority of the population, with resignation.

[45] Cited in "Shel soldat. . . . ," *Komsomol'skaia pravda*, 28 April 1990.
[46] Cited in Elizar Mal'tsev, "Ne izmeniaia sebe," *Literaturnaia gazeta*, 18 February 1987, 8.
[47] Vladislav Serikov, "Dogovor po sovesti," *Roman-gazeta*, 1986, No. 7: 9.

Far from all problems inherited from the war, however, belonged to the normal category. The plenipotentiaries of the Central Committee were forced to admit as much after examining the conditions of life in different regions of the country. In December 1945 a delegation from the Agitation and Propaganda Department of the Central Committee undertook an inspection of the coal-mining industry in Shchekinsk District of Tula Province in central Russia. The results were alarming. The living conditions of the workers were recognized as "very difficult," and the repatriated and demobilized workers lived especially poorly. Many of them lacked underwear, and the little that was available was worn out and dirty. They went for months without soap, the dormitories were very crowded, the inhabitants slept on wooden platforms or similar double-tiered bunks (for which they paid 10 percent of their monthly income). They received enough bread, 1200 grams a day, but its quality was poor. There was not enough butter, and petroleum products were used as butter substitutes.[48]

There were many signs of poor food supply in the localities. Groups of workers from Penza and Kuznetsk wrote letters to Politburo members V. M. Molotov, M. I. Kalinin, and A. I. Mikoyan, complaining of the difficult material conditions of life and the absence of the majority of necessary goods from the market.[49] In response to these letters a commission of the People's Commissiariat of Trade investigated and determined that the workers' complaints were well-founded.[50] In Nizhnyi Lomov of Penza Province the workers of factory No. 255 spoke out against the delay in the issuance of bread cards, and the workers of the plywood and match factories complained of long delays in receiving their pay.[51] The difficult working conditions at the war's end persisted in restored enterprises. Many people continued to work without shelter, in the open air, and during the winter, knee-deep in snow. Workplaces were often not lighted or heated, and people were poorly clothed for winter conditions. For this reason the secretaries of many local party committees in Siberia turned to the Central Committee with an unprecedented request: to allow them to skip the annual revolutionary anniversary celebration of 7 November 1946 on account of the "inadequate clothing of the population."[52]

---

[48] Informatsiia Upravleniia propagandy i agitatsii TsK VKP(b) "O material'no-bytovom polozhenii rabochikh ugol'noi promyshlennosti Tul'skoi oblasti," January 1946; RTsKhIDNI, f. 17, op. 125, d. 421, ll. 2–3.
[49] Informatsiia Upravleniia propagandy i agitatsii TsK VKP(b) o polozhenii del v Penzenskoi oblasti v sviazi s podgotovkoi k vyboram v Verkhovnyi Sovet SSSR, January 1946; ibid., d. 420, l. 40.
[50] Ibid.
[51] Ibid.
[52] Informatsiia Upravleniia propagandy i agitatsii TsK VKP(b) o podgotovke k prazdnovaniiu 29oi godovshchiny Oktiabr'skoi revoliutsii, November 1946; ibid., d. 421, l. 102.

Poor living conditions were one of the chief sources of dissatisfaction and agitation among the workers of the Urals and Siberia, most of whom were evacuees from the combat zones farther west. At war's end these people naturally wanted to return home. A commission of the Central Committee reviewed the situation of a series of defense plants in September and October 1945. It found distressing conditions, particularly in a tank factory in Omsk.

> The insistent demands of the workers to return to their former places of residence are prompted by the difficult living conditions [and by] dissatisfaction with the supply of clothes and shoes as well as food products. . . . Houses and dormitories are poorly constructed and not suitable for Siberian wintertime conditions. . . . The workers and their families endure extremely acute shortages of clothing, shoes, and linens. Annual production of textile goods is about .38 items per worker and of shoes .7 pairs per worker. Some workers are so poorly clothed that they cannot show up at their place of work.[53]

The workers protested against such living conditions. They refused to work more than eight hours a day, expressed open displeasure at the administration of enterprises, demanded their immediate return to former places of residence (the majority of the workers in Omsk had been evacuated from Leningrad, Voroshilovgrad, and other such cities). The situation was similar in the factories of the Urals and Siberia.[54] In order to forestall the further development of such attitudes among evacuated workers, special orders were issued forbidding them to leave their place of work under threat of legal liability. Not even threatening measures, however, sufficed to stop the elemental movement to return home. In August 1945 the People's Commissariat of Military Censorship registered 135 letters from Omsk workers addressed to relatives and friends, complaining of bad living conditions. "Conditions of life in the factory are terrible," according to one of these letters. "People are putting together a pack of supplies and fleeing, especially Leningraders. About four hundred have left recently. The order of the Commissar Malyshev is to return all those fleeing to Omsk and to prosecute them. We'll see what develops."[55] The writers of some letters expressed them-

---

[53] Dokladnaia zapiska zaveduiushchego otdelom Upravleniia kadrov TsK VKP(b) Borodina o polozhenii del na tankovom zavode v gorode Omske, 18 September 1945; ibid., op. 117, d. 530, ll. 37–8.

[54] Iurii Aksiutin, "Pochemu Stalin dal'neishemu sotrudnichestvu s soiuznikami posle pobedy predpochel konfrontatsiiu s nimi: Nekotorye sotsial'no-psikhologicheskie aspekty vozniknoveniia kholodnoi voiny," in M. M. Narinskii et al., eds., *Kholodnaia voina: Novye podkhody, novye dokumenty* (Moscow, 1995), 52–3.

[55] Vyderzhki iz pisem rabochikh zavodov g. Omska, zaderzhannykh Voennoi tsenzuroi NKGB SSSR, 19 September 1945; RTsKhIDNI, f. 17, op. 117, d. 530, l. 54.

selves more decisively: "The workers have given all their strength to defeat the enemy, and they want to return home, to their own people, their own homes. And now it turns out we have been deceived. They've shipped us out of Leningrad, and they want to leave us in Siberia. In this case we workers should say that our government has betrayed us and our work. They might imagine what kind of humor this leaves us in."[56]

Workers' demonstrations took place in several defense plants of the Urals and Siberia from July to September 1945. The situation grew so acute that on 4 August 1945 the Secretariat of the Central Committee gave special attention to the question. It ordered the administration in three factories where working conditions were most distressing to take urgent measures for the satisfaction of the legal demands of their employees (that is, with the exception of their demand to return home).[57]

The situation was scarcely better in the villages, many of which, especially in the regions subjected during the war to German occupation, were virtually depopulated. The population of the collective farms (including persons demobilized) toward the end of 1945 comprised only 85 percent of that of 1940; and the able-bodied proportion, only 67.5 percent of the prewar level.[58] The number of able-bodied men was reduced from 16.9 million in 1940 to 6.5 million at the beginning of 1946.[59] In several regions, for example in northern Russia, there were villages to which no live adult male returned.[60] Sown acreage was naturally reduced during the war, which of course depressed the harvest yield. The productivity of the collective farm lands fell as a result of the deterioration of work in the fields and the decline of the level of scientific agronomy. Women constituted the basic element of the able-bodied population of the village. They had to do all of the heavy work, and the administrative responsibilities were handled after the war by men. Collective farm production at the end of the war was in a critical condition, the peasants living essentially from their own private plots.

Besides destruction and ruin the war left another singular legacy, the growth of crime. This problem was felt especially acutely by the

---

[56] Ibid., l. 57.

[57] Postanovlenie Sekretariata TsK VKP(b) "O meropriiatiiakh po uluchsheniiu massovo-politicheskoi raboty i material'no-bytovogo obsluzhivaniia rabochikh zavodov No. 22, 174 i 179," 4 August 1945; ibid., ll. 11–12.

[58] I. M. Volkov, *Trudovoi podvig sovetskogo krest'ianstva v poslevoennye gody: Kolkhozy SSSR v 1946–1950 godakh* (Moscow, 1972), 21.

[59] Ibid.

[60] V. F. Zima, *Golod v SSSR 1946–1947 godov: Proiskhozhdenie i posledstviia* (Moscow, 1996), 159.

inhabitants of cities and industrial centers. If we judge by the letters that people wrote to government organs and to the newspapers, the struggle against crime in many cities after the war turned into a struggle for survival. The workers of Saratov wrote to *Pravda* in fall 1945 that "since the beginning of fall Saratov has been terrorized by thieves and murderers. To be forced to undress on the street, to have watches snatched from the wrist has become an everyday occurrence. . . . The life of the city simply ceases as darkness approaches. The inhabitants have grown accustomed to walking in the streets rather than on the sidewalks, and they watch suspiciously everyone who approaches them."[61] "A day doesn't pass without someone in Saratov being murdered or robbed, often in the very center of the city in broad daylight. . . . It's gone so far that the only people who go to the theater or the movies are those who live next door [to the theater]. The Karl Marx Theater, located in the suburbs, is empty in the evenings."[62] The workers of the Moscow suburb Podolsk shared the same problems.

> Marauding bandits and thieves detain peaceful citizens . . . not only in the evening, but kill, undress, and rob them in broad daylight, and not only in the obscure alleyways but on the main streets as well . . . even around the local party headquarters and the city soviet. After work, people gather in groups in order to protect themselves on their way home. Thus meetings after work are poorly attended, because workers are afraid to remain, afraid of being attacked on the way home. And it is no longer safe at home, either, because robberies take place there day and night.[63]

If it was unsafe to walk on the streets, it was equally unsafe to ride commuter trains, where special bands of criminals operated. People not only were afraid to remain for meetings after work but began to leave work before dark.[64] Such behavior reflected both the reality of crime and the spread of various kinds of rumors both in conversation as well as in spontaneously circulated leaflets describing alleged assaults and murders.[65] Some of these fears stemmed from elementary lack of information about the real state of affairs, and the authorities made no effort to share such information.

[61] Svodka pisem, postupivshikh v gazetu "Pravda" o banditizme, vorovstve i khuliganstve, 17 November 1945 g.; RTsKhIDNI, f. 17, op. 122, d. 118, l. 92.
[62] Ibid., ll. 92–3.
[63] Ibid., l. 93.
[64] Dokladnaia zapiska upolnomochennogo Komissii partiinogo kontrolia pri TsK VKP(b) po Vladimirskoi oblasti Shkol'nikova "O neudovletvoritel'noi rabote organov militsii, suda i prokuratury Vladimirskoi oblasti v bor'be s khuliganstvom, krazhami, grabezhami i drugimi prestupleniiami," 12 December 1945 g.; ibid., d. 103, l. 217.
[65] Ibid.

Statistical accounts of crime in the postwar years were incomplete and contradictory and, as a rule, included all categories of crime classified by Soviet legislation as liable to prosecution. Thus people committing minor offenses, those late to work or absent from work, were counted along with the real criminals. The figures of the Ministry of Internal Affairs are more accurate on the number of crimes investigated by the police. In 1946 there were 430,071 such cases; in 1947, 404,167; and in 1948, 191,720.[66] The figures prepared in 1948 by the Ministry of Internal Affairs on *all* crimes differ somewhat from those given above: 546,275 in 1946 and 453,165 in 1947.[67] By comparison, in 1940 a total of 1,253,947 crimes were recorded.[68] Thus even if we take into account the incomplete nature of the data, the postwar crime rate was on the whole significantly lower than the prewar rate. The popular perception, however, indicates that the criminal activity was considerably more serious than is suggested by the statistics. As we observed above, the people's fear of the criminal element stemmed not so much from reliable information as from the lack of it and the dependence on rumor instead. Robbery was in the circumstances more than conventionally threatening, as it often cost people their last meager possessions. It was poverty that explained the scale of fear, just as it explained the crime wave itself. This does not mean, of course, that the problem of crime after the war existed only in people's imaginations. The authorities also perceived it as one of their most serious problems, at least during the first two postwar years.[69] As the population confronted the problem, however, it began at once to recede. Hunger took its place. The hungry years, the worst of which were 1946 and 1947, scarcely spared anyone. Even those who did not literally go hungry recall these years as the worst.

Further Reading: The Second World War and Postwar Years

John D. Barber and Mark Harrison, *The Soviet Home Front 1941–1945: A Social and Economic History of the USSR in World War II* (London, 1991).
John Erickson, *The Road to Stalingrad* (London, 1975).

---

[66] Dokladnaia zapiska ministra vnutrennikh del SSSR S. Kruglova o sostoianii ugolovnoi prestupnosti v SSSR v 1948 g., 18 January 1949; GARF, f. 9401, op. 2, d. 234, l. 20.
[67] Dokladnaia zapiska ministra vnutrennikh del SSSR S. Kruglova o sostoianii ugolovnoi prestupnosti v SSSR za 1947 g., 4 February 1948; ibid., d. 199, l. 184.
[68] Ibid.
[69] Informatsiia Upravleniia po proverke partiinykh organov TsK VKP(b) "O faktakh uvelicheniia prestupnosti i khuliganstva," 10 February 1947; RTsKhIDNI, f. 17, op. 122, d. 289, ll. 1–6.

John Erickson, *The Road to Berlin* (Boulder, Co., 1983).

Werner Hahn, *Postwar Soviet Politics: The Fall of Zhdanov and the Defeat of Moderation 1946–1953* (Ithaca, 1982).

Susan J. Linz, ed., *The Impact of World War II on the Soviet Union* (Totowa, NJ, 1985).

William O. McCagg, *Stalin Embattled, 1943–1948* (Detroit, 1978).

William Moskoff, *The Bread of Affliction: The Food Supply in the USSR during World War II* (New York, 1990).

Mark von Hagen, "From 'Great Fatherland War' to the Second World War: New Perspectives and Future Prospects," in Ian Kershaw and Moshe Lewin, eds., *Stalinism and Nazism: Dictatorships in Comparison* (New York, 1997).

Amir Weiner, *Making Sense of War: The Second World War and the Fate of the Bolshevik Revolution* (Princeton, 2001).

Alexander Werth, *Russia at War, 1941–1945* (New York, 1964).

Alexander Werth, *Russia: The Postwar Years* (New York, 1971).

Index

Abdulin, Mansur, 295
aberration thesis, 70, 77
abortion, 214, 228–9
Abramov, Fedor, 292
accidental elements, 168
acculturation process, 49, 137, 244,
    266, 267, 270
activists
    diaries, 195, 197, 200, 204
    exiled kulaks' insurrectionary
        organization, 90
    female political, 230–1, 235
    housewife, 204
    military tribunals, 264
    Soviet, 145, 188–9, 265
    Ukrainian, 25, 264
    village and kolkhoz, 98, 197,
        200
administration see bureaucracy
adventure tales, 294–5
affirmative action, 172
Afinogenov, Aleksandr, 201
agriculture see collectivization;
    kolkhoz peasantry
Allilueva, Nadezhda, 29
amnesty legislation, 241, 250,
    252–3, 263, 264–5
Andreevskii raion, 96

anti-cosmopolitan campaign, 266
anti-insurgency campaigns, 140–1
anti-semitism, 241, 265–8, 271
anti-Soviet elements
    archival information, 131, 154,
        155
    collaborators, 241, 242, 250–3,
        262–5
    German villages, 255
    Great Terror, 84, 88, 89–90, 91,
        92, 93, 94, 99
    kulaks, 256
    national minorities, 241, 242,
        246–8, 255
    NKVD investigation of criminal
        contacts, 99
    OGPU investigations, 25
    Politburo quotas, 84
    Politburo resolution (1937), 90,
        146, 256
    Trotskyist–Zinovievist center, 88
Antonov movement, 140, 143
apparatchik, 32, 53
(apparaty) bureaucrats see
    bureaucrats (apparaty)
archives, 87, 153–5, 162, 190n
Arendt, Hannah, 133n, 148, 185n,
    245

Arkhangel'sk concentration camp, 144
Arkhangelskaia, Tatiana, 295
army *see* Red Army
Arrow Cross, 251
artificial insemination technology, 270
Astrakhan Province, 284
authoritarianism, 20, 293
  family policy, 225
  as legacy of Tsarist autocracy, 66–7
  long Russian history of, 121
  role of women, 231
  social structure as breeding ground for, 4, 41, 56–61
autobiographical narratives, 182, 185–6, 186n, 187–8, 207–8
  see also diaries
autocracy, 54, 71–3, 77, 279, 292
  Stalin's personal, 16, 29, 30
  Tsarist legacy, 52, 66, 69
Avdeenko, Alexander, 292–3

Babel, Isaak, 186
"Back Streets" (Smirnov), 288
backwardness, 69, 71, 73, 109, 121
  and culture, 173–4
  heavy heritage of, 77
  peasant population, 4, 191
  rural economy, 57
  social origins of Stalinism, 4
  Stalinism's unwillingness to accept, 20
  Stalinist terror, 129
Bahry, Donna, 18–19n
Baker, Keith, 111n
Baldwin, Peter, 121n
banditism, 140–1
Barkov, 90
Barmin, A., 29
Bauman, K. Ia., 23
Bauman, Zygmunt, 244
Bazarov, V., 25
Bebel, August, 150
Belgium, 250, 253, 262, 263
Belobrov, Andrei P., 142–3

Bendix, Reinhard, 50
Berezhnaia, Antonina, 208, 208n
Beria, L. P., 33, 34
Berliner, Joseph, 168
Bialer, Severyn, 33
Birobidzhan, 268
birth-rate, 213, 214, 218, 224, 228–9
Blackbourn, David, 120n
blood pedigree theory, 273
blue Danubes, 288, 289
Bolsheviks, 2n
  building socialism, 122, 123
  cataloguing of individuals, 153
  class analysis, 43
  coercive road to socialism, 68
  culture, 29, 266
  discontinuity with Stalinism, 3, 15
  eschatology, 146, 244
  failure of, 59
  Green Army uprising, 114n
  seizure of power, 2–3, 39, 85
  source of Stalin's policies, 71
  Stalin's deviation from, 15
  Stalin's executions of, 15
  state violence, 133–4, 135, 138, 141, 147, 155
  subjectivization policy, 186
  support of soldiers, 3
  support of workers, 3, 39
  transformation of, 50
  use of the term "terror," 147
  women's liberation and equality, 213–14
  see also Communist Party; October Revolution (1917)
Bonapartist dictatorship, 111
Borovets, Maksim, 261
Bourdieu, Pierre, 123n
bourgeois elements, 182
bourgeois order, 203
bourgeois privacy, 203
bourgeois specialists, 170
bourgeois values, 28, 239
bourgeoisie, 112, 115, 120, 120n, 136, 269

boyar aristocracy, 72
brigade diaries, 189n
Britain, 85
Brzezinski, Zbigniew, 30
Bukharin, Nikolai, 20, 68
  alliance with Stalin, 26
  as alternative to Stalin, 116n
  fall of, 21
  Great Offensive, 75, 103
  growing into socialism, 74
  incomplete socialism, 77
  Leninism, 116
  medieval principle, 55
  Stalin's climb to dictatorship, 70
  Stalin's unhappiness, 31–2
  state violence, 131–2
  statistical bureaus, 150
  trust in Stalin, 29n
Bulat, 98
Bul'ba, 261
Bulgakov, Mikhail, 168
bureaucracy
  anti-Soviet conspiracy stories, 25
  arbitrariness of, 164
  expansion of, 46, 50, 53, 115
  heavy heritage of, 77
  in loco parentis, 174
  need for stability and discipline,
    227
  need for tenure, 54
  as a principle of foreign
    domination, 148
  security of, 29
  sovereignty, 54
  Stalin's dominance of, 116
  support for Stalin, 3, 3–4n
  supremacy of, 57
  Tsarist Russia, 130–1
bureaucrats (apparaty), 49, 169
  defence of the people from, 100
  as detrimental social force, 40
  diaries, 190n
  growth of, 46
  military statistics, 136
  purges, 32, 40, 53, 54
byt (everyday life), 192–4, 194n

cadres revolution, 100
capitalism
  class analysis, 43, 58
  class exploitation, 271
  enemies of socialism, 241
  growing role of state, 44
  kulaks, 46–7, 74
  Marx's violent revolution, 109
  muzhik, 45
  Party's ideological distrust of, 74
  Riutin group, 23n
  socialism's assault on, 78
  suppression of fundamental
    elements of, 67, 77
  Trotsky's warnings on restoration
    of, 102
  Tsarist Russia, 57
  United States, 65
capitalist encirclement, 21, 85, 115,
  252
card indexes/files, 153–5
Carr, E. H., 44, 117n, 122n
Carrel, Alexis, 269–70
censuses, 118, 118n, 131, 149, 240
Central Committee
  anti-Soviet reports, 25
  attitude toward peasantry, 22
  employment of women, 219
  Great Terror, 88, 90–1, 92, 93,
    96, 103
  inspection of coal-mining industry,
    296
  Khrushchev's election to, 76
  kulaks as principal anti-Soviet
    element, 256
  post-war living and working
    conditions, 282, 296, 297, 298
  registration of ethnic Germans,
    255
  Trotskyist–Zinovievists, 88
  Ukrainian nationalists, 265
Central Control Commission, 23n, 25
Central State Archive, 153, 154
ceremonies, 51
Certeau, Michel de, 124–5n
Chesnokov, Dmitrii, 248

child care, 167, 214, 217, 219, 221, 224, 226
childbirth, 122, 167
childraising, 108, 213, 214, 230
children
    births in post-war Soviet Union, 281
    during Second World War, 281–2
    education, 227
    granting of passports, 98
    homeless, 214
    orphaned, 114, 282
    removal from negligent parents, 108
    socialization of, 217
    teenagers' working conditions, 282
China, 186n
Chinese Cultural Revolution, 273
Christian Church, 50
church history, 50
Churchill, Winston, 73
Civil War
    Don Cossacks, 254
    effect on economic and social structures, 40
    foreign threat, 85
    passportization, 150
    revolutionary utopianism, 113
    violence, 131, 137, 138–9
clan diaries, 189n
Clark, Katerina, 109n
class analysis, 43–4, 46, 58, 148
class antagonisms, 170, 255
class divisions, 108, 112
class struggle, 21, 254
    diaries, 191, 192
Cold War, 65, 291
collective victimization, 171
collectivization
    aims of, 59–60
    as clash between state and peasantry, 45–9, 59–60
    at end of Second World War, 298
    consequences of, 161
    depeasantizing policy, 59–60

diaries, 191–2, 196–7
ethnic minorities, 254
explanations of, 2
forced pace of, 68, 86
open resistance to, 21, 162
as particular feature of Stalinism, 2, 27, 74, 86, 225–6
peasant migration, 40, 47–8, 224
radical revisionists, 4
as "revolution from below," 4, 18
and women's roles, 216–17, 218
colonial techniques, 148
commemoration, hierarchies of, 249
Commission for Legal Matters, 95
Commodus, Emperor, 70
communal apartments, 176, 217, 288
communal institutions, 214, 217, 221–2, 224–5, 231
Communist Party, 2n
    belief in Marxian socialism, 67
    building of socialism, 74–7
    class war to the death, 73
    culture, 14
    employment of women, 219
    growth of, 216, 216n
    Jewish membership, 241
    lack of constraints on ambitions of, 130
    national elites, 240
    NEP, 115
    population's resentment of, 163, 170
    revisionism, 3
    self-presentation, 187
    Stalin's control of, 3, 14
    Tenth Party Congress (1921), 114, 114n
    terror, 2, 13, 40, 83, 88–90, 93, 99–100, 147, 147n
    see also Bolsheviks; Politburo
concentration camps, 56, 129, 141–2, 143–4, 245
Condorcet, 111, 111n
Cossacks, de-Cossackization, 131, 139

crime, growth of, 298–300
Crimean peninsula, 141
Crimean Tatars, 241
cultural conservatism, 15
cultural history, 1, 4, 109n
cultural revolution, 26, 28, 221
cultural traditionalism, 26, 226
culture, 5, 59, 173–4, 226
  Church's fight against, 50
  commodification of, 109n
culture, Bolshevik, 29, 266
culture, Communist Party, 14
culture, peasant, 47
culture, political, 1, 20–1, 226
culture, traditional folk, 109n
Czechoslovakia, 253

Dan, Fedor, 29n, 31
Dan, Lydia, 31
Dashnaks, 91
Davies, Joseph E., 102
Davies, Robert, 6–7
de-Cossackization, 131, 139
Decembrists, 285, 286
deculturation, 49, 56, 59
dekulakization, 21, 48, 97, 101,
  133, 145–6, 154
democracy, 41, 58, 59, 103, 112,
  120, 293
democratic states
  growing role of the state, 44,
    182n
  Western liberal, 5n, 182n
demography, 280–1
demonstrations, 279, 298
deportations, 2, 27, 129–30
  Armenians, 33
  Balts, 136–7
  children, 281
  Crimean Tatars, 241
  ethnic minorities, 33, 92, 131,
    161, 240, 241, 249, 253,
    254–5, 257, 258–9, 262
  from western borderlands during
    First World War, 136–7
  Germans, 92, 131, 136–7, 249,
    255, 257

Jews, 131, 249, 267
Koreans, 92
kulaks, 145–6, 165, 254–5
peasants, 161, 165
Poles, 249, 254, 257
Ukrainian nationalists, 241, 262
Destruction Battalions, 263
determinism, modernization theory,
  5n
Deutscher, Isaac, 85, 102–3
diaries, 6, 166–7, 182–3, 184, 185,
  186n, 188–91, 188n, 189n,
  190n
  as chronicles of socialist
    construction, 191–8, 193n,
    194n, 196n, 197n
  introspective and self-
    transformative functions of,
    198–203
  public and private spheres, 202–7,
    205n
dignity, 186
divorce, 232
Djilas, Milovan, 259–60
Doctors' Plot (1953), 33, 241, 247,
  267
domestic violence, 174, 189–90
Don region, 139, 140, 254
drunkenness, 167, 174
Duma, 71

Economic Problems of Socialism in the
  USSR, 246
edinonachalie, 53
education, 18, 175, 227
  abolition of coeducation, 231–2
  sense of self, 182, 187
  women, 217, 219, 224, 226
Eikhe, R. I., 89, 90
election campaigns, 18
elite politics, 39
Enchmen, Emmanuil, 149–50
enemies of the people, 40, 55, 152,
  154, 167, 189
Engels, Friedrich, 112–13, 200, 269
Enlightenment, 108, 108n, 111,
  112, 113, 118–19, 122

equality, 1, 67, 77, 111
  women, 213–14, 215, 230–5
Erenburg, Ilia, 189*n*
ethnic minorities, 6, 131, 239–41,
  253–9
  deportation by Stalin, 33, 92, 131,
    161, 240, 241, 249, 253,
    254–5, 257, 258–9, 262
  forced deportation during First
    World War, 136–7
  see also Jewish minority; Ukrainian
    nationalist movement
ethnic particularism, 241, 253, 272
ethnocentrism, 5*n*, 23
eugenics, 134, 245, 249, 269, 270
European Court, 253
euthanasia, 249, 269, 270
Ezhov, N. I., 31, 31*n*, 88, 94, 95, 96,
  103

factory history project, 182
fairy tales, 294–5
family
  attempts to abolish, 213, 214
  promotion of importance of, 214,
    227–31
  socializing functions of, 230
  weakening of, 213–14
Family Edict (1944), 232
family life, 204
family policies, 213–14, 218,
  225–35
family values, 19
famine (1932–3), 161
fatalism, 162, 164
fatherhood, 230
Fedotov, Georgii, 117*n*, 292, 293
fifth columns, 85, 99, 102, 103,
  247
Le Figaro, 268
filtration process, 142–3, 153
First World War, 165
  collaborators, 250
  deportations from western
    borderlands, 136–7
  state violence, 130, 131, 135,
    136–8

Fitzpatrick, Sheila, 4, 30–1,
  161–77
Five-Year Plans, 20, 27, 78, 102,
  168, 198
  unemployment, 218*n*
  and women's roles, 216–17, 218,
    219, 220, 221, 224
food supply, 296
Foucault, Michel, 124–5, 124*n*
Fourier, Charles, 113
France, 85, 251, 252, 263, 264
French Revolution, 108, 111–12,
  120, 135
Freud, Sigmund, 272
Frinovskii, M. P., 91
Fritzsche, Peter, 134
Frye, Northrop, 119*n*

Galin, Boris, 294
Galton, Francis, 152
Gan, 267
gardening state, 188, 244, 245–6,
  248, 255, 272
Garros, Véronique, 184*n*
Gefter, Mikhail, 285, 293
Geldern, James van, 28
gender roles, 6, 213–15
  see also women
Genghis Khan, 68, 69
genocide, 271–2
Genocide Convention, 271
Georgian Mensheviks, 91
Germany, 27, 86
  see also Nazi Germany
Getty, J. Arch, 30, 84
Goebbels, Joseph, 265
The Golden Calf, 169
Good Soldier Schweik, 169
Gorbachev, Mikhail, 66, 70*n*, 77
Gorkii Oblast, 282
Gorky, Maxim, 201, 268
gosudarstvennost', 53
grain requisitions, 2, 96, 97,
  113–14, 161, 163
Great Break, 68, 73–4, 115
Great Retreat, 26
Groman, V. G., 25

Grossman, Vasilii, 266
gulag prison camps, 1, 118*n*, 182, 187, 257

Halfin, Igal, 184*n*
Hannerz, Ulf, 119*n*
Harbintsy, 92
Harvard Project interviews, 18–19*n*, 164, 167, 170, 171
Hasek, Jaroslav, 169
health passports, 150
Hegel, Georg W. F., 75, 112
Hellbeck, Jochen, 181–209
heredity, 266, 269, 271
hidden transcripts, 184
historical agency, 181–2
History, end of, 245
Hitler, Adolf, 27, 33, 33*n*, 69, 85, 261, 277
Hobsbawm, Eric, 43
Hoffmann, David, 184*n*
Holocaust, 270
Holquist, Peter, 129–56, 184*n*
homeless children, 214
Homo Sovieticus, 169, 174, 175, 176
homosexuality, 228
housewife activists, 204
housework, 221–2, 229
humanistic discourse, 186
Hungary, 251
hunger, 163, 279, 281, 300

Iakir, Iona, 24
Iakovlev, Ia. A., 25
identity, national, 239–40
ideology
    diaries, 199–200
    and violence, 260
    see also socialist ideology
Ilf, I., 169
illegitimacy, 232
imperialism, 148
Inber, Vera, 199, 202–3
individualism, 109*n*, 182*n*, 282
industrial managers, 168
Industrial Revolution, 120

industrialization
    autobiographical domain, 182, 188
    diaries, 191
    factory history project, 182
    forced pace of, 68, 86
    modernization theory, 5*n*
    opposition to, 21
    as particular feature of Stalinism, 2, 18, 60, 74, 86, 225–6
    peasant migration, 40, 47–8
    radical revisionists, 4
    "revolution from below," 4, 18
    and women, 213, 214, 217, 218–25, 226
inflation, 223
informers, 167, 175, 176
Institute of Medical Genetics, 270
intelligentsia, 30*n*, 32, 166, 168, 170, 171
internationalism, 15, 19
invalids, 284–5, 291
Irkutsk province, 283–4
iron curtain, 291
Iudaizm bez prikras (Kychko), 268
Ivan the Terrible, 16, 52, 67, 69, 71–3
Izvestiia, 248

Japan, 85
Jewish Anti-Fascist Committee, 267
Jewish minority, 241, 249, 265–8, 271

Kagan, 267
Kaganovich, Lazar, 24, 25, 31, 33, 34, 76, 96, 103, 241, 271
Kaganovich, Mikhail, 27
Kalinin, Mikhail I., 25, 98, 192–3, 296
Kamenev, Lev B., 88, 116*n*
Kaminskii, G., 23
Karaganda, 118
Katsenelson, Ilia, 267
Kazakevich, Emmanuil, 286–7, 289, 294
Kazakh nationalism, 19–20

Ketlinskaia, Vera, 287
KGB archives, 87, 265
Khlevnyuk, Oleg, 83–104
khoziaistvenniki, 25
Khrushchev, Nikita, 54, 60, 76, 95
  Jewish minority, 267–8
  Stalin's trust, 34
  Ukrainian nationalists, 261
Kirov, Sergei, 21, 23n, 24, 29, 30
kolkhoz peasantry, 27n, 46, 47, 48, 60, 75, 169–70
  denial of governmental awards, 264
  deportations, 257
  diaries, 191–2, 193, 197, 200
  Great Terror, 98, 100–1
  migration to cities, 223
Kollontai, Aleksandra, 213, 231
Kolomenskyi locomotive building works, 89
Komsomol, 187
Komsomolsk-na-Amure, 118
Kondrat'ev, N. D., 25
Kondratiev, Viacheslav, 287
Korenevskaya, Natalya, 184n
Kornai, Janos, 174
Korotchenko, D. S., 96
Kosior, S. V., 23
Kosterina, Nina, 167
Kotkin, Stephen, 107–26
krai committees, 89, 90, 91–2
Krasnaya nov', 51
Krasnoe Sormovo, 89
Krasnoyarsk obkom, 96
Kratkii kurs, 34
Krokodil, 267
krupnyi gosudarstvennyi deyatel', 53
Krupskaia, Nadezhda, 231
Krylenko, Nikolai V., 98
Kuban Cossacks, 295
Kubanskie kazaki, 295
kulaks, 115, 117, 165, 254–5
  capitalism, 46–7, 74
  deportations, 145–6, 165, 254–5
  diaries, 191–2
  elimination as a class, 46–7
  military service, 257–8

Party's ideological distrust of, 74
passportization, 150
as principal anti-Soviet element, 256
rehabilitation of, 256, 257–8
Riutin group, 23n
secret bureau registration, 151
terror, 84, 89, 90–1, 94, 97, 99, 145
see also dekulakization
Kursk oblast, 101
Kuznetsk, 296
Kychko, Trohym, 268

labor books, 150
labor camps, 48, 131, 231
Lahusen, Thomas, 184n
Lapidus, Gail Warshofsky, 6, 213–36
Laue, Theodore von, 86
leadership cults, 18
Lenin Mounted Brigade, 262–3
Lenin, Vladimir, 2n, 13, 51, 57, 75, 114, 117
  abolition of family, 214
  comparison to Stalin, 20, 68, 172
  death of, 116
  democratic solutions, 58
  housework, 229
  nationality policy, 239
  noble origins, 269
  Stalin's deviation from, 14, 15, 19
  as Stalin's ideological reference, 71
  Stalin's rudeness, 73
Leningrad Affair (1947), 33
Leninism, 42, 52, 53, 116–17, 116n
Lewin, Moshe, 17, 26, 29–30, 32, 39–61, 65, 185n, 217
liberal discourse, 204
liberalism, 111
libraries, 294
Lieutenant Kizhe, 169
Life and Fate (Grossman), 266
Lipman-Blumen, Jean, 231n
literary intelligentsia, 168
Livonian war, 72
Livshits, 267
Livshits, Iakov, 269

Lominadze, Vissarion, 22, 22n
lynch trials, 271–2
Lysenkoism, 270

Madison, Bernice, 121–2n
Magnitogorsk, 75, 110, 118–19,
    118n, 122, 146
Makarenko, Anton, 230
Malenkov, G. M., 31, 33, 34, 88–9,
    93
Malia, Martin, 4, 65–79
Mal'tseva, M. D., 101
Manchuria, 85
Mankov, Arkadii, 166–7, 193–4,
    194n
marriage
    promotion of importance of, 214,
        227–8, 230, 232, 233
    rejection as support for women,
        234–5
Marx, Karl, 108–9, 112, 113, 200,
    269
Marx–Engels–Lenin Institute, 116n
Marxism, 2n, 53
    demise of, 66
    enemies of socialism, 241
    and nationality, 240
    scientific claims, 113
    social historians, 65–6
    as a sociological science, 269
    Stalin cult, 52
    as Stalin's ideological reference, 71
Mayer, Arno J., 120n
Mechanical Engineering, 206
medical knowledge, 107
Medvedev, Dmitrii, 260–1
Medvedev, Roy, 77
memoirs, 189
mentally retarded, 269
middle class, 28
Mikoyan, A. I., 24, 31, 33, 34, 296
military service, 214, 224, 231
military statistics, 136, 137
Ministry of Internal Affairs, 300
Mironov, 90
Mirzoian, Levon, 19–20
modernization theory, 5n

Molodtsov, Vladimir, 197n, 199–200
Molotov Factory, 282
Molotov, Viacheslav, 31, 33, 145,
    296
    anti-Soviet elements, 25
    Great Terror, 85, 89, 96, 103
    industrial targets, 24
    Stalin turns against, 34
    Stalin's private letters, 24
Moscow, 118n, 299
Moscow Ball Bearing Works, 89
Moscow Cheka, 142
moshchi, 51
motherhood, 213, 214, 228, 232
Muller, Hermann, 270
Mumford, Lewis, 119n
Muslim Communists, 19
Mussavats, 91

nachal'stvo, 49
Napoleon, 278
Narkomyust, 93, 98
narodnost', 52
national minorities *see* ethnic
    minorities
National Socialism, 134
    see also Nazi Germany
national-uklonizm (national
    deviationism), 19
nationalism, 19–20, 21, 52, 148,
    239–40
nationality policy, 6, 19–20, 23–4,
    239–40, 248, 253
    see also ethnic minorities
nationalization, 47, 53, 58–9, 114,
    226
nature, tension with nurture, 241–2,
    243–74
Nazi Germany, 5n, 15, 244
    biological/racial paradigms, 134,
        244
    clan diaries, 189n
    collective diaries, 189n
    euthanasia, 270
    Hitler's control of army, 33n
    invasion of Soviet Union, 277
    military build-up, 85

non-aggression pact with Soviet Union, 16
racial-biological enterprise, 249
Nekrasov, Viktor, 292
neo-traditionalism, 109n
Nepmen, 115
Netherlands, 250, 262
New Economic Policy (NEP), 114, 114n, 115, 115n
  comparison to post-NEP situation, 171, 172
  ending of, 17
  peace and stability of, 17
  remembered with nostalgia, 60
  state violence, 144
New England, 188n
Nicholas II, Tsar, 85, 103
Nikolaev, Leonid, 189n
Nikolskii, B. I., 118n
Nizhnyi Lomov, 296
NKVD, 243
  archival system, 154, 155
  diaries, 189
  Great Terror, 84, 87, 88, 90, 91, 92, 94, 95, 96, 97, 99, 146–7
  nationalist conspiratorial groups, 19
  prosecution of kulaks, 258
  public opinion, 171–2
  secret reports and interrogations, 184
  Ukrainian nationalists, 262
NKVD Military Tribunals, 263
Norway, 251
Novokuznetsk, 118
nurture, tension with nature, 241–2, 243–74

oblast committees, 90, 91–2
"Obshchestvennitsa," 204
October Revolution (1917)
  autobiographical domain, 185–6, 188, 207
  Bolshevik seizure of power, 2–3, 39, 85
  and Enlightenment, 112
  exclusion of Jews, 268
  promises of, 1
  revisionists, 3, 39, 66
  role of soldiers, 3
  role of workers, 3, 39
  sense of self, 185–6, 185n
Odessa oblast, 101
OGPU, 19, 25, 145, 151, 154
Omsk, 297–8
one-man management, 53
Oprichnina, 52, 72
Orel province, 142
Organization of Ukrainian Nationalists (OUN), 262, 264, 265
Organizational Bureau of the Central Committee, 255
Orgburo, 255
Orjonikidze, Sergo, 24, 25, 75
otvetrabotnik, 53
Out of the Night (Muller), 270
Ovechkin, Valentin, 252
Owen, Robert, 113

paganism, 50
Parallel Anti-Soviet Trotskyist Centre, 88
Parsonian sociology, 234
passportization, 131, 149–53, 223, 240, 257
paternalism, 174
paternity suits, 232
patriarchal authoritarianism, 4
patriarchy, 20
patriotism, 20, 33, 173, 175
Paul I, 70
Peasant Brest-Litovsk policy, 113–14
peasant patriarchalism, 4
peasants
  backwardness of, 4, 191
  central institutions attitude toward, 22
  concessions to, 27
  depeasantizing policy, 59–60
  deportations, 161, 165
  Green Army uprising against Bolsheviks, 114n
  legal regimen, 27n

peasants *cont.*
  migration to cities, 40, 47–8, 223
  open resistance to collectivization,
    21, 162
  pivotal role, 45–9
  "revolution from below," 18
  serfdom, 71, 72
  social mobility, 18
  see also kolkhoz peasantry;
    smychka
pensions, 109, 121*n*, 122
Penza Province, 296
People's Commissariat of Labor,
  220
People's Commissariat of Military
  Censorship, 297
People's Commissariat of Trade,
  296
Peregudov, A. V., 195–6, 196*n*
Peter the Great, 52, 60, 67, 69,
  71–3
Peter III, 70
petit bourgeois, 46, 50, 73
Petliura, Symon, 268
Petrograd Naval Academy, 142
Petrov, L., 169
petty-bourgeois egalitarianism,
  226
Peukert, Detlev, 139
physiological passports, 149
Piatakov, Iurii, 75
Piatnitskaia, Iuliia, 206–7
Plaggenborg, Stefan, 185*n*
Platonov, Andrei, 186
Podlubnyi, Stepan, 150–1, 166, 200,
  201, 202, 203, 205–6
Podolsk, 299
Pokrovskii, Mikhail N., 153
Poland, 251
police, 25, 32, 125
  Oprichnina, 52, 72
  state violence, 83, 131, 163, 171
  Sultan-Galiev counter-
    revolutionary organization, 19
  see also NKVD
Polish Organisation of Military
  Personnel, 92

Politburo
  attitude toward peasantry, 22
  deportation of ethnic minorities,
    254–5
  Great Terror, 84, 87, 88, 89–90,
    92–3, 94, 95–6, 98, 100–1,
    146, 147, 256
political agitation, 182, 187
political initiative, 184
political liberalization, 279
political rituals, 18
Popok, 89
post-revisionism, 4–5, 181–2
post-war literature, 233–4
Potemkin, Leonid, 199, 208
praktiki, 30*n*
Pravda, 227–8, 289, 299
Preobrazhenskii, E. A., 75
Presidential archives, 87
private property rights, 182*n*
private spheres, 184, 202–7
privilege, 25, 50, 165, 169, 170
  bureaucrats, 40, 52, 53, 54
  resentments against, 32
progressive modernity, 109, 121
Prokofiev, Serge, 169
propaganda, 16, 18, 49, 171, 184
  equal opportunities for women,
    213–14
  fascist, 248
  gender roles, 214–15
  open trials, 92
  sense of self, 182
  victory over Nazism, 33
  women's reproductive obligations,
    214
  see also Stalin cult
prostitution, 214, 228
Prussia, 72
pseudonyms, 266–7
psycho-biograms, 150
psychoanalysis, 182*n*
psychology, diaries, 199–200
public celebrations, 18
public opinion, 171–2
public services, 224–5
public spheres, 202–7

purges
  bureaucrats/Party officials, 32, 40,
    53, 54, 83, 84, 147
  collaborators, 241, 242, 250–3,
    262–5
  radical revisionists, 4
  Stalin's personal role in, 14, 15,
    30–2, 84
  see also purification drive; terror
purification drive, 6, 129, 206, 241,
    243
  collaborators, 241, 242, 250–3,
    262–5
  evolution of, 245
  Jewish minority, 241, 249, 265–8,
    271
  radicalization of policies, 244
  specific sites of, 249
  Ukrainian nationalist movement,
    241, 249–50, 260–5
Puritanism, 187n, 188n
Pushkin centennial, 18
Puzanov, Tikhon, 196–7

questionnaires, 131, 149, 152
quicksand society, 185n, 217

Rabinow, Paul, 119n, 120n
race, as a principle of the body
    politic, 148
Ramzin, L. K., 25
Red Army, 22, 115, 141, 173, 175
  arrests in leadership, 90
  defeat of Green Army, 114n
  ethnic minorities, 257, 258
  prosecution/execution of
    partisans, 263
  psychological pressure, 284
  veterans, 278–9, 283–91, 294
Red Army notebook, 188
Red Chemist factory, 284
Red militarism, 24
Reingol'd, I. I., 139
religion, 50–1
religious confession, 182n
republicanism, 111
resistances, 124, 125n

resocialization, 250
revisionism, 3–4, 39, 65–6, 83–4
  bourgeoisie, 120n
  resistance to Stalinism, 162
  sense of self, 181
The Revolution Betrayed (Trotsky), 227
revolutionary politics, 108, 111–12,
    184, 185
revolutions see French Revolution;
    October Revolution (1917)
Ribbentrop, Joachim von, 29
risk communities, 121n
risk-taking, 162, 167–8
Rittersporn, Gabor, 84
rituals, 51
Riutin, Martem'ian Ivanovich, 23,
    23n, 76
Riutin Platform and Appeal, 22
Romantic anticapitalism, 109n
Russian Revolution see October
    Revolution (1917)
Rychkov, 143–4

samoderzhavie, 52
Sanov, Lazar Samilovich, 267
Saratov, 299
science, 111, 130–1, 135–6
scientific elite, 111n
scientific socialism, 113
Scott, James, 184, 184n
Scott, John, 192
Scott, Masha, 192
Second World War, 249–53, 257–9,
    277–9, 280–301
  children, 281–2
  collaborators, 241, 242, 250–3,
    262–5
  invalids, 284–5, 291
  Soviet casualties, 277, 280–1
  Soviet material losses, 280
  veterans, 278–9, 283–91, 294
  women's role, 220–1, 224, 231
sects, 50
self
  sense of, 181–3, 184–91, 207–8
  see also diaries
self-constitution, 187n

self-improvement, 181
self-interest, 181
self-reflection, 183
Serdyuk, Z. T., 95
Serebriakov, Leonid, 269
Serikov, V. P., 295
sexual deviance, 228
sexual morality, 232
Shaginian, Marietta, 202–3
Shakhty affair, 76, 170–1
Shaporin, Iurii, 166
Shaporina, Liubov, 166
Shchekinsk District, 296
shelter society, 282
Shiryaevskii raion, 101
Shklovsky, V., 134, 135
Shnaider, Boguslav, 284
shock brigades, 246
Sholokov, Mikhail, 22, 103*n*
Short Course, 256
show trials, 18, 40, 55, 92–3, 94,
   101
Shtange, Galina, 167, 194, 204–5
Shtrom, Vera, 198
Siberia, 18, 296
   anti-Soviet elements, 89, 90
   evacuation during war, 278, 279
   living conditions, 297–8
   national minorities deported to,
     163
   tax-in-kind, 114*n*
Sich, Ivan, 194*n*
Simonov, Konstantin, 294
skepticism, 168–9
Skrypnyk, Mykola, 23
Slater, Philip, 232
Smirnov, Tolmachev, and Eismont
   opposition, 22
Smirnov, Viktor, 288
Smulson, Lazar, 267
smuta, 72
smychka, 17, 19
social activation, 186*n*
social cataloguing, 5, 129, 131, 136,
   148–55
social conservatism, 26, 225
social dislocation, 217, 225

social emancipation, 186, 207
social engineering, 45, 244–5, 253,
   254
social history, 1, 4, 39, 42, 65–6
social insurance, 122
social intervention, 5, 107–8, 125*n*,
   129–30, 135
social mobility, 18, 48, 221*n*, 225
social order, 108, 111, 112
social origins, 1, 3, 39–61
social problems, 214
social realm, 125*n*, 135–6
social regulation, 120
social science, 107, 135
social stabilization, 214
social statistics, 107, 129, 130–1,
   136, 137
social structure, 40, 44, 45
   and authoritarianism, 56–61
social transformation, 2, 18, 108,
   129, 217, 225
socialism, building of, 74–7, 115,
   122, 123, 131, 163
   diaries, 182–3, 194
   Magnitogorsk as encapsulation of,
     118
   sabotaging of, 21
   sense of self, 182, 186
   tied to imperial Russian history,
     117
socialist ideology, 1, 65–79
   condemnation of, 2
   Engels, 112–13
   Marx, 112, 113
   range of political thought, 2*n*
   role of, 2–4
society, scientific conception of, 111,
   130–1, 135–6
soldiers, 3
   see also Red Army
Solzhenitsyn, Aleksandr, 145, 172
Soviet Union
   collapse of, 65–6
   foreign threat, 85–6, 102–3
   influence on western world, 122*n*
   non-aggression pact with Nazi
     Germany, 16

post-war, 277–301
Sovnarkom USSR, 98–9, 98*n*
Sovnarkom-Central Committee, 94
spontaneity, 96–7, 168
spravki, 88–9, 98
SRs, 91
Stakhanovites, 163, 164, 172
stakhanovtsy, 27
Stalin cult, 15, 20, 40, 52, 69, 172
Stalin, Joseph
    abolition of family, 214
    bid for absolute power, 117*n*
    building hegemony in the 1930s,
        17–21
    characterizations of, 13–15, 20,
        24–5, 29–30, 66, 68–70, 73
    claim to have established
        socialism, 2*n*, 21, 109
    class struggle, 254
    comparison to Lenin, 20, 68, 172
    as conservative revolutionary,
        26–30
    control of Communist Party, 3, 14
    creation of state-run economy, 17
    denunciations of, 162
    during Second World War, 32–3
    eugenics, 270
    family policy, 214
    foreign threat, 85, 102–3
    higher stages of communism, 246
    as highest form of subjectivity,
        188*n*
    ideological references, 71
    invocation of past Tsars, 117*n*
    left opposition, 117*n*
    Leninism, 116–17, 116*n*
    martial qualities of Slavs, Germans
        and Jews, 266
    nationality policy, 239, 248
    new type of internal enemy, 247
    opposition to, 21–6
    origins of Second World War, 252
    origins of Stalinism, 1, 13–35,
        68–70
    "proposition of the screws,"
        290–1
    revisionism, 3

revolution from above, 18, 69, 71,
    72, 117*n*, 225
right to appeal guidelines, 268–9
rise to power, 13–14
shifting positions, 14
socialist ideology, 66–7, 71, 72–3,
    75
support from Soviet bureaucracy,
    3, 3–4*n*
and the term "Trotskyism," 116*n*
terror and autocracy, 13, 16,
    30–2, 55, 68–9, 71–3, 83,
    84–6, 95–6, 161–2, 268–9
victory in Second World War,
    289–90, 292–3
war casualties, 280
Wrangelite officer corps, 141
Stalingrad, 277
Stalinism
    consequences of, 5–6
    definition of, 2
    origins of, 1–5
    particular features of, 2
    resistance to, 4, 6, 162–3, 169,
        181
    revisionism, 3–4, 39
    Stalin's personal blame for, 1,
        13–35, 68–70
    widespread opposition, 6
Stalinsk, 118
Starr, S. Frederick, 221*n*
Stasova, Elena, 231
state
    dominant role of, 44
    growth of, 17
    interplay with society, 40, 44, 56
    limits of power, 17–18
    revisionists, 3, 39
    revolution from above, 18
    self-interested subjects, 182*n*
    see also bureaucracy
State Defense Committee, 257
state exploitation, 172
state intervention, 5, 107–8, 125*n*,
    129–30, 135
State Military Archive, 154
state ownership, 54

state violence *see* purges; purification
  drive; terror
state welfare *see* welfare state
state-run economy, 2, 15, 17, 109
statehood, 53
statization, 56, 58, 59
Stebun, Ilia Isaakovich, 267
sterilization, 130, 269
Stolypin, P., 45
subjectivity, 110, 124, 181–3,
  184–91, 207–8
  see also diaries
Sukhanov, N. N., 25
Sultan-Galiev, M. Kh., 19
Suny, Ronald Grigor, 13–35, 65
Syrtsov–Lominadze Right–Left Bloc,
  22, 22n

Tambov province, 140, 143–4
Tamerlane, 68
tavern (*shalmannaia*) democracy, 288
tax-in-kind, 113–14, 114n
technical intelligentsia, 26
terror
  arbitrariness of, 164
  ideology, 54–6
  objectives of Great Terror, 83–104,
    133, 146–7, 155, 252, 256,
    268–9
  Stalin's personal role in, 13, 16,
    30–2, 55, 68–9, 83, 84–6,
    95–6, 161–2, 268–9
  state violence as prophylactics,
    138–47
  state violence as technique, 5,
    129–56
  see also purges; purification drive
Tiumen, 284
Tocqueville, Alexis de, 135
totalitarian model of government,
  2–3, 5n, 83, 162, 181
Tovstukha, I. P., 20n
Trainin, Aron, 271–2
Transcaucasian federation, 22
travel diaries, 196
troiki, 90, 91–2, 94, 95
Trotskyists, Great Terror, 88

Trotsky, Lev, 13, 20, 68, 77
  as alternative to Stalin, 116n
  campaign against Stalin's
    "mistakes," 76
  family policy, 227
  Leninism, 116
  warnings of a prolonged war, 102,
    102n
  Wrangelite officer corps, 141
Trotskyism, 116n
Tsarist Russia, 43, 49
  capitalist sector, 57
  scientific conception of society,
    130–1, 135–6
  state violence, 136–7
  universal service, 71–2
TsIK USSR, 98
Tucker, Robert, 117n
Tukhachevskii, Mikhail, 24
Tula Province, 296
Turkmeniya troika, 96
Tvardovski, Aleksandr, 169
Twelve Chairs, 169

udarniki, 27
Ukrainian Central Committee, 254
Ukrainian Communist Party, 23,
  265
Ukrainian Insurgent Army (UPA),
  262, 264, 265
Ukrainian nationalist movement,
  241, 249–50, 260–5
Ulam, Adam, 171
Ul'ianov, Anatolii, 194–5, 198–9,
  200–1
unemployment, 108, 114, 122, 218,
  218n, 219
Union of Marxist–Leninists, 23
United Nations, 271
United States, 85
unpredictability, 162, 165
Urals, 297–8
uravnilovka, 26
urbanization, 5n, 118–20, 118n,
  217, 223
utopian socialism, 113, 243, 245–6
utopianism, 221, 221n, 222–3

vanguard concept, 174
Vareikis, I. M., 23
Vasilii Terkin, 169
Veresaev, V., 51
veterans, 278–9, 283–91, 294
victimization, 171
vintiki, 17
Vishnevskii, Vsevolod, 196
Vladimir Province, 284
Vogeler, Heinrich, 201–2
Volga Germans, 258
Voroshilov, K., 24, 33, 34, 96
vydvizhentsy, 30n
Vyshinskii, A. Ya., 25, 93, 101

wages, 26, 27, 223, 226
Ward, Chris, 14
Weber, Max, 50
Weiner, Amir, 6, 239–74
welfare state, 5, 107–8, 109,
    120–2, 121–2n, 125n, 126,
    130, 174
White movement, 91, 103, 131,
    138, 141, 142
will, diaries, 199–200
women, 6, 19, 213–36
    collectivization, 216–17, 218
    education, 217, 219, 224, 226
    Five-Year Plans, 216–17, 218,
        219, 220, 221, 224
    industrialization, 213, 214, 217,
        218–25, 226
    liberation and equality, 213–14,
        215, 230–5
    natural role as mothers, 213
    post-war Soviet Union, 281
    redefinition of roles, 225–35
    reproductive obligations, 213,
        214, 228–9
    unemployment, 218, 218n
women's movement, 204
worker resistance, 172

workers
    demonstrations, 279, 298
    diaries, 193, 194n
    evacuation of, 277–8, 279
    living conditions, 296, 297
    needs and demands of, 17
    remuneration system, 27
    "revolution from below," 18
    role in October Revolution, 3, 39
    social mobility, 18
    strike action, 162
    support for Bolsheviks, 3, 39
    wish to return home after
        evacuation, 297–8
    women, 213, 214, 217, 218–25,
        226
    working conditions, 296
    see also smychka
Workers and Peasants Inspection of
    the RSFSR, 221
working class, 46, 113, 118, 121,
    170, 172
World War I *see* First World War
World War II *see* Second World War
Wrangelite officer corps, 141
Wright, Gwendolyn, 119n

Yagoda, G. G., 88, 90
Yugoslavia, 253

Zambrowski, Roman, 267
"Zaulki" (Smirnov), 288
zemstvos, 71
Zhadanov, 267
Zhdanov, A., 31
Zhelenzniakov, Aleksandr, 197–8,
    200
Zhmerynka, 267
Zhuravlev, Nikolai, 192–3
Zinoviev, Grigorii, 20, 88
Zinovievists, Great Terror, 88
Zubkova, Elena, 6, 277–301

CPSIA information can be obtained
at www.ICGtesting.com
Printed in the USA
FSHW022242260719
60440FS